RAISED
ON THE
THIRD DAY

Defending the Historicity
of the Resurrection of Jesus

RAISED
ON THE
THIRD DAY

W. David Beck
& Michael R. Licona, Editors

Essays in Honor of Dr. Gary R. Habermas

LEXHAM PRESS

Raised on the Third Day: Defending the Historicity of the Resurrection of Jesus

Copyright 2020 W. David Beck & Michael R. Licona

Lexham Press, 1313 Commercial St., Bellingham, WA 98225
LexhamPress.com

Print ISBN 9781683594321
Digital ISBN 9781683594338
Library of Congress Control Number 2020945451

Lexham Editorial: Elliot Ritzema, Matthew Boffey, Erin Mangum, Abby Salinger
Cover Design: Lydia Dahl
Book Design: Abigail Stocker
Typesetting: Danielle Thevenaz

CONTENTS

Introduction   ix
Michael R. Licona and W. David Beck

Note from Gary Habermas   xiii

1   On Habermas's Minimal Facts Argument   1
Robert B. Stewart

2   The Soul and Near-Death Experiences:
A Case for Substance Dualism   15
J. P. Moreland

3   The Image on the Shroud:
A Best Explanations Approach   37
Mark W. Foreman

4   The Uniqueness of Christianity in
a World of Religions   61
Craig J. Hazen

5   John Rawls's Political Liberalism and
the Problem of Taking Rites Seriously:
From Abortion to Same-Sex Wedding Cakes   75
Francis J. Beckwith

6   On the Organic Connection between
Jesus' Atoning Death and Resurrection   89
William Lane Craig

7   The Moral Argument and the Minimal Facts   105
David Baggett

8   The Logical Structure of Moral Arguments   129
W. David Beck

9   The Testimony of Josephus and
    the Burial of Jesus   143
    Craig A. Evans

10 Near-Death Experiences and
    Christian Theology   159
    Dale C. Allison, Jr.

11 The Deaths of the Apostles and Belief in
    Jesus' Resurrection   179
    Sean McDowell

12 The History and Current State of
    Modern Shroud Research   201
    Barrie M. Schwortz

13 Racing toward the Tomb:
    Purity and Sacrifice in the Fourth Gospel   225
    Beth M. Sheppard

14 A Note on Women as Witnesses and
    the Empty Tomb Resurrection Accounts   257
    Darrell L. Bock

15 Historical Epistemology and Divine Action   263
    Benjamin C. F. Shaw

16 The Primacy of Paul in Discussions on
    Jesus' Resurrection   289
    Michael R. Licona

17 What Aspiring (and Veteran) Apologists
    May Learn from Gary Habermas   315
    Alex McFarland

18 What Everyone Should Learn
    from Gary Habermas   325
    Frank Turek

    List of Contributors   339

INTRODUCTION

Michael R. Licona and W. David Beck

This volume was a labor of love to honor our colleague and friend Gary Habermas. His accomplishments in apologetics, especially his work on the resurrection of Jesus, puts him at the very top of his field. That alone warrants a book in his honor. But additionally, Gary has always seen his scholarship as a means of ministering to others. The crowd that will surround him in heaven to thank him for his help dealing with their doubts and puzzlements through letters and email is inestimable.

However, first and foremost, Gary is our good friend, and that is what motivates us most. So we begin with brief personal reflections from the two editors.

Licona

In fall 1985, during my final semester of graduate school, something happened that I never anticipated: I began questioning the truth of the Christian faith. Until that point, my faith had been strong. I had a passion to know God and a love for exegeting the Greek New Testament. I had little concern at that time for the matters of higher criticism. In my mind, the Bible is God's holy word. So I did not concern myself with those whose views about the Bible differed from my own. As a result, I had done just enough to squeak out a B in Introduction to the New Testament. That turned out to be a huge mistake.

Toward the end of my final semester, a number of issues began to shake my faith. I was doing my degree at Liberty University, and although there were some stellar faculty members in the theology department at the time, I suppose I felt a bit embarrassed to voice the questions that were troubling me. One of my roommates, an Australian named Jeff Jack who was in the process of earning a master's degree in Christian apologetics, suggested that I speak with his professor, Gary Habermas.

Until that time, I had no interest in apologetics. But I decided to pay Professor Habermas a visit.

I had never taken a course with him, since he taught in the philosophy department. Still, he welcomed me when I knocked on his office door and asked to speak with him. I found him approachable and authentic. That would be our first of countless discussions that have occurred over more than thirty years. Professor Habermas was exactly what I needed. He allowed me to share my concerns and ask any question. He listened. He understood. And he provided reasonable answers. I doubt whether I would be a follower of Jesus today had it not been for Professor Habermas.

Since that first meeting, we have become friends, very close friends, as close as any family member. Other than my wife Debbie, I do not have a closer or better friend than Gary. He and his wonderful wife, Eileen, have been spending a week with our family every year for more than two decades. Debbie and I love them dearly. My two children, Allie and Zach, know him as "Uncle Gary," as does our son-in-law, Nick.

I could never repay Gary for the time he invested in me. This book is offered as a small demonstration of my respect, appreciation, and love for him.

Beck

I first met Gary at the annual meeting of the Evangelical Philosophical Society (EPS) in 1979. He read a paper on Averroes that piqued my medievalist attention. We talked afterward and I immediately knew we shared common interests and would be friends. A year later I was allowed to hire him, and he was at Liberty starting our MA in Apologetics. Our wives became good friends, as did our kids who are around the same ages.

Forty years later, I am pleased and proud to call Gary my best friend. I admire his incredible memory for facts, his dogged determination to get the evidence for every detail of an argument, his willingness to talk through difficult personal and family matters, and his great example in ministry.

Gary and I have attended EPS most of the forty years since then, always insisting on sharing a hotel room. We are both *very* late night owls and not early risers. As a result, we have spent countless hours discussing, well, whatever. There are a number of issues on which we disagree, which only makes our friendship more enjoyable. He remains an unrepentant Cartesian dualist, which effects numerous philosophical issues. I have tried my best, Lord! These arguments have been going on for most of those forty years, and they have served to deepen our friendship.

We have always lived near each other, shared lunch, gone to (or skipped) faculty meetings together, and shared each other's burdens. Between our two large families, someone always needs prayer, and I can always count on my good friend to share those needs. Thank you, Gary.

When Mike brought up the idea of a Festschrift, I was eager to join in. This was a meaningful and joyous work in dedication to one of God's best.

NOTE FROM GARY HABERMAS

The occasion of this Festschrift came to me as a genuine surprise. During the initial call from the editors, Dave Beck and Mike Licona, I was informed that the secret had stayed secure for more than one year, without so much as a guess or even a hint on my part. This was no small feat considering that the editors and authors are good friends with whom I quite frequently cross paths. But no slips occurred! The result was completely unexpected and I was overwhelmed. To simply say that I am humbled and grateful to be in this position would be a vast understatement.

The first thing that caught my eye when I skimmed the table of contents was the absolutely outstanding lineup of scholars that Beck and Licona had assembled. Time and again as I scanned the list of names and topics, I thought, "Really? Wow! This or that scholar agreed to be involved?" The next thing I noticed was the quite natural division of the essays and topics into two major areas. From philosophy and philosophical theology in the initial section, followed by history, resurrection, and New Testament in the next division, it was all well arranged from first to last.

Further, the volume's topics largely revolve around the research areas that I have pursued most over the years. Near-death experiences (J. P. Moreland, Dale Allison), the death and burial of Jesus (Craig Evans, Beth Sheppard), the theological significance of these events (William Lane Craig), and the resurrection and its results (Mike Licona, Darrell Bock, Sean McDowell, Robert Stewart) form quite a swath of territory. Even the Shroud of Turin made it into the mix (Barrie Schwortz,[1] Mark Foreman).

---

1. While not attempting to single out many specific details from the individual contributions, I would be remiss not to mention here that just as my long-time friend Barrie Schwortz documents in his own essay, he was the official scientific photographer for the famous Shroud of Turin Research Project (STURP). Most intriguingly, Barrie is a Jewish scholar and non-Christian who still thinks through his many years of scientific research that this burial cloth actually did wrap the dead body of Jesus after his crucifixion.

Other relevant topics in this volume include the existence of God and related worldview issues (Dave Beck, Dave Baggett), Jesus' uniqueness among the world religions (Craig Hazen), and the question of whether historians can legitimately identify any particular event as most likely involving a miracle (Ben Shaw). Frank Beckwith follows with some thoughts on more practical applications of philosophy to specific insights in the realms of political and ethical theory. Alex McFarland and Frank Turek address issues of ministry application and allowing our lives to speak as loudly as our words.

One could hardly be more pleased with how this text has turned out. The scholars' competencies are off the charts, and the chosen topics likewise. I have nothing but admiration for the exceptional job done here by editors Beck and Licona.

The Minimal Facts Argument

A number of the essays in this text mention and/or discuss what I have termed the *minimal facts method or approach to New Testament matters.* This general angle is the one used most frequently throughout my writings. Though I have applied it often in published formats to several other research topics, I have employed it far more regularly over the years when examining the subject of Jesus' resurrection. As such, it is not surprising that it has shown up in one way or another in several of the essays in this volume.

The chief idea behind the minimal facts argument is to use only those historical facts that fulfill two chief criteria. First, each event must itself be confirmed by an array of indications from various angles that establish the strong likelihood of its occurrence. In my now-massive resurrection magnum opus that has become my constant research companion for more than the past five years, literally several dozen pointers exist that confirm just these facts, even when derived by more skeptical standards of research. Many of these indicators are drawn from the very early creedal confessions as well as the strict application of the New Testament criteria to the available data.

Second, due to the strength of the backup information that favors just these few facts, the vast majority of recent critical specialists has affirmed the historicity of these early events. Of these two criteria, the first is by far the most crucial, since the multiple evidential pointers that establish the likelihood of each event are sufficient to make the case by themselves, whether or not the scholarly tide remains supportive, as it has been in recent decades. After all, scholarly convictions may change, no longer affirming this foundation.

Actually, a number of critical New Testament historians, theologians, and other scholars in recent years have also begun their search for the historical Jesus by delineating a list of those events that researchers consider to be well-established. Their lists of historical facts form their own foundation, with which they begin their study. By comparison, their lists are always longer than the truncated one used on behalf of the resurrection appearances of Jesus,[2] hinting at the strength of the more skeptically derived minimal facts method. After providing their own lineups of what they consider the known data, these contemporary scholars then move forward to work from their own starting points.

For the Sake of Ministry

Another area of study that is probably shared even more regularly and wholeheartedly by scholars across all sides of the theoretical perspectival divide is that, given the appropriate textual, philosophical, theological, and scientific foundational structure, sound theory must lead inexorably to good pastoral, ethical, social, and even political applications and practices. Of course, there will always be wide varieties of views on *how* some of the finer points of these applications ought to be pursued, but the idea that there must be ministry application itself is widely agreed upon. Even as Jesus taught us, the hungry, the homeless, the sick, and others, particularly those who cannot care for themselves, need to be fed and otherwise cared for. As Jesus told the lawyer who asked, this is our second greatest duty of all.

In this way, a firm theoretical foundation must lay the groundwork for good ministry. But as I remind myself regularly, our constant preoccupation with theoretical issues alone cannot absolve us of our practical responsibilities. A few of the essays in this text have varied from offering hints to providing more urgent reminders pertaining to some of these moves, calling us to our more practical responsibilities.

---

2. Of course, these other studies cover more areas of Jesus' life, too.

Conclusion

We end where we began. The honor bestowed upon me on the occasion of this Festschrift was a truly humbling as well as totally unexpected experience. This is especially the case when the reputations of the individual contributors are considered along with these works that are drawn from their own areas of expertise. I thank profusely each of these scholars, friends, and colleagues.

Further, David Beck and Michael Licona have both been fantastic friends and so much more than that for several decades, and I will never forget the love that they have shown by making such an involved time commitment in the midst of their own exceptionally busy schedules. Though it is far too inadequate to simply say so, I thank each of them for that.

To the readers, I wish you many pleasant hours of thoughtfulness and study. May we all march forward together from our callings, jobs, and disciplines to being just as committed to personal ministry.

 PART 1

On PHILOSOPHY, PHILOSOPHY OF RELIGION, *and* PHILOSOPHICAL THEOLOGY

1

ON HABERMAS'S MINIMAL
FACTS ARGUMENT

Robert B. Stewart

I am not aware of anyone who has studied the historicity of the resurrection of Jesus longer and more deeply than Gary Habermas has.
As of 2004, Habermas had completed an overview of more than 1,400
sources on the resurrection of Jesus published since 1975, and he had
catalogued about 650 of these texts in English, German, and French.[1] By
the year 2012, that number had increased to around 3,400 sources.[2] Has
anyone ever read even half that many unique books and/or articles on
the resurrection of Jesus? From time to time, Habermas has reported on
his findings, although the sum total of his research is a moving target. To
his credit, Habermas has been insistent on including atheist, agnostic,
and liberal scholars in his catalog, along with mainline and evangelical
scholars. He does this in order to ensure that nobody can say that he
only surveyed his own scholarly group.

He has also pioneered a "minimal facts" method of arguing for the
resurrection of Jesus. This essay will be an appreciative critique of that
method. For more than thirty-five years, Habermas has argued that "surrounding the end of Jesus' life, there is a significant body of data that
scholars of almost every religious and philosophical persuasion recognize

---

1. Gary R. Habermas and Michael R. Licona, *The Case for the Resurrection of Jesus* (Grand Rapids:
Kregel, 2004), 60.

2. Gary R. Habermas, "The Minimal Facts Approach to the Resurrection of Jesus: The Role of
Methodology as a Crucial Component in Establishing Historicity," *Southeastern Theological Review*
3.1 (Summer 2012): 18.

as being historical. The historicity of each 'fact' on the list is attested and supported by a variety of historical and other considerations."[3]

Explaining the "Minimal Facts" Method

Habermas has two criteria for an occurrence to be designated a minimal fact:

1. Each event has to be established by more than adequate scholarly evidence, and usually by several critically ascertained, independent lines of argumentation.

2. Additionally, the vast majority of contemporary scholars in relevant fields have to acknowledge the historicity of the occurrence.

One must note the difference in nature between these two criteria: the first is established by evidence, the second by consensus of scholarly opinion. The first is much more firm; past events are not subject to change, although our knowledge of evidence related to them and our interpretation of that evidence may change. The second is indeed subject to change because all of us, from time to time, change our opinions on matters, whether for good or ill.

Habermas is well aware of the difference between his two criteria in terms of sources and natures. This awareness leads him to state:

> Of the two criteria, I have always held that the first is by far the most crucial, especially since this initial requirement is the one that actually establishes the historicity of the event. Besides, the acclamation of scholarly opinion may be mistaken or it could change.[4]

---

3. Habermas, "Minimal Facts," 15. Examples of Habermas arguing from a recognition of this agreed-upon body of facts include but are not limited to the following works: *The Resurrection of Jesus: An Apologetic* (Grand Rapids: Baker, 1980), 22–41; *Ancient Evidence for the Life of Jesus: Historical Records of His Death and Resurrection* (Nashville: Thomas Nelson, 1984), 124–134; with Antony Flew, *Did Jesus Rise from the Dead? The Resurrection Debate*, edited by Terry L. Miethe (San Francisco: Harper and Row, 1988), 19–27, 42–46, 155–158; *The Historical Jesus: Ancient Evidence for the Life of Christ* (Joplin, MO: College Press, 1996), 152–170; "Resurrection Research from 1975 to the Present: What are Critical Scholars Saying?" *Journal for the Study of the Historical Jesus* 3:2 (June 2005): 135–53.

4. Habermas, "Minimal Facts," 16.

All along, Habermas has produced two lists of facts, the first list being longer and more inclusive, the second shorter and more exclusive. He states it thus:

> The longer list was usually termed the "Known Historical Facts" and typically consisted of a dozen historical occurrences that more generally met the above criteria, but concerning which I was somewhat more lenient on their application. This would apply especially to the high percentages of scholarly near-unanimous agreement that I would require for the shorter list. From this longer listing, I would extrapolate a briefer line-up of from four to six events, termed the Minimal Facts.[5]

Something that is sometimes overlooked concerning Habermas's method is that a minimal fact is not simply the agreed-upon opinion of the vast majority of scholars. He does not fall prey to the fallacy of appealing to majority belief or *consensus gentium*. Both criteria are necessary; one without the other is insufficient to produce a minimal fact. Minimal facts are "established by more than adequate scholarly evidence" *and* "the vast majority of contemporary scholars in relevant fields [acknowledging] the historicity of the occurrence." In other words, a bare consensus of scholarly opinion is just that—naked shared belief. Each criterion is a necessary condition, but neither taken by itself is a sufficient condition to establish a minimal fact. It is the shorter, more exclusive, "minimal facts" list—and the method that drives it—that interests me and is the focus of this essay.

What Are Habermas's "Minimal Facts"?

In *The Case for the Resurrection of Jesus*, Habermas and Michael R. Licona argue for four minimal facts.[6]

- Fact #1: Jesus died by crucifixion.

- Fact #2: Jesus' disciples believed that he rose and appeared to them.

---

5. Habermas, "Minimal Facts," 16. Habermas notes that his earliest publications sometimes listed those events that comprised his shorter, more exclusive list as "core facts," but that he early on settled on the designation "minimal facts."

6. Habermas has presented lists of varying lengths over the years as he has refined this method. This essay will work from the list in *The Case for the Resurrection of Jesus*.

- Fact #3: The church persecutor Paul was suddenly changed.

- Fact #4: The skeptic James, brother of Jesus, was suddenly changed.

Each of these four facts was affirmed by 90 percent or more of the scholars that Habermas had studied in his voluminous cataloguing of sources on the resurrection of Jesus.[7]

Interestingly enough, in 2010, with the publication of his *The Resurrection of Jesus: A New Historiographical Approach*,[8] Licona trimmed (with Habermas's agreement) their earlier list of four facts to three, which he termed "historical bedrock."[9] Which criterion was discarded and why? The castaway was fact four, that James was suddenly changed. Did the percentage fall below the requisite threshold of at least 90 percent affirmation? No, but the sample size was deemed too small compared to the sample size of the other three minimal facts for this highly-agreed-upon fact to be retained. Apparently there is a required sample size as well as a required percentage, although neither Habermas nor Licona state exactly what that sample size needs to be.

The (minimal) elephant in the room is the absence of one other historical statement that both Habermas and Licona, along with the majority of scholars that Habermas cataloged, personally affirm: the empty tomb. Why do they exclude the empty tomb as a minimal fact? Because it does not rise to the level of at least 90-percent agreement among the scholars that Habermas has catalogued. A large majority of scholars, across the theological divide—skeptical, liberal, mainline, and conservative—conclude that the tomb was empty, but not 90 percent. In other words, it was left out because the percentage of scholars that affirmed it was not high enough. *It had nothing to do with the evidential support or the epistemic justification for the proposition itself.*

Nevertheless, in *The Case for the Resurrection of Jesus* (2004), Habermas and Licona designate the empty tomb as a "Plus One" fact. They grant that less than 90 percent of scholars writing on the

---

7. Habermas, "Minimal Facts," 17.

8. Michael R. Licona, *The Resurrection of Jesus: A New Historiographical Approach* (Downers Grove: InterVarsity, 2010).

9. Licona notes: "Although he has provided lists of varying lengths in the past, Habermas now identifies three minimal facts that are regarded as indisputable by almost all scholars writing on the subject." Licona, *The Resurrection of Jesus*, 302.

resurrection affirm the empty tomb as a fact, but they give the empty tomb significant attention because "there is strong evidence for it, and it is accepted as a fact of history by an impressive majority of scholars." Habermas estimates that 75 percent of scholars affirm it.[10]

In Licona's tome, he offers up four "second-order" facts: (1) the conversion of James, (2) the empty tomb, (3) Jesus' predictions of his violent, imminent death as well as his resurrection afterwards, and (4) that the earliest apostles held that Jesus appeared in a bodily form.[11] Habermas seems to agree with Licona on these points.[12]

I mention this to point out that even Habermas and Licona seem to want to include more than their method allows. I wonder if there is something driving this desire that warrants attention.

Analysis and Critique

There are thirteen points I want to make about this method: some positive, some negative.

1. Habermas's minimal facts method is *evidential*. Although rational belief in God's existence may not require evidence, belief in an event in history seems to require evidence. In other words, given that history is a public discipline, one arguing for a historical event needs to argue from evidence that anyone can access and critique, and by doing so reach a reasonable conclusion regarding the claim that has been made. Habermas appeals to the most certain and widely attested evidence, i.e., that evidence most likely to be publicly affirmed, and thus his argument for the resurrection is based on a very solid foundation.

2. The minimal facts approach is simpler than others. In other words, by limiting the data that one is considering, the method focuses one's attention on a few truly important issues, thus keeping potential objections to a minimum. Minimal facts arguments are less vulnerable to criticism because there are fewer points to be challenged. This focus is good, although it may overlook otherwise significant issues. One generally reliable rule of thumb is this: address the central issues and the peripheral ones will fall into line. Additionally, historians, like

---

10. Habermas and Licona, *Case for the Resurrection*, 70.

11. Licona, *The Resurrection of Jesus*, 468–69.

12. Habermas, "The Minimal Facts Approach to the Resurrection of Jesus: The Role of Methodology as a Crucial Component in Establishing Historicity," 23.

scientists, need to keep the principle of parsimony (Ockham's razor) in mind. All other things being equal (and they almost never are), the simpler solution is generally to be preferred. Although Ockham's razor applies to solutions, not methods, perhaps something similar is true concerning methods to arrive at a solution. Even if such is not the case, the simplicity of the method must still be appreciated.

3. On the other hand, comprehensiveness is also a good thing. In historical investigation, one should take note of *all* the relevant data. All other things being equal, the explanatory theory, or hypothesis, that can make sense of the most data should be preferred. Focus is a good thing, but so is comprehensiveness. *Simplicity* has a mirror twin, and her name is *sufficiency*. To its credit, Habermas's method fares well in terms of focus and simplicity, but it does not fare as well in terms of comprehensiveness.

4. Habermas's minimal facts method "has the benefit of bypassing the often protracted preliminary discussions of which data are permissible."[13] This is one of its strengths. Frequently the first step to resolving disagreements is to find that on which all (or most) parties can agree, and then work from that starting point. This allows the apologist to fight as few battles as necessary to achieve his or her aim.

5. Minimal facts does not mean minimal information. *The Case for the Resurrection of Jesus* is 352 pages; *The Resurrection of Jesus: A New Historiographical Approach* is 718 pages. The minimal facts method is thus one way to give maximal attention to the most widely accepted propositions concerning the death and resurrection of Jesus, and thus to draw out all the implications of these central historical facts. In this way, the objections to conclusions in favor of Jesus' resurrection drawn from these minimal facts can be thoroughly assessed.

6. Habermas's minimal facts method does not downplay the importance of biblical reliability. Instead, the method focuses one's attention on a few nearly universally acknowledged facts without denying other less widely affirmed claims of Scripture. Nowhere, that I'm aware of, does Habermas ever indicate that the reliability of the New Testament should be doubted or denied, or that biblical reliability is unimportant. Still, it is true that the method does not depend upon biblical reliability. But this is a strength, not a weakness, in that his method can be

---

13. Habermas, "Minimal Facts," 16–17.

used effectively with skeptics because it does not allow them to disregard facts supporting the conclusion that Jesus was raised from the dead simply by denying the inspiration and/or inerrancy of Scripture.

7. A clearly stated method that is consistently followed levels the playing field. We will never overcome our worldviews completely (although worldviews can be challenged, critiqued, and changed); but unless we state our methods, and then seek to justify them in public dialogue, we will never even *limit* their influence on us as to what we believe. Simply put, method matters. Habermas recognizes this, and he receives some support from an unlikely source in the person of John Dominic Crossan, who states it well:

> Method, method, and once again, method. Method will not guarantee us the truth, because nothing can do that. But method, as self-conscious and self-critical as we can make it, is our only discipline. It cannot ever take us out of our present skins and bodies, minds and hearts, societies and cultures. But it is our one best hope for honesty. It is the due process of history.[14]

Though no method can ensure success in this endeavor, in my opinion this method has at least as good a chance as any other in this regard because it is a clearly stated method. (As an epistemic particularist, I feel obliged to point out that this is not epistemic methodism.)

8. One concern is that this method, with its insistence upon 90-percent or higher consensus, may be too clever by half. By requiring at least 90-percent agreement, it may force historians to ignore facts that are potentially even more helpful in discovering the truth than those that Habermas accepts as minimal facts. This is so because sometimes a proposition fails to achieve 90-percent affirmation, not because skeptics deny it, but because conservative scholars hold to positions regarding those propositions that even more strongly support the Christian case.

A personal story may help illustrate my concern. Several years ago, Habermas and I were speaking at the same conference. I presented an argument for the historicity of Jesus contra mythicism, one I now term an "argument from critical scholarship." I accepted for the sake of

---

14. John Dominic Crossan, *The Birth of Christianity: Discovering What Happened in the Years Immediately After the Execution of Jesus* (San Francisco: HarperSanFrancisco, 1998), 44.

argument the standard form-critical date for Mark's Gospel of AD 70 or shortly thereafter (Bart Ehrman's dating) and argued along form-critical lines, including the four-source solution to the synoptic problem that included the hypothesis of Q, in this way:

1. If the Synoptic Gospels were written around AD 70 or a little later, then Q was obviously written earlier, say from the late 50s to the mid-60s;

2. If Q was written in the late 50s to the mid-60s, then the formal traditions from which Q came were written earlier, say from the late 40s to mid-50s;

3. If the formal tradition which predated Q was situated in the late 40s to mid-50s, then the informal stories from which the formal tradition came were even earlier, say from the late 30s to the mid-40s;

4. If that's the case, then there simply wasn't enough time for legends about Jesus to grow up (particularly when one considers the presence of Aramaisms in the Synoptic Gospels).[15]

At the outset of my presentation, I announced that I was going to make an argument inspired by Habermas's minimal facts approach. At lunch afterwards, he insisted to me—*correctly, given his stated method*—that my argument was *not* a minimal facts argument because the standard form-critical view as to the dating of the Synoptics was not agreed on by 90 percent or more of the guild. He was correct on that point. I agree. My argument was not and is not a minimal facts argument. It was, however, *somewhat like* a minimal facts argument in that it worked from a starting point that the vast majority of skeptical scholars would affirm. It is better described as an argument from "critical scholarship," "liberal source critical dating," or "critical consensus." Habermas's catalog count concerning the dating of Mark to around AD 70 does not rise to the 90-percent or more level primarily because conservatives like

---

15. The presence of Aramaisms suggests that the stories from which the written Gospels came were told in Palestine, which was where the Christian movement began. This would indicate that those who originally told these stories were very close to the events they narrated both in geographic and temporal terms. This, of course, would be very relevant with regard to the historicity of Jesus' resurrection.

myself or Craig Blomberg think that Mark's Gospel should be dated *earlier* than AD 70.[16] (One should note that there are some liberals, like John A. T. Robinson, or non-theists, like James Crossley, who also think along these lines.)[17] If the standard critical hypothesis that the oral tradition formalized over time (which led to written sources prior to Mark) is correct, and Mark was written earlier than the 70s, then my argument works even better, because then all the other components of the view, including the dating of Q, the formal stories from which Q came, and the informal traditions that later were formalized have to be even earlier. Unfortunately, Habermas's minimal facts method doesn't allow for it because of the requirement for at least 90-percent consensus on the issue!

9. Another concern is that Habermas's method demands that he ignore propositions for which he has good reasons to believe—indeed, propositions that he does believe. I think this is why Habermas and Licona insist on mentioning "Plus One" or "Second Order" facts. Even they are uneasy with this unfortunate result of their method. But to their credit, they maintain their method, which is the methodologically responsible thing to do.

10. Having more true beliefs rather than fewer is almost always advantageous, *so long as one doesn't just believe irresponsibly*. (The gullible person who believes anything for any reason, or without reason, will always have more true beliefs than the epistemically responsible person—but the gullible person will also have *far more false beliefs* than the epistemically-responsible person.) Of course, if we knew which propositions were true, then we wouldn't need to discuss historical method. It seems, however, that for the most part, we can agree upon which beliefs are justified. Yet the minimal facts method

---

16. Given the absence of a single reference to the destruction of the temple as a past event in any of the NT Gospels, I am inclined to think that all of our canonical Gospels were written before AD 70. Furthermore, if one accepts the traditional date for Paul's execution (mid-60s under Nero), then the case to date the Synoptic Gospels earlier is strengthened, if one also concludes that the reason Luke failed to record the outcome of Paul's trial was because Paul's trial was still ongoing when Luke concluded his second treatise to Theophilus. Cf: Craig L. Blomberg, *The Historical Reliability of the New Testament: Countering the Challenges to Evangelical Christian Beliefs*, Studies in Christian Apologetics, ed. Robert B. Stewart (Nashville: B&H Academic, 2016), 13–15. NB: Blomberg and I part company on the dating of John. I think John was likely written prior to AD 70, and he does not. Neither of us would affirm a date of around AD 70 for Mark, however.

17. John A. T. Robinson, *Redating the New Testament* (London: SCM Press, 1976), 13; James G. Crossley, *The Date of Mark's Gospel: Insight from the Law in Earliest Christianity*, The Library of New Testament Studies (London: T&T Clark, 2004), 22–24.

requires that we exclude many propositions that are very well justified simply because only a clear majority—as opposed to the vast majority—of scholars affirm them. But justification is not something that is dependent upon being believed by anyone—propositions are justified or unjustified even if nobody believes them. Responsible belief is based on justification, not vice versa. This is an apparent problem for the minimal facts method.

11. Another concern is that the scholarly consensus will almost certainly change (as Habermas acknowledges).[18] In fact, the scholarly consensus could change so drastically that Habermas would have fewer minimal facts from which to argue (although I am not expecting that to happen anytime too soon). Still, quantitatively speaking, the shift would not need to be that large for one or more of his minimal facts to drop below the 90-percent affirmation threshold. If that happened, then Habermas would be left with one or two minimal facts rather than three. In fact, given Habermas's criteria, it could even be the case that the scholarly consensus would change so drastically that there would be *no* minimal facts from which to argue, even if there were multiple lines of evidence for several facts concerning the resurrection of Jesus. This is at least possible. On Habermas's criteria, a minimal facts method today could leave us with a no facts method tomorrow.

12. I am struck by the fact that if one ends Mark's Gospel at Mark 16:8—which most critical scholars do—not every New Testament Gospel records an appearance of Jesus, which is one of Habermas's minimal facts. Yet all of the New Testament Gospels mention the empty tomb. If the Holy Spirit thought it best to include the empty tomb in each of our Gospels, then perhaps the empty tomb should be part of our method of arguing for the resurrection.

On the other hand, it is also true that the earliest New Testament witness to the resurrection, 1 Corinthians 15, mentions numerous appearances of the risen Jesus but says nothing about an empty tomb: Jesus died, was buried, was raised, and appeared to many believers—some of whom (e.g., Paul) were not believers until Jesus appeared to them.

Still, one can pretty safely assume that an empty tomb was entailed in Jesus being raised. After all, if he was in Galilee after his resurrection (Matt 28:16), then he was not in a tomb in or near Jerusalem.

---

18. Habermas, "Minimal Facts," 16.

Furthermore, the empty tomb establishes an important point concerning the nature of Jesus' resurrection: it involved the resurrection of an embodied person. That is, he was raised bodily from the dead.

13. A further question concerning Habermas's minimal facts method is this: Why is it not one of Habermas's minimal facts that the Christian movement begins in Jerusalem? Are there not multiple lines of evidence for this being the case? Do less than 90 percent of critical scholars affirm this? This seems to be a significant fact. There is little doubt that the earliest Christians declared the resurrection of Jesus in Jerusalem in the earliest days of the Christian church. But it seems obvious, at least to me, that they could not have preached the resurrection of Jesus in Jerusalem at this time if Jesus' body were still in the tomb. It strains the imagination to believe that the earliest disciples preached that Jesus was raised from the dead in the same city where he was executed and buried fifty days after his crucifixion if the tomb were not empty. So why is the fact that the Christian movement began in Jerusalem not one of Habermas's minimal facts? Perhaps the reason is because this fact is so widely recognized that few, if any, scholars question it. If this is so, then why have so few written on Jerusalem being the place where the Christian movement began? The answer seems obvious: you don't have to argue for things that everybody believes. But then this calls into question the necessity of the unstated criterion of a sufficient sample size for a fact to be considered a minimal fact.

Trying the Case (Thinking Juristically)

Perhaps it will help to assess Habermas's minimal facts method in a different way. I am the son of a judge. Growing up with a judge as a father is like living with a human lie detector. A constant refrain in our home was, "Boys, I hear better liars than you every day." Worse, when we misbehaved, we got sentenced. Most important for this essay is that judges like to say, "What matters is not what you *know*; but what you can *show!*" In my view, the minimal facts method works best as a strategy for *showing what you know* rather than for *knowing what you show*. It works best as a strategy to *argue a case*, rather than a strategy to *discover the facts* of a case. It works best not as a *method of discovery*, but rather as *a presentation method*; it's not about *epistemology*, but instead about *persuasion*.

The minimal facts method is akin to the case a lawyer makes when the judge has ruled one or more items of evidence out of order. It is not all the evidence that you have at your disposal, but it is all the evidence that you're allowed to present, or at least everything this particular court will consider. It is not the whole story, but it might still be enough of the story for you to persuade a jury to rule in favor of your client.

The mentioning of second-order facts seems to support my position that the minimal facts method is a way to present a case rather than a way to discover the facts. In other words, Habermas did not reach his conclusions on the basis of minimal facts. Instead, he reached his conclusions on the basis of his first (and admittedly most important) criterion—multiple lines of evidence pointing in that direction.

That the minimal facts argument gets off the ground is testimony to how strong the historical evidence for the resurrection actually is. The argument demonstrates that there is more than enough evidence for an objective person to conclude that it is very likely that Jesus was raised from the dead, or at least to admit that it is possible that Jesus was raised from the dead. At the very least, Habermas's minimal facts argument demonstrates that those denying the historicity of the resurrection of Jesus have not proved their case beyond a reasonable doubt.

The minimal facts method is therefore an exercise in *a fortiori* reasoning. Note that there is a difference between *a fortiori* reasoning and an *a fortiori* argument. An argument is a set of statements in which there are clearly stated premises that offer support for a conclusion, while some particular type of reasoning is often simply thinking in a general way. One can reason in an *a fortiori* manner without making an explicit *a fortiori* argument. (Generally, *a fortiori* reasoning can be translated into one or more *a fortiori* arguments, although the reasoning may not be explicitly stated.[19]) The following is an example of *a fortiori* reasoning:

> If I am too old to play Little League baseball, then obviously my father is too old, too.

---

19. A useful book-length treatment of *a fortiori* reasoning is Avi Sion, *A Fortiori Logic: Innovations, History and Assessments* (Geneva: Avi Sion, 2013). Sion estimates that there are at twenty-eight instances of a fortiori reasoning in the New Testament.

Minimal facts arguments appear to argue along this line:

> If the resurrection of Jesus is probable with only three facts being admitted as evidence for it, then obviously the resurrection of Jesus is even more likely if more evidence in favor of Jesus' resurrection is admitted.

Conclusion: If It Helps, Use It

Apologists should always size up their apologetic context, including their audience, and then proceed accordingly. If you can use more evidences, then do so. If you can lead someone all the way from skepticism to Christian faith, then do so. Much of the time, doing so is not possible in one conversation—nor the result of one argument—because of the worldview or mindset of your dialogue partner. Worldviews typically change over time, not as a result of one argument or conversation.

Additionally, it is often better to take one less step in presenting the evidence for the Christian worldview than to take one step too many. *Logically*, one line of argument or evidence that fails to persuade is simply one line of argument that failed. But *psychologically*, one failed line of argument can tarnish the other lines of argument or evidence even if your interlocutor has no reason for rejecting those particular lines of evidence. Psychologically, taking one step too many often functions like the legal concept of "fruit of a poisonous tree." Recognize also that sometimes placing a bit of doubt into the mind of an assured skeptic is the best that one can hope for. Sometimes showing them the inconsistency of their control beliefs is what is most needed at that moment. Sometimes one has to settle for partial rather than complete success. This means that sometimes a minimal facts argument is just what the doctor ordered.

The minimal facts method is thus a means of contextualization. In particular, in an academic guild in which skepticism is the default mode, Christian scholars are working in an environment where many, if not the majority, are predisposed to dismiss all but the most uncontroversial of claims. In this context, arguing from minimal facts is often how one must begin.

A minimal facts approach to arguing for the resurrection of Jesus is not the right approach to take in every context, nor with every person.

But what approach is? If there were any argument for any part of the Christian worldview that worked with everyone, then we would only need one theistic argument, or one argument for the resurrection, or for the deity of Christ, or for any number of positions. Habermas and Licona would have done better to title their book, *A Case for the Resurrection of Jesus* rather than **The** *Case for the Resurrection of Jesus*. But it is nevertheless a substantial and logically consistent case. Furthermore, the attention they give to reasons for and against their minimal facts is extremely well-reasoned and impressive.

My own personal preference is to try to get all the evidence I can into consideration whenever I can, but I freely admit that minimal facts arguments are a good way to argue much of the time. In fact, Habermas's minimal facts argument is the best way to argue some of the time.

2

THE SOUL AND NEAR-DEATH EXPERIENCES: A CASE FOR SUBSTANCE DUALISM

J. P. Moreland

I was part of the philosophy faculty at Liberty University from 1987–1990. I enjoyed my teaching and research there immensely. But by far the greatest thing that happened to me during my sojourn at Liberty was meeting, befriending, and laboring alongside Gary Habermas. We clicked the first time we met, and he has now been a loving, close friend for thirty-two years. He is a man thoroughly committed to the Lord Jesus, the spread of his kingdom, and the defense of Christianity. I love and admire him deeply. In fact, for many years now, most scholars (including me) have recognized Habermas as the top expert on Jesus' resurrection. It is for this and other reasons that I am honored to be his friend and to contribute to this book.

Gary has always done his work as a scholar strategically for the kingdom. Early in his graduate education and the early years of his career, Gary the philosopher saw a significant lacuna in the defense of the gospel, and he stepped up to the plate to fill that need: working on miracles, the historicity of the New Testament and the bodily resurrection of Jesus, and the reality of near-death (they should be called "after death") experiences (NDEs).[1] These all have an empirical flavor to them, and Habermas

---

1. In 1992, Gary and I coauthored *Immortality: The Other Side of Death* (Nashville: Thomas Nelson, 1992). Cf. *Beyond Death* (with Gary Habermas, Wheaton, IL: Crossway Books, rev. ed., 1998). The book is now available with Wipf & Stock. He had been thinking about NDEs for years before we wrote this. For a recent publication by Habermas on NDEs, see Gary Habermas, "Evidential Near-Death Experiences," in *The Blackwell Companion to Substance Dualism*, eds. Jonathan J Loose, Angus J. L. Menuge, and J. P. Moreland (Oxford: Blackwell, 2018), 227–46.

has masterfully combined philosophy with empirical research for decades. The church and I myself owe him a great debt. In my view, he is the leading expert on Jesus' resurrection in North America, perhaps in the world. And he is the leading evangelical expert on NDEs.

In what follows, I will lay out a case for generic substance dualism (SD) and show how one argument—the modal argument—has been strengthened by NDEs.

What Is SD?

By "generic substance dualism" I mean the view according to which (1) there is a substantial self, soul, or ego that is spiritual and immaterial, (2) that substantial self, soul, or ego is the bearer/ground of strict, Leibnizian diachronic personal identity, and (3) that self, soul, or ego is not identical to the body or any of its physical parts.[2]

SD has a reciprocal epistemic relationship with NDEs. Since NDEs involve disembodied existence, if a good case can be made for SD, then it provides background knowledge for raising the probability of NDEs. Put simply, if physicalism is true regarding human persons, then disembodied existence as characteristic of NDEs is simply impossible in the actual world. But if human persons are souls, then (obviously) the possibility of NDEs follows and their probability increases.

Conversely, the reality of NDEs provides evidence for dualism, as can be seen from the following:

$$P(h/e\&k) = P(h) \times P(e/h\&k)$$

$$P(\neg h/e\&k) \quad P(\neg h) \quad P(e/\neg h\&k)$$

Here h = SD, e = NDEs, and k = background knowledge. Thus, the probability (P) of SD given NDEs and k over the probability of not-SD given NDEs, and k is a function of two other probabilities: the prior probability of SD over the prior probability of not-SD times the fittingness of NDEs given SD and k over the fittingness of NDEs given not-SD & k. For the sake of argument, let us take physicalism and SD as our only two options and, thus, not-SD = physicalism.

---

2. See the introduction by Jonathan J Loose, Angus J. L. Menuge, and J. P. Moreland in *The Blackwell Companion*, 1–21.

The fittingness ratio is the most important one for our purposes. Again, for the sake of argument, we can grant that the prior probability of SD is, say, .3, and that of physicalism is .7. But the fittingness of NDEs given SD is extremely high, say .99. This is because the fittingness of NDEs given physicalism approximates zero, but let's give it a value of .01. Given this form of Bayes' Theorem, it is evident that the probability of SD given NDEs is much, much higher than the probability of physicalism given NDEs. As we shall see later, NDE accounts provide strong support for the modal argument for SD.

The Irrelevance of Neuroscience for Discovering the Nature of Consciousness and Its Possessor

The central ontological issues in philosophy of mind regarding the nature of consciousness and its bearer/possessor—What is a thought, feeling, or belief? What is that to which I myself am identical?—are basically commonsense and philosophical issues for which neuroscientific discoveries are irrelevant. Neuroscience is helpful in answering questions about what factors in the brain and body generally hinder or cause mental states to obtain, but it is silent about the nature of mental properties/states and the self.

To see this further, consider the following. It seems that we have discovered that if a certain type of neuron—a mirror neuron—is damaged, then one cannot feel empathy for another person. How are we to understand this? To answer this question, we need to get before our minds the notion of empirically equivalent theories. If two or more theories are empirically equivalent, then they are consistent with all and only the same set of empirical observations. Thus, an appeal to empirical data cannot be made in favor of one of such theory over the others.

Three empirically equivalent explanatory theories regarding the discovery of the function of mirror neurons come to mind. Each would give a different answer to the question, "What is and what possesses empathy?" These are strict physicalism (in some way or another, a firing of mirror neurons is identical to a feeling-empathy event), mere property dualism (a feeling-empathy event is irreducibly mental; it is caused by the firing of mirror neurons, and both events occur in the brain), and SD (the firing of mental neurons in the brain causes a feeling-empathy event in the soul). Of these three views, no empirical datum can pick which is correct, nor does an appeal to epistemic simplicity help. Epistemic simplicity is a tie-breaker, and the substance dualist will insist as I do later that the arguments and evidence for SD are probative.

A Case for SD

At least five arguments have been offered in the recent literature for some form of SD.

A. Our Basic Awareness of the Self

Stewart Goetz has advanced the following type of argument for the nonphysical, spiritual nature of the self, which I have modified:[3]

1. I am essentially an indivisible, simple, spiritual substance.

2. Any physical object is essentially a divisible or complex entity (any physical object has spatial extension or separable parts).

3. The law of identity (necessarily, if x is identical to y, then whatever is true of x is true of y, and vice versa).

4. Therefore, I am not identical with any physical object (e.g. my living body, brain, or other physical part of my body).

5. If I am not identical with a physical object, then I am a soul.

6. Therefore, I am a soul.

Premise (2) is pretty obvious, and (5) is commonsensical. The body and brain are complex material objects made of billions of parts—atoms and molecules. And for most people, the live options are that I am either some physical object or a soul. Premise (3) is the law of identity and uncontroversial.

Premise (1) is controversial and, without evidence, question-begging. Fortunately, Goetz provides that evidence. Regarding premise (1), we know it is true by introspection, direct awareness of our self.

---

3. Stewart Goetz, "Modal Dualism: A Critique," in *Soul, Body and Survival*, ed. Kevin Corcoran (Ithaca, NY: Cornell University Press, 2001), 89.

When we enter most deeply into ourselves, we become aware of a very basic fact presented to us: we are aware of our own self (ego, I, center of consciousness) as being distinct from our bodies and from any particular mental experience we have, and as being an uncomposed, spatially unextended, simple center of consciousness. In short, we are just aware of ourselves as simple, conscious things. This fundamental awareness is what grounds my properly basic belief (one rational to have that is not based on other beliefs) that I am a simple center of consciousness. On the basis of this awareness and premises (2) and (3), I know that I am not identical to my body or my conscious states; rather, I am the immaterial self that *has* a body and a conscious mental life.

An experiment may help convince you of this. Presently, I am looking at a chair in my office. As I walk toward the chair, I experience a series of what are called phenomenological objects or chair representations. That is, I have several different chair experiences that replace one another in rapid succession. As I approach the chair, my chair sensations vary. If I pay attention, I am also aware of two more things. First, I do not simply experience a series of ownerless sense-images of a chair. Rather, through self-awareness, I also experience the fact that it is I myself who has each chair experience. Each chair sensation produced at each angle of perspective has a perceiver who is I. An "I" accompanies each sense experience to produce a series of awarenesses—"I am experiencing a chair sense-image now."

I am also aware of the basic fact that the same self that is currently having a fairly large chair experience (as my eyes come to within twelve inches of the chair) is the very same self as the one who had all of the other chair experiences preceding this current one. Through self-awareness, I am aware of the fact that I am an enduring I who was and is (and will be) present as the owner of all the experiences in the series.

These two facts—I am the owner of my experiences, and I am an enduring self—show that I am not identical to my experiences. I am the conscious thing that has them. I am also aware of myself as a simple, uncomposed and spatially nonextended center of consciousness (e.g. the range of objects in my visual field is spatially extended, but my visual field itself is not, nor is the entity—I—that possesses it). In short,

I am a mental substance. Moreover, I am fully present throughout my body; if my arm is cut off, I do not become four fifths of a self. My body and brain are divisible and can be present in percentages (there could be 80 percent of a brain present after an operation). But I am an all-or-nothing kind of thing. I am not divisible; I cannot be present in percentages.

Of course, one could simply deny that we have such self-awareness. But I do not find such a denial reasonable. Consider the following proposition, which we may call the causal-acquaintance principle:

$$(CA) \ \Box(s)(x)(y)(Kasx\tilde{O}Kasy)$$

Where s ranges over knowing subjects, x ranges over causal facts (e.g., a hammer's causing a nail to move), and y ranges over the associated causal objects that constitute their causal facts (e.g., the hammer). K_a is "has knowledge by acquaintance with." CA says that, necessarily, if a subject s has knowledge by acquaintance with a causal fact x, then s has knowledge by acquaintance with the relevant causal object y. For example, if s is directly aware of a hammer's causing a nail to move, then s is directly aware of the hammer. CA seems to account for a wide range of cases and is highly justified.

Now, there is a difference between active and passive thoughts. A passive thought is one that happens to me as a patient when I am, say, listening to someone talk. By contrast, an active thought is one that I exercise active power with respect to and entertain freely as an agent. We are quite capable of knowing the difference between active and passive thoughts, but we do not vouchsafe such knowledge by gaining further knowledge about the causal pedigree of the two types of states, as a compatibilist would have it. No, we are directly acquainted with the difference and can be aware of it by simply attending to the relevant mental states. Take as a causal fact my causing an active thought. It would seem to satisfy the antecedent of CA. If so, then it follows that I have knowledge by acquaintance with myself.

B. Unity and the First-Person Perspective

Consider the following argument:

1. If I were a physical object (e.g., a brain or body), then a third-person physical description would capture all the facts that are true of me.

2. But a third-person physical description does not capture all the facts that are true of me.

3. Therefore, I am not a physical object.

4. I am either a physical object or a soul.

5. Therefore, I am a soul.

A complete physical description of the world would be one in which everything would be exhaustively described from a third-person point of view in terms of objects, properties, processes, and their spatiotemporal locations. For example, a description of an apple in a room would go something like, "There exists an object three feet from the south wall and two feet from the east wall, and that object has the property of being red, round, sweet," and so on.

The first-person point of view is the vantage point that I use to describe the world from my own perspective or standpoint. Expressions of a first-person point of view utilize what are called *indexicals*—words like "I," "here," "now," "there," "then." "Here" and "now" are where and when I am; "there" and "then" are where and when I am not. Indexicals refer to me, myself. "I" is the most basic indexical, and it refers to my self that I know by acquaintance with my own self in acts of self-awareness. I am immediately aware of my own self and I know to whom "I" refers when I use it; it refers to me as the self-conscious, self-reflexive owner of my body and mental states.

According to a widely accepted form of physicalism, there are no irreducible, privileged first-person perspectives. Everything can be exhaustively described in an object language from a third-person perspective. A physicalist description of me would say, "There exists a body at a certain location that is five feet and eight inches tall, weighs 160 pounds," and so forth. The property dualist would add a description of the properties possessed by that body, such as the body is feeling pain or thinking about lunch.

But no amount of third-person descriptions captures my own subjective, first-person acquaintance of my own self in acts of self-awareness. In fact, for any third-person description of me, it would always be an open question as to whether the person described in third-person terms was the same person as I am. I do not know my self because I know some third-person description of a set of mental and physical properties and also know that a certain person satisfies that description (namely, me). I know my self as a self immediately through being acquainted with my own self in an act of self-awareness. I can express that self-awareness by using the term "I."

"I" refers to my own substantial soul. It does not refer to any mental property or bundle of mental properties I am having, nor does it refer to anybody described from a third-person perspective. "I" is a term that refers to something that exists, and "I" does not refer to any object or set of properties described from a third-person point of view. Rather, "I" refers to my own self with whom I am directly acquainted and whom, through acts of self-awareness, I know to be the substantial uncomposed possessor of my mental states and my body.

A related argument has been offered by William Hasker:[4]

1. If I am a physical object (e.g., a brain or a body), I do not have a unified visual field.

2. I do have a unified visual field.

3. Therefore, I am not a physical object.

4. I am either a physical object or a soul.

Therefore, I am a soul. To grasp the argument, consider one's awareness of a complex fact, say one's own visual field consisting of awareness of several objects at once, including a number of different surface areas of each object. Now one may claim that such a unified awareness of one's visual field consists in the fact that there are a number of different physical parts, each of which is aware only of part of and not the whole of the complex fact. Indeed, this is exactly what physicalists say. We now know that when one looks at an object, different regions of the brain process different electrical signals that are

---

4. William Hasker, *The Emergent Self* (Ithaca, New York: Cornell University Press, 1999), 122–44.

associated withdifferent aspects of the object (e.g., its color, shape, size, texture, location).[5] However, this claim will not work, because it cannot account for the fact that there is a single, unitary awareness of the entire visual field.[6] There is no region in the brain that "puts the object back together into a unified whole." Only a single, uncomposed mental substance can account for the unity of one's visual field or, indeed, the unity of consciousness in general.

C. Free Will, Morality, Responsibility, and Punishment

Consider the following argument:

1. If I am a physical object (e.g., a brain or a body), then I do not have free will.

2. But I do have free will.

3. Therefore, I am not a physical object.

4. I am either a physical object or a soul.

5. Therefore, I am a soul.

When I use the term free will, I mean what is called libertarian freedom. I can literally choose to act or refrain from choosing. No circumstances exist that are sufficient to determine my choice. My choice is up to me. I act as an agent who is the ultimate originator of my own actions. Moreover, my reasons for acting do not partially or fully cause my actions; I myself bring about my actions. Rather, my reasons are the teleological goals or purposes for the sake of which I act. If I get a drink because I am thirsty, the desire to satisfy my thirst is the end for the sake of which I myself act freely. I raise my glass *in order to* drink.

If physicalism is true, then human free will does not exist. Instead, diachronic and synchronic determinism are true. The former refers

---

5. For more on the unity of consciousness, the binding problem and split-brain phenomena, see Tim Bayne, "The Unity of Consciousness and the Split-Brain Syndrome," *The Journal of Philosophy* 105, no. 6 (2008): 277–300; Tim Bayne and David Chalmers, "What is the Unity of Consciousness?" in *The Unity of Consciousness*, ed. Axel Cleeremans (Oxford: Oxford University Press, 2003), 23–58. Cf. J. P. Moreland, "Substance Dualism and the Unity of Consciousness," *Blackwell Companion*, 184–207. For an empirical argument against physicalism that centers on some of these considerations, see Eric LaRock, "An Empirical Case against Central State Materialism," *Philosophia Christi* 14, no. 2 (2012): 409–26.

6. Hasker, *The Emergent Self*, 122–46.

to determinism over time. The latter refers to determinism at a given moment. Regarding diachronic determinism, If I am just a physical system, there is nothing in me that has the capacity to freely choose to do something. Material systems, at least large-scale ones, change over time in deterministic fashion according to the initial conditions of the system and the laws of chemistry and physics. A pot of water will reach a certain temperature at a given time in a way determined by the amount of water, the input of heat, and the laws of heat transfer.[7]

Besides diachronic determinism, physical macro-objects such as human persons are characterized by synchronic determinism. Why? Because according to physicalists, ordinary physical objects and all their characteristics and behaviors are determined at any given time by the sum of their ultimate micro-physical parts. This is called "bottom-up determinism," and attempts to solve this problem within a physicalist framework have failed.[8]

Now, when it comes to morality, it is hard to make sense of moral obligation and responsibility if determinism is true. They seem to presuppose libertarian freedom. If I *ought* to do something, it seems to be necessary to suppose that I can do it, that I could have done otherwise without anything needing to be different, and that I am in ultimate control of my actions. No one would say that I ought to jump to the top of a fifty-floor building and save a baby, or that I in 2020 ought to stop the American Civil War, because I do not have the ability to do either. If physicalism is true, I do not have any genuine ability to choose my actions. Further, free acts seem to be teleological. We act for the sake of goals or ends. If physicalism (or mere property dualism) is true, there is no genuine teleology and, thus, no libertarian free acts.

It is safe to say that physicalism requires a radical revision of our common-sense notions of freedom, moral obligation, responsibility, and punishment. On the other hand, if these common-sense notions are true, physicalism is false.

---

7. For two reasons, quantum indeterminacy is irrelevant here: (1) The best interpretation of quantum indeterminacy may be epistemological and not ontological. (2) If quantum indeterminacy is real, events still have their chances fixed by antecedent conditions, and this is inconsistent with libertarian freedom, since on this view nothing fixes the chances of a free action.

8. See J. P. Moreland, "Why Top-Down Causation Does Not Supply Adequate Support for Mental Causation," in *Body and Soul: Recent Debates*, eds. Thomas M. Crisp, Steve L. Porter, Gregg A. Ten Elshof (Grand Rapids: Eerdmans, 2016), 51–73.

The same problem besets (mere) property dualism. There are two ways for property dualists to handle human actions. First, some property dualists are epiphenomenalists. A person is a living physical body having a mind, the mind consisting, however, of nothing but a more-or-less continuous series of conscious or unconscious states and events which are the effects but never the causes of bodily activity. Put another way, when matter reaches a certain organizational complexity and structure, as is the case with the human brain, then matter produces mental states like fire produces smoke, or like the structure of hydrogen and oxygen in water produces wetness. The mind is to the body as smoke is to fire. Smoke is different from fire (to keep the analogy going, the physicalist would identify the smoke with the fire or the functioning of the fire), but fire causes smoke, not vice versa. The mind is a by-product of the brain and causes nothing; the mind merely *rides* on top of the events in the brain. Hence, epiphenomenalists rejects free will, since they deny that mental states cause anything.

A second way that property dualists handle human action is through a notion called "event-event causation."[9] To understand event-event causation, consider a brick that breaks a glass. The cause in this case is not the brick itself (which is a substance), but an event, viz., the brick's being in a certain state—a state of motion. And this event (the brick's being in a state of motion) was caused by a prior event, and so on. The effect is another event, viz., the glass's being in a certain state—breaking. Thus, one event—the moving of a brick—causes another event to occur—the breaking of the glass. Further, according to event-event causation, whenever one event causes another, there will be some deterministic or probabilistic law of nature that relates the two events. The first event, combined with the laws of nature, is sufficient to determine or fix the chances for the occurrence of the second event. Events form causal chains according to natural laws, and each member of the chain is a passive happening that is triggered by another passive happening.

---

9. Timothy O'Connor has argued that agent causal power could be an emergent property over a physical aggregate. See his *Persons and Causes* (NY: Oxford, 2000). Subsequently, O'Connor has changed his view and opted for the idea that the agent is an emergent individual. See Timothy O'Connor, Jonathan D. Jacobs, "Emergent Individuals," *The Philosophical Quarterly* 53 (October 2003): 540–55. For a critique of O'Connor, see J. P. Moreland, *Consciousness and the Existence of God* (London: Routledge, 2008), ch. 4.

Agent action is an important part of an adequate libertarian account of freedom of the will. One example of agent action is this typical case: raising my arm. When I raise my arm, I, as a substance, simply act by spontaneously exercising my active powers. *I* raise my arm; I freely and spontaneously exercise the powers within my substantial soul and simply act. No set of conditions exists within me that is sufficient to determine that I raise my arm. Moreover, this substantial agent is characterized by the power of active freedom, conscious awareness, the ability to think, form goals and plans, to act teleologically (for the sake of goals), and so forth. Such an agent is an immaterial substance and not a physical object. Thus, libertarian freedom is best explained by an SD and not by physicalism or mere property dualism.

Unfortunately for mere property dualists, event-event causation is deterministic. Why? For one thing, there is no room for an agent, an ego, an "I" to intervene and contribute to one's actions. I do not produce the action of raising my arm; rather, a state of desiring to raise an arm is sufficient to produce the effect. There is no room for my own self, as opposed to the mental states within me, to act.

For another thing, all the mental states within me (my states of desiring, willing, hoping) are states that were deterministically caused (or had their chances fixed) by prior mental and physical states outside of my control, plus the relevant laws. "I" become a stream of states/events in a causal chain that merely passes through the physical object identical to me. Each member of the chain determines that the next member occurs.

In summary then, mere property dualism denies libertarian freedom, because it adopts either epiphenomenalism or event-event causation. Thus, mere property dualism, no less than physicalism, is false, given the truth of a libertarian account of free will, moral ability, moral responsibility, and punishment. Our commonsense notions about moral ability, responsibility, and punishment are almost self-evident. We all operate toward one another on the assumption that they are true (and these common-sense notions seem to assume libertarian free will). However, if physicalism or mere property dualism is true, we will have to abandon and revise our common-sense notions of moral ability, responsibility, and punishment, because free will is ruled out.

D. Sameness of the Self over Time

Consider the following argument:

1. If something is a physical object composed of parts, it does not survive over time as the same object if it comes to have different parts.

2. My body and brain are physical objects composed of parts.

3. Therefore, my body and brain do not survive over time as the same object if they come to have different parts.

4. My body and brain are constantly coming to have different parts.

5. Therefore, my body and brain do not survive over time as the same object.

6. I do survive over time as the same object.

7. Therefore, I am not my body or my brain.

8. I am either a soul or a body or a brain.

9. Therefore, I am a soul.

Premise (2) is commonsensically true. Premise (4) is obviously true as well. Our bodies and brains are constantly gaining new cells and losing old ones, or at least, gaining new atoms and molecules and losing old ones. So understood, bodies and brains are in constant flux. I will assume that (8) represents the only live options for most ordinary people. This leaves premises (1) and (6).

Let's start with (1). Why should we believe that ordinary material objects composed of parts do not remain the same through part replacement?[10] To see why this makes sense, consider five scattered boards, A–E, each located in a different person's back yard. Commonsensically, it doesn't seem like the boards form an object. They are just isolated boards. Now suppose we collected those boards and put them in a pile with the boards touching each other. We would now have, let us

---

10. For more on problems of material composition, see ed. Michael Rea, *Material Constitution: A Reader* (Lanham, Maryland: Rowman & Littlefield: 1996); Christopher M. Brown, *Thomas Aquinas and the Ship of Theseus* (London: Continuum, 2005).

suppose, an object called a pile or heap of boards. The heap is a weak object, indeed, and the only thing unifying it would be the spatial relationships between and among A–E. They are in close proximity and are touching each other.

Now, suppose we took away board B and replaced it with a new board F to form a new heap consisting of A and C–F. Would our new heap be the same as the original heap? Clearly not, because the heap is just the boards and their relationships to each other, and we have new boards and a new set of relationships. What if we increased the number of boards in the heap to one thousand? If we now took away one board and replaced it with a new board, we would still get a new heap. The number of boards does not matter.

Now imagine that we nailed our original boards A–E together into a makeshift raft. In this situation, the boards are rigidly connected such that they do not move relative to each other; instead, they all move together. If we now took away board B and replaced it with board F, we would still get a new object. It may seem odd, but if we took board B away and later put it back, we would still have a new raft, because the raft is a collection of parts and bonded relationships to each other. Thus, even though the new raft would still have the same parts (A–E), there would be new bonding relationships between B and the board or boards to which it is attached.

Now think of a cloud. From a distance, it looks like a solid, continuous object. But if you get close to it, say in an airplane, it becomes evident that it is a very loose collection of water droplets. The boundaries are vague, and for any droplet near the "edge," it is pretty arbitrary whether or not it is a genuine part of the cloud or simply a droplet outside the cloud. The cloud is like a heap of boards or a raft. If new droplets are added and some removed, it is, strictly speaking, not the same cloud.

Now consider our bodies and brains and assume they are mere physical objects composed of billions of parts. From our daily vantage point, they appear to be solid, continuous objects. But if we could shrink down to the atomic level, we would see that, in reality, they are like a cloud—gappy, largely containing empty space, and composed of billions of atoms (molecules, cells) that stand in various bonding relations between and among those parts. If we were to take a part away and replace it, we would have a new object. The body and brain are like the cloud or our raft. Besides the parts and the relationships among them, there is nothing in the body or brain to ground its ability to remain the same through part replacement. This is the fundamental insight behind the view that the body and brain cannot remain the same if there is part alternation.[11] Since the body and brain are constantly changing parts and relationships, they are not the same from one moment to the next in a strict philosophical sense (though, for practical day-to-day purposes, we regard them as the same in a loose, popular sense).

So much for premise (1). What about premise (6)? Why should we think we survive as the same object over time? Suppose you are approaching a brown table and in three different moments of introspection you attend to your own awareness or experiences of the table. At time t_1 you are five feet from the table and you experience a slight pain in your foot (P_1), a certain light brown table sensation from a specific place in the room (S_1), and a specific thought that the table seems old (T_1). A moment later at t_2, when you are three feet from the table, you experience a feeling of warmth (F_1) from a heater, a different table sensation (S_2) with a different shape and slightly different shade of brown than that of S_1, and a new thought that the table reminds you of your childhood desk (T_2). Finally, a few seconds later (T_3) you feel a desire to have the table (D_1), a new table sensation from one foot away (S_3), and a new thought that you could buy it for less than twenty-five dollars (T_3).

In this series of experiences, you are aware of different things at different moments. However, at each moment of time, you are also aware that there is a self at that time that is having those experiences and that unites them into one field of consciousness. Moreover, you are also aware that the very same self had the experiences at T_1, T_2,

---

11. The view I am advancing is called *mereological essentialism* (from the Greek word *meros*, which means "part"). Mereological essentialism is the idea that an object's parts are essential to its identity such that it could not sustain its identity to itself if it had alternative parts. Animalists and constitutionalists deny mereological essentialism. For a brief exposition of these views, see Eric Olson, *What Are We?: A Study in Personal Ontology* (Oxford: Oxford University Press, 2007), chs. 2 and 3. In different ways, each view claims that, under certain circumstances, when parts come together to form a whole, as a primitive fact, the whole itself just is the sort of thing that can survive part alteration. In my view, this is just an assertion. The whole is just parts and various relations, and neither the parts nor the relations can sustain identity if alternatives are present. The whole is not a basic object—it is identical to its parts and relations.

and T_3. Finally, you are aware that the self that had all the experiences is none other than you yourself. This can be pictured as follows:

Original position   Table

$$\{P_1,S_1,T_1\} \qquad \{F_1,S_2,T_2\} \qquad \{D_1,S_3,T_3\}$$

$$I_1 \qquad\qquad I_2 \qquad\qquad I_3$$

$$I_1=I_2=I_3=I \text{ Myself}$$

Through introspection, you are aware that you are the self that owns and unifies your experiences at each moment of time and that you are the same self that endures through time. This is pretty obvious to most people. When one hums a tune, one is simply aware of being the enduring subject that continues to exist during the process. This is basic datum of experience.

Moreover, fear of some painful event in the future or blame and punishment for some deed in the past appear to make sense only if we implicitly assume that it is literally I myself that will experience the pain or that was the doer of the past deed. If I do not remain the same through time, it is hard to make sense of these cases of fear and punishment. We would not have such fear or merit such punishment if the person in the future or past merely resembled my current self in having similar memories, psychological traits, or a body spatiotemporally continuous with mine or that had many of the same parts as my current body.[12]

Finally, some have argued that to realize the truth of any proposition or even entertain it as meaningful, the very same self must be aware of its different parts (e.g., those expressed by the associated sentence's subject, verb, and predicate). If one person-stage contemplated

---

12. Some claim that what unites all of one's various psychological stages into the life of one single individual is that the latter stages stand in an immanent causal relation to each other. But an immanent causal relation is one that holds between two states in the same thing. Thus, before a causal relation can be considered an immanent one, there must already be the same thing that has the two states. Because the immanent causal relation presupposes sameness of the thing in question, it cannot constitute what it is for the thing to be the same. Further, the immanent causal view confuses what causes an object to endure over time with what it is for the object to remain the same.

the subject, another stage the verb, and still another the predicate, literally no self would persist to think through and grasp the proposition as a whole.

E. The Modal Argument

This brings us to the modal argument for which NDEs are very relevant. The core of the modal argument for the soul is fairly simple: I am possibly disembodied (I *could* survive without my brain or body), my brain or body are not possibly disembodied (they *could not* survive without being physical), so I am not my brain or body. Thus, there is something true of me—I have the modal property of being possibly disembodied—that is not true of my brain or body, so I cannot be my brain or body. I am either a soul or a brain or a body, so I am a soul. In the argument, "possibility" means "metaphysical possibility" or, if you prefer, "logical possibility." Let's elaborate on the argument.

Thought experiments have rightly been central to debates about personal identity. For example, we are often invited to consider a situation in which two persons switch bodies, brains, or personality traits or in which a person exists disembodied. In these thought experiments, someone argues in the following way. Because a certain state of affairs S (e.g., Smith existing disembodied) is conceivable, this provides justification for thinking that S is metaphysically possible. Now if S is possible, then certain implications follow about what is/is not essential to personal identity (e.g., Smith is not essentially a body).

We all use conceiving as a test for possibility/impossibility throughout our lives. I know that life on other planets is possible (even if I think it is highly unlikely or downright false) because I can conceive it to be so. I am aware of what it is to be living and to be on earth, and I conceive no necessary connections between these two properties. I know square circles are impossible because it is inconceivable, given my knowledge of being square and being circular. To be sure, judgments that a state of affairs is possible/impossible grounded in conceivability are not infallible. They can be wrong. Still, they provide strong evidence for genuine possibility/impossibility. In light of this, I offer the following criterion:

> For any entities *x* and *y*, if I have good grounds for believing I can conceive of *x* existing without *y* (e.g., a dog without being

colored brown), or vice versa, then I have good grounds for believing x (being brown) is not essential or identical to y (being a dog), or vice versa.

Let us apply these insights about conceivability and possibility to the modal argument for SD. The argument comes in many forms, but it may be fairly stated as follows:[13]

1. The law of identity: necessarily if x is identical to y, then whatever is true or possibly true of x is true or possibly true of y, and vice versa.

2. I can strongly conceive of myself as existing disembodied. (For example, I have no difficulty believing that near-death experiences are possible; that is, they *could* be true.)

3. If I can strongly conceive of some state of affairs S (e.g., my disembodied existence) that S possibly obtains, then I have good grounds for believing of S that S is possible.

4. Therefore, I have good grounds for believing of myself that it is possible for me to exist and be disembodied.

5. If some entity x (for example, I myself) is such that it is possible for x to exist without y (for example, my brain or body), then x (for example, my self) is not identical to y (my brain or body), and y (my brain or body) is not essential to x (my self).

6. My body (or brain) is not such that it is possible to exist disembodied, i.e., my body (or brain) is essentially physical.

7. Therefore, I have good grounds for believing of myself that I am not identical to my body (or brain) and that my physical body is not essential to me.

A parallel argument can be advanced in which the notions of a body and disembodiment are replaced with the notions of physical objects. So understood, the argument would imply the conclusion that I have

---

13. Cf. Keith Yandell, "A Defense of Dualism," *Faith and Philosophy* 12 (October 1995): 548–66; Charles Taliaferro, "Animals, Brains, and Spirits," *Faith and Philosophy* 12 (October 1995): 567–81.

good grounds for thinking that I am not identical to a physical object nor is any physical object essential to me. A parallel argument can also be developed to show that possessing the ultimate capacities of sensation, thought, belief, desire, and volition are essential to me; that is, I am a substantial soul or mind and could not exist without the ultimate capacities of consciousness.

I cannot undertake a full defense of the argument here, but it would be useful to a say a bit more regarding (2). There are a number of things about ourselves and our bodies of which we are aware that ground the conceivability expressed in (2). I am aware that I am unextended (I am *fully present* at each location in my body, as Augustine claimed; I occupy my body as God occupies space by being fully present throughout it); I am not a complex aggregate made of substantial parts, nor am I the sort of thing that can be composed of physical parts. Rather, I am aware that I am a basic unity of inseparable faculties (of mind, volitions, emotion, etc.) that sustains absolute sameness through change; and I am not capable of gradation (I cannot become two-thirds of a person).[14]

In NDEs, people report themselves to have been disembodied. They are not aware of having bodies in any sense. Rather, they are aware of themselves as unified egos that have sensations, thoughts, and so forth. And we have no difficulty conceiving (note: conceiving is not the same thing as imagining) of someone having an NDE as existing in a disembodied state. Thus, this provides grounds for thinking that this is a real possibility (even if disembodied existence never actually happens, though of course I believe it does), and thus, one cannot be one's body, nor is one's body essential to him. Instead, one is a soul.

There is a physicalist response to this argument that goes like this. The notion of "possibility" used in the argument is not metaphysical or logical possibility; rather, it is epistemic possibility. Epistemic possibility means "for all we know, such and such may be metaphysically/logically possible, and such and such may not be metaphysically/logically possible."

To illustrate, suppose that unknown to me, a table in my kitchen is actually made of particleboard, though I believe it is made of wood.

---

14. In normal life, I may be focusing on speaking kindly and be unaware that I am scowling. In extreme cases (multiple personalities and split brains), I may be fragmented in my functioning or incapable of consciously and simultaneously attending to all of my mental states, but the various personalities and mental states are still all mine.

My son-in-law Carlos asks me, "Isn't it possible that the table is made of particleboard?" What am I to say? Well, if I am right that the table is actually made of wood, then it is not metaphysically possible for that very table to exist and be made of particleboard. A table so made would clearly be a different table. But if I have never taken the time to inspect the table, I might say, "Well, I must admit, for all I know it might be made of particleboard. I guess that is possible." I am using an epistemic sense of possible: "I guess it's possible (epistemically) that I am wrong and that the table is made of particleboard and not wood. But if it is, in fact, made of wood, then it is not possible (metaphysically) for that very table to be made of particleboard."

This last statement shows that something can be epistemically possible (for all I know, the table is made of particleboard, and people exist disembodied) without being really/metaphysically possible (if the table is made of wood, it just can't be the same table if it were made of particleboard; if people are physical objects, then their disembodiment is metaphysically impossible).

Does this objection (the modal argument uses epistemic possibility, not metaphysical possibility, and no real possibilities follow from mere epistemic possibility) work? Not really, and to see why, consider the following account of a real NDE.[15] The case involves a woman named Kimberly Clark Sharp who worked at Harborview Hospital in Seattle. While attempting to resuscitate a clinically dead young patient—Maria—the patient suddenly became conscious, grabbed Kim's arm, and reported that she had left her body, floated out and above the hospital roof, and had seen a large, old blue shoe with a little bow worn to the threads and with the lace tucked under the heel on an upper ledge of the hospital roof! The ledge was not accessible to anyone but hospital personnel or visible from buildings nearby, and Maria had never been to the hospital before. With her curiosity aroused about this bizarre story, Kim was shocked to find the shoe just as Maria had described in just the correct location! Maria was interviewed by other witnesses that day who corroborate the incident.

It is important to note that this is just one of millions and millions of accounts of NDEs. The account you just read is quite typical. For our purposes, note that the account does not contain any combination

---

15. See Peter Shockey, *Reflections of Heaven* (New York: Doubleday, 1999), 147–48.

of states of affairs that are not metaphysically compossible or logically consistent. I have read hundreds of NDE accounts, and not one of them contained logically inconsistent or metaphysically incompossible states of affairs. Even if all NDE accounts are false, it is crystal clear when you read them that they are surely metaphysically possible. The only argument against their metaphysical possibility would be a disqualifying, question-begging assumption of physicalism before considering the evidence.

The truth is that almost everyone, including well-educated atheists, recognize that NDEs are metaphysically possible. How do I know this? Because virtually everyone is willing to hear the evidence for NDEs and decide on that basis whether or not they are real. On April 12–13, 2012, Gary Habermas, Peter Kreeft, and I did a two-day debate on life after death with opponents Michael Shermer, Victor Stenger, and Keith Parsons. Here's the interesting thing to note: everyone in the debate was willing to allow the evidence to settle whether or not NDEs were real.

Shermer, Stenger and Parsons disputed the evidence and argued that it was inadequate. But note, the very fact that they let evidence or the lack thereof settle the issue shows that they assumed that NDEs were metaphysically possible! No one would let the evidence settle the claim that a group of people had discovered a field of square circles in Montana. When NBC's "Dateline" does a show on NDEs, millions of people watch it, including millions of very skeptical people. Why? Because they want to know the evidence. But those same people would never watch a program on the discovery of square circles in Montana. Square circles are metaphysically impossible, and we don't need to look for evidence to know they aren't real. But it's different with NDEs. We watch or we debate the evidence because we know that NDEs just might be real because they are at least metaphysically possible. In this way, NDE accounts provide strong evidence for premise (2) in the modal argument for the soul's reality.

Conclusion

Among contemporary intellectual elites in Western culture, there is a widespread belief, though unexamined and ill-informed, that claims that the soul is real are best left for *The National Inquirer*. Nothing can be further from the truth. I have tried to present arguments for SD, albeit in precis form. And I have illuminated how it is that there is a reciprocal epistemic relationship between SD and NDEs. Gary Habermas has devoted much work to defending the reality of NDEs, and I have done the same with SD. Once again, it is a joy and honor to be teammates with my dear friend and colleague.

3

THE IMAGE ON THE SHROUD: A BEST EXPLANATIONS APPROACH

Mark W. Foreman

On the weekend of June 18–20, 1999, I accompanied Gary Habermas on a trip to Mary Mother of the Church Abbey in Richmond, VA, for a conference on the Shroud of Turin. The abbey had recently opened a new study center on the Shroud and this was to be its first major event. A number of notable scholars in Shroud studies were present, including John Jackson, Ian Wilson, Alan and Mary Wagner, Alan Adler, Thomas D'Muhula and Barrie Schwortz. Jackson, Adler, D'Muhula, and Schwortz were all members of the Shroud of Turin Research Project (STURP) that led to the 120-hour investigation of the Shroud in 1978. Most attendees presented papers, including Gary, who presented on the topic "Historical Epistemology, Jesus' Resurrection, and the Shroud of Turin."

I have known Gary Habermas as a student, colleague, and friend for over thirty years. While we have had many conversations about philosophy, apologetics, and religion, the area where we have connected the most has been our shared interest in the Shroud of Turin. My own interest began in high school, when, as a Roman Catholic, I first heard of the Shroud in a talk at my local church, during which slides were presented of the Giuseppe Enrie 1931 photos. I was immediately fascinated about the idea that there was a cloth purported to contain the actual image of Jesus Christ—not just a painting, but the real image, like a photograph. I tried to find out what I could, but at that time of no internet, sources were limited to just a few references I could find in books and encyclopedias. Eventually my interest waned, though it never completely disappeared. In 1978, I found a copy of Ian Wilson's book *The Shroud of Turin:*

The Burial Cloth of Jesus Christ?.[1] It was the first book on the Shroud I had ever seen and became my first real foray into Shroud studies.

Habermas's interest in the Shroud began later in life. He writes:

> I got into the Shroud not long after finishing my PhD dissertation on the resurrection & then moving back to Detroit from Montana. It was reported that the Shroud contained evidence for the resurrection, so that's all it took! I contacted one of the two biggest researchers at that time, Eric Jumper of the Air Force Academy, who put me in contact w/ Ken Stevenson. As they say, the rest is history![2]

In 1981, Habermas and STURP researcher Kenneth E. Stevenson coauthored the book *Verdict on the Shroud: Evidence for the Death and Resurrection of Jesus Christ.*[3] It was my introduction to Gary Habermas. A few years later, after the report on the carbon dating of the Shroud was released in 1990, Habermas and Stevenson followed up *Verdict* with *The Shroud and the Controversy: Science, Skepticism, and the Search for Authenticity.*[4] Since that time Habermas has done a number of presentations on the Shroud as well as articles and interviews.

When one approaches the problem of the authenticity of the Shroud as the burial cloth of Jesus of Nazareth, two major questions emerge. First, is there plausible historical, medical, scientific, and textile evidence that the Shroud is the genuine article? Second, what is the best explanation for how the image was formed on the Shroud? I will not address the first of these questions, except to say that all evidence we have, save one, points to an affirmative answer to the question of authenticity. I will not discuss this but will point the reader to the score of academic books and articles that have cataloged the evidence.[5] The only evidence proposed that points to inauthenticity is the 1988 Carbon-14 tests, in which researchers proposed a date of 1260–1390 for the Shroud. I will also not address this evidence, as it

---

1. New York: Doubleday, 1978.

2. Personal correspondence, May 29, 2019.

3. G. R. Habermas and K. E. Stevenson, *Verdict on the Shroud: Evidence for the Death and Resurrection of Jesus Christ* (London: Hale, 1981).

4. G. R. Habermas and K. E. Stevenson, *The Shroud and the Controversy: Science, Skepticism, and the Search for Authenticity* (Nashville: Thomas Nelson, 1990).

5. I provide a list of some of these at the end of the chapter.

is very well addressed by Barrie Schwortz in another chapter in this volume.[6] The purpose of this chapter is to address the second question: which theory best explains how the image was formed? I will begin by listing twenty-four features of the Shroud. I then will survey the main theories that have been suggested as to how the image was formed.[7] The basis for our evaluation will be the ability of each to explain all twenty-four features. At the end of the article, I shall offer some thoughts on the apologetic significance of the Shroud of Turin.

It needs to be noted at the beginning that research on the Shroud is extremely challenging for at least two reasons. First, access to the object of research, the Shroud itself, is extremely limited. It has only been exhibited a handful of times, and few of these have allowed for any sort of scientific investigation. It is analogous to investigating the back of the moon: few have actually seen it, so for most of us all we have to go on are photographs.

The first photographs of the Shroud were those of Pia Secondo during an 1898 exposition of the Shroud. This was the first time the details of the Shroud, best seen when looking at a negative image, were seen. The Shroud was not publicly displayed again until 1931, when Giuseppe Enrie again photographed it on the first of a twenty-one-day exposition. These were the most popular photos up until the STURP photos were distributed. It would not be seen again in public until 1973. However, in 1969 a private investigation of the Shroud was held for three days to examine the condition of the Shroud and determine the feasibility of a C14 test to be performed. The Shroud was photographed again for the first time in color.

In 1978, the longest and most in-depth scientific investigation occurred under the auspices of the Shroud of Turin Research Project (STURP), a team of thirty-three American scientists. The team was granted 120 hours of access to the Shroud and performed a host of scientific tests on the Shroud; many photographs in many different

---

6. Schwortz adopts the reweaving hypothesis as the solution to the C-14 anomaly. Many Shroud researchers have abandoned that hypothesis due to lack of evidence. I tend to side with Mark Antonacci, who is a proponent of the radiation theory of formation and believes neutron radiation also explains why the C-14 was skewed. See below.

7. Due to space constraints, I cannot detail each and every theory that has been suggested, but will select the main candidates, lumping some together as they have the same features or problems.

EM spectrums were taken.[8] Most of the scientific information we have comes from this investigation. In 1988 the custodians of the Shroud allowed a sample to be cut for C-14 testing. In 2002 a symposium was held to consider the preservation of the Shroud. At that time the patches covering the burn holes as well as the Holland backing were removed, the back of the Shroud was lightly vacuumed, new spectro-photometry and digital scanning were performed, and new high-definition photographs were taken. The Shroud was then placed in a new hermetically sealed modern reliquary pumped full of argon for preservation. Since then the Shroud has had only four public viewings in 2010, 2013 (television only), 2015 and 2020 (television only) where no scientific investigations were performed.

The second challenge in researching the Shroud is that scientific investigation is only one kind of evidence; historical investigation also needs to be performed. Tracing the history of an object of ancient or even medieval times is often extremely difficult. For the Shroud, much of this is due to the fact that the same cloth-bearing image can be referred to by a number of different names. What we know today as the "Shroud of Turin" has only become known by that name since coming to Turin in 1585. Since the Shroud does not have an established moniker passed down in history, we need to be open to the idea that a variety of names and phrases, such as "Image of God Incarnate," Acheriopoieta ("not made by human hands"), Image of Edessa, and Mandylion may be possible references to the same image-bearing cloth. Also, premodern historical records are often incomplete, partial, or missing altogether. One often must piece bits of the historical record together to arrive at a plausible theory of an ancient object's movement through history. If the Shroud is an object of first-century Palestine that traveled through the Mideast and much of southern Europe for over 1500 years, we should expect its history to be sketchy and would be suspicious of any cleaned-up and obvious answers. It is the nature of ancient history that mysteries will remain.

Finally, a word needs to be said about the approach I am taking in this chapter. It is not my purpose to prove definitively anything positive or negative concerning the authenticity of the Shroud. As with

---

8. See Barrie Schwortz's chapter in this volume, "The History and Current State of Modern Shroud Research," for an excellent summary of the work and conclusions of the STURP team.

most items and literature from ancient history, conclusions must necessarily be tentative. Because evidence is often incomplete and fragmented, one is frequently forced to speculate to fill in the gaps. Many unanswered questions about the Shroud abound, and more research and scientific study needs to be performed before any definitive conclusions can be reached.[9] Hence, my goal is somewhat modest. I want to suggest what I believe is the best explanation for the current evidence in addressing how the Shroud image was formed on the linen cloth. A best-explanation approach is a form of abductive reasoning that considers the theory with the largest explanatory scope, most explanatory power, plausibility in relation to background information, and illumination of cognate areas, and that is minimally ad hoc to be the best theory available.

Some Basics about the Shroud of Turin

A shroud (sindon) is a long cloth wrapped around a corpse in preparation for burial. It was common in ancient days for a person to be wrapped in a shroud and be buried in the ground with no coffin. In first-century Palestine, Jewish corpses were wrapped in a shroud and placed in a temporary grave, such as a small cave, and to allow the body to decay for a period of about a year. At the end of that period, the cave was opened and the leftover bones removed and placed in an ossuary for permanent burial. Unlike the Egyptians, who mummified the dead using several strips of linen wrapped horizontally around the body, the shrouds of ancient Palestine were made of one long single piece of linen that was wrapped vertically around the body.

Since 1578, a shroud has been housed at the Cathedral of St. John the Baptist in Turin, Italy. The shroud measures at fourteen feet, six inches long by three feet, nine inches wide. Ancient tradition has claimed that this is the original burial cloth that held the crucified body of Jesus of Nazareth. This shroud contains the image of a man that has a number of striking elements consistent with that of a man who has undergone crucifixion, including some very unique features described in the Gospel accounts of Jesus' crucifixion. Most of these are observable by carefully examining the Shroud. Among them are:

---

9. Even the title of Mark Antonacci's 2015 book, *Test the Shroud at the Atomic and Molecular Levels* (Ashland, OH: Forefront Publishing Co., 2015), promotes the need for more research.

1. The frontal and dorsal image is of a five-feet, ten-inch naked male weighing an estimated 170 pounds.

2. The image is a high-resolution, clear, and detailed image with no distortions.

3. The image appears to be in a state of rigor mortis, lying flat with arms crossed down over the abdomen and one leg raised at the knee.

4. A puncture wound in the right wrist (the left wrist is hidden from view) consistent with wounds from being nailed to a cross is apparent. The thumbs are folded under the long distended fingers.

5. Scourge wounds on the chest, legs, and back, which match a Roman flagrum commonly used to beat a man in first-century Palestine, can be seen. It is estimated that there are over 120 wounds.

6. Puncture wounds in the scalp and head are consistent with a cap of thorns.

7. A wound in the right side is consistent with a stabbing. From it exudes a pool of blood and clear liquid that is judged to be serum.

8. A puncture wound is identifiable around the feet, and one nail goes through both feet.

9. Blood surrounds the wrist and scalp wounds, including blood flowing up the arms consistent with blood from the wrists flowing down from suspended arms.

10. The face appears to have been beaten, with a left swollen cheek and raised right eyebrow. Blood is spattered on the face and in the beard.

11. The hair is long and appears to be tied in the back. The beard has a distinct "divided" look, and parts of it may be missing.

12. Abrasions are identifiable on the nose and knees consistent with a man falling down. Dirt has been identified in the abrasions.

13. On the dorsal side, abrasions are identifiable on the shoulders consistent with the carrying of a heavy object.

14. The image on the Shroud is a negative image, meaning that normally light areas appear dark and dark areas appear light. This became apparent when the first photographs were taken of the Shroud in 1898.

15. In addition to the image, the Shroud also contains a number of scorch marks, holes, and, until recently, patches over holes as well as water stains. This is due to a 1532 fire that broke out in the church in Chambery, France, where the Shroud was being housed. Silver on the casket holding the Shroud melted and poured down on the folded Shroud within. The holes were patched in 1534, and a backing was attached to the Shroud. In 2002, the backing and patches were removed and a new backing sewn on.

16. The linen is a 3:1 (three over one) herringbone weave consistent with a first-century weave pattern but not with any European fabric of the Middle Ages.

In addition to the above observations, the following were determined by the 1978 STURP investigations:

17. The image is a superficial image lying on the utmost top fibers of the thread making up the linen. A thread is made up of about one-hundred to two-hundred fibers, and depth of the image is about 0.2 microns of a single fiber deep.

18. The frontal side of the image has double superficiality. The image not only appears on the top layers of threads, but a fainter duplicate image appears on the other side of the cloth, also on the top layers.

19. The image contains 3-D information with no distortion. "The image-density distribution of both front and back

images can be correlated to the distance between an object having the shape and contours of a human body and a cloth covering that body."[10] When subjected to VP8 image analyzer, the 3-D information can be observed.

20. When laid flat, the image has vertical mapping. "The mapping of image features from the body to the cloth of the frontal image is more or less vertical, corresponding to the direction of gravity."[11]

21. The blood on the Shroud was tested and found to be type AB human blood. There is no image underneath the blood. There are no brush strokes indicating that the blood was painted on.

22. The image contains no pigments, no dyes, no brush-strokes, no cementation between fibers, no clumping, and no capillary flow, all of which would be evidence of painting, dyeing, or staining. "The image fibers are colored (straw-yellow) due to chemical reactions involving poly-saccharides composing the linen fibers: oxidation, dehy-dration and conjunction."[12] No substance has been added to create the image.

23. The image enveloped a dead human body that showed no signs of decomposition and no putrefaction.

24. When placed under enhanced lighting, an x-ray is pro-duced which shows bones, especially in the fingers of the hands and the teeth.

It cannot be emphasized enough how unique many of these features are. Take, for example, the superficiality of the image (17). The Shroud is made of thousands of linen threads. Each thread is composed of hundreds of fibers. A typical fiber is about twenty microns in width.[13]

---

10. John Jackson, *The Shroud of Turin: A Critical Summery of Observations, Data and Hypotheses* (Colorado Springs: The Turin Shroud Center of Colorado, 2017), 71.

11. Jackson, *The Shroud of Turin*, 72.

12. Jackson, *The Shroud of Turin*, 69.

13. To get a perspective, a quarter of an inch is equivalent to about six hundred microns, which is thirty times the size of a fiber.

The Shroud image is no deeper than 0.02 microns of a single fiber. It is the upper-upper top of the upper-upper fibers of the upper-upper threads of the linen. It is extremely superficial. For another example, take the 3-D information. A VP8 imaging analyzing computer is designed to produce an isometric projection or brightness map where white represents a higher elevation, black represents lower, and midrange appears between these two extremes. When we observe the image, it appears as 3-D to our minds. When the analyzer is applied to a normal 2D photograph, it tends to distort the image when portrayed in 3-D. However, the photographs of the Shroud show a non-distorted 3-D image. This leads researchers to conclude that some sort of 3-D information was encoded into the Shroud when the image was created. These are just two examples of very unique features of the Shroud. A satisfactory theory must be able to explain these and the rest of the twenty-four features of the Shroud.

When it comes down to it, there are only two general options for how the image on the Shroud was formed. Either it occurred through some natural process of physics or chemistry or it was man-made. We will look at the early naturalistic theories first and then turn to the man-made theories. We will then turn to enhanced naturalistic theories.

Early Naturalistic Theories

The earliest scientific explanation of the formation of the Shroud image attributes it to some natural process involving a dead corpse. One of the earliest Shroud researchers was Paul Vignon. In 1902, he wrote the earliest book about the Shroud, *The Shroud of Christ*, just four years after Pia Secondo took his 1898 photographs. In 1937, Vignon published an article in *Scientific American* about his research. His first hypothesis was that the image was produced when the Shroud came into direct content with a dead corpse that was wet with sweat, embalming oils, and other liquids. These liquids would have made the Shroud stick to the body and would have left a stain on the Shroud. Vignon quickly abandoned this theory, as there would be too many distortions and this image presents no distortions (2). The contact theory is problematic as well, as there would be no superficiality (17), there would be capillarity and cementation from an added substance

(22), and it provides no explanation for a negative image (14), 3-D information (19), vertical mapping (20), or x-ray images (24). This theory also requires the corpse to have begun decomposition and purification, which is not evident on the Shroud (23).

Vignon's second hypothesis was that the beaten and crucified corpse would emit ammoniac vapors due to urea in sweat and blood, and that these may have caused the image. This is often referred to as the gas diffusion theory. STURP chemist Ray Rogers thought there was something to this hypothesis. He proposed that a Maillard reaction between amino acids could be generated from a decomposing body. Rogers proposed that a thin layer of starch might have been left on the linen during its manufacturing, and this would provide the amino acids for the reaction. However, the chemical tests on the Shroud found no evidence of starch on the linen (22). Also, it is highly questionable if the image would be non-distorted (2), as vapors do not travel in a straight line and the image seems to be directly vertical in relation to a dead body (20).

Man-Made Theories

On October 13, 1988, an announcement was made about the results of carbon-14 testing of the Shroud. C-14 testing dated the Shroud to a date of 1260–1390 with 95 percent accuracy. It was announced that, rather than being the actual burial cloth of Jesus, the Shroud was a thirteenth- or fourteenth-century forgery. At the press announcement, Edward Hall, director at the Oxford carbon dating laboratory, said, "There was a multimillion pound business in making forgeries during the fourteenth century. Someone just got a bit of linen, faked it up, and flogged it."[14] Critics and skeptics are quick to affirm the forgery hypothesis, but often they do not offer an explanation as to how the forgery might have taken place. Claiming forgery and proving forgery are two very different things.[15]

---

14. Quoted in Jackson, *The Shroud of Turin*, 92.

15. From this point on I will refrain from referring to the Shroud as a forgery. Forgery carries with it the concept of intent and implies that the creator of the Shroud, if there was one, intended to deceive people into believing this was the actual burial cloth of Jesus. While that is certainly possible, it is not necessarily the case. The artist could have intended that the Shroud just be a remarkable work of art and everyone just assumed a deceitful intention. We have no evidence of the intention of the artist, assuming there was one. Therefore, the term "forgery" is

Due to the C-14 testing, the painting hypothesis is by far the most popular theory of the formation of the image, especially among the uninformed. However, it is not new. It is probably the earliest attempt put forth to explain the image on the Shroud. In 1389, Bishop Pierre D'Arci wrote a memorandum to Pope Clement VII claiming that his predecessor, Bishop Henri of Poiters, had investigated the Shroud thirty-five years earlier and declared it a fake. This is often claimed to be the first documented evidence we have of the Shroud's existence.[16] We have no idea if the message was ever sent or even completed. The fact that these are drafts implies that the actual memorandum was never sent. According to the note, Bishop Henri had heard that a "cunning artist" had painted the image and that he had confronted the artist, who admitted to painting it. The D'Arci Memorandum is often quoted by skeptics as proof the Shroud is man-made. However, there are problems with the memorandum. Several scholars raise questions about the desire of D'Arci to uncover false relics, and this third-hand account may have been motivated by that. Ian Wilson comments that there may be a translation error from the Latin and that the phrase "the truth being attested by the artist who had painted it" could easily be translated as "the truth being attested by an artist who copied it."[17] Given the scientific evidence we now have in our possession, the fact that this is third-hand testimony, and that the draft of the memo is incomplete, most Shroud researchers discount the D'Arci Memorandum.[18] But not all.

The painting hypothesis has come down through history, some even claiming it was painted during the Renaissance by Leonardo Da Vinci. The most recent proponent was the late Walter McCrone. McCrone was a world-renowned microscopist who had obtained sticky-tape samples gathered off the Shroud during the 1978 STURP investigation.

---

misapplied and has the misfortune of immediately biasing one against any serious consideration of the Shroud. I will simply refer to this as the "man-made theory."

16. Though the 1192–1195 Hungarian Pray Manuscript contains an image that portrays the herring-bone pattern of the Shroud and the distinctive L-shaped burn holes and therefore could be considered the earliest documentary evidence of the Shroud. Thank you to Robert Rucker for making this point.

17. I. Wilson, *The Shroud: Fresh Light on the 2000-Year-Old Mystery ...* (London: Bantam Press, 2010), 145.

18. See R. Rucker, "Evaluation of 'A BPA Approach to the Shroud of Turin'" (Nov 2018), for a more detailed assessment of the D'Arci memorandum (http://www.shroudresearch.net/hproxy .php/Evaluation-of-A-BPA-Approach-to-the-Shroud-of-Turin--Rev-0.pdf?lbisphpreq=1).

McCrone reported the presence of iron oxide on the Shroud, which is a substance used in tempera paint, and, armed with the D'Arci memorandum, McCrone concluded that the Shroud was painted. He also discovered minute flecks of paint on the Shroud, supporting his conclusion. Even though challenged, McCrone was adamant about his conclusions and eventually wrote a book on it, which has become the primary resource for many skeptics.[19] McCrone may not have been aware that STURP researchers had already discovered iron oxide on the Shroud, but it wasn't just on the image areas; it was all over the Shroud in non-image areas as well. The researchers concluded that iron oxide was probably introduced to the linen fabric when the flax was soaked in pond water in preparation for weaving. As far as the minute flecks of paint, it was common during the Renaissance for paintings of the Shroud to be made and then pressed against the Shroud in order to sanctify them, and this would explain the presence of the flecks. As a variation on the painting hypothesis, Emily A. Craig and Randall R. Bresee used a dusting method of painting to obtain an image that at first glance is very similar to the Shroud image. They used powdered pigments on paper that they then transferred to linen, which was heated to set the image.[20]

While the painting hypothesis is popular, it has serious problems when considering the twenty-four facts for which it needs to account. First, the shroud is a negative image (14). While it is not impossible to paint a negative image, from where would a medieval artist have even conceived of the idea? Negative images were not created until the invention of photography, over four hundred years later than the C-14 date. Second, paint was one of the main factors the STURP team went after in its investigation of the Shroud. Literally hundreds of chemical and spectrometry tests were performed on the image of the Shroud. No substances were discovered (22). Mark Antonacci summarizes the conclusion of the paint investigation:

> To summarize, inorganic elements in paint (such as iron oxide and vermilion) as well as organic compounds (including gelatin) should have revealed themselves through sharp and identifiable

---

19. W. McCrone, *Judgment Day for the Shroud of Turin* (Amherst, NY: Prometheus, 1999).

20. E. A. Craig and B. R. Bresee, "Image Formation and the Shroud of Turin," *Journal of Imaging Science and Technology* 34:1 (February 1994).

features in STURP's many spectral studies. None were found—
not in all the ultraviolet, X-ray, and visible light studies that
measured fluorescence, absorption, reflectance, and emission
features of the Shroud body and blood images. As STURP members put it, the tests detected "none of the spectral characteristics expected form normal dyes, stains, and pigments..." This
important evidence confirms the fact that neither organic nor
inorganic compounds can be responsible for the body and blood
images on the Shroud of Turin.[21]

There are other problems with the painting hypothesis. It cannot
account for the superficiality of the image (17), as any sort of painting
would involve capillary flow and cementation between the fibers (22)
and would be absorbed deeper into the cloth. It cannot account for the
3-D-encoded information (19). Any normal painting would come out
vastly distorted under the VP-8 analyzer. Also a painting alone cannot
account for the presence of human blood on the Shroud (21), nor the
way the blood is splattered on the image (4–9), nor the fact that there
is no image under the blood (21). Finally, a painting cannot account
for the x-ray images on the Shroud (24).

Bas Relief and Scorching

A number of individuals have suggested a theory that depends on
using a heated metal bas relief of an image like on the Shroud. A linen
cloth, possibly soaked, is placed on the metal image, and the linen was
scorched with a copy of the metal image. This produces an image that
has some of the features found on the Shroud, such as a negative image
(14). However, in order to achieve the superficiality of the Shroud (17),
incredible control would have had to have been maintained over the
amount of time for the Shroud to be scorched. John Jackson theorizes
that at 200°C, a linen cloth could only be on the bas relief for 1/100 to
1/10 of a second. It seems extremely remote that anyone could have

---

21. M. Antonacci, *The Resurrection of the Shroud: New Scientific, Medical and Archeological Evidence* (New York: M. Evans and Company, 2000), 51. The quote is from R. N. Rogers and L. A. Schwalbe, "Physics and Chemistry of the Shroud of Turin," *Proceedings of the United States Conference of Research on the Shroud of Turin* (Albuquerque, NM: Holy Shroud Guild, March 1977), 21.

that kind of control, especially without modern technology.[22] This method also cannot account for the blood stains (21), especially that there was no image under the blood stains. Finally the x-ray features are not accounted for under this theory (24).

Bas Relief and Frottage

A similar theory was proposed by Luigi Garlaschelli, in which he claimed he definitively proved the Shroud was a fake. Again, bas relief was used for the face of the image, while a human body was used for the remaining image. Garlaschelli produced a full reproduction of both frontal and dorsal images of the Shroud using a frottage or rubbing technique. The linen was prepared with acidic compounds in a water-based slurry and placed over the body (and later over the bas relief of the head). It was then rubbed against the body/bas relief. Afterward, scourging marks and blood were added using a diluted pigment and then brushed on. Finally, the cloth was aged through heating. The result was an image that was "pseudo-negative, is fuzzy with half-tones, resides on the topmost layers of the cloth, [and] has some 3-dimensional properties."[23] However, while this image is similar to that of the Shroud, it differs in significant ways. One of the characteristics of the superficial image (17) on the Shroud is that the image-containing fibers are coated all the way around. This does not seem to be the case with Garlaschelli's image. Also, one would have assumed that evidence of the slurry, and certainly of the pigments, would have been detected if the Shroud was created in this fashion, and none was (22). The image is not as high-resolution, clear, and distinct as the Shroud (2). While the image contains some 3-D elements, it is mostly an image of flat plateaus and valleys, lacking the detail we find on the Shroud (24). And finally, there are no x-ray features on Garlaschelli's image (24).

---

22. Jackson, *The Shroud of Turin*, 105.
23. Jackson, *The Shroud of Turin*, 81.

Medieval Photography

One theory suggested by Nicholas Allen is that the Shroud was an example of a medieval photo-like process using a camera-obscura technique.[24] Camera obscura is a simple technique that most of us are familiar with; it's what we use when viewing a solar eclipse through a pinhole box projector. Allen used a life-sized sculpture of a body in bright sunlight focused through a lens made of a six-inch piece of quartz, which conveyed the image to a linen cloth covered with silver nitrate and located in a dark chamber. He produced a compelling image that showed many, but not all, of the features of the Shroud. However, one problem is that there is simply no evidence of any process like this having been used in medieval times. Not one example of this process has ever been found. Also, it is questionable if the superficiality would be retained, since silver nitrate is liquid and capillary action would have soaked it further into the image. (17). As a foreign substance, traces of it would have been detected (22). It does not account for the blood on the cloth, that there was no blood under the image (21), the 3-D information, (19] or the x-ray features (24).

The Shadow Hypothesis

Our final candidate for a man-made method is the shadow hypothesis, promoted by Nathan D. Wilson. This process also uses sunlight. A cloth is first aged by heating and is laid out in sunlight. Painted glass of differing shades is placed between the cloth and the sunlight. The painted cloth casts a shadow on the cloth. The shadow doesn't create a positive image, but a negative one, as the sunlight bleaches the unprotected portions of the cloth. Blood would then have been added to the cloth. While the negative image would have been achieved by this process, one wonders how a medieval forger would even conceive of producing a negative image. This method does not account for superficiality (17, 18). (The suggestion was made that a forger could bleach the other side of the fabric to create a superficial image, but why would he do that?) It also cannot account for the 3-D information (19), the blood and no image under the blood (21), and the x-ray image of bones and teeth (24).

---

24. Allen, N.P. "Verification of the Nature and Causes of the Photo-negative Images on the Shroud of Lirey-Chambery-Turin," *De Arte 51, Pretorua UNISA* (1995).

In the spirit of Gary Habermas, one can formulate a minimal facts argument against any forger theory. While Habermas uses minimal facts to argue in *favor* of the resurrection, I would like to suggest a minimal facts approach to argue *against* all the man-made theories. While I have stated that any theory must address all twenty-four of the features of the Shroud listed above, I think only a handful of those facts rule out the man-made theories. That is simply because we have no way of even conceptualizing how a medieval artist could have produced these features. I am speaking specifically of four facts: superficiality (17), double superficiality (18), 3-D information (19), and x-ray elements (24). These facts alone rule out any of the man-made theories. In fact, I think an argument can be made based on only one fact: superficiality (17). There doesn't seem to be any way the image can be produced that matches the extreme superficiality we see on the Shroud. Perhaps Thibault Heimberger expressed it best when he commented (specifically about Garlaschelli's theory) that

> "modern artists and researchers" (including [Garlaschelli]) know that they have to work in such a way that they have to produce a Shroud-like image with these properties. ... Up to know [*sic*] they all failed. What is the probability for a medieval forger, who obviously could not have in mind these properties, to produce by chance an image having the properties?[25]

Enhanced Naturalistic Theories

I refer to this final group of theories as "enhanced naturalistic theories" because, while the process involves a natural process (radiation), it is enhanced in that there is no real scientific explanation as to what would generate the process, at least to the level that it would have produced the image on the Shroud. Yet, if we are to follow the evidence to where it leads, I do believe it brings us here.

The Corona Discharge Model

A corona discharge (CD) is a natural electrical discharge brought on by the ionization of air surrounding a conductor in the presence of a strong electric field. Giulio Fanti is the main researcher suggesting

---

25. Quoted in Jackson, *Shroud of Turin*, 106.

that this may be how the image on the Shroud was formed. According to this theory, when a CD event occurs it normally emits light in the ultraviolet range, and this can cause an image to arise. According to Rose Sinclair, writing in *Textiles and Fashion,* "Corona discharge is an atmospheric pressure plasma process that exposes the fabric to high-energy electrons that can cause chemical and physical changes on the fabric surface."[26] Fanti and his team used a metalized mannequin covered with a cloth in a high-energy electric field that produced a CD. An image was left on the cloth that produced a number of Shroud-like features. It was a superficial image with some 3-D characteristics. However, the image was very distorted and had very little clarity [2]. Other experiments have had success at clear high-resolution images of smaller areas, like hands, but nothing clear has come of larger bodies. Fanti himself raises one major problem with this theory when he comments on the experiment above. "In this case almost all the chemical-physics characteristics match those of the Shroud, but one question remains: what could have developed a 300,000 V discharge in the sepulcher?"[27] Some have suggested a massive earthquake could have caused a sufficient electric discharge, especially if enough radon were present to ionize the air. Radon gas is often found in confined spaces in the vicinity of Jerusalem.

The Radiation Hypothesis

The view that seems best to address all of the features on the Shroud is the radiation hypothesis. While there are variations of the hypothesis, I will stay with the hypothesis suggested by Mark Antonacci, which he calls the "historically consistent hypothesis."[28] This hypothesis suggests that the Shroud was irradiated with particle radiation. Particle radiation occurs when protons and neutrons are emitted from atoms. When protons irradiate cellulose, it turns it into a straw-yellow color. That is the color of the image on the Shroud. Robert Rucker writes:

---

26. R. Sinclair, *Textiles and Fashion: Materials, Design and Technology* (Cambridge: Woodhead Publishing C., 2015), obtained online at https://www.sciencedirect.com/topics/engineering/corona-discharge.

27. G. Fanti and P. Malfi, *The Shroud of Turin: First Century after Christ!* (Singapore: Pan Stanford Publishing, 2015), 29.

28. Antonacci, *Test the Shroud*, 233.

The discoloration is caused by a rearrangement of the electron bonds of the carbon atoms that were already in the cellulose molecules of flax fibers in the linen threads, so that the discoloration does not result from new atoms being added to the cloth! The discoloration results from single electron bonds, that bond the carbon atoms to the surrounding atoms, being changed to double electron bonds. This change from single to double electron bonds of the carbon atoms took place in a pattern to create the front and back images of the crucified man on the Shroud! Thus, the discoloration is due to energy added to the cloth but without substance, i.e. atoms, being added to the cloth. The energy was evidently added to the cloth in one or more very short powerful bursts of radiation so that the electron bonding could be altered before the energy penetrated beyond the top one or two layers of fibers in a thread.[29]

However, where would this radiation come from? Antonacci and Rucker maintain that it could only have come from one source, the body itself. Again, Rucker explains,

The mechanism that discolored the fibers required energy to drive it and information to control it. Energy was necessary to change the single electron bonds of the carbon atoms into double electron bonds. Information was necessary to control which fibers were discolored and the length of that discoloration, so that the pattern of discoloration could form the image of a crucified man. ... This information could have only come from the body that was wrapped in the Shroud.[30]

Radiation has the benefit that it not only explains how the image was formed but also explains all twenty-four features listed above. More than that, it explains why the C-14 dating could have been skewed. In the burst of radiation, neutrons were emitted along with protons. While protons explain how the image was formed, neutrons explain why the C-14 dating was off. Carbon-14 is a rare isotope that

29. R. A. Rucker, "Status of Research on the Shroud of Turin" (Apr 18, 2019), 5, http://www.shroudresearch.net/hproxy.php/Status-of-Research-on-the-Shroud-of-Turin.pdf?lbisphpreq=1.
30. Rucker, "Status of Research."

is created in the upper atmosphere when a nitrogen-14 atom absorbs a neutron produced by a cosmic ray coming into our atmosphere. If neutrons were emitted in the burst of radiation that formed the image, then this same reaction (N-14 + neutron → C-14 + proton) would produce new C-14 on the Shroud, shifting the carbon date on the Shroud by up to thousands of years, depending on the location on the Shroud. This is the neutron absorption hypothesis.[31] Antonacci explains,

> C-14 is also created at very precise rates within any irradiated material containing nitrogen atoms, such as linen or blood. If the Shroud was irradiated by neutrons, new C-14 atoms would have also been created throughout this unique burial cloth. Neutron radiation would have substantially increased the C-14 content within the cloth making it appear much younger than its actual age.[32]

Even the scientists involved in the original C-14 dating acknowledged that neutron radiation would have significantly altered the date of the Shroud and invalidated the C-14 dating.

> When asked by a journalist soon after their results were announced whether such a process could have caused an incorrect dating of the Shroud, Michael Tite, who coordinated the carbon dating of the Shroud for the British Museum, commented: "It is certainly possible if one gave the Shroud a large dose of neutrons to produce C-14 from the nitrogen in the cloth." Robert Hedges, one of the scientists who participated in the carbon dating of the Shroud at the Oxford laboratory, also acknowledged to the journalist that a "sufficient level of neutrons from radiation on the Shroud would invalidate the radiocarbon date we obtained."[33]

It seems that the radiation hypothesis is currently the best explanation for how the image was formed on the Shroud, as it has the largest explanatory scope, greatest explanatory power, and is the most

---

31. The author is thankful to Robert Rucker for his input on this explanation.

32. M. Antonacci, *Test the Shroud at the Atomic and Molecular Levels* (Ashland, OH: Forefront Publishing Co., 2015), 119.

33. Antonacci, *Test the Shroud*, 123.

plausible defense (with all of the other evidences) for the Shroud's authenticity. Of course this does not mean it is problem free. The idea of a body releasing radiation in one powerful burst is, at present, scientifically unexplainable. It is certainly not a common event. However, eliminating scientism,[34] if one is open to the possibility of events occurring outside of our current understanding of science, then one should follow where the evidence leads. That seems to be that radiation left the body in the Shroud, causing both the image to transfer with all of its features and skewing the C-14 test to a younger date.

One additional benefit of Antonacci's hypothesis is that it is testable. Neutron radiation also affects the most common form of chlorine (Cl-35) and calcium (Ca-40), converting them to new elements by adding a neutron, creating Cl-36 and Ca-41. These atoms do not exist in nature. Therefore, all one would need to do is to test the Shroud for the presence of these two elements. Their presence would go a long way toward scientifically confirming that the Shroud was irradiated with neutrons. Currently there are no plans for scientific testing on the Shroud, hence the title of Antonacci's book is a plea: *Test the Shroud at the Atomic and Nuclear Levels.*

An Apologetic Assessment

Considering all the evidence for the authenticity of the Shroud, including the image characteristics; scientific, historical, and medical evidence; and the best theory for the formation of the image on the cloth, I believe a plausible and reasonable argument can be made that the best explanation for the identity of the Shroud is that it is the actual burial cloth of Jesus. However, we have yet to discuss its apologetic value. For even if it is the authentic burial shroud of Jesus, one can easily say, "Well, so what?"

I remember years ago reading an editorial in response to the original published findings of the 1978 STURP investigation in which the author said (I am paraphrasing here), "Ultimately, it really doesn't make any difference to one's faith. Skeptics won't believe it, and believers

---

34. "Roughly, scientism is the view that the hard sciences—like chemistry, biology, physics, astronomy—provide the only genuine knowledge of reality." J. P. Moreland, *Scientism and Secularism: Learning to Respond to a Dangerous Ideology* (Wheaton, IL: Crossway, 2018), 25.

don't need it." I am not so sure that is entirely true, and so I would like to explore those two options.

At face value, it does seem that most skeptics will not even consider discussion of the Shroud as a live option. This is probably the case for the confirmed religious skeptic, one who is staunchly entrenched in his or her skepticism. Such a person is usually close-minded to any argument or evidence that comes close to affirming the truthfulness of a religious belief. However, not all skeptics are of this variety. Some approach religious questions with a naturalistic bent but are open to hearing other arguments and following the evidence where it leads. True, they will be suspicious of religious claims and will always look for naturalistic alternative explanations, giving such explanations priority over claims that, while not religious in themselves, reach religious conclusions. I find such skepticism healthy. We should not accept evidence uncritically, and we should have a healthy skepticism when we hear claims that are outside of what others and we have experienced in life. When I am told that an individual who was diagnosed with terminal stage-four cancer is suddenly and inexplicably cancer free after friends prayed for him, I am initially skeptical. It is not that I don't believe that God can miraculously heal; I am just initially skeptical that he did it this time. I want to explore alternative possibilities and see if they offer a better explanation before I adopt the miracle view.

I think for the healthy skeptic, the evidence for the Shroud might have some positive effect. She might not buy everything, but if she is open to seeking the truth, the evidence for the Shroud might open the door to further explorations to the claims of Christianity. Much would depend on how the material is presented. I think one should start first by just observing the image characteristics in light of the Gospel accounts. Then one might go into the scientific evidence, as that is usually where most modern skeptics believe truth can be found. There are some debatable lines of evidence that I would avoid with our skeptic. One does not want to embroil her in a debate that even Shroud experts are not sure of (the coins over the eyes being a good example). Stick with those lines of evidence that are the most strong and convincing; revisit the controversies later.

Do believers need the Shroud? The obvious answer is no. The Shroud could turn out to be a forgery or fake news and it would not affect any belief about Jesus Christ as the son of God or what he did on earth or his death and resurrection. There is plenty of evidence of these cardinal beliefs apart from the Shroud. The Shroud is not necessary to support the truth of any aspect of Christianity. However, I would stop short of saying it has no value.

Some have suggested that, given its extraordinary features and the best explanation we have of its origin, the Shroud constitutes definitive evidence of the resurrection. While it is true that the radiation event we discussed would be a rare anomaly, perhaps having occurred just once, I would be cautious of such a claim. The fact is, we simply do not know what a resurrection event would look like, nor what residual effects it might leave behind. To make any such claims is to go beyond the evidence, even if the Shroud is the authentic burial cloth of Jesus. I am open to the radiation hypothesis as being in line with the resurrection, but I would not claim it is evidence of it. One might say that while the Shroud does not prove the resurrection of Jesus, his resurrection might explain the Shroud. It is reasonable to expect that something like a resurrection, in which a normal human body would become a resurrection body, would leave residual effects, and that one of them would be an image on a shroud.

Assuming its authenticity, I think its greatest apologetic value is that it confirms the Gospel accounts of the events surrounding the passion of Jesus. The Gospels report that he was beaten and flogged (Mt 27: 26, 30; Mark 15:15, 19; Luke 22: 64; John 19:1), and we clearly see on the Shroud what would be marks on the legs, back, and face. The Gospels report that he was crowned with a crown of thorns (Matt 27:29; Mark 15:17; John 19:2), and we see puncture marks from a crown. The Gospels report that he was crucified (Matt 27:35; Mark 15:24; Luke 23:33; John 19:18), and we see punctures in the wrist and feet and blood flowing down from extended arms. Finally, John's Gospel specifically mentions that a soldier, having seen that Jesus was already dead, pierced his side, and that blood and water then emerged (John 19:34). The water, most likely being serum separated from the blood, which one would expect to see of a post-mortem wound, is likely what we see on the Shroud. So what the Shroud does supply is empirical evidence supporting the Gospel accounts as reliable concerning the passion of Jesus.

In the end, questions and mysteries remain, some of which may never be answered. If asked how probable I think it is that Shroud is the authentic burial cloth of Jesus, I am not sure I can arrive at a percentage, as my friend Gary Habermas is often inclined to do. I do think that it is currently the best explanation for the existence and features of the Shroud. That may be the best one could ever say.[35]

My List of the Best Shroud Books and Websites

For those who want to do serious study, there are hundreds of books to choose from. In my humble opinion, these are the best out there:

Books

Antonacci, Mark. *The Resurrection of the Shroud: New Scientific, Medical, Archaeological Evidence.* New York: M. Evans and Company, 2000.

——. *Test the Shroud at the Atomic and Molecular Levels.* Ashland, OH: Forefront Publishing Co, 2015.

Fanti, Gulio, and Pierandrea Malfi. *The Shroud of Turin: First Century After Christ!* Singapore: Pan Stanford Publishers, 2015.

Habermas, Gary. R., and Kenneth. E. Stevenson. *Verdict on the Shroud: Evidence for the Death and Resurrection of Jesus Christ.* Servant Books, 1981.

——. *The Shroud and the Controversy: Science, Skepticism, and the Search for Authenticity* Nashville: Thomas Nelson Inc., 1990.

Jackson, John. *The Shroud of Turin: A Critical Summery of Observations, Data and Hypotheses.* Colorado Springs, CO: The Turin Shroud Center of Colorado, 2017.

Whanger, Alan, and Mary Whanger. *The Shroud of Turin: An Adventure of Discovery.* Franklin, TN: Providence House Publishers, 1998.

Wilcox, Robert K. *The Truth about the Shroud of Turin.* Washington, DC: Regnery Publishing, 2010.

Wilson, Ian. *The Shroud: Fresh Light on the 2000-Year Old Mystery...* London: Bantam Books, 2010.

---

35. I wish to express thanks to Robert Rucker for his review and comments on an earlier draft of this paper.

www.shroud.com, run by Barrie Schwortz, who was the official documentation photographer for STURP; great photographs with the best collection of articles, papers and other resources.

www.shroudresearch.net, run by Robert Rucker, a nuclear scientists who has written many excellent papers.

www.shroudofturin.com, run by John Jackson and the Shroud Center of Colorado; they put together an updated Critical Summary of Observations, Data and Hypotheses.

www.testtheshroud.org, Mark Antonacci's site promoting further research on the Shroud.

www.shroudcenter.com, Ross Bereaukt's site; Ross has been working on the Shroud for over 25 years.

www.shroudphotos.com, by Vernon Miller, the main scientific photographer for STURP.

4

THE UNIQUENESS OF CHRISTIANITY
IN A WORLD OF RELIGIONS

Craig J. Hazen

G ary Habermas's lifelong research and teaching on the resurrection of Jesus naturally calls for a comparative study. Even if one is convinced of Jesus' resurrection by the kinds of evidence and arguments unearthed and published by Habermas, one is then compelled to ask at least one more important apologetic question: Did anything comparable take place in any of the other historic world religions?

Habermas himself explored this comparative path briefly in a wonderful little web publication in 2016 titled, "The Uniqueness of Jesus among the Major World Religions" (www.garyhabermas.com/evidence2). I want to pick up on that thread and add some other unique features of Christianity that I have explored over the years through my own work in comparative religion. In my view, Habermas is right to focus on the claims of the historical Jesus and the demonstration of the truth of those by means of the resurrection. But I don't think followers of Christ would be surprised at all to find that Jesus left for us other important points of uniqueness and authenticity that follow closely in the wake of his conquest of death.

One afternoon I received a call in my office at Biola University from a teaching assistant at a local community college. He was contacting me on behalf of a professor in a religious studies course who was looking for representatives from various spiritual traditions to come and speak in his classroom. The professor wanted the students to hear firsthand from a wide range of religious thinkers and devotees—an admirable idea in my view. I was free on the morning they were asking about, so I was delighted to go and address the group.

A couple of days later I found myself in the classroom, and, after a few announcements, the professor began to introduce me as the morning's speaker. "This is Craig Hazen, and he will be interacting with us this morning from the standpoint of his religious tradition, fundamentalist Christianity."

The label caught me off guard. I thought I was coming to talk about a much broader category, such as Christianity in general, or maybe Protestant Christianity, or even evangelical Protestant Christianity—all of which I could claim as my tradition. The term "fundamentalist" used to carry a noble meaning but had lost its cachet long, long ago.

In the brief introduction, the professor did not mention that I had earned a PhD in religious studies at the University of California, that I had studied at the International Institute for Human Rights in Strasbourg, France, or that I had run a biology research laboratory. Perhaps he didn't mention these because they do not fit the stereotype of a fundamentalist, which has come to mean, among other things, a kind of anti-intellectualism and separation from mainstream society. He knew that I was a professor of some kind myself, but he probably assumed that my graduate education consisted of memorizing obscure verses from the King James Bible at "Grover's Bible College and Feed Lot."

In order to paint a more positive picture as quickly as possible, I reintroduced myself and gave them a little bit of background about my interest in the study of religions from around the world, human rights, and science. This caused the students a little bit of confusion, because they did not connect fundamentalists with serious academic work—especially in these kinds of subjects.

I made a snap decision really to turn the tables on them that morning by doing something much different than a standard presentation about biblical Christianity. I told them that given my background in religious, scientific, and cultural studies, I wanted to impart to them something very valuable—some practical knowledge that would help them in tangible ways.

I assumed something about the students that turned out to be correct. Many of them were taking the popular religious studies survey class because they were very curious about the various traditions. In some respects, they were using the class to take some of these religions out for a kind of non-threatening test drive.

What I proposed to do that morning was to give them an expert guided tour on just how a clear-thinking person would go about a religious quest. Here you are at the college, I told them, attempting to use analytic skills and careful reasoning to gain knowledge and insight into subjects ranging from music appreciation to organic chemistry. Why shouldn't we use those same cognitive tools to help us make sense of the seemingly crazy world of religion, especially since many of you are doing some very careful evaluation about what religion you might embrace yourself one day? In other words, how would a thoughtful person go about a religious quest?

Well the students were genuinely interested in this idea. It did not dawn on me until later why they were so fascinated at this prospect. As it turned out, in their experience no one had ever linked the ideas of clear thinking or rational assessment with the pursuit of religion. It is as if they were separate categories (rationality and religion) and "never the twain shall meet." Nevertheless, they really thought this was a novel idea and a great gesture. It was already toward the end of the term, and the professor had never offered anything along these lines, nor had any of his guest speakers. The students were very enthusiastic, but the whole topic had the added side bonus of helping the students to forget all about "fundamentalism." So with a willing nod from the professor of the class—who later told me he, too, wanted to hear what I had to say about such a novel topic—I started.

The first point I made in my impromptu presentation was actually a setback for my hope of shedding the fundamentalist label the professor had pinned on me. The students recoiled at the first proposition to come out of my mouth. In all honesty, looking back I probably said it without much nuance in order to stir things up a bit. Maybe deep down I wanted to get the students to a full and verifiable state of consciousness before I got onto the details of my talk. It worked. In fact, one sleepy surfer in the back of the room came alive after my statement and was even waving a skateboard with one hand to emphasize certain points when he joined the discussion.

What was this unsettling statement I made that attracted the momentary ire of the college class and caused the bags under their eyes to disappear? It was this: I made the unabashed claim that any thoughtful person who was on a religious quest would obviously start that quest by exploring Christianity first. In other words, a person eventually has to make a choice about where to start any kind of journey. If one is looking to buy a new car, one needs to decide if he should first visit the Daewoo or the BMW dealership. There must be some rational, objective criteria that a person uses to decide where to go first to kick the tires—price, proximity, status, reputation, quality, and a whole range of personal preferences. To at least some extent, the same should be true with religious traditions if you are intentionally setting out to explore them. Remember, I'm not trying to decide which tradition is *true* at this point, but rather with which tradition it makes the most sense to start the quest. A person has to start somewhere. I think Christianity is, by any rational measure, the obvious place for a thinking person to start the exploration.

After a few moments of mostly good-hearted heckling from the students, I told the class that I would give them four reasons why a thoughtful person on a religious quest would obviously start with exploring Christianity. I spent the rest of my time with them that morning presenting this case with a lot of spirited interaction.

What follows is the case I made to the class: "Four Reasons Why a Thoughtful Person on a Religious Quest Should Start That Quest with Christianity." Of course, I've done a lot of thinking about my off-the-cuff lecture and have fleshed it out a bit in these pages. But the basic four points are the same.

1: Christianity Is Testable

I told the students that morning that at the heart of the Christian tradition are some claims about Jesus—his life, his teaching, his death, and his resurrection—that are testable. What I mean by this is that these claims are such that any thinking person can examine the evidence and reasonably determine whether or not the claims are historically accurate or justified. I think this is one of the primary reasons why a thoughtful person sorting through the various religious traditions would obviously start with Christianity. Christianity is unique in that it actually *invites* people to investigate carefully its claims about God, humankind, the universe, and the meaning of life.

There is a passage in the Bible that supports this notion—and I consider it to be one of the strangest passages in all of religious literature. In the New Testament, the Apostle Paul writes something that is a bit shocking given the way we normally think about religion and faith in the modern world. In this passage Paul is giving a discourse on the Christian view of life after death. But then in the midst of this he says something that seems startling to our common sensibilities about religion. He says, "If Christ has not been raised [from the dead], our preaching is useless and so is your *faith*" (1 Cor 15:14). Maybe just to make sure we would not be confused about what he is saying here, he repeats the idea several verses later. "And if Christ has not been raised, your *faith* is futile" (1 Cor 15:17a).

Now why would I consider this to be one of the strangest passages in all of religious literature? For this reason: I have not been able to find a passage in the scriptures and teachings of the other great religious traditions that so tightly links the truth of an entire system of belief to a single, testable historical event. Real faith in these statements seems to be invariably linked to the truth of a real-world occurrence. What the Apostle Paul said here was radical in the context of most religious traditions. He was saying, in essence, that if Jesus did not come back from the dead (in his own body, as the witnesses and Scriptures declared), if this did not really take place in time and space, then Christianity is bunk—our Christian faith is worthless, useless, or futile.

This idea that the truth of Christianity is linked to the resurrection of Jesus in a testable way really does set Christianity apart from the other great world religious traditions in a dramatic fashion. Historic Asian religions, by and large, don't even argue with the point. When it all boils down, Hinduism, Buddhism, and the like are about inner personal experience and not about objective public knowledge. There are other traditions that *seem* to be about objective knowledge, until you probe a little more deeply. Mormonism, for instance, seems to be about hidden gold plates, Jesus' ancient visit to the western hemisphere, and latter-day prophets—things that could certainly be, in principle, evaluated in an objective way. However, when facing evidence contrary to these claims, the Mormon missionary, scholar, or apostle steps back and begins to talk about the special inner knowledge, a "burning in the bosom," that is the only confirmation that really counts about these unusual stories. At the end of the day, the Mormon is no different than the Buddhist in that they both rely on inner experience as their ultimate source and warrant for religious knowledge.

This is why Christianity is unique and why a thoughtful person on a religious quest would be wise to start the quest with Christianity—it really is testable. If Jesus did not come back from the dead after being executed by a Roman crucifixion team in first-century Jerusalem, then, according to the apostle Paul, Christianity is simply not true. It openly invites people to investigate its claims objectively.

2: In Christianity, Salvation Is a Free Gift from God

Almost every time I speak on a college campus about why a thoughtful person would start her religious quest with Christianity, I wonder if I really need all four reasons. The first two reasons are so powerful that in my mind they can carry the day without much help from the other two that I present.

This isn't a hard conclusion to come to. Think about it. What if someone were to come up to you on a street corner and present to you a new path to God? During the presentation it becomes clear that the ideas being offered are in no way testable, so you can never, in principle, objectively know whether or not they are true. In addition, the picture painted of God is that he requires a great deal from you. You must strive heroically to change the way you think, feel, and behave in every corner of your life in order to please the deity and move forward on the path of salvation or enlightenment. Indeed, it might be the case that you will need to strive heroically for many lifetimes in order to reach the mark. Of course, there is a final logical twist here. If you have no way to gauge whether the basic religious system is true, you could also never know whether or not your intense striving to please the deity was enough or if you were doing the right things in the right way. Even if at the end of the day a religious system like this *is* true, it doesn't make a whole lot of sense for someone exploring the various religious options to *start* the exploration with such a system.

By way of contrast, what if someone were to come up to you on the same street corner and present to you a religious system that was testable—hence opening the door for you to do a vigorous investigation of its claims? In addition, the system sets forth a picture of God as a loving father who wants to give the free gift of salvation to anyone who will receive it. Do I need to say more? If this testable and free system accurately describes Christianity, and if the untestable and arduous system accurately describes the other religious options, then I don't see how a reasonable person would not start their search with Christianity. It seems like a no-brainer of Olympic proportions.

Christianity is unique in its offer of salvation by grace alone—a free gift from God to anyone who will receive it. In the history of religion, there have only been a couple of instances of a religious movement that considered salvation or enlightenment to be a free gift from a deity. But even in those cases (such as in *Amida* Buddhism or a certain form of *bhakti* Hinduism) it is not a no-strings-attached kind of gift. There is still work to be done on the part of the devotees.

Hence, the Christian tradition stands in a solitary spot in the spectrum of world religions when the apostle Paul writes in Ephesians 2:8–9, "For it is by grace you have been saved, through faith—and this not from yourselves, it is the gift of God—not by works, so that no one can boast."

Salvation in Christianity is a free gift, and hence it is equally available to anyone. You don't need to be a spiritual superstar, of noble birth, or highly educated. Anyone can come, as they sometimes sing at revival meetings, "just as I am." This is a very attractive and unique feature and makes Christianity an obvious choice as a starting place for a religious quest.

3: In Christianity, You Get an Amazing Worldview Fit

If you are trying to prioritize a group of religions in order to know which one you ought to check out first, it would be extremely helpful to know which of the religions painted a picture of the world that seemed to be a very tight match with the way the world really is. If such a match could be determined, I know it would give reasonable people a lot of confidence that they were making a good choice about their starting point.

Let me come at this from the other direction. It seems reasonable to me that a thoughtful person would not want to start her religious quest with a religion that seemed to have tremendous difficulty making sense of the world that we encounter. The problem here is that the world we bump into on a daily basis is one of the only sources of data we have to work with in evaluating all kinds of claims, including religious claims.

So if you have a choice to study under a guru whose mission it is to reveal to the world that the moon's surface is made of spumoni ice cream, or under one who thinks the moon's outer layer is primarily anorthosite rock, I think a reasonable person would go with the one whose teaching seems to have the closest match to the way the universe really is. That is the general principle I am trying to communicate with this third claim.

It is a bold claim to say that the Christian worldview fits best with the way the world really is, simply because so much would need to be examined to find out if this assertion is justified. After all, the list of things to compare seems endless. But from my perspective, what I have learned about the various religions and about the world in general makes this claim totally plausible. Since I obviously cannot explore every aspect of the world (from cosmology to cosmetology) to demonstrate in just a few pages that this is reasonable, I shall use one very profound example to illustrate the point: the problem of evil, pain, and suffering.

Every human being observes evil and experiences pain and suffering on almost a daily basis. It seems obvious to me that any religion that does not do justice to these common human experiences should probably not be at the top of the list for a thoughtful religious seeker. How do the various religious traditions explain these phenomena or make sense of them?

Devotees of Eastern religious traditions, such as Buddhism and Hinduism, certainly encounter the same kinds of evil, pain, and suffering that other people around the globe experience. But teachers, thinkers, and leaders in these movements have a very different way of dealing with the experience than we normally do in the western world. Eastern traditions normally put evil, pain, and suffering in the category of illusion. Suffering can therefore be overcome through the understanding of its true nature. Evil and pain will fade away as the devotee gains enlightenment about the illusory nature of the phenomenal world. As a famous Tibetan lama once wrote to me after I had given a lecture on Buddhism, "Evil and suffering are real only as long as the ego believes them to be real." The Lama put it in the simplest words possible for practical purposes. His solution to evil and suffering was to change what we believe about them. They will then cease to be real.

Well, it's time to finally ask the big question. If we are in search of a worldview that matches the way the world really is, then how do we evaluate these approaches to evil? After having some dialogue with the students for a short time on this question, I gave them the following illustration.

I have twin boys, and when they were babies, together they played a character on a highly rated television sitcom. My wife and I would be on the set quite often, taking care of them when they were not rehearsing or filming. Several of the writers and cast members heard that I was some sort of religion professor and found it interesting to discuss some of their religious ideas with me. One time, over dinner before an evening filming, I remember listening at length to one of them describe in great detail the teachings of a new guru she was following. Although some of it sounded a bit off kilter to me, it was easy to sit and listen because it was so very interesting to see how Eastern religious concepts were being enfolded into a Hollywood mindset. One of the points this woman was making was that her guru thought that good and evil were ultimately not real and could be transcended through right views. After I'd had several plates of food (the catered cuisine was outstanding on the day of the performance) and a couple of cappuccinos, the woman finally asked me for my reaction to all of this—and she had covered a range of topics. I only asked one question, and I didn't ask it to be provocative or cheeky. I was genuinely curious about the answer. I thought it would simply keep the conversation going. I asked, "What would your guru say about the Holocaust?"

Several things happened the moment I asked the question. I hadn't realized that a number of people sitting nearby had already been tuned into our conversation for some time. But now they weren't pretending to pick at their food any more. They lifted their heads and turned them in our direction. It turns out that a good number of the cast, crew, and production staff were Jewish. As you can imagine, they were also very interested in the answer to the question. The woman I was dialoguing with hadn't noticed the audience subtly growing around us. She was busy thinking through the implications of the question. She had a bit of a blank stare, and from the look on her face it seemed as if her whole worldview was imploding inside her head. You see, she too came from a Jewish family. And although she was far too young to be involved in the horror herself and did not even practice her family's faith, she knew very well from her family, extended family, and her Jewish cultural connections that the Holocaust was a defining chapter in her own identity and approach to life. The Holocaust was real and could not be denied in any sense—not historically, not emotionally, not morally.

Somehow (and I've seen this happen often) this woman had been completely blind to a gaping hole in her view of things as she was learning from her new guru. How could she so thoroughly buy into her guru's teaching about evil being an illusion and still take seriously the unthinkable suffering that the Jews of Europe endured? She couldn't. And it certainly wasn't anything I said. I just happened to be there when she had a moment of enlightenment of a very different kind: a realization that a worldview that attempts to dismiss such profound evil, pain, and suffering as illusion is simply not a viable guide to life.

Every religion has to attempt to make sense of evil because it is such a pervasive and serious phenomenon. And every religion struggles in the task. The Scriptures of Christianity confront the issue of evil head-on, starting with the first pages of Genesis. There is a whole section of the Bible, the book of Job, dedicated to the unanswerable questions that are involved in personal suffering. Although the Bible never answers the "why" question in cases of individual instances of suffering (such as, Why did the drunk driver crash into *me*?), it does provide the most satisfactory context for coming to terms with the existence of evil.

Although I believe the biblical approach to the problem of evil to be true, I am not arguing for it here (there are many persuasive books that do argue it very effectively). I am trying to make the more modest claim that if given the choice between a worldview that simply dismisses pain and suffering as ultimately not real and a worldview that admits that they do indeed exist, the choice is obvious. You would choose the latter. This really is tightly analogous to the question I asked at the beginning of this section. Would you be more inclined to follow a guru who taught that the surface of the moon was made of spumoni ice cream or one who taught that it was made of anorthosite rock? Saying that evil is an illusion is like saying that the moon's surface is made of spumoni. We can rightly claim to have knowledge that both claims are not true. A good worldview deals with the obvious; it does not dismiss it.

My bold assertion at the outset was that the picture Christianity paints of the world actually matches, better than any other option available, the way the world really is. Of course, as I predicted at the beginning, I didn't even come close to proving this point, because I would have had to explore so many issues in great depth. But I (and, more importantly, a whole host of people much smarter than me in our own day and throughout history) have come to the conclusion that the basic Christian view of the world is the only viable option.

4: Christianity Has Jesus at the Center

My time with the students was almost over. I was talking fast all morning to try to pack in all of my reasons for why a thoughtful person on a religious quest would start with exploring Christianity. I thought I had made a pretty good case. The students were very attentive, and hence I assumed interested in what I had to say. However, when I presented my fourth reason, things unexpectedly turned sour for a moment. I claimed that a good reason to start with Christianity was that it had Jesus as the indisputable center of the tradition. The student with the skateboard immediately chimed in. He remarked that it was interesting I waited until the end to slip in such a loaded reason—a reason that sounded a lot more like straightforward evangelism than anything else.

I looked at the professor for the class, who was sitting at the far end of the first row. I asked him if he had a chance during the semester to go over the views about Jesus among the religions of the world. He said he hadn't and gave me permission to address it if I wanted to. I took him up on the offer.

I could understand why skateboard guy and others in the class had an initial problem with my point about Jesus. They were missing some crucial information, so they were misunderstanding where I was going with my remarks. Jesus is, without doubt, the closest thing the world has to a universal religious figure. Almost every religious tradition wants to claim him as its own in one way or another. My comment that "Christianity has Jesus at the center" is not a raw assertion of my own religious position. Rather, it is an argument that if Jesus is such an attractive figure that the religious people of the world want to co-opt him for their own traditions, then it makes perfect sense to give special attention to Christianity, the tradition that plants Jesus firmly at its center and claims him as its founder.

This is certainly not a raw assertion of religious favoritism—just the opposite. It is another very strong reason for a thoughtful person to start their religious exploration with Christianity: everybody wants to claim Jesus as their own.

Take Hinduism, for example. There are many teachers and scholars who have proclaimed Jesus to be one of the ten avatars of Vishnu, alongside Rama and Krishna. Vishnu is one of the major deities in the Hindu pantheon of gods, and an avatar is "one who descends." Hence, it is not uncommon to find Jesus set forth as a kind of incarnation of Lord Vishnu. This is certainly not the documented historical picture of Jesus, but it does demonstrate the respect and influence he commands among many faithful Hindus. It is not unusual for a Hindu to revere Jesus to the point of veneration because he is such an impressive figure.

Likewise, it is not at all unusual for Buddhists of the later Mahayana traditions to see Jesus as a preeminent spiritual figure. Often, he is considered to be a great "bodhisattva," that is, one who is motivated by compassion to step back from the brink of nirvana in order to help others along the path to awakening. Buddhists often believe that, during his day, Jesus offered all of the Buddhist teaching (dharma) to which his generation was open. A few even see him as the maitreya bodhisattva, an enlightened messianic being in the Tusita heaven awaiting his last reincarnation. The Tibetan Buddhist leader, the Dalai Lama, has said on several occasions that he is not worthy to be compared with Jesus, believing that Jesus is a "fully enlightened being."

Islam is an especially interesting case. One would not glean from popular treatments of Islam that Jesus even enters into the religious picture. But knowledgeable Muslims and their texts give the fuller view. If the Muslim prophet, Muhammad, and Jesus went head-to-head in a simple contest where their special attributes were tallied up, Jesus would win by at least six to one. Muhammad was a prophet. According the Qur'an and Islamic tradition, Jesus was also a prophet. However, unlike Muhammad, Jesus was also born of a virgin, was a worker of miracles, was carried to heaven by Allah without tasting death, was called the Word of God, and will return to appear to all before the final judgment—all according to the Qur'an. Now clearly Muhammad is considered the greatest prophet because he carried the final message of Allah to humankind. But Jesus is a revered figure who is second only to Muhammad in honor and respect. Muslims certainly do not consider him to be divine, but they do consider him a pinnacle of righteousness and a non-negotiable object of belief.

Of course, the parade of Jesus enthusiasts does not end there. It is hard to find a major tradition or a minor movement that does not give him a very special place of honor and find significant ways to fold him into their system of beliefs. The Baha'i, the Sikhs, the Mormons, the New Age Movement, the Unitarians, Religious Science, the Jehovah's Witnesses, the Jains, the Deists, and many more all find a way, as the 1970 Anne Murray hit song says, to put their "hand in the hand of the man from Galilee."

Since Jesus is, by any measure, the only universal religious person, a figure so towering that almost every religious body has to find a way to bring him aboard in some capacity, it makes perfect sense to me that anyone on a religious quest would know just where to start.

Conclusion

My official time in front of the class of college students had ended, but the discussion certainly did not. At least a dozen students followed me out the door, and we sat at some tables outside and discussed big religious issues for several more hours. Even though my talk ended up being quite a Christo-centric presentation, the students were not put off by that. These are difficult issues, and they seemed to appreciate not just that I took a position, but that I invited careful scrutiny of my own conclusions. As one young woman said at the end of our time together, "What are we so afraid of? We ought to be asking the toughest questions and religious leaders and teachers should be prepared with honest answers. If there is a God, one thing is certain: he made us thinking people. As long as we are kind to each other, we should be able to discuss these things openly."

She was right; we shouldn't be afraid. Her comment reminded me of a famous saying of the apostle Peter from the New Testament—really a command to all Christian believers: "Always be prepared to give an answer to everyone who asks you to give the reason for the hope that you have. But do this with gentleness and respect" (1 Pet 3:15).

5

JOHN RAWLS'S POLITICAL LIBERALISM AND THE PROBLEM OF TAKING RITES SERIOUSLY: FROM ABORTION TO SAME-SEX WEDDING CAKES

Francis J. Beckwith

I first met Gary Habermas in 1986 when I was a PhD student at Fordham University in New York City. While doing research for what would eventually become my doctoral dissertation,[1] I came across Gary's 1980 book *The Resurrection of Jesus: An Apologetic*.[2] It was one of several of Gary's books that I would read over the next year in preparation for defending my dissertation proposal. Because there was no email or social media in those days, when I had several questions about Gary's work, I simply called him on the telephone. To my surprise, he not only answered the phone—we talked for nearly ninety minutes. He was sincerely interested in my project and, in the course of our conversation, made several important suggestions that I would later incorporate into my dissertation. This was the first of scores of conversations that we would have over the phone for well over a decade. Through those years, we stayed in each other's homes, were roommates at academic conferences, contributed to the same books, and participated together in both lay and professional events.

---

1. Francis J. Beckwith, "David Hume's Argument against Miracles: Contemporary Attempts to Rehabilitate It and a Response" (PhD diss., Fordham University, 1988).

2. Gary Habermas, *The Resurrection of Jesus: An Apologetic* (Grand Rapids: Baker Book House, 1980; republished by University Press of America, 1984).

In those days, I was, like Gary and most other Christian philosophers, primarily interested in questions having to with the rationality of Christian belief and the contemporary challenges to it. Although I still think those questions are important,[3] and I occasionally teach courses that address them, my interests have shifted dramatically toward political and legal philosophy, and in particular the debates about the place of religious reasons in public life.[4] It may surprise some of Gary's readers to learn that he has had an interest in these questions for quite some time, though to my knowledge he has never addressed them in his scholarship. He has, however, discussed them privately with friends and colleagues for decades. (How could he not, given the important place in American politics played by the Rev. Jerry Falwell, Sr. [1933–2007], the larger-than-life founder of Liberty University, the academic institution Gary has called home for nearly four decades and at which he serves as a distinguished professor?)

In this chapter, I want to honor Gary by offering an original contribution in which I briefly reflect on the work of the late political and social philosopher John Rawls (1921–2002) and its application to one of the most hotly contested questions on religious liberty: should vendors have a right to refuse to cooperate with the celebration of a same-sex wedding for religious reasons? Because he died in 2002, Rawls never addressed this question. Nevertheless, as I argue below, I think we can gain some insight into how Rawls could have answered this question if we look at how he wrestled with the issue of legal restrictions on abortion.

---

3. See, e.g., Francis J. Beckwith, *Never Doubt Thomas: The Catholic Aquinas as Evangelical and Protestant* (Waco, TX: Baylor University Press, 2019); Francis J. Beckwith, "All Worship the Same God: Referring to the Same God View," in *Do Christians, Muslims, and Jews Worship the Same God?: Four Views*, eds. Ronnie P. Campbell and Christopher Gnanakan (Grand Rapids: Zondervan, 2019); Francis J. Beckwith, *Return to Rome: Confessions of An Evangelical Catholic* (Grand Rapids: Brazos Press, 2009); Francis J. Beckwith, William Lane Craig, and J. P. Moreland, eds., *To Everyone an Answer: A Case for the Christian Worldview* (Downers Grove, IL: InterVarsity Press, 2004).

4. See, e.g., Francis J. Beckwith, *Defending Life: A Moral and Legal Case Against Abortion Choice* (New York: Cambridge University Press, 2007); Francis J. Beckwith, *Politics for Christians: Statecraft as Soulcraft* (Downers Grove, IL: InterVarsity Press, 2010); Francis J. Beckwith, Susan McWilliams, and Robert P. George, eds., *A Second Look at First Things: A Case for Conservative Politics* (South Bend, IN: St. Augustine's Press, 2013); Francis J. Beckwith, *Taking Rites Seriously: Law, Politics, and the Reasonableness of Faith* (New York: Cambridge University Press, 2015)

The year 2018 marked the twenty-fifth anniversary of the publication of the first edition of John Rawls' *Political Liberalism*.[6] He famously, and repeatedly, tells us that the project of this book is to answer the question: "How is it possible that there may exist over time a stable and just society of free and equal citizens profoundly divided by reasonable religious, philosophical, and moral doctrines?"[7]

As with much of the philosophical literature on religion and politics published between roughly the early 1970s through the late 1990s, *Political Liberalism* confronted the question of whether religious citizens could justly pass laws, informed by their faith, which coerced citizens who did not share that faith.[8] The stock examples at the time (though not all employed by Rawls) were laws that prohibited the propagation and use of obscene materials, severely limited or banned access to abortion or birth control, proscribed physician-assisted suicide, favored one religion over another, and restricted sexual relations to marital acts between men and women. For, as was evident to anyone who had eyes to see, the opposing camps on these moral issues ran largely (though not entirely) along religious lines.

During this era, the conventional wisdom, at least among a certain cadre of philosophers, was that on matters of deep moral disagreement (such as the ones just mentioned) the state should restrain its coercive hand, even if a majority of citizens on one side of the dispute thinks it has the better argument for what it believes is the correct moral position on the matter. According to Rawls, these disagreements arise as

---

5. What follows in this chapter is a revised version of a paper I first presented at the 2019 Eastern Division Meeting of the American Philosophical Association in New York City (January 7–9), as part of the symposium "Religious Philosophers on Neutralist Liberalism: 25 Years of Rawls's *Political Liberalism*." I would like to thank the other panelists—Paul Weithman (Notre Dame), Jorge L. A. Garcia (Boston College), and Christopher J. Eberle (US Naval Academy)—as well as several audience members for their important feedback.

6. John Rawls, *Political Liberalism* (New York: Columbia University Press, 1993). In all later editions, including the 1995 paperback edition and the 2005 expanded edition, the pagination of what was the first edition remains the same. Because throughout this paper I will be referring to portions of the latter editions, I will only be citing from the expanded edition: *Political Liberalism*, expanded ed. (New York: Columbia University Press, 2005).

7. Rawls, *Political Liberalism*, xv.

8. Rawls does not single out religious belief, as do other writers, like Robert Audi, who hold similar views. See Robert Audi, *Religious Commitment and Secular Reason* (New York: Cambridge University Press, 2000). Rather, Rawls includes religion as one of many possible "reasonable comprehensive doctrines." See Rawls, *Political Liberalism*, 13–15, 58–66.

a consequence of the pluralism that results from the flourishing of free institutions in a society consisting of citizens from a wide variety of differing cultural, social, and ethnic backgrounds and historical experiences.[9] This is why most citizens enter the public square with sometimes radically different, though not unreasonable, evidential *sets*, as Christopher Eberle calls them.[10] One's evidential set—which includes what one thinks are reliable background beliefs and sources of authority—influences, if not largely determines, how one weighs evidence and assesses the strength of moral and political considerations in making judgments on matters of public and private concerns.

But, as Rawls points out, once one accepts the burdens of judgment—that is, the variety of factors that account for reasonable disagreement in a free society—one should be skeptical of policy proposals, based on any comprehensive doctrine, that attempt to coerce our compatriots on matters of constitutional essentials (or basic rights). Once we realize that the existence and persistence of reasonable disagreement is inevitable in a free society—that almost all of us arrive readied with deeply held beliefs that other equally reasonable citizens may think false even when we are convinced otherwise—we should embrace the limitations of public reason. "Our exercise of political power is proper and hence justifiable only when it is exercised in accordance with a constitution the essentials of which all citizens may reasonably be expected to endorse in light of principles and ideals acceptable to them as reasonable and rational," writes Rawls.[11] Hence, on the issues mentioned earlier—obscenity, abortion, birth control, physician-assisted suicide, religious establishment, and consensual non-marital sex—the state, under political liberalism, has no justification for coercing its citizens to obey the dictates of a reasonable comprehensive doctrine, religious or otherwise, unless it can provide to its citizens reasons that they would be irrational in rejecting. For this reason, Rawls and other like-minded liberals—such as Ronald Dworkin and Thomas Nagel—have defended laws supporting tolerance and

---

9. Rawls, *Political Liberalism*, 54–58.

10. Christopher Eberle, *Religious Reasons in a Liberal Democracy* (New York: Cambridge University Press, 2002), 61–62.

11. Rawls, *Political Liberalism*, 217.

individual liberty on these matters.[12] This, we are told, is the consequence of the liberal neutrality implied by the constraints of public reason, which suggests a type of epistemic modesty on the part of the state, and *not* a commitment to advancing as correct the convictions of some citizens whose comprehensive doctrines endorse religious skepticism, sexual libertinism, abortion, physician-assisted suicide, and obscenity as actual goods.[13]

Rawls on Abortion

Take, for example, how Rawls' comments on the right to abortion developed between the first edition of *Political Liberalism* (in 1993) and his 1997 article, "The Idea of Public Reason Revisited."[14] In a famous footnote in the first edition, he asks us to "consider the question of abortion in terms of these three important political values: the due respect for human life, the ordered reproduction of political society over time, including the family in some form, and finally the equality of women as equal citizens."[15] He then concludes that any reasonable public policy on the matter would balance these considerations and allow for abortion in the first trimester, and that a call for a ban on abortion would be unreasonable, since it would not properly balance these political values and thus would run afoul of public reason. Early reviewers of the first edition of *Political Liberalism* singled out this reasoning for special critique,[16] pointing out that opponents of abortion do in fact offer public reasons for their view, and thus provide a contrary answer to the same question that their detractors ask—Does the fetus have more status?—that results in a different, though obviously not unreasonable, balance of political values. Michael Sandel, for example,

---

12. See, e.g., Ronald Dworkin, *Is Democracy Possible Here?: Principles for a New Political Debate* (Princeton, NJ: Princeton University Press, 2006); and Thomas Nagel, "Moral Conflict and Political Legitimacy," *Philosophy and Public Affairs* 16 (1987). Although it is clear that Rawls agreed with Dworkin and Nagel on the legal permissibility of abortion, birth control, physician-assisted suicide, religious disestablishment, and non-marital sex, I could not find any work in which Rawls addressed the issue of obscenity.

13. This insight I gleaned from comments made by Nagel in his "Rawls and Liberalism," in *The Cambridge Companion to Rawls*, ed. Samuel Freeman (New York: Cambridge University Press, 2003), 74–75.

14. Rawls, "The Idea of Public Reason Revisited (1997)," in *Political Liberalism*, 440–490, originally published in the *University of Chicago Law Review* 64.3 (Summer 1997): 765–807.

15. Rawls, *Political Liberalism*, 243 n. 32.

16. See, e.g., Kent Greenawalt, "Some Problems with Public Reason in John Rawls's *Political Liberalism*," *Loyola of Los Angeles Law Review* 28 (June 1995): 1303–17.

writes, "But if the Catholic Church is right about the moral status of the fetus, if abortion is morally tantamount to murder, then it is not clear why the political values of toleration and women's equality, important though they are, should prevail."[17] In light of these critiques, Rawls clarifies his initial remarks in a new introduction to the second edition of *Political Liberalism.* In a new footnote, he claims that he was not making an argument for the right to a first trimester abortion, but rather was providing an illustration on what a proper balance of political values on a contested issue might look like.[18] As an example of the sort of balancing he was trying to illustrate, he conscripts a 1995 article authored by Judith Jarvis Thomson.[19] In that piece, Thomson argues that even if it is not unreasonable for the abortion opponent to hold that the early embryo has protected moral status, a just government should still not restrict a woman's right to abortion, since it has an obligation to err on the side of liberty when advocates on both sides of a question are not unreasonable. Writes Thomson:

> One side says that the fetus has a right to life from the moment of conception, the other side denies this. Neither side is able to prove its case. ... [W]hy should the deniers win? ... The answer is that the situation is not symmetrical. What is in question here is not which of two values we should promote, the deniers' or the supporters'. What the supporters want is a license to impose force; what the deniers want is a license to be free of it. It is the former that needs justification.[20]

What is important to recognize here is how Rawls (through Thomson) envisions how the government ought to think of coercion when there are competing interests and the exercise of a basic right is at stake: individual liberty, on balance, should be accorded special deference. Nevertheless, explains Rawls, if the opponent of abortion can offer an "equally reasonable balance, or ordering, of public reason that argues

---

17. Michael Sandel, "Political Liberalism," *Harvard Law Review* 107 (1994): 1778 (review of *Political Liberalism* by John Rawls).

18. Rawls, *Political Liberalism*, liii–liv n. 31.

19. Rawls, *Political Liberalism*, lii n. 31.

20. Judith Jarvis Thomson, "Abortion: Whose Right?," *Boston Review* 20.3 (1995), available at http://bostonreview.mit.edu/BR20.3/thomson.html (no pagination). For a response to Thomson, see Francis J. Beckwith, "Thomson's 'Equal Reasonableness' Argument for Abortion Rights: A Critique," *American Journal of Jurisprudence* 49.1 (2004).

for the denial of that right,"[21] then a ban on abortion may in fact not run afoul of public reason. To make this point, Rawls references an article authored by the late Joseph Cardinal Bernadin (1928–1996),[22] about which Rawls writes:

> The idea of public order that the Cardinal presents includes these three political values: public peace, essential protections of human rights, and the commonly accepted standards of moral behavior in a community of law. Further, he grants that not all moral imperatives are to be translated into prohibitive civil statutes and thinks it essential to the political and social order to protect human life and basic human rights. The denial of the right to abortion he hopes to justify on the basis of those three values. I don't assess his argument here, except to say it is clearly cast in the form of public reason.[23]

It is apparent from these remarks that Rawls had backed away from his claim in the first edition that "any comprehensive doctrine that leads to a balance of political values excluding that duly qualified right [to abortion] in the first trimester is to that extent unreasonable."[24]

What makes abortion a peculiarly difficult issue for Rawls, as it is for other citizens, is that unlike public questions that involve self-regarding acts between consenting adults—in which the dispute is over the extent to which the state ought to regulate an alleged private vice—the conflict over abortion requires that the government, at some point, address the question of whether the fetus is a subject of rights and thus a potential victim of unjustified homicide in a typical abortion. I suspect this is why Rawls comes to doubt that there is one right neutralist liberal answer in the abortion debate. As he notes, "[D]isputed questions, such as that of abortion, may lead to a stand-off between different political conceptions, and citizens must simply vote on the question."[25] For this reason, in both the second edition of *Political Liberalism* as well as "The Idea of Public Reason Revisited," he even suggests that if

---

21. Rawls, *Political Liberalism*, liv n. 31.

22. Joseph Cardinal Bernardin, "The Consistent Ethics: What Sort of Framework?" *Origins* 16 (Oct. 30, 1986): 345, 346–50.

23. Rawls, *Political Liberalism*, liv n. 32.

24. Rawls, *Political Liberalism*, 243 n. 32.

25. Rawls, *Political Liberalism*, liii.

abortion opponents were able to persuade a majority of voters to ban abortion, such a law would not violate the canons of public reason:

> Some may, of course, reject a legitimate decision [of a majority of citizens to vote for a particular law], as Roman Catholics may reject a decision to grant a right to abortion. They may present an argument in public reason for denying it and fail to win a majority. But they need not themselves exercise the right to abortion. They can recognize the right as belonging to legitimate law enacted in accordance with legitimate political institutions and public reason, and therefore not resist it with force. Forceful resistance is unreasonable: it would mean attempting to impose by force their own comprehensive doctrine that a majority of other citizens who follow public reason, not unreasonably, do not accept. Certainly Catholics may, in line with public reason, continue to argue against the right to abortion. Reasoning is not closed once and for all in public reason any more than it is closed in any form of reasoning. Moreover, that the Catholic Church's nonpublic reason requires its members to follow its doctrine is perfectly consistent with their also honoring public reason.[26]

What stands out about these comments is the way in which Rawls conceptualizes how neutralist liberalism may secure the right of religious conscience for those who lose at the ballot box while protecting the integrity of our democratic institutions against forceful resistance by those very same citizens. The government may permit abortions, but it may not coerce others to undergo or perform them. Opponents of abortion—if they are not able to enact their view into law—may not engage in civil disobedience to prevent others from exercising that right. On my reading of Rawls, he is making a good faith effort to fend off the charge suggested by some—and to which I alluded earlier—that neutralist liberalism collapses into (or is a cover for) a comprehensive liberalism that endorses certain policies as advancing actual goods that citizens who embrace other reasonable comprehensive doctrines reject.

---

26. Rawls, "The Idea of Public Reason Revisited (1997)," in *Political Liberalism*, 480 (notes omitted). This paragraph is nearly word-for-word identical, including footnotes, to a paragraph on pages liv-lv in the second edition of *Political Liberalism*.

With Rawls's deliberations on abortion in mind, I would like to move from the 1990s and the abortion debate to the 2010s and recent religious liberty claims that have arisen as a result of the application of anti-discrimination laws and the legal recognition of same-sex marriage. I would like to briefly explore how an advocate of Rawls's neutralist liberalism could assess this issue.[27] Take, for example, a 2018 case decided by the U.S. Supreme Court, *Masterpiece Cakeshop v. Colorado Civil Rights Commission*.[28] In this case, Jack Phillips, the owner of Masterpiece, declined to design and create a custom wedding cake for a same-sex couple. He claimed that as a Christian who believes that same-sex relations are immoral, the act it would violate his conscience to cooperate with a ceremony that celebrates such unions. However, because Masterpiece is a public accommodation, it is subject to a Colorado statute that forbids discrimination based on sexual orientation. For this reason, the same-sex couple filed a complaint against Masterpiece to the Colorado Civil Rights Commission. After victories before the commission and in state court, the couple eventually lost in the US Supreme Court. Ruling in favor of Masterpiece, the Supreme Court found that because some of the commission's members had made disparaging comments about Phillips' religious beliefs, and thus

---

27. As far as I can tell, the first time Rawls explicitly addresses the issue of same-sex marriage is in his 1997 article "The Idea of Public Reason Revisited," in which he writes, "Finally, consider the state's interest in the family and human life. How should the political value invoked be specified correctly? Traditionally it has been specified very broadly. But in a democratic regime the government's legitimate interest is that public law and policy should support and regulate, in an ordered way, the institutions needed to reproduce political society over time. These include the family (in a form that is just), arrangements for rearing and educating children, and institutions of public health generally. This ordered support and regulation rests on political principles and values, since political society is regarded as existing in perpetuity and so as maintaining itself and its institutions and culture over generations. Given this interest, the government would appear to have no interest in the particular form of family life, or of relations among the sexes, except insofar as that form or those relations in some way affect the orderly reproduction of society over time. Thus, appeals to monogamy as such, or against same-sex marriages, as within the government's legitimate interest in the family, would reflect religious or comprehensive moral doctrines. Accordingly, that interest would appear improperly specified. Of course, there may be other political values in the light of which such a specification would pass muster: for example, if monogamy were necessary for the equality of women, or same-sex marriages destructive to the raising and educating of children" (779; citation omitted). He clarifies this paragraph in the footnote that follows: "Of course, I don't here attempt to decide the question, since we are concerned only with the kinds of reasons and considerations that public reasoning involves" (779 n. 38).

28. *Masterpiece Cakeshop v. Colorado* 584 U. S. ____ (2018) (slip opinion).

undermining the commission's role as a fair and impartial tribunal, Phillips' religious free exercise rights had been violated.

Suppose we ground the legal recognition of same-sex marriage in something like Rawls's neutralist liberalism, as several scholars have done.[29] Not surprisingly, in *Obergefell v. Hodges* (2015), the Supreme Court case that found a constitutional right for same-sex marriage, the Court offers a rationale along Rawlsian neutralist liberal lines:

> Many who deem same-sex marriage to be wrong reach that conclusion based on *decent and honorable religious or philo- sophical premises*, and neither they nor their beliefs are dispar- aged here. But when that sincere, personal opposition becomes enacted law and public policy, the necessary consequence is to put the imprimatur of the State itself on an exclusion that soon demeans or stigmatizes those whose own liberty is then denied.[30] (emphasis added)

The justice who penned those words, Anthony Kennedy, is the same one who bemoaned, in similar language, the treatment of Mr. Phillips before the Colorado Civil Rights Commission:

> To describe a man's faith as "one of the most despicable pieces of rhetoric that people can use" is to disparage his religion in at least two distinct ways: by describing it as despicable, and also by characterizing it as merely rhetorical—something insubstan- tial and even insincere. The commissioner even went so far as to compare Phillips' invocation of his sincerely held religious beliefs to defenses of slavery and the Holocaust. This sentiment is inappropriate for a Commission charged with the solemn responsibility of fair and neutral enforcement of Colorado's

---

29. See, e.g., Elizabeth Brake, "Minimal Marriage: What Political Liberalism Implies for Gay Marriage," *Ethics* 120.2 (2010): 302–37; John Scott Gray, "Rawls's Principle of Justice as Fairness and Its Application to the Issue of Same-Sex Marriage," *South African Journal of Philosophy* 23.2 (2004): 158–70; Linda C. McClain, "Deliberative Democracy, Overlapping Consensus, and Same- Sex Marriage," *Fordham Law Review* 66 (1997–98): 1241–52; Frank I. Michelman, "Rawls on Constitutionalism and Constitutional Law," in *The Cambridge Companion to Rawls,* ed. Samuel Freeman. (New York: Cambridge University Press, 2003), 394–425; Martha Nussbaum, "A Right to Marry?: Same Sex Marriage and Constitutional Law," *Dissent* (Summer 2009): 43–55; Dworkin, *Is Democracy Possible Here?*, 1–24, 86–89.

30. *Obergefell v Hodges*, Nos 14–556, 14–562, 14–571, 14–574, 2015 US LEXIS 4250, at *36 (June 26, 2015).

anti-discrimination law—a law that protects discrimination on the basis of religion as well as sexual orientation.[31]

Justice Kennedy avoids the question of what should be done if a more circumspect and respectful Civil Rights Commission had issued the same judgment against Masterpiece. Like the dispute over abortion, under Rawls' neutralist liberalism, this is a difficult question to answer. On the one hand, it is clear to most of us that the legal recognition of same-sex marriage seems to naturally follow from Rawls' neutralist liberalism. On the other hand, it's not so clear that is the case with the rigid enforcement of anti-discrimination laws when it involves events that have been historically tightly tethered to religious moral and liturgical traditions. Take, for example, the fictional case of the Orthodox Jewish photographer, Abraham Zimmerman, owner and operator of Zimmy's Photography. Its employees consist of Abraham (or Abe), his wife, Betty, and his two children Robert and David, all of whom share the same religious faith. Suppose one Monday morning a local Christian minister, Mr. Paul, contacts Abe in order to procure his services. Mr. Paul wants to hire Zimmy's to take professional photographs at the church's upcoming baptismal ceremony so that the congregation can post the pictures on its website and on social media for the purpose of announcing and celebrating the church's newest converts. Abe then asks Mr. Paul, "What is the name of your church?" He replies, "The Messianic Jewish Church of Denver." Mr. Paul goes on to explain, "We are a congregation consisting exclusively of Jewish converts to Christianity, some of whom are former members of your synagogue." Stunned by this answer, Abe responds, "I'm really sorry to have to say this, but I cannot in good conscience cooperate with the celebration of a liturgical event that I believe is a public act of apostasy. I hope you understand." Seeing that the expression on Mr. Paul's face indicates that he does not understand, Abe goes on to explain that Zimmy's would not object to photographing any of the church's ministers or members in or near any body of water, even the very lake in which the baptisms are supposed to take place. But, he explains, these baptisms are different, since they are liturgical events that, in this case, are public expressions of the renunciation

---

31. *Masterpiece Cakeshop*, 584 US, 13 (slip opinion).

of his Jewish faith. For this reason, Abe pleads, "It's not that I will not participate. It's that I *cannot* participate." Mr. Paul, offended by Abe's answer, files a complaint with the Colorado Civil Rights Commission, arguing that Abe's denial of services violates the state's prohibition of discrimination based on religion. In court, Abe's lawyer argues that Abe is not denying services because of Mr. Paul's religion, but rather, because of the nature of the ceremony for which Mr. Paul is requesting Abe to exercise his artistic gifts in celebrating. Abe's lawyer explains that for Mr. Paul, the baptisms will be performed out of obedience to what Christ commands in the New Testament, while for Abe they are acts of apostasy performed in disobedience to what he believes God commands in the Torah. However, the Colorado Civil Rights Commission is not convinced:

> The Supreme Court has recognized that, in some cases, conduct cannot be divorced from status. This is so when the conduct is so closely correlated with the status that it is engaged in exclusively or predominantly by persons who have that particular status. We conclude that the act of baptism constitutes such conduct because it is "engaged in exclusively or predominantly" by Christians. Therefore, Mr. Zimmerman's distinction between not serving Christians and not cooperating with the celebration of a baptism is one without a difference. But for his religion, Mr. Paul would not have sought to baptize his congregants, and but for his intent to do so, Mr. Zimmerman would not have denied Mr. Paul his services.

Our fictional commission is effectively re-describing a liturgical practice in language that would seem foreign to those, both disciples and dissenters, who take the baptismal rite seriously. For this reason, it would seem odd under Rawlsian neutralist liberalism for one to agree with the commission's verdict, since it would put the government in the position of telling the Zimmerman family that the only way to avoid violating the state's anti-discrimination laws in cases like this is to "join in the Worship of Ceremonies of another Church,"[32] as John Locke once put it. This fictional verdict, I should

---

32. John Locke, *A Letter Concerning Toleration* (1689), trans. William Popple, ed. James H. Tully (Indianapolis: Hackett Publishing, 1983), 48.

note, is modeled nearly word for word after the real Colorado Court of Appeals' opinion in the case of Masterpiece Cakeshop,[33] which, as we seen, was overturned by the Supreme Court when it ruled in favor of the vendor (Jack Phillips).

But for religious believers like Phillips, weddings are more like baptisms and bar mitzvahs than they are like baby showers and bachelor parties. This is why many religious groups have elaborate and sophisticated rules on whether or not a wedding conducted under the auspices of the government or another faith counts as legitimate in the eyes of God. In fact, at the very beginning of Christian history, St. Paul maintained that a non-Christian marriage is still a licit and binding union after one of the partners converts and may very well become a means of grace (1 Cor 7:12–14). In the Christian Bible that Phillips believes is authoritative, the marriage between a husband and a wife is used as an analogy to explain Christ's relationship to his church (Mt 9:15, Mark 2:19, Luke 5:34, John 3:29, 2 Cor 11:2, Eph 5:25, Eph 5:31–32, Rev 19:7, Rev 21:2, Rev 21:9, Rev 22:17).

Abe's judicial loss seems almost like a paradigm case of the government *violating* Rawls' neutralist liberalism, insofar as it is coercing a citizen to cooperate with practices that, given his reasonable comprehensive doctrine, he has good nonpublic reasons to reject. In this sense, it is analogous to Rawls' comments on the abortion opponent's right to follow her church's teachings while still honoring public reason. The Jewish photographer may not forcefully resist the Messianic Jewish congregation's right to baptize its converts, even if the photographer believes it is an act of apostasy, just as Phillips may not forcefully resist a same-sex couple's right to marry, even if Phillips believes that it as an act of grave sin. On the other hand, neither the church nor the couple has the right to conscript the power of the state to force Abe or Phillips to cooperate with the performance of

---

33. "In these decisions, the Supreme Court recognized that, in some cases, conduct cannot be divorced from status. This is so when the conduct is so closely correlated with the status that it is engaged in exclusively or predominantly by persons who have that particular status. We conclude that the act of same-sex marriage constitutes such conduct because it is 'engaged in exclusively or predominantly' by gays, lesbians, and bisexuals. Masterpiece's distinction, therefore, is one without a difference. But for their sexual orientation, Craig and Mullins would not have sought to enter into a same-sex marriage, and but for their intent to do so, Masterpiece would not have denied them its services" (*Craig v. Masterpiece Cakeshop* [2015] Court of Appeals of Colorado, No. 2015COA115, ¶ 34).

liturgical events contrary to their respective faiths, just as the pro-life advocate does not have the right to forcefully interfere with a woman's right to terminate her pregnancy.[34]

Conclusion

Neutralist liberalism, as conceived by figures like Rawls, Dworkin, and Nagel, is a political theory whose purpose is to provide a framework by which citizens holding a variety of contrary and reasonable views may live in peace with one another. To illustrate this point, Rawls argued that if the pro-choice view on abortion emerges out of the democratic process as the law of the land, pro-life advocates should not be required to support abortion or procure one in violation of their conscience. It would seem to follow from this that the neutralist liberal should take the side of vendors like Jack Phillips.

---

34. I am not suggesting that abortion ought to be legal. I am merely arguing that if Rawls were alive today, and consistently applied what he said about abortion to the disputes over the religious liberty of wedding vendors, he would side with Phillips (though in other cases, under a different set of facts, he may not).

6

ON THE ORGANIC CONNECTION BETWEEN JESUS' ATONING DEATH AND RESURRECTION

William Lane Craig

P enal substitution in a theological context may be defined as the doctrine that God inflicted upon Christ the suffering which we deserved as the punishment for our sins, with the result that we no longer deserve punishment.[1] Theories of the atonement in which penal substitution plays a central role focus quite properly on Jesus' death as the means by which atonement for sins is achieved. The message of the NT is that God, out of His great love, has provided the means of atonement for sin through Jesus' sacrificial death on the cross.

The predominant motif used in the NT to characterize the atonement is the portrayal of Jesus' death as a sacrificial offering to God on our behalf. Joel Green provides a pithy summary:

---

1. Notice that this explication leaves open the question whether Christ was punished for our sins. Some defenders of penal substitution hold that God afflicted Christ with the suffering which, had it been inflicted upon us, would have been our just desert and, hence, punishment. In other words, Christ was not punished, but he endured the suffering which would have been our punishment had it been inflicted on us. We should not exclude by definition such accounts as being penal substitutionary theories, since Christ on such accounts suffers as our substitute and bears what would have been our punishment, thereby freeing us from punishment. These features serve to distinguish such accounts from satisfaction theories like Anselm's. On a penal substitutionary account, in contrast to satisfaction theories, the harsh treatment deserved by sinners is still administered or vicariously endured, even if it is not punishment. For discussion of what they characterize as penal substitution theories of various strengths, i.e., the degree to which they affirm that God punished Christ, see Daniel J. Hill and Joseph Jedwab, "Atonement and the Concept of Punishment," in *Locating Atonement: Explorations in Constructive Dogmatics*, eds. Oliver D. Crisp and Fred Sanders (Grand Rapids: Zondervan, 2015), 139–53.

In their development of the saving significance of Jesus' death, early Christians were heavily influenced by the world of the sacrificial cult in Israel's Scriptures and by the practices of animal sacrifice in the Jerusalem temple. ... The expression *'Christ died for all,'* widespread in this and variant forms throughout the NT (e.g., Mark 14:24; Rom 5:6, 8; 15:3; Gal 2:21; 1 Pet 3:18), is thematic in this regard, as are references to the salvific effects of *the blood of Christ* (e.g., Acts 20:28; Rom 5:9; Col 1:20). Jesus' death is presented as a *covenant sacrifice* (e.g., Mark 14:24; 1 Cor 11:25; Heb 7:22; 8:6; 9:15), a *Passover sacrifice* (e.g., John 19:14; 1 Cor 5:7–8), the *sin offering* (Rom 8:3; 2 Cor 5:21), the *offering of first fruits* (1 Cor 15:20, 23), the sacrifice offered on *the Day of Atonement* (Heb 9–10), and an offering reminiscent of *Abraham's presentation of Isaac* (e.g., Rom 8:32). The writer of Ephesians summarizes well: 'Christ loved us and gave himself up for us, a fragrant offering and sacrifice to God' (Eph 5:2).[2]

Thus, "the cross" came to be a metaphor epitomizing the gospel message, such that Paul could call the gospel "the word of the cross" (1 Cor 1:18), reminding his Corinthian converts that "I decided to know nothing among you except Jesus Christ, and him crucified" (1 Cor 2:2).[3] Hence, Paul would glory in nothing "except the cross of our Lord Jesus Christ" (Gal 6:14).

Paul quotes the earliest summary of the gospel message, a four-line formula dating to within five years of Jesus' crucifixion, reminding the Corinthian believers:

I delivered to you as of first importance what I also received:
that Christ died for our sins in accordance with the Scriptures,
that he was buried,
that he was raised on the third day in accordance with the Scriptures,
and that he appeared to Cephas, then to the Twelve.
(1 Cor 15:3–5 ESV)

This is the message, Paul says, that was proclaimed by all the apostles (1 Cor 15:11), and it is the message that dominates the NT. The first

---

2. Joel B. Green, "Kaleidoscopic View," in *The Nature of the Atonement*, ed. James Beilby and Paul R. Eddy (Downers Grove, IL: IVP Academic, 2006), 172 (my emphases).

3. Unless otherwise noted, all Scripture quotations in this chapter are in the NRSV.

line of the pre-Pauline formula encapsulates in a pithy way the NT doctrine of the atonement.

The importance of the death of Christ for the NT church may be seen in the disproportionate space the four Gospels devote to Jesus' so-called "passion," the final week of his suffering and crucifixion, thereby emphasizing his death. Of course, Jesus' death is not the end of the passion story: the Gospels all conclude with the proclamation of Jesus' victorious resurrection, vindicating him as God's chosen one. The death and resurrection of Jesus are two sides of the same coin: as Paul wrote, he "was put to death for our trespasses and raised for our justification" (Rom 4:25).

A common criticism of penal substitutionary theories is that due to their myopic focus on Jesus' death as the means of atonement, his resurrection seems to be a superfluous add-on. What does it mean to say, for example, that he was "raised for our justification"? How is his resurrection connected with our justification? Had Christ not been raised, he still would have "borne our sins in his body on the tree" (I Pet 2:24), thereby expiating our guilt. Just as the Levitical animal sacrifices offered in the tabernacle and the temple, which NT writers see as a type of Christ, did not require the revivification of the sacrificial animal in order to be efficacious in achieving atonement, so Christ's self-sacrificial death seems to have no organic connection with his resurrection, according to penal substitutionary theories.[4]

By contrast, in other atonement theories, like the Christus Victor model, Jesus' resurrection is vitally connected with his victory over Satan, death, and hell. According to this theory, Christ by means of his death and resurrection delivered mankind from bondage to Satan and from corruption and death, which are the consequences of sin.[5]

---

4. By an "organic connection" I mean a natural connection, where one element flows out of the other, rather like the connection between a leaf and a branch, in contrast to the connection between a Christmas ornament and a branch.

5. Sometimes, church fathers like Origen interpreted Jesus' ransom saying (Mark 10:45) very literally to mean that Christ's life was offered to Satan as a payment in exchange for human beings. Having secured the release of the hostages held by Satan, Christ then rose from the dead, thus triumphing over him. But not everyone agreed with Origen's ransom model. A different version of the Christus Victor theory is to be found, especially among the Latin fathers, according to which Christ was not given as a ransom to Satan but rather was the victim of Satan's unjust and deadly attack. Often confused with the ransom model, this so-called political model of Christus Victor attributes Satan's undoing to an overreach of authority on the devil's part. The role of Christ's resurrection in breaking Satan's power remains the same as on the ransom model.

What Satan did not realize in claiming Christ's life was that Christ, as the second person of the Trinity, could not be held by him. Raising Christ from the dead, God defeated Satan, leaving him without captives. Irenaeus explains,

> But inasmuch as God is invincible and long-suffering, He did indeed show Himself to be long-suffering in the matter of the correction of man and the probation of all, as I have already observed; and by means of the second man did He bind the strong man, and spoiled his goods, and abolished death, vivifying that man who had been in a state of death. For at the first Adam became a vessel in his [Satan's] possession, whom he did also hold under his power, that is, by bringing sin on him iniquitously, and under colour of immortality entailing death upon him. For, while promising that they should be as gods, which was in no way possible for him to be, he wrought death in them: wherefore he who had led man captive, was justly captured in his turn by God; but man, who had been led captive, was loosed from the bonds of condemnation.[6]

In the Christus Victor model, Jesus' resurrection is organically connected with his death as the means of God's achieving victory. By contrast, for all its superiority as an account of how forgiveness of sin and reconciliation with God are achieved,[7] the theory of penal substitution seems to lack any tight connection between Jesus' atoning death and resurrection. Given that Paul connects the two, this poses a challenge for penal substitutionary atonement theorists.

Multifaceted Atonement Theories

Now, in a certain sense, the above criticism is unfair. For penal substitutionary theorists are not typically myopically focused on penal substitution, as though it were the entirety of one's atonement theory. Theologians have often remarked on the multiplicity of metaphors and

---

6. Iraneus, *Against Heresies* 3.23.

7. The Christus Victor theory is so wanting in this respect that Albrecht Ritschl, in his monumental history of atonement and justification, simply passes over the patristic period and begins his history with Anselm (Albrecht Ritschl, *A Critical History of the Christian Doctrine of Justification and Reconciliation* [1870], trans. John S. Black [Edinburgh: Edmonton and Douglas, 1872], Introduction).

motifs characterizing Christ's atonement found in the NT.[8] The biblical doctrine of the atonement may be aptly compared to a multi-faceted jewel, each facet contributing to the beauty of the whole gem. The various facets of a gem are transparent to and refracted in one another, thereby increasing the brilliance and beauty of the whole. Sacrifice, ransom, governmental and judicial motifs, moral influence, and so on, are all facets of a full atonement theory. Hence, it is not so important if certain motifs, like Jesus' resurrection, are more organically connected to some facets rather than to others. Together they build a full-orbed theory.

A complete atonement theory may, and I think should, include both the motif of Christus Victor and penal substitution, as did, for example, Augustine's account. For Augustine, Christ did not conquer Satan simply by power (through his resurrection) but also, and more profoundly, by righteousness (through penal substitution). "He conquered the devil first by righteousness, and afterwards by power: namely, by righteousness, because He had no sin, and was slain by him most unjustly; but by power, because having been dead He lived again, never afterwards to die" (*On the Trinity*, 13.14.18).[9]

This raises the question, "What, then, is the righteousness by which the devil was conquered?" The answer: "What, except the righteousness of Jesus Christ?" (13.14.18). The further question then arises: "And how was he conquered?" Augustine answers,

> Because, when he found in Him nothing worthy of death, yet he slew Him. And certainly it is just, that we whom he held as debtors, should be dismissed free by believing in Him whom he slew without any debt. In this way it is that we are said to be justified in the blood of Christ. For so that innocent blood was shed for the remission of our sins. (13.14.18)

The initial answer, more superficial, seems to be that Christ conquered through righteousness in that he, being righteous, was unjustly treated by Satan. But this answer would not suffice to explain how we are

---

8. See Leon Morris, *The Atonement: Its Meaning and Significance* (Downers Grove, IL: IVP, 1983); Green, "Kaleidoscopic View," 157–85; I. Howard Marshall, *Aspects of the Atonement: Cross and Resurrection in the Reconciling of God and Humanity* (London: Paternoster, 2007).

9. Translations of Augustine in this chapter are from the Nicene and Post-Nicene Fathers, Series 1. Available at https://www.newadvent.org/fathers/, ed. Kevin Knight.

freed from our just desert and forgiven of our sins by believing in him. The deeper answer is therefore that "innocent blood was shed for the remission of our sins."

Here we connect with the motif of penal substitution. The principalities and powers could justly demand our death as the penalty for sin. But Christ's innocent death was undeserved and could therefore serve as a sacrifice that removes sin and obviates its penalty: "We, indeed, came to death through sin; He through righteousness: and, therefore, as our death is the punishment of sin, so His death was made a sacrifice for sin" (4.12.15). God's love is proved in that Christ should "without any evil desert of His own, bear our evils" (13.10.13).

In his treatise *Against Faustus*, Augustine makes explicit his affirmation of Christ's being substitutionally punished. He says, "Christ, though guiltless, took our punishment, that He might cancel our guilt, and do away with our punishment" (14.4). He interprets Galatians 3:13 to mean by "curse" the punishment of death which is due for sin:

> As He died in the flesh which He took in bearing our punishment, so also, while ever blessed in His own righteousness, He was cursed for our offenses, in the death which He suffered in bearing our punishment. ... The believer in the true doctrine of the gospel will understand that Christ is not reproached by Moses when he speaks of Him as cursed, not in His divine majesty, but as hanging on the tree as our substitute, bearing our punishment. (*Against Faustus*, 14.6–7)

Augustine says, "The curse is pronounced by divine justice, and it will be well for us if we are redeemed from it. Confess then that Christ died, and you may confess that He bore the curse for us" (*Against Faustus*, 14.7).

Comparing the conquering of Satan by power and by righteousness, Augustine reflects:

> It is not then difficult to see that the devil was conquered, when he who was slain by Him rose again. It is something more, and more profound of comprehension, to see that the devil was conquered when he thought himself to have conquered, that is, when Christ was slain. For then that blood, since it was His who had no sin at all, was poured out for the remission of our sins;

that, because the devil deservedly held those whom, as guilty of sin, he bound by the condition of death, he might deservedly loose them through Him, whom, as guilty of no sin, the punishment of death undeservedly affected (*On the Trinity*, 13.15.19).

Here we find an admirable integration of the motifs of Christus Victor and penal substitution. Christ bore undeservedly the punishment of sin that we deserved—namely, death, so that by his death our sins are remitted. This is how he through righteousness achieves victory over the devil. Augustine muses that although God's power is more greatly manifested by raising Christ from death than by preventing his death, that is not why God permitted Satan to so afflict Christ. Rather, says Augustine, the reason why we are justified in the blood of Christ is different: "When we are rescued from the power of the devil through the remission of sins: it pertains to this, that the devil is conquered by Christ by righteousness, not by power" (*On the Trinity*, 13.14.18). Thus, Augustine wonderfully confesses Christ as "both Victor and Victim, and therefore Victor, because the Victim" (*Confessions*, 10).

Ratification of Jesus' Atoning Death

Still, it deserves to be asked if the penal substitutionary facet of one's atonement theory might not be more directly related to Christ's resurrection than as an indirect condition of Christ's conquering Satan. It can be plausibly argued, I think, that the resurrection serves an evidentiary function vis-à-vis penal substitution in that it ratifies Jesus' messianic claims and so vindicates the efficacy of his atoning death.

It is difficult to exaggerate how countercultural was the image of the Messiah presented by Jesus of Nazareth. The prevailing Second-Temple expectation was of a warrior-king who would cast off the yoke of Israel's enemies (read: Rome), restore the throne of David in Jerusalem, and command the respect of Jew and gentile like. Against this background, the skepticism of the chief priests about Jesus of Nazareth must elicit a good deal of sympathy. It is no wonder that Mark portrays them as standing at the foot of the cross and mocking Jesus, "He saved others; he cannot save himself. Let the Messiah, the King of Israel, come down now from the cross, that we may see and believe" (Mark 15:31–32). It would have seemed absurd that such a pathetic and helpless figure could have been the Messiah.

But the resurrection of Jesus showed that God had dramatically vindicated Jesus. No matter how out-of-the-mold Jesus' understanding of his messiahship may have been, that understanding had been unequivocally confirmed by God's miraculously raising him from the dead. Peter declares, "This Jesus God raised up, and of that we all are witnesses. ... Let all the house of Israel therefore know assuredly that God has made him both Lord and Messiah, this Jesus whom you crucified" (Acts 2:32–36).

Jesus' messianic mission was therefore seen to be, not aborted by his crucifixion, but fulfilled in it. Jesus had understood his impending death in this same light. He predicted his death (Mark 10:33–34) and even provoked it by his messianic actions in Jerusalem (Mark 11:1–10, 13–18). As he celebrated with his disciples his final Passover meal, he "took a loaf of bread, and after blessing it he broke it, gave it to them, and said, 'Take; this is my body.' Then he took a cup, and after giving thanks he gave it to them, and all of them drank from it. He said to them, 'This is my blood of the covenant, which is poured out for many'" (Mark 14:22–24).[10] Jesus saw his death symbolized in the elements of the Passover meal. It was the blood of the Passover lamb smeared on the doorposts of Jewish homes that had saved the Jewish people from God's judgement. Jesus' blood, soon to be poured out for many, would accomplish the same purpose. The fact that the disciples then share symbolically in partaking of his body and blood shows that his death is meant to encompass them; it is a death on their behalf.

Moreover, the expression "this is my blood of the covenant"[11] recalls Moses' words at the inauguration of the old covenant, "See the blood of the covenant that the Lord has made with you" (Exod 24:8). The only other OT passage that mentions "the blood of my covenant with you" is Zech 9:9–12, a proclamation of the advent of a messianic king who will restore Israel's fortunes. Jesus the Messiah is inaugurating by his death the new covenant prophesied by Jeremiah, which would bring restoration and forgiveness of sin:

---

10. See discussion of the authenticity and meaning of Jesus' words by Joachim Jeremias, *The Eucharistic Words of Jesus*, trans. Norman Perrin (New York: Charles Scribner's Sons, 1966), ch. 5; Brant Pitre, *Jesus and the Last Supper* (Grand Rapids: William B. Eerdmans, 2015), ch. 5.

11. Paul and Luke have explicitly "this cup is the new covenant in my blood" (1 Cor 11:25; Luke 22:20).

The days are surely coming, says the LORD, when I will make a
new covenant with the house of Israel and the house of Judah.
It will not be like the covenant that I made with their ancestors
when I took them by the hand to bring them out of the land of
Egypt—a covenant that they broke, though I was their husband,
says the LORD. But this is the covenant that I will make with
the house of Israel after those days, says the LORD: I will put my
law within them, and I will write it on their hearts; and I will
be their God, and they shall be my people. No longer shall they
teach one another, or say to each other, 'Know the LORD,' for
they shall all know me, from the least of them to the greatest,
says the LORD; for I will forgive their iniquity, and remember
their sin no more. (Jer 31:31–34)

Jesus saw his death as not merely averting God's judgment but as
expunging Israel's sin and restoring fellowship with God.

Moreover, the words "poured out for many" hark back to Isaiah's
prophecy of the servant of the Lord, who:

poured out his soul to death,
and was numbered with the transgressors;
yet he bore the sin of many,
and made intercession for the transgressors. (Isa 53:12)

In Luke 22:37, Jesus, on the night of his arrest, cites this very Scripture
in application to himself. "For I tell you that this Scripture must be fulfilled in me: 'And he was counted among the transgressors.' For what
what is written about me has its fulfillment" (ESV). The "many" whose
sin the servant bears include the gentiles, to whom the servant would
be a light of salvation (Isa 42:6; 49:6). Jesus saw himself as the suffering servant of Isaiah 53, who "makes himself an offering for sin" (Isa
53:10). Earlier, Jesus had said of himself, "the Son of man came not to
be served but to serve, and to give his life a ransom for many" (Mark
10:45).[12] The Son of Man is a divine-human figure from Daniel's proph-

---

12. For a discussion of the authenticity and interpretation of this saying, see Peter
Stuhlmacher, *Reconciliation, Law, and Righteousness: Essays in Biblical Theology* (Philadelphia:
Fortress Press, 1986), chap. 2: "Vicariously Giving his Life for Many, Mark 10:45 (Matt. 20:28),"
16–29; cf. idem, "Eighteen Theses on Paul's Theology of the Cross," in *Reconciliation, Law, and
Righteousness*, 165.

ecy whom "all peoples, nations, and languages should serve" (Dan 7:14).
In his paradoxical statement, Jesus stands things on their head, declaring that the Son of Man has come in the role of a servant and, like the
servant of Isaiah 53, gives his life as a ransom for many. Only in Isaiah
53 do we find in the OT the complex idea of a "serving" figure who, in
an eschatological context, gives his life for "the many."[13]

According to the Gospels, then, Jesus saw his death as a redemptive
sacrifice, like the Passover sacrifice, and himself as a sin-bearer, like
Isaiah's servant of the Lord, inaugurating, like the Mosaic sacrifice, a
fresh covenant between God and the people. The success of his messianic mission is ratified by God's raising him from the dead. In the
absence of his resurrection, an indelible question mark would remain
behind Jesus' iconoclastic person and mission. His resurrection tells
us that he was not delusional, as many believed, but was in fact the
Messiah and Savior.

Resurrection and Satisfaction of Divine Justice

This is all well and good, but it remains the case that Jesus' resurrection is thus related to the atoning work of the cross only externally.
The resurrection serves as evidence of the efficacy of Christ's atoning
death, but is there an even more organic connection between them?
I think that there is.

Any biblically adequate atonement theory must include the notion
of propitiation, the appeasement of God's just wrath against sin.[14] The
source of God's wrath is his retributive justice,[15] and so appeasement of

---

13. Rikki E. Watts, "Jesus' Death, Isaiah 53, and Mark 10:45: A Crux Revisited," in William H.
Bellinger, Jr. and William R. Farmer, eds. *Jesus and the Suffering Servant: Isaiah 53 and Christian
Origins* (Harrisburg, PA: Trinity Press International, 1998), 143.

14. For a discussion of the biblical basis of propitiation, see Morris, *The Atonement*, chapter
7; Marshall, *Aspects of the Atonement*, chapters 1 and 2. Paul's crowning statement concerning
Christ's atoning death (Rom 3:21–26) comes against the backdrop of his exposition of God's
wrath upon and condemnation of mankind for its sin. Something in Paul's ensuing exposition
of Christ's death must solve this problem, averting God's wrath and rescuing us from the death
sentence hanging over us. The solution is found in Christ, "whom God put forward as a *hilas-
tērion* in his blood" (3:25).

15. Theories of justice may be classified as broadly retributive or consequentialist. Retributive
theories of justice hold that punishment is justified because the guilty deserve to be punished.
Consequentialist theories of justice hold that punishment is justified because of the extrinsic
goods that may be realized thereby, such as deterrence of crime, sequestration of dangerous
persons, and reformation of wrong-doers. Consequentialism seems ill-suited to serve as a theory
of divine justice because God's judgment is described in the Bible as ultimately eschatological.
Punishment imposed at that point could seemingly serve no other purpose than retribution. In

wrath is a matter of the satisfaction of divine justice. Biblically speaking, the satisfaction of God's justice takes place, not as Anselm thought, through compensation, but through punishment.[16] In the view of the Protestant Reformers, the just desert of those outside of Christ is borne in their proper persons, whereas Christ bears the just desert of those who are united with Christ by faith.[17]

Contemporary theologians have distinguished between exclusionary place-taking (German *exkludierende Stellvertretung*) and inclusionary place-taking (*inkludierende Stellvertretung*).[18] This important distinction requires a word of explanation about substitution and representation, respectively. In cases of simple substitution, someone takes the place of another person but does not represent that person. For example, a pinch hitter in baseball enters the lineup to bat in the place of another player. He is a substitute for that player but in no sense represents that other player. That is why the batting average of the player whom he replaces is not affected by the pinch hitter's performance. On the other hand, a simple representative acts on behalf of another person and serves as his spokesman but is not a substitute for that person. For example, the baseball player has an agent who represents him

---

any case, the biblical view is that the wicked deserve punishment (Rom 1:32), so that God's justice must be in some significant measure retributive. Over the last half-century or so there has been a renaissance of theories of retributive justice, accompanied by a fading of consequentialist theories, so that retributivism has come to be the standard view.

16. Especially important in this regard is Isaiah 53 and its New Testament employment. See the essays by Bailey, Farmer, and Watts in *Jesus and the Suffering Servant: Isaiah 53 and Christian Origins*, eds. William H. Bellinger, Jr. and William R. Farmer (Harrisburg, Penn: Trinity Press International, 1998); also the essays by Hermisson and Hofius in *The Suffering Servant: Isaiah 53 in Jewish and Christian Sources*, eds. Bernd Janowski and Peter Stuhlmacher [1996], trans. Daniel P. Bailey (Grand Rapids: Wm. B. Eerdmans, 2004). With regard to Anselm's theory of compensation (*satisfactio*) given to God, Pannenberg rightly comments, "Without this vicarious penal suffering, the expiatory function of the death of Jesus is unintelligible, unless we try to understand his death as an equivalent offered to God along the lines of Anselm's satisfaction theory, which has no basis in the biblical data" (Wolfhart Pannenberg, *Systematic Theology*, 3 vols., trans. Geoffrey W. Bromiley [Grand Rapids: William B. Eerdmans, 1991], 2.427).

17. See, e.g., Martin Luther, *Commentary on St. Paul's Epistle to the Galatians*, trans. Theodore Graebner (Grand Rapids: Zondervan, 1939), 63–64; John Calvin, *Institutes of the Christian Religion* II.16.2.

18. Alternatively, *ausschliessende vs. einschliessende Stellvertretung*. See, e.g., the influential work of Hartmut Gese, "The Atonement," in *Essays on Biblical Theology*, trans. Keith Crim (Minneapolis: Augsburg, 1981), 106; Otfried Hofius, "Sühne und Versöhnung: Zum paulinischen Verständnis des Kreuzestodes Jesu," in *Paulusstudien*, 2nd rev. ed., WUNT 51 (Tübingen: J.C.B. Mohr [Paul Siebeck], 1994), 41. The distinction is already to be found in Albrecht Ritschl, *The Christian Doctrine of Justification and Reconciliation: The Positive Development of the Doctrine*, ed. Alexander Beith Macauley and H. R. Mackintosh (Clifton, N.J.: Reference Book Publishers, 1966), 163–75.

in contract negotiations with the team. The representative does not replace the player but merely advocates for him.[19]

These roles can be combined, in which case we have neither simple substitution nor simple representation but rather substitutional representation (or representative substitution). A good illustration of this combination of substitution and representation is to be found in the role of a proxy at a shareholders' meeting. If we cannot attend the meeting ourselves, we may sign an agreement authorizing someone else to serve as our proxy at the meeting. He votes for us, and because he has been authorized to do so, his votes are our votes: we have voted via proxy at the meeting of shareholders. The proxy is a substitute in that he attends the meeting in our place, but he is also our representative in that he does not vote instead of us but on our behalf, so that we vote. This combination is an inclusionary place-taking.

The Swiss Reformed theologian Francis Turretin believed that Christ, in bearing our punishment, was both our substitute and our representative before God. He states that "the curse and punishment of sin which he received upon himself in our stead secures to us blessing and righteousness with God in virtue of that most strict union between us and him by which, as our sins are imputed to him, so in turn his obedience and righteousness are imputed to us."[20] This relation is not one of simple substitution; there is an inclusive union here, which is the basis of the imputation of our sins to Christ and of his righteousness to us. According to Turretin, so long as Christ is outside of us and we are outside of Christ, we can receive no benefit from his righteousness. But God has united us with Christ by means of a twofold bond, one natural (namely, communion of nature by the incarnation), the other mystical (namely, the communion of grace by Christ's mediation), in virtue of which our sins might be imputed to Christ and his righteousness imputed to us. Christ was punished in our place and bore the suffering we deserved, but he also represented

---

19. Representation in this sense needs to be distinguished from representation in the sense of symbolization. A baseball scorecard is a representation of the playing field, and marks on it represent hits, outs, runs, and so on. Christ's death as a representation in this sense would be akin to the popular misunderstanding of Hugo Grotius' governmental theory of the atonement as a representation to the world of what it would look like if Christ were punished for our sins.

20. Francis Turretin, *Institutes of Elenctic Theology*, 3 vols., ed. James T. Dennison, trans. George Musgrave Giger (Phillipsburg, NJ: Presbyterian and Reformed, 1992), vol. 2, Topic 16, Question 3.

us before God, so that his punishment was our punishment. Christ was not merely punished instead of us; rather, we were punished by proxy.[21] For that reason, divine justice is satisfied.

How does it come to pass that we are so represented by Christ? As mentioned, Turretin proposed two ways in which we are in union with Christ: first, by way of his incarnation and, second, by way of our mystical union with him. Although theologians often appeal to this latter union of believers with Christ to explain the efficacy of his atonement,[22] such an account seems to be viciously circular.[23] Turretin emphasized that it is our union with Christ that is the basis of the imputation of sins to Christ and of our justification.[24] But the problem is that the mystical union of believers with Christ is the privilege only of persons who are regenerate and justified. There is here a vicious explanatory circle: in order to be in mystical union with Christ, one must first be justified, but in order to be justified, one must first be in mystical union with Christ. What is needed is a union with Christ which is explanatorily prior to (even if chronologically simultaneous with) imputation and justification.

Turretin's first proposal is therefore to be preferred.[25] In virtue of Christ's incarnation (and, I should say, his baptism, whereby Jesus

---

21. Contemporary atonement theorists have identified examples of such punishment by proxy even in human affairs, such as a team captain's being punished for his team's failings or a squad leader's being punished for his troops' failings (Steven L. Porter, "Swinburnian Atonement and the Doctrine of Penal Substitution," in *Faith and Philosophy* 21, no. 2 [2004]: 236–37). Of course, Christ has been uniquely appointed by God to be our proxy, which may make his case *sui generis*.

22. See, e.g., Steve Jeffery, Michael Ovey, and Andrew Sach, *Pierced for Our Transgressions: Rediscovering the Glory of Penal Substitution*, foreword by John Piper (Wheaton, IL: Crossway Books, 2007), 144–47, 242–43. While recognizing a problem of "timing" occasioned by the fact that neither we nor our sins existed at the time of Christ's death, the authors do not seem cognizant of the logical problem of vicious circularity.

23. As recognized by Reformed theologian Henri Blocher, "Justification of the Ungodly (*Sola Fide*): Theological Reflections," in *Justification and Variegated Nomism: A Fresh Appraisal of Paul and Second Temple Judaism*, 2 vols., ed. D. A. Carson, Peter T. O'Brien, and Mark A. Seifrid, vol. 2: *The Paradoxes of Paul*, Wissenschaftliche Untersuchungen zum Neuen Testament (Tübingen: Mohr Siebeck, 2004), 497–8. Cf. the discomfiture of Bruce L. McCormack, "What's at Stake in Current Debates over Justification? The Current Crisis of Protestantism in the West," in *Justification: What's at Stake in the Current Debates*, eds. Mark Husbands and Daniel J. Treier (Downers Grove, IL: InterVarsity Press, 2004), 101–2.

24. He calls our union with Christ the "cause and foundation" of our sharing in all his benefits, including justification (remission of sins and adoption as sons) (Turretin, *Institutes of Elenctic Theology*, 2.16.6).

25. So-called realist accounts of the union, which appeal to mereological fusions like "fallen humanity" and "redeemed humanity" as a basis for original sin and Christ's redemption (Oliver

identified himself with fallen humanity), Christ is appointed by God to serve as our proxy before him. The *logos*, the second person of the Trinity, has voluntarily consented to be appointed, by means of his incarnation and baptism, to serve as our proxy before God so that by his death he might satisfy the demands of divine justice on our behalf.

The Unitarian theologian Faustus Socinus, in his withering attack on the Reformers' theory of penal substitution in *On Jesus Christ our Savior* (1578),[26] had argued that Christ did not, in fact, render satisfaction for our sins, since the penalty each of us faces is eternal death, and Christ did not literally endure this (III.4). Among contemporary atonement theorists, Eleonore Stump has voiced the same objection: "On orthodox theological doctrine, the penalty for sin is damnation, permanent absence of union with God. And yet it is not the case on any version of the Anselmian interpretation, even Calvin's, that Christ suffered permanent absence of union with God, so that this variation on the Anselmian interpretation has to construct some equivalence to human damnation that Christ does undergo."[27] It seems to me, however, that Turretin adequately responded to Socinus on this score by doing exactly as Stump suggests.[28] According to Turretin, Christ was forsaken by God the Father by His withdrawing from him the beatific vision and by suspending the joy and comfort and sense and fruition of full felicity. While Christ's punishment was not infinite as to duration, still in its intensity it was equivalent to the eternal suffering of

---

D. Crisp, "Original Sin and Atonement," in *The Oxford Handbook of Philosophical Theology*, eds. Thomas P. Flint and Michael C. Rea [Oxford University Press, 2009], 437–46; cf. Oliver D. Crisp, *The Word Enfleshed: Exploring the Person and Work of Christ* [Grand Rapids, MI: Baker Academic, 2016], 137–41), are implausible and unavailing, being dependent upon a principle of apparently unrestricted mereological composition and a tenseless theory of time, and implying a view of human personhood incompatible with divine punishment and rewards (William Lane Craig, *Time and Eternity: Exploring God's Relationship to Time* [Wheaton, IL: Crossway, 2001], chapter 5; William Lane Craig, *God Over All: Divine Aseity and the Challenge of Platonism* [Oxford: Oxford University Press, 2016], chapter 6).

26. Remarkably, an English translation of this epochal work has never been published. The works of Socinus are included in the *Bibliotheca Fratrum Polonorum quos Unitarios vocant*, ed. Andreas Wissowatius (Amsterdam: Irenopoli, 1668). Alan Gomes, to whom I am indebted, has translated the crucial Part III of Socinus' *De Jesu Christo Servatore* in his unpublished doctoral dissertation, "Faustus Socinus' 'De Jesu Christo Servatore,' Part III," with a historical introduction, translation, and critical notes by Alan Gomes (Ann Arbor, MI: University Microfilms International, 1990). A detailed summary of the argument of the entire work is available in John Charles Godbey, "A Study of Faustus Socinus' *De Jesu Christo Servatore*" (PhD Dissertation, University of Chicago Divinity School, 1968).

27. Eleonore Stump, *Atonement* (Oxford: Oxford University Press, 2019), 25; cf. 78.

28. Turretin, *Institutes*, 2.14.11.

the damned in hell on account of the infinite dignity of the person suffering.[29] In that case, Christ could be said to suffer subjectively the same pains as the damned. Turretin says that we cannot doubt the infinite value of Christ's satisfaction, for although his human nature was finite, the satisfaction is infinite, since it is relative to the person, who is the efficient cause and to whom the obedience and suffering are to be attributed.[30]

Herein we see the organic connection between Christ's incarnation, death, and resurrection. God's raising Jesus from the dead is not only a ratification to us of the efficacy of Christ's atoning death; it is a necessary consequence of it. For by his substitutionary death Christ fully satisfied divine justice. The penalty of death having been fully paid, Christ can no more remain dead than a criminal who has fully served his sentence can remain imprisoned. Punishment cannot justly continue; justice demands his release. Thus, Christ's resurrection is both a ratification and a necessary consequence of his satisfaction of divine justice.

Understanding Christ's resurrection as a necessary consequence of his atoning death enables us to read Paul's affirmation "Jesus our Lord ... was put to death for our trespasses and raised for our justification" (Rom 4:25) in a surprising new light. Commentators have puzzled over the fact that παρεδόθη διὰ τὰ παραπτώματα ἡμῶν καὶ ἠγέρθη διὰ τὴν δικαίωσιν ἡμῶν, when read with the standard meaning of the preposition διά + accusative, does not seem to make sense.[31] If we take διά to mean "on account of" or "because of," Paul's affirmation means that Jesus died on account of our sins and was raised on account of our justification. While Christ's dying on account of our sins makes perfect sense on the view that Christ endured the suffering which we deserved as the punishment for our sins, it seems to make no sense

---

29. Stump objects, "No matter what sort of agony Christ experienced in his crucifixion, it certainly was not (and was not equivalent to) everlasting damnation, if for no other reason than that Christ's suffering came to an end" (Stump, *Atonement*, 78). This is an obvious non-sequitur, since intensity can more than make up for limited duration. Indeed, since the future is merely potentially infinite, at no point will the damned ever have experienced more than finite suffering. Stump also asserts that suffering cannot be both voluntary and punishment. This seems evidently false, since a person may volunteer—and doubtless many have volunteered, such as in cases of civil disobedience—to be punished.

30. Turretin, *Institutes*, 2.14.12.

31. See, e.g., Douglas J. Moo's comments on Rom 4:24–25 in his *The Epistle to the Romans*, New International Commentary on the New Testament (Grand Rapids: William B. Eerdmans, 1996).

to say that Christ was raised from the dead on account of our being justified. Seemingly, one would want to say quite the reverse that our justification is on account of Christ's being raised; because he is risen, somehow we are justified. This aporia has led many commentators to construe the two instances of διά + accusative in Paul's sentence to have two different meanings, first "on account of" and then a different meaning like "with a view toward": Christ was put to death on account of our sins and raised for the sake of our justification. But the view of satisfaction defended here enables us to read Romans 4:25 in a straightforward and univocal way: Jesus was put to death on account of our sins and raised on account of our justification.[32] The resurrection of Jesus is a necessary consequence of his satisfying divine justice for us by his atoning death.

Conclusion

The resurrection of Jesus, on a penal substitutionary understanding of the atonement, is thus organically connected with his atoning death. Not only is Jesus' resurrection a vital part of a full-orbed atonement theory which features both Christus Victor and penal substitutionary motifs (not to mention other motifs as well), and not only is Jesus' resurrection a dramatic divine ratification of the efficacy of Jesus' atoning death, but also Jesus' resurrection is more directly a necessary consequence of his complete satisfaction of divine justice on our behalf. The penalty of death having been fully paid, Jesus can no longer be justly held by it: he must rise from the dead.

---

32. Of course, the view of the organic connection between Jesus' atoning death and resurrection here defended does not depend on so interpreting this verse.

7

THE MORAL ARGUMENT AND
THE MINIMAL FACTS

David Baggett

I f we were to picture the array of apologetic resources as a star-studded
baseball team, the case for the resurrection would likely reside at the
center of the diamond as the prize pitcher. Nobody can take the mound
and make that pitch better than Gary Habermas. Habermas has devoted
his life to exploring the case for the resurrection of Jesus, the truth of
which enables one to arrive at the essential truth of Christianity quite
quickly. Perhaps more than anyone else, he has done the most remarkable work in making the historical case for the resurrection.

Extending the baseball analogy, perhaps the wide-ranging center
fielder is the moral argument. When William Lane Craig has been asked
which argument for God's existence he finds to be the most effective on
the college campuses he visits, he says it's the moral argument (though
the resurrection argument, he affirms, is the most central).[1] And some
were surprised to hear that Alvin Plantinga, when asked which argument
from natural theology he thought to be the best, similarly answered the
moral argument.[2]

---

1. Craig's personal favorite is the Kalam argument, but he says it is the moral argument that has
tended to make the biggest impact. The moral argument is sometimes, of course, deployed for the
purpose of arguing for the afterlife, largely owing to Kant's influence, who offered the argument as
a way of rationally postulating both God and the afterlife. Kant's moral argument for immortality,
unfortunately, departs from the Christian insistence that the sanctification process for believers
actually reaches its culmination in complete conformity to the image of Christ. In principle it is
possible to confine the moral argument just to a conclusion about the afterlife, but an argument
encompassing both conclusions is arguably the more natural fit. To take just one example, consider
C. Stephen Layman's argument that will be summarized later.

2. Jerry L. Walls and Trent Dougherty, eds., *Two Dozen (or So) Arguments for God* (New York:
Oxford University Press, 2018), 447. Plantinga put it this way: "I'm inclined to think the moral

Because of the straight line from resurrection to Christianity, Habermas is wont to characterize the resurrection argument as a one-step apologetic approach. Rather than arguing first for theism, and then for the resurrection—a two-step procedure—he aims to get the job done in one fell swoop. In contrast to the argument from the resurrection, the moral argument is more typically seen as a two-stepper: first, a general argument for bare or classical theism, and then, more specifically, the move to Christianity in particular.

Rather than accentuating contrasts between Habermas's minimal facts case (henceforth MFC) for the resurrection and the moral argument as I tend to envision it, I intend here to lay out various points of resonance and strategic comparisons between them. Their underlying logic, after all, is remarkably similar, conforming to the same general epistemological pattern. It will be assumed that readers are already largely familiar with the contours of MFC, so here we can focus on variants of the moral argument that bear striking similarities to aspects of his MFC. To locate the relevant examples, I will honor Habermas's affinity for history by dipping into the rich pool of historical luminaries in the field of moral apologetics to highlight sometimes forgotten but poignant and germane examples.

Then I can identify a half dozen ways the moral argument paves the way to Christianity. Before getting to those suggestive pointers, let's first quickly canvass the history of the moral argument, especially in Western Europe and America in the modern era. This will be a quick, cursory examination for the sake of establishing the big picture, from which we can then pluck relevant details as needed. Then I will quickly explain the general structure of the moral argument and note its similarities to the structure of Habermas's MFC, along with resemblances between Habermas himself and several of the luminaries discussed.

---

arguments the most compelling. I find it hard to see how there can be genuine moral obligation apart from a divine command. And since I think there really is genuine moral obligation—I'm wholeheartedly committed to that—that seems to me to be an argument with a very strong premise and a pretty good connection between premise and conclusion."

Precursors to Kant

Let's begin this aerial view of the history of the moral argument by tipping our hat in the direction of a few thinkers who came before Kant, who is largely recognized as the first significant figure in a grand story that includes dons, deans, and dinosaurs—and even a British prime minister.[3]

Alfred North Whitehead once famously said that all of Western philosophy is a footnote to Plato (427–348 BC), and the history of the moral argument might provide some measure of confirmation. William Lane Craig has suggested that the history of the moral argument traces all the way back to Plato.[4] George Mavrodes notes that the Good, in Plato's thought, is somehow fundamental to what *is* as well as to what *ought to be*.[5] There we find the notion that things have goodness insofar as they stand in some relation to the Good. With the advent of Christian theism, the Good became naturally identified with God himself.[6] It is no accident that there is a long tradition of theistic (and even Christian) Platonism, running from Augustine to Robert Adams; it's almost irresistible for a Platonist to consider what it says about the nature of ultimate reality that moral truths are deep truths about the universe.[7]

For present purposes, consider Plato's teacher Socrates (470–399 BC), and note a conspicuous similarity between Socrates in the *Apology* and Saint Paul in Acts 17 at Mars Hill. Socrates (like Paul) saw himself as under a divine mandate and was a firm believer in objective moral obligations, but he famously claimed ignorance about many things, such as the exact nature of piety. Interestingly enough, though, just like Paul in Acts 17 would later echo, Socrates repeatedly affirmed his conviction

---

3. Jerry L. Walls and I offer a sustained account of this history in our *The Moral Argument: A History* (Oxford University Press, 2019).

4. William Lane Craig, *Reasonable Faith: Christian Truth and Apologetics*, 3rd ed. (Wheaton, IL: Crossway, 2008), 104.

5. George Mavrodes, "Religion and the Queerness of Morality," in *Ethical Theory: Classical and Contemporary Readings*, 2nd ed., ed. Louis P. Pojman (New York: Wadsworth, 1995), 587.

6. The irony is that Plato also wrote the early Socratic dialogue *Euthyphro*, to which many point as definitive evidence against the propriety of locating holiness or justice in the divine realm, owing to the famous "Euthyphro Dilemma." The tenth book of Plato's *Laws* has also proven to be important to aspects of moral apologetics.

7. Thanks to C. Stephen Evans for this insight.

that there would be an ultimate reckoning for how we live our lives; concerning that prognostication he didn't express any doubts. There is actually a long litany of other similarities between Socrates and Paul that won't detain us here, but instead let us take note of one radical difference. Whereas Socrates's recurring refrain on a range of vexed matters moral and metaphysical was one of *ignorance*, Paul—several hundred years later in that same location, the birthplace of Western philosophy—said that the hour of ignorance was over (Acts 17:30), a reference not likely lost in that fabled context. And why was the time of ignorance past? Because of *anastasis*—the resurrection of Jesus—thus imbuing warnings of a coming judgment with all the greater urgency.

Plato's protégé, Aristotle (384–322 BC), took a different approach to ethics from that of his mentor. Aristotle was more inclined to speak of a thing's *flourishing*. A knife's goodness depends on the effectiveness with which it serves its purpose, for example. Likewise with human beings: how effectively do they serve their purpose? And this question raises another, namely, *what is* the purpose, goal, or end of human beings? Much of the Judeo-Christian tradition would share with Aristotle a strong sense of human and moral teleology. A life of virtue, for example, is thought to fit our nature somehow, Aristotelian and Christian ethicists would agree. For Aristotle, the highest activity in which we can be engaged is contemplation of the divine. This is the apex of the life of rational contemplation. Aristotle conceived of God as a magnet drawing people to himself.[8] The ease with which one like Aquinas could incorporate Aristotle's philosophy into a framework of divine law reveals quite a bit of consistency between aspects of Aristotelian and Christian thought.

Plato and Aristotle exerted a huge influence on medieval Christian thinkers, including Augustine (AD 354–430), Thomas Aquinas (1225–1274), and many others. We could discuss such writers—the way, for example, the goodness of God was a central, if not *the* central, feature of Augustine's thought, or how he endorsed the classical moral psychology according to which we do all that we do in relation to what we take to be our *summum bonum* (highest good).[9] Or Aquinas's rich account of goodness and his famous "Fourth Way." For that matter, before getting to Kant we could spend time on other medievals, like

---

8. A difference in this regard is that the God of Christianity also actively pursues us.

9. David Horner, "Too Good Not to be True," https://www.youtube.com/watch?v=sBSK4Hw1XoY (accessed February 11, 2019).

Anselm of Canterbury (1033–1109), Duns Scotus (1266–1308), or William of Ockham (1285–1347). Or we could visit additional modern figures like George Berkeley (1685–1753) and Bishop Butler (1692–1752), René Descartes (1596–1650) and Blaise Pascal (1623–1704), John Locke (1632–1704) and Thomas Reid (1710–1796), because all of them were legitimate precursors to Kant on the moral argument. For now, let's skip ahead to the most famous moral apologist of all, the sage of Königsberg.

Immanuel Kant

Immanuel Kant (1724–1804) offered two main moral arguments for God's existence. Here is a discursive formulation of his *argument from grace.*

1. Morality requires us to achieve a standard too exacting and demanding to meet on our own without some sort of outside assistance.

2. Exaggerating human capacities, lowering the moral demand, or finding a secular form of assistance aren't likely to be adequate for the purpose of closing the moral gap.

3. Divine assistance is sufficient to close the gap.

4. Therefore, rationality dictates that we must postulate God's existence.[10]

This argument pertains to the possibility of the moral life; if *ought implies can*, then the requirements of morality, if they are to be met, have to be within our reach. With God's help, and only with God's help, they are. This is the first half of "Kantian moral faith."

Here's Kant's other argument, the *moral argument from providence*:

1. Full rational commitment to morality requires that morality is a rationally stable enterprise.

2. In order for morality to be a rationally stable enterprise, it must feature ultimate correspondence between happiness and virtue.

---

10. Much credit goes to John Hare for providing resources and language to formulate Kant's argument so concisely. See his *Moral Gap: Kantian Ethics, Human Limits, and God's Assistance* (Oxford: Clarendon Press, 1997).

3. There is no reason to think that such correspondence obtains unless God exists.

4. Therefore, rationality dictates the postulation of God's existence.[11]

This argument pertains to the *coincidence thesis*, which earlier arose in various forms in Locke, Descartes, Pascal, Reid, and Butler. It pertains to the idea that virtue and ultimate well-being coincide, which is the other half of Kantian moral faith.

Between Kant and C. S. Lewis

Mention of the moral argument usually invokes the specter of either Immanuel Kant or C. S. Lewis, but there were plenty of good moral apologists who came between them—even largely setting aside notable Germans like Hermann Lotze (1817–1881) and others.[12] Subsequent to Kant, John Henry Newman (1801–1890) was a significant British figure during the nineteenth century. He exemplified the fact that the history of apologetics is very much a story about epistemology. His rich epistemological insights served as the foundation of his moral argument. His broad epistemology and expansive empiricism recognized that we are more than narrow logic choppers. He likened the quest for truth to a vaulted ceiling that ingeniously throws its weight in a variety of directions. We gradually come to the conclusions we do through a complicated process of considering a great number of evidences, not just through tight discursive analyses. The phenomenology of conscience, in particular, can prove telling, as we have direct experience of the One to whom we are responsible, before whom we are ashamed, whose claims on us we fear, making possible what he called a *real assent* and sense of deep assurance.[13]

---

11. Kant gave this argument in the Dialectic of the *Critique of Practical Reason* and at the beginning of *Religion within the Boundaries of Mere Reason* and the end of the first and third *Critiques*.

12. Lotze, especially because of his powerful insistence on the metaphysical importance, indeed primacy of morality to metaphysics, wielded considerable influence on such thinkers as Sorley and Taylor, discussed below.

13. See John Henry Newman, *An Essay in Aid of a Grammar of Assent* (Notre Dame, IN: University of Notre Dame Press, 1979 [1870]). For an excellent contemporary application of a Newmanesque explication of moral phenomenology, especially in conversation with William May, Germain Grisez, and John Finnish, see John F. Crosby, "The Personal Encounter with God in Moral Obligation," in Crosby's *Personalist Papers* (Washington, D.C.: Catholic University of America Press, 2004), 64–92.

Born in 1838, Henry Sidgwick (1838–1900) would identify the dualism of practical reason as a problem confronting the ethical enterprise. This is the tension between one's own happiness and the happiness of others, or between rational self-love and rational benevolence. Sidgwick thought these impulses equally legitimate, yet on occasion they encounter an intractable tension. The full rationality of morality requires the resolution of this dualism, but Sidgwick did not see such a rapprochement as forthcoming. The only potential solution he could see was a theistic one, according to which a providential God ensures their harmony, but Sidgwick himself refused to follow this path. Nevertheless, his writings include the seeds for such a moral argument, predicated on the full rationality of morality.[14]

Born four years after Sidgwick was William James (1842–1910), whose work would eventually offer several resources that a moral apologist can deploy. He saw it as irrational to embrace a rule of reasoning that precludes finding truth that is really there to be found and argued that the category of moral regret is a bad fit with a naturalistic worldview. Like Newman and others, his was an expansive empiricism that included considering the evidential value of relational, aesthetic, and ethical deliverances.[15]

His contemporary, British Prime Minister Arthur Balfour (1848–1930), who, like James, gave Gifford lectures that touched on the moral argument, similarly recognized the moral deficiencies of naturalism. He was particularly intent on underscoring the ways in which deflationary analyses of moral values and duties are better at explaining them *away* than at actually explaining them. The published version of his first Gifford lectures, *Theism and Humanism*, was one of C. S. Lewis's ten favorite books.[16]

It is an application that insists on closely attending to the datum of moral obligation and, in the process, defending a central thesis of Spanish philosopher Francisco Suárez (1548–1617).

14. Readers can probably detect that this is part of the ongoing discussion of the Coincidence Thesis. See Henry Sidgwick, *The Methods of Ethics*, 7th ed. (Indianapolis, IN: Hackett, 1981).

15. In his consistently excellent commentary, Crosby thinks James only considered moving from the idea of God as infinite demander to obligation experienced as imperative, rather than the reverse path; but I'm not so sure, since this is based only on *Varieties*, which was originally to be just the first half of his analysis. He didn't end up writing the second, which may well have featured movement in the other direction. Crosby, op cit., 86–87. At any rate, see William James, *The Will to Believe and Other Essays in Popular Philosophy* (Cambridge, MA: Harvard University Press, 1979 [1897]), especially "The Dilemma of Determinism," and *Varieties of Religious Experience* (New York: The Modern Library, 1994).

16. Arthur James Balfour, *Theism and Humanism* (London: Hodder and Stoughton, 1915).

William Sorley, born in 1855, argued that God provides the best and most rational and unified view of reality, the ground of both the natural and moral orders. A close look reveals that Sorley's approach, rather than dated, remains a lively, instructive, and powerful model to follow. Whether he was integrating or reconciling various pieces of natural theology, the causal and moral, the is and ought, reality and value, life and work, finite and infinite goods, the temporal and transcendent, the moral law and evil, philosophy and poetry, or morality and metaphysics, his was an expansive and integrative mind and an open and capacious heart, and his prescient insights have proven the test of time. He demonstrated, as has Habermas, what long and intimate acquaintance with the world of ideas and living with an argument can accomplish, and his enduring example can serve as an inspiration and corrective for apologetics today.[17]

Andrew Seth Pringle-Pattison (1856–1931) struck a number of similar chords as other notable moral apologists, while distinguishing himself in a few salient respects. He lauded Kant on the issue of value, tracing that line of argument to focus on the principled reason to side with Kant over Hume on the problem of evil. Still, though, he was critical of Kant in other respects, thinking Kant paid God's immanence inadequate attention. Pringle-Pattison saw clearly various implications of the moral argument for the character of God, not just the matter of God's existence, and he intentionally launched criticisms at Hume's narrow empiricism.[18]

Anthony Thiselton writes that in the nineteenth and early twentieth centuries, the most convincing advocate of the moral argument was perhaps Hastings Rashdall (1858–1924). Rashdall critiqued Sidgwick's inability to see that rational benevolence has primacy over rational self-love, so while recognizing the dualism of practical reason, Rashdall underscored the strength of at least certain versions of theism to account for the priority of benevolence and altruism. As both a moral apologist and a kind of utilitarian, Rashdall also demonstrated that agreement on normative ethical theory is not a prerequisite for proponents of the moral argument. What is needed more centrally is

17. William Sorley, *Moral Values and the Idea of God*, 3rd ed. (New York: MacMillan, 1930).

18. Andrew Seth Pringle-Pattison, *The Idea of God in the Light of Recent Philosophy: The Gifford Lectures Delivered in the University of Aberdeen in the Years 1912 and 1913* (New York: Oxford University Press, 1920).

recognition of an essential dependence relation of morality on God, not agreement on the peripheral matter of fine-grained normative analysis. Rashdall argued that a generous empiricism will not domesticate morality, watering its authority down, but instead insist on allowing the deliverances of morality, the binding nature of the moral law, and the transcendent implications and aspirations of the moral good to inform metaphysics. Like many others, he thought the moral argument works best when combined with other pieces of natural theology.[19]

Clement Webb (1865–1954) usually did work on the moral argument in the context of his wider theological interests. He primarily looked to Plato for inspiration on the nature of moral goodness, and to Kant on the nature of moral duties. Although he initially thought Kant had reduced religion to morality, he eventually softened on that conviction.[20] As empirical experience justifies belief in an external world, he took our moral experience as solid justification for belief in moral duties. Inspired by Martineau,[21] Webb argued that the phenomenology of moral duties (that Kant explained so well) warranted belief in departing from an overambitious kind of Kantian autonomy that precludes belief in a "Higher than ourselves" that gives us the moral law. For Webb, sanction for belief in such an ultimate source is found in morality, a source both immanent and transcendent.[22]

Born in 1866, W. G. de Burgh did not think moral evidence entailed theism, but that it did incline toward it. Such evidence includes both goodness and rightness, and he endorsed a cumulative case for God's existence. He thought it took Kant's work on obligations to give the moral argument its teeth and momentum. Consciousness of moral obligations implies the reality of a moral order, which then implies God as its author and sustainer. Likewise with moral values, which are better explained by a personal God than by an impersonal Platonic realm. When it came to God's love, he departed from the tradition

---

19. Hastings Rashdall, *The Theory of Good and Evil: A Treatise on Moral Philosophy*, Vol. 1 (Oxford: Clarendon Press, 1907).

20. A more recent vindication of Kant on this score can be found in Stephen Palmquist's "Does Kant Reduce Religion to Morality?" *Kant-Studien*, Jan 1992: 129–48.

21. James Martineau, *A Study of Religion: Its Sources and Content*, Vols. 1–2 (Oxford: Clarendon Press, 1888); *Types of Ethical Theory*, Vols. 1–2 (New York: Cosimo Inc., 2006).

22. See Clement Chares Julian Webb, *Studies in the History of Natural Theology* (Oxford: Clarendon Press, 2012); *Divine Personality and Human Life* (Aberdeen: University of Aberdeen, 1920); and *Kant's Philosophy of Religion* (Oxford: Clarendon Press, 1926).

of analogical predication at points, thinking it inadequate for a full appreciation of the incarnation.[23] He also argued that divine holiness without divine love would call into question God's goodness.[24]

A. E. Taylor (1869–1945), in an effort to carve out evidential space for morality, argued at length against an artificial dichotomy between fact and value. Divorcing facts and values is like trying to separate the sounds of a great symphony from its musical quality. More important than what we do is who we are, he thought, and what is needed is an adequate account for the sort of external assistance we desperately require to be radically transformed—after all, we can't pull ourselves up by our own hair. The inherent features of moral guilt point in the direction of a personal and perfectly loving God as our First and Final Cause. He counseled close and sustained attentiveness to moral evidence and modeled a laudably expansive epistemology.[25]

Walter Robert Matthews (1881–1973) found the moral argument (along with the teleological argument) the most persuasive of all the theistic arguments. When reflecting on the moral evolution of mankind, he asked what it implies concerning the nature of the universe. When discussing the conscience, he inquired into the grounds of its characteristic property, and when pondering the nature of the good, he asked, "What is the place of the Good in the general structure of the universe?" In each case he was led to the theistic hypothesis.

From Lewis to Now

Probably the most famous moral argument of all is the popular version that C. S. Lewis (1898–1963) developed at the beginning of his enormously influential book *Mere Christianity*. Lewis started with the common sense observation that we make moral judgments about right and wrong that we take to be objectively true. This suggests a reality

---

23. Of course this issue is at the heart of one of the debates between classical theists and theistic personalists.

24. W. G. de Burgh, *From Morality to Religion: Being the Gifford Lectures, Delivered at the University of St. Andrews, 1938* (Port Washington, NY: Kennikat Press, 1938) and *The Legacy of the Ancient World* (Harmondsworth: Penguin Books, 2 vols., 1955).

25. A. E. Taylor, *Socrates* (Boston: The Beacon Press, 1951); *Faith of a Moralist* (New York: Macmillan, 1930); and *Does God Exist?* (New York: Macmillan, 1947). In *Does God Exist?*, Taylor ends with an argument for the resurrection of Jesus to augment his earlier popular version of the moral argument, their conjunction facilitated without the constraints and strictures of the Gifford lectures.

beyond and behind the moral law that Lewis went on to argue is like a mind, which points ultimately to a theistic explanation. Around the same time Lewis articulated this argument, he spelled out another version for a more academic audience based on the claim that if we are to have morality at all, we must take our basic moral judgments as self-evidently true. Lewis also developed other variations of the moral argument in his essays "The Poison of Subjectivism" and "De Futilitate," the latter of which argued that our condemnation of cruelty and indifference gives us the substance of a moral argument.[26]

A. C. Ewing (1899–1973) worked extensively on moral goodness, while Elton Trueblood (1900–1994) directed his attention to the conception of the universe that imbues the moral law with understandability. Austin Farrer (1904–1968), a friend and colleague of Lewis's, focused on the intrinsic, intuitively accessible value and dignity of persons, while George Mavrodes (b. 1923) underscored the ontologically odd nature of binding moral obligations in a naturalistic world. Basil Mitchell (1917–2011) demonstrated how secular ethics illegitimately borrow from theism.[27]

G. E. M. Anscombe (1919–2001), famed student of Wittgenstein's and the one person reputed to have beaten C. S. Lewis in a debate, wrote a landmark piece in 1958 called "Modern Moral Philosophy,"[28] in which she gave a powerful, historically informed semantic consideration that can be construed as good evidence that we should look beyond history and semantics into questions of the ultimate foundations of morality. To understand the way the moral language game is played, we have to see the way it developed out of a specifically theistic context in the Western world. In this context, oughtness and rightness and other moral concepts were tied to the commands of God. Lacking such undergirding assumptions, our moral terminology lacks

---

26. C. S. Lewis, *Mere Christianity* (HarperSanFrancisco, 2001); "De Futilitate" and "The Poison of Subjectivism," in *Christian Reflections*, ed. Walter Hooper (Grand Rapids: Eerdmans, 1995).

27. A. C. Ewing, *Value and Reality: The Philosophical Case for Theism* (New York: Humanities Press, 1971); Elton Trueblood, *Philosophy of Religion* (Westport, Connecticut: Green Publishing Group, 1975); Austin Farrer, *Reflective Faith: Essays in Philosophical Theology* (Eugene, OR: Wipf & Stock, 2012); George Mavrodes, "Religion and the Queerness of Morality," in *Ethical Theory Classical and Contemporary Readings*, 2nd ed., ed. Louis P. Pojman (New York: Wadsworth, 1995); and Basil Mitchell, *Morality, Religious, and Secular* (Oxford: Oxford University Press, 1980).

28. G. E. M. Anscombe, "Modern Moral Philosophy," reprinted in *The Collected Philosophical Papers of G. E. M. Anscombe*, Vol. 3: *Ethics, Religion, and Politics* (Oxford: Basil Blackwell, 1981), 26–42.

not only important historical foundations but also persuasive rational warrant, and it retains force only insofar as it illegitimately borrows against that history.[29]

H. P. Owen (1926–1996) was a wonderfully systematic thinker, and his work is a joy to read. Like Habermas, he was a student of history. As such, his moral argument is couched in what was one of the better cursory sketches of the history of the moral argument. On the shoulders of Newman, Sorley, Taylor, and others, he constructs an intelligent moral argument. Distinguishing between self-evidence and self-explanation, he argues that various moral phenomena, though they fall into the former category, don't fall into the latter, so they cry out for an adequate account. In discussing the deliverances of morality and delineating their salient features, he patiently demonstrates their theistic implications without pretending to have offered anything in the vicinity of a logical proof or demonstration. Significantly, he extends his case not just to theism generally, but to Christianity particularly.[30]

Clement Dore (1930–2016) argued that morality gives us reasons to believe in a being with God-like power and knowledge.[31] John Warwick Montgomery, born in 1931, offered a variety of evidential arguments for God's existence; among them he put forth a moral argument to the effect that classical theism provides the necessary explanation of human dignity and human rights.[32] Robert Adams (b. 1937) did groundbreaking work in theistic ethics and offered innovative variants of the moral argument on that foundation, while his wife Marilyn (1943–2017) demonstrated how God's incommensurable goodness can help defuse the most otherwise intractable versions of the problem of evil.[33] Linda Zagzebski (b. 1946) identified three ways we need moral confidence and how theism provides it. C. Stephen Evans (b. 1948) defended

---

29. Evans questions this analysis by showing that Socrates, well before Christianity, was able to apprehend the salient features of moral obligations, namely, (a) a judgment about a moral obligation is a kind of verdict on my action; (b) a moral obligation brings reflection to closure; (c) a moral obligation involves accountability or responsibility; and (d) a moral obligation holds for persons simply as persons. See his *God and Moral Obligation* (Oxford: Oxford University Press, 2013), ch. 2.

30. H. P. Owen, *The Moral Argument for Christian Theism* (London: George Allen & Unwin, 1965), and *The Christian Knowledge of God* (London: The Athlone Press, 1969).

31. Clement Dore, *Theism* (Dordrecht: D. Reidel Publishing Company, 1984).

32. John Warwick Montgomery wrote *The Law above the Law* (Irvine, CA: New Reformation Publications, 1975) and *Human Rights and Human Dignity* (Irvine, CA: New Reformation Publications, 2019).

33. Robert Adams, *Finite and Infinite Goods* (Oxford: Oxford University Press, 1999).

divine command theory and a natural signs approach to apologetics.[34] J. P. Moreland (also b. 1948) constructed an argument on the basis of recalcitrant moral facts, and John Hare (b. 1949) did landmark work on Kantian moral arguments.

William Lane Craig (also b. 1949) has used the moral argument to a powerful effect in numerous books and debates. He has popularized this modus tollens discursive account:

1. If God does not exist, then there are no objective moral values and duties.

2. There are objective moral values and duties.

3. So, God exists.[35]

C. Stephen Layman (b. 1955) began his moral argument with what he calls the *Overriding Reason Thesis* (ORT), which says the overriding (or strongest) reasons always favor doing what is morally required, and the *Conditional Thesis* (CT), which says that if there is no God and no life after death, then the ORT is not true. Since there are compelling reasons to reject neither, what follows is either God's existence or the existence of an afterlife in which virtue is rewarded. But in light of the incalculable complexity of a system like karma and the transmigration of souls, the moral order postulated by nontheistic reincarnation paradoxically provides evidence for the existence of a personal God after all.[36]

R. Scott Smith (b. 1957), Mark Linville (b. 1957), Angus Menuge (b. 1963), and Angus Ritchie (b. 1974) have all offered distinctive, brilliant, epistemic moral arguments, and Paul Copan (b. 1962) has used history to augment the moral argument, extend it to Christianity, and defend the character of the God of the Old Testament.[37]

---

34. Linda Zagzebski (2004), "Does Ethics Need God," *Faith and Philosophy* 4: 294–303; *Divine Motivation Theory* (Cambridge: Cambridge University Press, 2004). C. Stephen Evans, *Natural Signs and Knowledge of God: A New Look at Theistic Arguments* (Oxford: Oxford University Press, 2010). Natural signs, on Evans's account, are both widely accessible and easily resistible—consonant with solid (Pascalian and other) grounds for a measure of divine hiddenness.

35. William Lane Craig, *Reasonable Faith: Christian Truth and Apologetics* (Wheaton, IL: Crossway, 2008).

36. C. Stephen Layman, "A Moral Argument for the Existence of God," in *Is Goodness without God Good Enough?*, eds. Robert K. Garcia and Nathan L. King (Lanham, MD: Rowman and Littlefield, 2009), 52.

37. R. Scott Smith, *In Search of Moral Knowledge: Overcoming the Fact-Value Dichotomy* (Downers Grove, IL: InterVarsity Press, 2014); Mark Linville, "The Moral Argument," in *The*

General Structure of the Moral Argument
and Its Resonances with Habermas's MFC

This broad array of variants of the moral argument underscores that the argument comes in many of shapes and sizes, but we can identify at least a general overall structure that tends to be held in common. It typically begins with some salient moral phenomenon in need of explanation, like moral duties, intrinsic human value, objective moral values, or the like. Then, there's an effort to identify either the only, the best, or at least eminently adequate explanation of the phenomenon. Finally, when appropriate, there is at least a tentative inference to that explanation as likely true for providing such an account.

There are usually three conceptually distinct components of moral arguments designed to evidentially point in the direction of God. First, there is some sort of realist assumption made or argument offered for objective moral realities in need of adequate explanation. This involves a tacit rejection of reductionist accounts that settle for explaining such phenomena away or domesticating them and robbing them of their teeth.[38] Second, a theistic account needs to be shown as especially effective at providing the explanation or account of the realities in question. Not all moral apologists need to agree on the precise way of construing the theistic account; such fine-grained details are at the relative periphery of the discussion. What is central, as we saw in our discussion of Rashdall, is that there's agreement on an essential dependence of whatever moral phenomena on God. Third, critiques of alternative accounts provided by secularists, nontheistic Platonists, Cornell realists, and the like are offered. If theism is going to be advanced as

---

Blackwell Companion to Natural Theology, eds. William Lane Craig and J. P. Moreland (Oxford: Blackwell Publishing Limited, 2009); Angus Menuge, "The Failure of Naturalism as a Foundation for Human Rights," https://www.moralapologetics.com/wordpress/the-failure-of-naturalism-as-a-foundation-for-human-rights; Angus Ritchie, *From Morality to Metaphysics: The Theistic Implications of our Ethical Commitments* (Oxford: Oxford University Press, 2012); Paul Copan, "A Moral Argument," in *To Everyone an Answer: A Case for the Christian Worldview*, eds. Francis Beckwith, William Lane Craig, and James Porter Moreland (Downers Grove, IL: InterVarsity Press, 2004); *Is God a Moral Monster? Making Sense of the Old Testament God* (Grand Rapids: Baker Books, 2011); with Matthew Flannagan, *Did God Really Command Genocide? Coming to Terms with the Justice of God* (Grand Rapids: Baker Books, 2014).

38. Three books written by nonnaturalist nontheists in recent years defending sturdy moral realism are David Enoch, *Taking Morality Seriously: A Defense of Robust Realism* (Oxford: Oxford University Press, 2011); Russ Shafer-Landau, *Moral Realism: A Defence* (Oxford: Clarendon Press, 2005); and Erik J. Wielenberg, *Robust Ethics: The Metaphysics and Epistemology of Godless Normative Realism* (Oxford: Oxford University Press, 2014).

the only or even merely the best explanation, this raises the burden to show that its explanations are superior to those provided by the alternative accounts. Abductivists tend to do this by using a principled set of criteria to narrow down the list of potential explanation candidates to the best explanation, which we can then tentatively infer as the likely true explanation.[39]

One way to capture a great deal of the import and history of the moral argument outlined above is to consider the four-fold cumulative, teleological, abductive case that Jerry Walls and I have advanced. It's an effort to tap into numerous strands of the moral argument that have surfaced throughout its rich and fertile history. The four components of our argument are these: (1) objective moral values and duties (and perhaps other moral facts like moral rights, moral freedom, moral regret, and the like); (2) moral knowledge; (3) moral rationality;[40] and (4) moral transformation. The phenomena to be explained encompass metaphysics, epistemology, and Kantian moral faith in both of its dimensions.[41]

These moral phenomena are similar to Habermas's minimal facts, requiring explanation. After identifying the moral fact(s) to be considered, we identify various explanation candidates, and then apply such criteria as explanatory scope and power, degree of ad hoc-ness, and conformity with other beliefs to make the case that their best explanation is God. If all goes to plan, the case is made that the divine loom weaves together the warp of moral ontology with the weft of moral knowledge and, by turns, the taut threads of moral faith.

This general methodology is not unlike Habermas's minimal facts case for the resurrection. In a similar fashion he argues for the resurrection as the better explanation of the minimal facts than those explanations provided by, say, the swoon or resuscitation hypotheses.

---

39. By "abductivists" I mean those who attempt to make an "inference to the best explanation." The inference from *best* explanation to *likely true* explanation is not logically guaranteed in light of the possibility of a bad pool of alternatives from which to choose, the likeliest of which is still intrinsically unlikely. Van Fraasen, Plantinga, and others have raised this matter, and, for some, it resides in the neighborhood of their a priori resistance to theism's inclusion in the original pool in the first place. The best initial reply is to show that neither bare nor classical theism is implicated in any logical contradictions.

40. The coincidence thesis rears its head again.

41. See David Baggett and Jerry L. Walls, *Good God: The Theistic Foundations of Morality* (New York: Oxford University Press, 2011) and *God and Cosmos: Moral Truth and Human Meaning* (New York: Oxford University Press, 2016). See also David Baggett and Marybeth Baggett, *The Morals of the Story: Good News about a Good God* (Downers Grove, IL: InterVarsity Academic, 2018).

Besides parities in strategy, it is worth mentioning that Habermas also reflects some of the character traits of the great luminaries from the history of moral apologetics. For now, four examples will suffice. First, his friendship with Antony Flew is a colorful illustration of his capacity for friendship with those with whom he disagrees.[42] For present purposes, it bears repeating that the history of the moral argument, with few exceptions, is marked with those who were remarkably respectful toward their interlocutors. And in some cases, as would later be the case with Habermas and Flew, it was in the context of a genuine, rich friendship with ideological foes that some of the best work in moral apologetics was done. Newman, for example, carried on a lifelong correspondence with his "dear friend" Froude, with whom he failed to see eye to eye, but the correspondence yielded great fruit, including many of the insights that made it into Newman's magisterial *Grammar of Assent*.[43]

Second, Habermas endured a bitter personal trial when he lost his first wife far sooner than he should have, and the way the resurrection sustained his hope and faith during that horrible time of loss has been a powerful testimony for many. It demonstrated the power of his argument and, more importantly, the power of the resurrection itself. C. S. Lewis, in the Second World War, and William Sorley, in the First, did much of their most important work on the moral argument during the throes of war. In Sorley's case, he was in the midst of writing his Gifford lectures on the topic when he received the horrible news of his son's death in the war. Apologetics and apologists that stand the test of time can endure the trials and drink the sufferings of this world to its dregs without losing the hope that won't disappoint.

Third, like the thinkers discussed above, Habermas has shown what it means to live with an argument. This takes prodigious perseverance in a world in such a hurry. Owen Barfield once said that the trouble in his day—and it's worse now—is that we have all gotten very clever, no longer capable of thinking deeply because we think too quickly. It

---

42. I have discussed this in print already. See David Baggett, ed., *Did the Resurrection Happen? A Conversation with Gary Habermas and Antony Flew* (Downers Grove, IL: InterVarsity Press, 2009), 13–20. That book later lists salient philosophical questions the resurrection debate raises. In retrospect I might have added to the list the matter of what constitutes the nature of nomological laws.

43. See Nicholas Lash's introduction to Newman's *Grammar*.

takes tremendous patience to feel the force of a disparate collection of reasons whose cumulative force is considerable, and such patience requires intentional cultivation and hard work. Especially in an age of social media, sounds bites, and mic drops, living with ideas and arguments has fallen out of vogue. Unless an argument is able to be encapsulated in a few sentences, it often gets dismissed as hopelessly unwieldy or impracticable, as if we ought to be allergic to anything requiring sustained effort and more than a modicum of investment. Time spent considering Habermas's life can serve as a corrective and antidote to such superficiality and frenetic rushes to judgment.

Fourth, like Newman, Sorley, Taylor, and others, Habermas embraces a rich, expansive epistemology and broad empiricism. The history of the moral argument is replete with careful examination of the logic, language, and phenomenology of moral realities. Similarly, in his zeal to avoid error, Habermas is careful not to miss the truth. Rather than resting content with something like Flew's longstanding *a priori* resistance to anything remotely smacking of the supernatural, Habermas was and is willing to follow the evidence where it leads. Not unlike A. E. Taylor's rigorous effort to delineate the features of moral guilt that we can glean from close examination of its phenomenology,[44] which can then potentially prove revelatory, likewise Habermas has shown a laudable rigorous attentiveness to the evidence. Great apologists do.

These personal traits that function so constitutively of a great apologist remind us of these important words Aristotle once wrote: "It is not true, as some writers assume in their treatises on rhetoric, that the personal goodness revealed by the speaker contributes nothing to his power of persuasion; on the contrary, his character may almost be called the most effective means of persuasion he possesses."[45]

Moral Apologetics and Christianity

In what remains, let us briefly look at ways in which the moral argument can be deployed as an argument not just for God generally, but for Christianity particularly. The claim is not that by moral apologetics

---

44. Condemnation, indelibility, demand for punishment, pollution, shame.

45. *The Rhetoric and the Poetics of Aristotle*, trans. Rhys Roberts (New York: McGraw-Hill, 1984), 25.

alone one can somehow *deduce* all the aspects of special revelation contained in Christianity, but rather this: in light of Christianity having been revealed, moral arguments for God's existence point quite naturally in its direction. The following list, far from exhaustive, offers six reasons to think this is so.

Christological

The final chapter of H. P. Owen's *Moral Argument for Christian Theism* points to New Testament teachings on goodness, duty, and beatitude that can both positively and negatively lead the mind to belief in the God of Christianity. Newman thinks that special revelation performs a sort of ampliative function in taking the deliverances of general revelation and focusing them into more fine-grained form, namely, of Christ. One of the great virtues of moral arguments for God's existence is that they point not just to the existence of God, but to a God of a particular nature: a God who is morally perfect—not just perfectly holy, but also perfectly loving. A. C. Ewing once said that the source of the moral law is morally perfect.[46] Such a notion is described in various ways: omnibenevolent, impeccable, essentially good, and the like. What does it look like when omnibenevolence takes on human form? Jesus is a powerful answer. Moral apologetics works best when it is Christological.

Trinitarian

To conceive of God as essentially and perfectly loving requires some sort of account. The right account, again, is not the sort of idea that we are able to generate on our own; we depend on special revelation to tell us what it is. But Christianity has provided us with an account of the divine nature that is Trinitarian in nature—we cannot deduce it, but we can recognize its truth once we see it. C. S. Lewis wrote in *Mere Christianity*, "All sorts of people are fond of repeating the Christian statement that 'God is love'. But they seem not to notice that the words 'God is love' have no real meaning unless God contains at least two Persons. Love is something that one person has for another person. If

---

46. Ewing, *Value and Reality*, 199.

God was a single person, then before the world was made, He was not love."[47] Moral apologetics works best when it is Trinitarian.[48]

Forgiveness

Under the performative or transformational variant of the moral argument can fit our need not just for transformation but forgiveness. Most all of us have on occasion shuddered and been riddled with guilt for having fallen short of a moral standard of which we can hardly help but be aware. In a paper on moral arguments for God, Robert Adams once wrote that standard fare in such philosophical discussions are ontological or epistemic arguments, but then he added, "I am keenly aware that they form only part of the total moral case for theistic belief. Theistic conceptions of guilt and forgiveness, for example ... may well have theoretical and practical moral advantages at least as compelling as any that we have discussed."[49] The moral argument, functioning as a prelude to the gospel, leaves one with a deep existential need for forgiveness for our moral failures. If that is the phenomenological question the moral argument raises, the death and resurrection of Jesus is the historical and theological answer Christianity provides. As Lewis once said, Christians offer an explanation of how we got into our present state of both hating goodness and loving it—and hope that our worst moments do not define us. Moral apologetics reminds us of our need for forgiveness; a test of the strength of a worldview is its ability to provide it. The good news of Christianity is that forgiveness is available.

Individual Transformation

Historically, Christianity has a demonstrated track record of reaching people of every race and ethnicity and socioeconomic background and radically transforming their lives. In *They Found the Secret*, a book

---

47. C. S. Lewis, *The Complete C. S. Lewis Signature Classics* (New York: HarperOne, 2002), 142–43.

48. For an excellent podcast on this topic, see Brian Scalise, "Brian Scalise on the Nature of Love in Islam and Christianity," March 15, 2012, in *Moral Apologetics,* https://www.moralapologetics.com/wordpress/podcast-brian-scalise-on-the-nature-of-love-in-islam-and-christianity.

49. See Robert Adams, "Moral Arguments for Theistic Belief," in *Rationality and Religious Belief,* ed. C. Delaney (Notre Dame, IN: University of Notre Dame Press, 1970), 116–40.

chronicling the spiritual lives of various Christian saints, can be found this description:

> Out of discouragement and defeat they have come into victory. Out of weakness and weariness they have been made strong. Out of ineffectiveness and apparent uselessness they have become efficient and enthusiastic. The pattern seems to be self-centeredness, self-effort, increasing inner dissatisfaction and outer discouragement, a temptation to give it all up because there is no better way, and then finding the Spirit of God to be their strength, their guide, their confidence and companion—in a word, their life.[50]

This isn't Pollyannaish. We can be not only forgiven our sins but delivered from sin itself. We can be changed, and ultimately entirely transformed; the very power that raised Jesus from the dead can be at work within us to change us from within, wholly and completely. Moral apologetics works best when it is individually transformational—indeed, Taylor preferred language of *transfiguration*.

Culturally Transformative

Paul Copan speaks of an historical aspect of moral apologetics: the historical role played by Christ and his devoted followers to promote social justice. Morality demands deep cultural transformation, too, including hard work to battle systemic evils. Copan cites specific cultural developments that can be shown to have flowed from the Jewish-Christian worldview, leading to societies that are "progress-prone rather than progress-resistant," including such signs of progress as the founding of modern science, poverty-diminishing free markets, equal rights for all before the law, religious liberty, women's suffrage, human rights initiatives, and the abolition of slavery, widow-burning, and foot-binding.[51]

Metaphysics scripts history. Derrida wrote that "the cornerstone of international law is the sacred ... the sacredness of man as your

---

50. V. Raymond Edman, *They Found the Secret: 20 Transformed Lives that Reveal the Touch of Eternity* (Grand Rapids: Zondervan, 1984), 12.

51. See Paul Copan, "Reinforcing the Moral Argument: Appealing to the Historical Impact of the Christian Faith," paper presented at the Evangelical Theological Society, November 2014, San Diego.

neighbor."[52] Today there is a growing opinion among Chinese social scientists that the Christian idea of transcendence was the historic basis for the concepts of human rights and equality. Atheist Richard Rorty admits that throughout history, societies have come up with various ways to exclude certain groups from the human family by calling them subhuman, and that, by contrast, Christianity gave rise to the concept of universal rights, derived from the conviction that all human beings are created in the image of God.

Jürgen Habermas (that *other* Habermas), who is not a Christian himself, writes the following:

> Christianity has functioned for the normative self-understanding of modernity as more than just a precursor or a catalyst. Egalitarian universalism, from which sprang the ideas of freedom and a social solidarity, of an autonomous conduct of life and emancipation, the individual morality of conscience, human rights, and democracy, is the direct heir to the Judaic ethic of justice and the Christian ethic of love. This legacy, substantially unchanged, has been the object of continual critical appropriation and reinterpretation. To this day, there is no alternative to it. And in light of current challenges of a postnational constellation, we continue to draw on the substance of this heritage. Everything else is just idle postmodern talk.[53]

Moral apologetics works best when it is culturally transformative.

Eschatological

The moral argument and the problem of evil are locked in a zero-sum game. One will win, and one will lose. Christianity offers principled reason to think that the glory to come will not just *outweigh* but definitely *defeat* the worst evils of this world. Christian philosopher Marilyn Adams writes, "If Divine Goodness is infinite, if intimate relation to It is thus incommensurably good for created persons, then we

---

52. Jacques Derrida, "To Forgive: The Unforgivable and Imprescriptible," in *Questioning God*, ed. John D. Caputo, Mark Dooley, and Michael J. Scanlon (Bloomington, IN: Indiana University Press, 2001), 70.

53. Jürgen Habermas, *Time of Transitions*, ed. and trans. Ciaran Cronin and Max Pensky (Cambridge, MA: Polity, 2006), 150–51.

have identified a good big enough to defeat horrors in every case."[54]
Moral apologetics works best when it is eschatological.

Universal

Christianity gives compelling reasons to think that every person possesses infinite dignity and value—a motif founds in the likes of Linville, Farrer, and Evans. To be loved by God, the very archetype of all goodness—each of us differently, but all of us infinitely—and to have been made a person in his image is to possess greater worth than we can begin to imagine. And humanity is not just valuable in the aggregate, according to Christianity. Rather, each person is unique, each is loved by God, and each is someone for whom Jesus suffered, died, and was raised. And in the book of Revelation, for everyone who lays down their arms and allows themselves to be vanquished by the overtures of God's perfect love, a white stone will reveal a unique name for each one of them—marking their distinctive relationship with God and vocation in him. Moral apologetics works best when it is universal—without neglecting the personal.

Final Thoughts

I finish with these two last thoughts. First, by way of putting all these considerations together, an analogy: like a labyrinthine maze of jumbled metal filings suddenly stands in symmetrical formation in response to the pull of a magnet, so the right organizing story—classical theism and orthodox Christianity—pulls all the moral pieces of evidence into alignment and allows a striking pattern to emerge. Various luminaries from the history of the moral argument embrace a method by which the strengths of a variety of evidences combine into a compelling cumulative case. Interestingly enough, we can see this dynamic at play even within a single argument, as our four-fold moral case demonstrates considerable resiliency and philosophical power. Combining the moral argument, then, with other arguments, including Habermas's signature case for the historicity of the resurrection, only increases their collective power and persuasive potential.

---

54. Marilyn McCord Adams, *Horrendous Evils and the Goodness of God* (Ithaca, NY: Cornell University Press, 1999), 82–83.

Second, on a personal note, Gary Habermas is the reason I came to teach at Liberty in 2006. I was teaching at a different college when I attended an Oxbridge conference in England in 2004, where I met him and his wife, Eileen. My mother was with me on the trip, and the four of us amidst the towering spires all got along swimmingly right from the start. Gary and my mom had both grown up in Detroit. She still loved it and pined for it with a nostalgia entirely incommensurate with reality, and Gary—suffice it to say—not so much. This led to endless fun frivolity between those two. Long story short, Liberty was hiring, the topic was broached, and eventually I made the move—where, among other things, I would eventually find my wife!—but none of it would have ever happened without my meeting this remarkable fellow.

Since then, we have collaborated on two books, my fondness and respect for him has only grown exponentially, and it has been a joy and honor to count him as a colleague and friend—even when he is mischievously mixing a metaphor or inexplicably raving about *The Walking Dead*.[55] In my mind, there is little doubt that, along with his rigor, scholarship, and insatiable[56] work ethic, it is Gary's amiability, likeability, and winsomeness that all collectively contribute to his being the premier, practically paradigmatic apologist that he is today. With the publication of his forthcoming magnum opus, it's my hope and prayer that his years of steadfast labor on the historicity of the resurrection could very well be quickly approaching a Gladwellian tipping point where we begin to see the fruition of his efforts like never before—which could do untold good for the kingdom. Seeing a good man operate on all thrusters so faithfully fulfilling and passionately pursuing his obvious God-given vocation, doing what he was born to do over the course of a lifetime, is nothing less than an ennobling inspiration. The chance to honor him and partially repay a mammoth debt of gratitude by participating in this volume has been a marvelous privilege.

---

55. Besides the aforementioned resurrection book, see David Baggett, Gary Habermas, Jerry L. Walls, eds., *C. S. Lewis as Philosopher: Truth, Goodness, and Beauty*, 2nd ed. (Lynchburg, VA: Liberty University Press, 2017).

56. Veritably freakish.

8

THE LOGICAL STRUCTURE
OF MORAL ARGUMENTS

W. David Beck

The Argument Base

Each one of the traditional arguments for God's existence begins with a simple observation of the world around us. We see ourselves living in a connected dependency of nature, an ecosystem in which things, including ourselves, are sustained by each other. We find ourselves living in productive patterns with other things in ways that allow us to prosper and extend our goals. And then there is this: we sense we need to live our lives in contexts of obligations to each other, as well as the things, especially animals, around us, seeking each other's well-being and minimizing our suffering and pain.

Each of the arguments then proceed to a stage in which alternative explanation scenarios are advanced and examined, sometimes quite explicitly but often not. This can vary depending on how many there might be, but also on how extensive the base observation is. This can be quite detailed, for example, if the base is the universe as a whole, which then demands some sort of universal principle.

With moral arguments, in their many different forms, this base can take on any number of different scenarios, depending on precisely where the argument seeks to locate our sense of morality. Stephen Evans, in his recent entry on this topic for the *Stanford Encyclopedia of Philosophy*,[1] notes four possible bases for the argument: a) a perception of objective

---

1. C. Stephen Evans, "Moral Arguments for the Existence of God," *Stanford Encyclopedia of Philosophy*, at http://plato.stanford.edu/entries/moral-arguments-god/.

moral requirement; b) direct moral knowledge or awareness; c) a perception of human dignity; or d) a practical perception of the reasonableness of acting morally. Each of these will dictate a somewhat different logic of elimination, nevertheless some commonalities remain. It is this common strategy or flow of logic that is the focus of this study.

Each of the a posteriori arguments concludes to a best (at times, the "last man standing") explanation. Since there are causal connections involved, this conclusion will also bring with it some characteristics of the base observations being explained. Hence the conclusion will contain more than just an existence mandate, but clearly also some implications regarding properties. This is especially crucial in any form of moral argument, and it is this step that we also want to examine more closely to see just how the flow of logic goes.

Finally, I should note in advance that, like the others, moral arguments come in all three logical argument patterns: deductive, inductive, and abductive. As Charles Peirce noted, all arguments are kinds of inferences to best explanations.[2] This may well stretch our analysis a bit, and, granted, there are examples, especially abductive ones, where the structure we are advocating is simply not explicitly there. Nevertheless, it is usually, admittedly not always, the case that the larger text at least suggests the flow of logic we identify below.

The Logic of the Argument Base

Evans' four categories are essential in determining the initial flow of argument. We will look at the categories briefly but our primary concern is finding commonalities that will set the stage for a unified first phase of any Moral Argument.

The starting point of any a posteriori argument is its specific choice of observational data. So moral arguments have differed in their selection of types of moral facts. One type is our perception that some of our social requirements carry a level of objectivity that goes beyond mere duty to obey the individual laws of our particular government. We can see many as helpful and important to enforce, such as driving on the right side of the road, but, nevertheless, as lacking any real moral authority. Others, however, such as protecting the lives of

---

2. See, e.g., Charles Peirce, "A Neglected Argument for the Reality of God," *Hibbert Journal* (1908), where he discusses the teleological argument as an example.

children, carry a force that transcends individual national or ethnic boundaries and form a broadly human moral obligatoriness. This, in turn, seems to demand explanation that goes beyond any individual society. Robert Adams' divine command argument is a good example.[3]

Some have argued for a second source: our apparently universal perception of human value, dignity, or worth. That such a general awareness underlies our sense of natural rights and grounds justice, is argued, for example, by Nicholas Wolterstorff.[4] Any such intrinsic value would seem to transcend humans and thus require explanation as to how it obligates us.

Third, there is the Kantian type of "practical" argument,[5] that we find ourselves postulating God as the only way to make sense of our perception of having a moral duty, and its pursuit being the only means to happiness.

A fourth type sees us as having straightforward awareness or knowledge of moral truth. Richard Swinburne has argued that moral facts are a priori truths, or at least grounded in them.[6] We simply find ourselves knowing that certain behavior patterns are binding for all of us. That might, as Swinburne thinks, eliminate the need for any empirical moral argument, but one might still think that such knowledge needs further explanation.

We now need to make some clear distinctions between argument types to see if this would impact the actual structure of content in a moral argument. First, what about the distinction between a priori and a posteriori claims as base for the argument?

As noted, some, such as Richard Swinburne, consider the moral argument to be a priori. The a priori elements are principle imperatives like, "Genocide is wrong," whereas the a posteriori concerns statements such as, "It is wrong for person Q to commit genocide on people R." There is nothing about the nature of a posteriori propositions that determines whether such propositions are right and wrong or good and bad. It's similar to stating, "This elephant is grey," and not

---

3. See Robert Adams, *Finite and Infinite Goods* (New York: Oxford University Press, 1999).

4. See Nicholas Wolterstorff, *Justice: Rights and Wrongs* (Princeton: Princeton University Press, 2007).

5. Found in several places, most importantly his 1788 *Critique of Practical Reason*.

6. See Richard Swinburne, *The Existence of God*, 2nd ed. (Oxford: Oxford University Press, 2004).

making the commitment that all elephants are grey, even though it very well may be the case.

However, the very concept and meaning of the word *"genocide"* seemingly denotes ethical judgments such as right or wrong. Those who consider the moral argument a posteriori would have to deny that genocide *denotes* wrongfulness; rather, it *connotes* wrongfulness. Swinburne and the like might claim that genocide denotes wrongfulness just as yellow denotes color. Perhaps such considerations shouldn't be discarded so soon. When hearing the word *"holocaust,"* it may bring about thoughts that immediately understand the meaning of the word to be wrong. This is likely influenced by historical events that did involve a holocaust, and those experiences rustle up emotions and ethical judgments. However, there are also phrases, like *"biological warfare,"* that may also immediately conjure up similar judgments, but such judgments are likely to be inferences to subjunctive conditionals, such as, "It would be wrong to engage in biological warfare." There haven't been major events that involved biological warfare like there have holocausts.

With a posteriori claims, there may be true counterfactuals, or at least counterfactuals that aren't nonsensical. "This elephant is grey" may have a counterfactual of "This elephant is not grey" that is not incoherent. Likewise, "This person should not cut this person open" has a true counterfactual: "This person should cut this person open." If the person performing the cut in the counterfactual claim is a surgeon attempting to save the other's life, then it is certainly permitted if not obligatory.

Synthetic a priori claims have no true counterfactuals. "Rape is wrong" does not have the counterfactual "Rape is permitted" or "Rape is right." The defense of such counterfactual considerations will be discussed at the end of phase two. Such inferences may not be drawn just yet in this rationale and are premature. So we leave them out of consideration of logical structure for now.

Moral arguments also differ in their form. Most have been deductive. In a sound deductive argument, if the premises are true the conclusion is true, regardless of whether or not further evidence is considered, so long as the rules of inference are followed. Typically, here the first premise is a statement of some moral phenomena followed by a series of premises that draw conclusions as to what must follow as to the cause or reason for such phenomena.

Some moral arguments, at least in their first phase, are inductive. Induction works, of course, by some sort of enumeration: as support for the conclusion that all p's are q's, for example, that each item in a list of behaviors is considered by everyone to be morally good. This makes for an ampliative argument in which the premises, while not entailing the truth of the conclusion, nevertheless provide good reason for accepting it. So examples of universally agreed-on morally good behaviors, perhaps along with the elimination of rival explanations, could lead to the conclusion that there is likely a cosmic moral decider.

Abduction, or inference to the best explanation, is similar to induction in that both methods are ampliative, but rather than the premises adding to the probability of the conclusion, the conclusion adds to the probability of the premises. Here, the inferences are used to connect evidence with theory. In this context, a metaethical theory is composed of axioms—primarily synthetic a priori, experiential evidence, and synthetic a posteriori—and are connected by inference. The aggregate of the theory serves to explain the data within itself and not the evidence explaining the theory. So moral arguments of this form might move from a posited God to show how well that explains what we know to be the case about moral phenomena.

The key point for abduction is the explanatory scope and power of the explanation. Abductive reasoning does not derive a certain conclusion (for one would then be guilty of affirming the consequent), but it makes an inference to the best explanation. Peirce's example was whether anyone should believe in the existence of Napoleon. He claimed that the past may be inferred from the study of present effects, namely, artifacts and records. Peirce concluded, "Though we have not seen the man [Napoleon], yet we cannot explain what we have seen without the hypothesis of his existence."[7]

Different as these approaches are in logical structure, they have three commonalities that give the moral argument a convergent logical flow. First, these are all claimed to be general and universal human observations. Though at some level internal and subjective, their

---

7. Charles Sanders Peirce, "Abduction and Induction," in *The Philosophy of Pierce*, ed. J. Buchler (London: Routledge, 1956), 375.

universality lends them objectivity. We think they hold everywhere in our world, and, in fact, the way we apply moral considerations to science fiction—like Star Trek, for example—seems to indicate that we expect they hold in every possible world and for any rational creature.

Second, their objectivity, their transcending reality, pushes us to seek and demand an explanation for the observations. We cannot leave them as brute givens any more than we can the law of gravity.

Third, and most importantly, none of these observations would make sense as moral reality unless there is a moral authority, that is, genuine obligation. Clearly, it is this demand for assent to a morality that initiates the moral argument. Thus, what these arguments typically trade on is not moral behaviors, sensibilities, feelings, intuitions, codes, cultural standards, evolved commonalities, or altruistic patterns, but rather actual obligations. But, it is typically argued, obligation makes no sense apart from a referent: it seems one could only be obligated *to* some authority.

It is for this reason, we think, that the argument runs into its fiercest opposition right at the start. This is not the case for either the cosmological or teleological argument. There, the first premise observation seems acceptable to everyone. But here, not so much!

Fortunately, however, we are here not interested in the soundness of the argument, or even the truth of any of the premises. So we are not going to respond to any objections, and we will not refer to specific examples of the argument but simply to a general format.[8] So we turn to the logic of the first phase of the moral argument.

The Logic of Phase One

The first phase of the argument seeks for possible alternate explanations of our moral obligations. Here, of course, there is a great variety of ways to proceed. Some forms, especially those from the late nineteenth and early twentieth century, do not explicitly consider any alternatives but simply move directly to a higher moral authority. Nevertheless, almost invariably the text will include consideration of alternate possible explanations, regardless of how quickly they are dismissed.

There are two immediate candidates that are typically advanced. The first is a natural causal explanation, the second a social influence

---

8. No doubt the classic example that roughly follows this format is C. S. Lewis.

one. That is, our observations of morality are to be attributed either to some naturally occurring process such as an evolutionary survival-of-the-fittest mechanism operating by means of, as most often advanced, altruism, or to some social enforcement process such as religion, cultural/educational factors, peer pressure, family values, and so on. So morality comes either from nature or from other persons.

Sam Harris manages to combine both of these approaches in his recent books *The Moral Landscape* and *Free Will*. In *The Moral Landscape*, he states, "Questions about values are really questions about the well-being of conscious creatures. ... I want to develop a science of human flourishing."[9]

What is interesting as we think of the logic here is that both of these options capture an important insight, and so their discussion and eventual elimination sets up both a set of negations as well as a set of affirmations. Here is what I mean. In the first case, nature or evolution, the argument will be something to the effect that causality cannot produce morality. Morality, it will be claimed, can only occur where there are free agents acting, at least to some extent, apart from external and even internal constraint. The common, if not universal, lack of conformity to perceived moral obligations is frequently cited as *prima facia* evidence. And so, the argument concludes, whatever else evolution is successful in explaining, say behaviors, compulsions, intuitions, preferences, customs, social norms, and the like, it says nothing about moral obligation.

So, such an argument negates causal explanations in general. At the same time, it affirms that the only explanatory context that could be acceptable would have to involve the reasons of free moral agents, that is, persons.

Similarly, the social hypothesis encounters the objection that other persons, precisely as free moral agents themselves, cannot authorize moral obligation on their equals. The authority status from which one could prescribe true obligation would demand an unequal and higher status than what is possible among equal human persons. Here again,

---

9. Sam Harris, *The Moral Landscape* (New York: Free Press, 2010), 7. Harris has attempted to redefine normative statements. He equates human wellbeing with the good and that which does not contribute to human wellbeing as not the good.

social rankings can explain behaviors, customs, codes, and the like, but not, it is typically argued, actual obligations.

So this counter would defeat any form of "other persons" explanation. Nevertheless, it affirms our intuition that any good explanation must treat all persons as morally equal and thus eliminate their moral authority over others.

Phase one of the argument, then, sets up and defeats the rival hypotheses for explaining moral obligation. I note again here that I am attempting only to clarify the logical flow of this argument, not establish the truth of any of these premises.

The Logic of Phase Two

The defeat of these two explanations now forms the logical dynamic of the second phase that brings us to the conclusion. Specifically, it leaves us with affirmations that form a dilemma from which there appears to be only one escape. The argument so far appears to establish two propositions. First, that moral obligations can only be explained by personal sources. Only persons have the capacities to understand, formulate, and hence elicit real moral obligations. Only persons have the intentionality that allows for an internal dialogue about right and wrong, and then to form entirely new beliefs about what one ought to do in the future.

Second, moral obligations cannot be explained by being sourced in other persons, since persons are inherently equal. We cannot originate moral obligations for each other: we lack any authority to do so. I can remind someone—my children, for example—of moral requirements. I can teach, encourage, persuade, and even force them. They remain, however, quite free to decide for themselves what their obligations are.

So the dilemma follows from the need to actually explain the source of moral obligation. It *must come* from another person, but it *cannot come* from another person. It appears that the only reasonable way out of the dilemma is to conclude that the best explanation for moral obligations is that there is a person who is, in fact, *somehow* authorized to establish such obligations for other persons: a cosmic moral-obligation-decider.

We should note that this is, at best, a rather thin conclusion. It says nothing about infinity, singularity, omniscience, and so on. It does, however, provide two important identity criteria. First, of course, the source must be (at least) a person possessing the capacities to reason, deliberate, assess, and evaluate situations; comprehend and apply the values of actions and persons; and more. And second, this source must have an identifiable authorization to be such a morality decider. Thin, but nevertheless there are some critical identity criteria here.

There is, of course, nothing in any form of this basic argument that seems to hint at what precisely this authorization is or even what the possibilities might be; of course, this has been a topic of much discussion. But as long as the moral arguer is content with thin conclusions, we need not demand more, especially if the moral argument is seen as merely a component in a larger "case."[10] One might at this point simply add to the conclusion the Thomistic mantra: "... and this we all know to be God." Clearly, however, that would eventually demand much intervening argumentation, though God does, after all, meet the identity criteria, and furthermore, it seems difficult to imagine who or what else would or even could.

So what I have argued is that the possible alternative explanations for moral obligations, causal and social, set up a dilemma premise from which the only escape is to combine both horns. "Must be a person" plus "cannot be another person" yields the conclusion "must be an authorized person."

Some Examples

This argument has a long history. It begins as a kind of teleological argument for the Stoics for whom there is an overarching *logos*, or cosmic lawfulness, that includes not just physical/natural law, but moral and social as well. Emperor Marcus Aurelius (AD 121–180) was the last of five emperors regarded as good. His principle writing, a collection of his philosophical thoughts about life, is *Meditations*. The pattern here is typical:

> If our intellectual part is common, the reason also, in respect of which we are rational beings, is common: if this is so, common also is the reason which commands us what to do, and what not to do; if this is so, there is a common law also; if this is so,

---

10. I mean this in the sense established by Basil Mitchell in *The Justification of Religious Belief* (New York: Seabury Press, 1974).

we are fellow-citizens; if this is so, we are members of some political community; if this is so, the world is in a manner a state. For of what common political community will anyone say that the whole human race are members? And from thence, from this common political community comes also our very intellectual faculty and reasoning faculty and our capacity for law; or whence do they come? For as my earthly part is a portion given to me from certain earth, and that which is watery from another element, and that which is hot and fiery from some peculiar source (for nothing comes out of that which is nothing, as nothing also returns to non-existence), so also the intellectual part comes from some source.[11]

Our perception of the moral law cannot be a function of our body, because it is a result of reasoning, and so it must be sourced in intellect. But it is common to all of us as human beings, and so it must have a source in an intellect that is beyond us. This argument is still fairly undeveloped, granted, but the basic logic is apparent. Morality is a function of persons, not physical causality, but we are all the same, and so there must be some person who is the true source of moral law.

Following Kant, there is a series of British idealists who develop a distinctive observation-based argument. The later of these, especially William Sorley (1855–1935), have to contend with evolution, understood as a total naturalism that explains everything. So now, that argument against physical causality as the source of moral law is fully developed. Sorley already has everything that Thomas Nagel will argue against neo-Darwinian materialism in his chapter on value in *Mind and Cosmos* almost 150 years later.[12]

Another good, and more current, example is the American philosopher, Elton Trueblood (1900–1994). He was still part of the British-Kantian tradition, but, chastened by early twentieth century positivism, his argument is more empirical. We recognize moral law by, in part, observing moral progress. Then he argues:

---

11. Marcus Aurelius, *Meditations*, trans. George Long (New York: Washington Square Press, 1964 [1862]), IV, 4, 22–23.

12. Thomas Nagal, *Mind and Cosmos: Why the Materialist Neo-Darwinian Conception of Nature Is Almost Certainly False* (Oxford: Oxford University Press, 2012).

The only sense in which progress is possible is the recognition that there is a difference between what the generality of mankind approves and what is really right.

This means that the only locus of the moral law is a superhuman mind. That it must be a mind is clear when we realize that law has no meaning except for minds, and that it must be superhuman is clear when we realize that it cannot be ours. ...

Only a personal being can appreciate a moral law or be a moral lawgiver. ... We do not feel shame or pollution when we harm *things* ... but we do feel these when we violate the rights of *persons*. ... The practice of the honest atheist frequently denies the conscious import of his words, because he is acting in a way which makes no sense *unless his conscious conclusions are untrue.*[13]

Here again, we see the underlying logic at work. It must be a mind, but not one of ours, so there must be a superhuman mind.

There are, of course, plenty of examples where this logic is far less evident, and some where it is simply assumed. Nevertheless, in general, I argue, this is the logical pattern that underlies the moral argument. Eliminating the two likely explanations, physical causality and social causes, yields a dilemma of two seemingly contradicting propositions: (1) the moral law must have its source in persons, and (2) the moral law cannot have its source in other persons. The only way out of the dilemma is to conclude that there must be a superperson: a person like us, but yet not one of us. That is, a person capable of understanding the contexts of moral law, yet authorized to dictate moral law to human persons. A thin conclusion indeed, but yet enough to establish a minimal theism and eliminate naturalism.

---

13. D. Elton Trueblood, *Philosophy of Religion* (New York: Harper & Row, 1957), 115.

 PART 2

On HISTORY, PHILOSOPHY OF HISTORY, THE RESURRECTION, *and* THE NEW TESTAMENT

9

THE TESTIMONY OF JOSEPHUS AND THE BURIAL OF JESUS

Craig A. Evans

A few scholars have expressed doubt that the crucified Jesus was given proper burial. It is speculated that he and the two men crucified with him (Matt 27:38; Mark 15:27; Luke 23:33; John 19:18) were left hanging on their crosses or, at best, were cast into shallow graves where dogs could have mauled their corpses.[1] The proposed nonburial of Jesus and the other two men flies in the face of archaeological evidence, Jewish customs, law, and practice, and all extant relevant literary and historical evidence. Not surprisingly, the proposal is widely rejected, if even acknowledged.[2] The most important written evidence comes from Josephus. One passage in particular deserves careful attention.

In his account of the Jewish rebellion against Rome, Josephus vents against the Idumean rebels who murdered some of the ruling priests and then did not see to the proper burial of their bodies. The actions of

---

1. See J. D. Crossan, "The Dogs beneath the Cross," in *Jesus: A Revolutionary Biography* (San Francisco: HarperOne, 1994), 123–58, here 154; idem, *Who Killed Jesus? Exposing the Roots of Anti-Semitism in the Gospel Story of the Death of Jesus* (San Francisco: HarperCollins, 1995), 188; B. D. Ehrman, *How Jesus Became God* (New York: HarperOne, 2014), 157–58, 377 n. 8.

2. J. Magness, "Jesus' Tomb: What Did it Look Like?" in *Where Christianity Was Born,* ed. H. Shanks (Washington, DC: Biblical Archaeology Society, 2006), 212–26. Magness concludes (224) that "the Gospel accounts describing Jesus' removal from the cross and burial are consistent with archaeological evidence and with Jewish law." See also B. R. McCane, "'Where no one had yet been laid': The Shame of Jesus' Burial," in *Authenticating the Activities of Jesus,* eds. B. D. Chilton and C. A. Evans, NTTS 28.2 (Leiden: Brill, 1998), 431–52. All four of the New Testament Gospels provide accounts of the burial of Jesus (Matt 27:57–61; Mark 15:42–47; Luke 23:50–56; John 19:38–42). Early Christian preaching presupposed the burial (cf. 1 Cor 15:4; Acts 2:24–32). Nothing is said of the burial of the other two men. No ancient tradition, whether supportive or challenging, raises any question about the burial of Jesus. Nonburial of three crucified men, just outside the walls of Jerusalem and on the eve of Passover, was unthinkable.

the rebels is not of interest in the present discussion; rather, it is what Josephus says about the expectations of burial:

314 Οὐκ ἐκορέσθησαν δὲ τούτοις οἱ θυμοὶ τῶν Ἰδουμαίων ἀλλ' ἐπὶ τὴν πόλιν τραπόμενοι πᾶσαν μὲν οἰκίαν διήρπαζον ἔκτεινον δὲ τὸν περιτυχόντα 315 καὶ τὸ μὲν ἄλλο πλῆθος αὐτοῖς ἐδόκει παρανάλωμα τοὺς δὲ ἀρχιερεῖς ἀνεζήτουν καὶ κατ' ἐκείνων ἦν τοῖς πλείστοις ἡ φορά 316 ταχέως δ' ἁλόντες διεφθείροντο καὶ τοῖς νεκροῖς αὐτῶν ἐπιστάντες τὸν μὲν Ἄνανον τῆς πρὸς τὸν δῆμον εὐνοίας 317 τὸν δὲ Ἰησοῦν τῶν ἀπὸ τοῦ τείχους λόγων ἐπέσκωπτον προῆλθον δὲ εἰς τοσοῦτον ἀσεβείας ὥστε καὶ ἀτάφους ῥῖψαι καίτοι τοσαύτην Ἰουδαίων περὶ τὰς ταφὰς πρόνοιαν ποιουμένων ὥστε καὶ τοὺς ἐκ καταδίκης ἀνεσταυρωμένους πρὸ δύντος ἡλίου καθελεῖν τε καὶ θάπτειν. (Josephus, J.W. 4.314–317)

314 The fury of the Idumeans being still unsatiated, they now turned to the city, looting every house and killing all who fell in their way. 315 But thinking their energies wasted on the common people, they went in search of the ruling priests; it was for them that the main rush was made, and they were soon captured and killed. 316 Then, standing over their dead bodies, they scoffed at Ananus for his benevolence toward the people and at Jesus for the address which he had delivered from the wall. 317 They actually went so far in their impiety as to cast out the corpses without burial, although the Jews are so careful about funeral rites that even malefactors who have been sentenced to crucifixion are taken down and buried before sunset.[3]

When Josephus wrote this, probably in AD 74 or 75, he knew perfectly well that Rome alone possessed capital authority in Judea and Samaria after the removal of Archelaus in AD 6. In fact, elsewhere he affirms it explicitly: "Coponius, a Roman of the equestrian order, was sent out as prefect, entrusted by Caesar with full powers, including capital punishment [μέχρι τοῦ κτείνειν]" (J.W. 2.117; lit. "up to killing").[4]

---

3. Translation based on H. St. J. Thackeray, *Josephus III: The Jewish War Books IV–VII*, LCL 210 (Cambridge MA: Harvard University Press, 1928), 93.

4. Translation based on H. St. J. Thackeray, *Josephus II: The Jewish War Books I–III*, LCL 203 (Cambridge MA: Harvard University Press, 1927), 367. Ananus, son of Annas the Great, was removed from office for convening the Sanhedrin for the purpose of condemning James, the

It is to this Roman authority that John 18:31 alludes: "It is not lawful for us to put any man to death [ἡμῖν οὐκ ἔξεστιν ἀποκτεῖναι οὐδένα]" (RSV). Pilate, in the Gospel of John, invites the accusers of Jesus to judge the Galilean according to their law (as, in effect, Gallio does when Paul in Corinth is accused by fellow Jews in Acts 18:12–17). But the judges of Jesus have called for his death, so they must defer to Roman authority. After the removal of Ethnarc Archaelaus, capital authority remained in the hands of the Roman prefects (later procurators), with the exception of the brief rule of Agrippa I (AD 41–44) until the destruction of the Jewish state.

The statement that "the Jews are so careful about funeral rites that even malefactors who have been sentenced to crucifixion are taken down and buried before sunset" is in reference to peacetime, before the Jewish rebellion erupted in AD 66.[5] However people died, whether by execution, misadventure, or natural causes, the Jewish people buried the dead, Jewish or Gentile, saint or sinner. Even if crucified (by the authority of Rome), the dead were buried.

Elsewhere in his writings, Josephus makes statements consistent with what he asserts in *J.W.* 4.317. In his description of Jewish piety and obligations, Josephus states: "We must furnish fire, water, food to all who ask for them, point out the road, not overlook an unburied corpse [ἄταφον μὴ περιορᾶν], show consideration even to declared enemies"[6] (*Ag. Apion* 2.211; cf. 2.205). It is important to observe here that burial of the dead is placed in the category of providing necessities for life, such as fire, water, and food. These kindnesses, extended even to "declared enemies," include burial. In his later twenty-volume *Antiquities*, Josephus restates this obligation in his discussion of capital punishment:

---

brother of Jesus (Josephus, *Ant.* 20.200–203). See A. N. Sherwin-White, *Roman Society and Roman Law in the New Testament: The Sarum Lectures 1960–61* (Oxford: Oxford University Press, 1963), 36: "Capital power was the most jealously guarded of all the attributes of government, not even entrusted to the principal assistants of the governors." Sherwin-White adds, "Though the local city councils and sanhedrins could arrest and punish robbers and brigands with imprisonment, execution for these offences depended on the procurator" (43).

5. During the war, especially the siege of Jerusalem (AD 69–70), thousands of Jews, many of them crucified, lay unburied (*J.W.* 5.449–451).

6. Translation based on H. St. J. Thackeray, *Josephus I: The Life, Against Apion*, LCL 186 (Cambridge MA: Harvard University Press, 1926), 379.

Let him that blasphemes God be stoned, then hung for a day, and buried without honor and in obscurity [κρεμάσθω δι᾽ ἡμέρας καὶ ἀτίμως καὶ ἀφανῶς θαπτέσθω]. (*Ant.* 4.202)

Let him be led forth ... and be stoned to death; and, after remaining for the whole day [δι᾽ ὅλης τῆς ἡμέρας] exposed to the general view, let him be buried at night [θαπτέσθω νυκτός]. So it shall be with all who are condemned by the laws to be put to death. Let burial be given even to your enemies; and let not a corpse be left without its portion of earth, paying more than its just penalty. (*Ant.* 4.264–265)

In these passages, Josephus does not quote from Deuteronomy 21:22–23, but he clearly presupposes the Mosaic law. "Let him be hung for a day" (κρεμάσθω δι᾽ ἡμέρας) in the first passage and δι᾽ ὅλης τῆς ἡμέρας ("the whole day") and θαπτέσθω νυκτός ("let him be buried at night") in the second passage echo Deuteronomy's κρεμάσητε αὐτὸν ἐπὶ ξύλου ("you should hang him on a tree") and ταφῇ θάψετε αὐτὸν ἐν τῇ ἡμέρᾳ ἐκείνῃ ("with burial you shall bury him that same day"). More will be said about Deuteronomy 21:22–23 shortly.

Josephus also speaks of the obligation to bury those who have killed themselves as well as enemies slain in battle: "With us it is ordained that those who kill themselves [τοὺς ... ἀναιροῦντας ἑαυτούς] should be exposed unburied until sunset [μέχρις ἡλίου δύσεως ἀτάφους ἐκρίπτειν], although it is thought right to bury even our enemies slain in war"[7] (*J.W.* 3.377). Josephus regards suicide as a serious crime against the life that God has provided: "But as for those who have laid mad hands upon themselves, the darker regions of Hades receive their souls, ... That is why this crime, so hateful to God, is punished" (*J.W.* 3.375–376; cf. 3.379: "impiety towards our creator"). Josephus implies that the law of Moses condemns suicide, but in fact the Torah says nothing about it. In context, Josephus is of course speaking of (and justifying) his decision not to take his life in the face of imminent capture by the Romans (*J.W.* 3.361–386). As it happens, Jewish tradition in the approximate time of Josephus is largely accepting of suicide, especially if linked in some way

---

7. Translation based on Thackeray, *Josephus II*, 683. Thackeray confusingly renders τοὺς ... ἀναιροῦντας ἑαυτούς as singular ("the body of a suicide").

to martyrdom or remaining loyal to the Mosaic law.[8] Notwithstanding the self-serving claims of Josephus, it is interesting that in *J.W.* 3.377, those who kill themselves and enemies slain in battle are treated side by side. Of all the dead, they are the most unworthy of funerary rites; yet even they are to be given proper burial.

Josephus also criticizes the zealots for preventing the burial of many fellow Jews who died during the siege of Jerusalem. The passage begins by relating the fate of those who attempted to flee the city, or at least contemplated it:

> Along all the highways the dead were piled in heaps; and many starting to desert changed their minds and chose to die within the walls, since the hope of burial made death in their native city appear more tolerable. The zealots, however, carried barbarity so far as to grant interment [lit. to provide earth] to none, whether slain within the city or on the roads; but, as though they had covenanted to annul the laws of nature along with those of their country, and in their outrages upon humanity to pollute even the Deity, they left the dead rotting in the sun [ὑφ' ἡλίῳ τοὺς νεκροὺς μυδῶντας ἀπέλειπον]. For burying a relative, as for desertion, the penalty was death.[9] (*J.W.* 4.381–382)

This passage is interesting at several points. There is little doubt that Josephus exaggerates, hoping to put the rebels in the worst possible light. Nevertheless, there is probably some truth in what he claims. To discourage desertion, the zealots killed those trying to flee from the besieged city, and in some instances they may have even killed those who attempted to "provide earth" (μεταδοῦναι γῆς) for the dead. Josephus describes the actions of the zealots as an "annulment" of the laws of nature, as well as annulment of the law of Moses. All cultures, including Roman, recognized the importance of proper burial. What makes the action of the zealots especially heinous from the Jewish point of view was its insult to God. Leaving the dead to rot in the sun, day after day, was "to pollute even the Deity [συμμιᾶναι καὶ τὸ θεῖον]."

---

8. D. Daube, "Death as a Release in the Bible," *Novum Testamentum* 5 (1962): 82–104. Nowhere in biblical literature is suicide condemned. Christian thinking was very similar to Jewish thinking until the time of Augustine, after which suicide was widely viewed as self-murder.

9. Translation based on Thackeray, *Josephus III*, 111, 113.

Here Josephus clearly presupposes the law found in Deuteronomy 21:22–23, which commands burial of the executed criminal at the setting of the sun, so that "you will not pollute [οὐ μιανεῖτε] the land, which the LORD your God gives you for an inheritance" (RSV). To pollute the land which God gave Israel is, in a sense, to pollute God himself. By refusing to bury the murdered ruling priests (*J.W.* 4.317), as well as those who were killed trying to flee the city (*J.W.* 4.381–382), the zealots, says Josephus, brought upon Israel the fulfillment of ancient prophecies that foretold the capture of Jerusalem and the fiery destruction of her famous temple (*J.W.* 4.386–388).

Burial is so important in Jewish thinking that some, during siege and battle, risked their lives to "throw a little dust" upon the dead (κόνιν αἴροντες χεροῖν ὀλίγην ἐπερρίπτουν τοῖς σώμασι) who had been cast out unburied (*J.W.* 4.330–332). Some died while trying to bury others (*J.W.* 5.514). There is archaeological evidence from Jotapata (Yodefat), whose capture in 67 BC basically ended Jewish resistance in Galilee, that the Romans deliberately made burial of the Jewish dead difficult if not impossible. There is evidence that in some cases, Jews may have buried their dead in temporary graves hoping to return later and complete the process.[10] Some of the skeletal remains found in the Naḥal Ḥever caves should probably be understood the same way.[11]

---

10. On skeletal and burial/nonburial evidence of Jotapata, see A. Mordechai, "Yodefat - Jotapata. A Jewish Galilean town at the end of the Second Temple period: The results of an archaeological project," in *Galilee in the Late Second Temple and Mishnaic Periods: Life, Culture, and Society*, ed. D. A. Fiensy and J. R. Strange, vol. 2 (Minneapolis: Fortress Press, 2015), 109–26, here 119–21. Mordechai discusses finding hastily or, perhaps, temporarily buried skeletons in miqvoth and cisterns. I should mention that in 2013–2014 at Khirbet el-Maqatir, about twelve kilometres north of Jerusalem, the site that may have been Ephraim (see John 11:54), Scott Stripling and his team excavated the skeletal remains of seven females ranging in age from six to sixty and one pre-adolescent male. Their attempt to hide in a subterranean complex in AD 69 failed, and they suffered violent deaths at the hands of the Romans. (I thank Dr. Stripling for sharing with me his final report.) At Masada, which fell to the Romans in AD 73, the skeletal remains of twenty-five men, women, and children were found in a cave at the north end of the mountain-top fortress, and three more skeletons in the Northern Palace itself. Mingled among the skeletal remains of those found in the cave were the bones of pigs, evidently intended as a post-mortem insult. See Y. Yadin, *Masada: Herod's Fortress and the Zealots' Last Stand* (New York: Random House, 1966), 193–201; D. Barag et al., *Masada IV: The Yigael Yadin Excavations 1963–1965 Final Reports. Lamps / Textiles / Basketry, Cordage and Related Artifacts / Wood Remains / Ballista Balls / Addendum: Human Skeletal Remains* (Jerusalem: Israel Exploration Society, 1994), 366–67.

11. The skeletal remains found in the Naḥal Ḥever caves are not easily interpreted. Yadin associated them with the Bar Kokhba rebellion, but the remains are likely those of refugees from the first rebellion (AD 66–73), as well as from the last great rebellion (132–135 CE). For images, as well as discussion, see Y. Yadin, *The Finds from the Bar Kokhba Period in the Cave of Letters* (Judean Desert Studies; Jerusalem: Israel Exploration Society, 1963), 33–34 + plates 6, 103, and 104–8;

In some cases, burial of the dead was not possible because there were too many dead: "As for burying their relatives, the sick had not the strength, while those with vigor that remained were deterred both by the multitude of the dead and by the uncertainty of their own fate; for many fell dead while burying others" (*J.W.* 5.514). Perhaps even more ghastly, the Jewish defenders who sallied forth to fight with the enemy had to trample upon the dead whose corpses covered the ground (*J.W.* 6.2–3).

The claim that "Jews used to take so much care of the burial of men [περὶ τὰς ταφάς]" is well documented in sources from Jewish late antiquity. The righteous Tobit is above all praised for his concern to bury the dead, even at personal risk (Tob 1:17–20; 2:3–8; 4:3; 12:12–13). In the first passage, burial of the dead is an act of charity comparable to providing food and clothing (esp. v. 17), which for Tobit puts his life at risk (vv. 19–20: "I bury them and then go into hiding"; cf. 2:7–8). Because of his great piety, especially with regard to providing proper burial for others, Tobit is told of God's approval (12:13) and at the end of his life is himself given a "magnificent funeral" (14:11).[12]

When and under what circumstances Tobit was written are unsettled questions. That the theme of burial is important in Tobit is quite clear. In this writing, θάπτειν ("to bury") occurs seventeen times, and τάφος ("grave") some half dozen. Tobit's burial of the unburied is his greatest virtue and, in the eyes of the pagan authority, his greatest offence. Frank Zimmermann concludes that because Antiochus IV Epiphanes "would not allow the burial of the Jewish slain," Tobit was probably written during the Maccabean struggle against the Seleucid king.[13] For evidence, Zimmermann appeals to 2 Macc 9:15, which reminds readers that before his fatal illness Antiochus had threatened

---

idem, *Bar-Kokhba: The Rediscovery of the Legendary Hero of the Last Jewish Revolt against Imperial Rome* (London: Weidenfeld and Nicolson, 1971), 60–65; R. A. Freund, *Secrets of the Cave of Letters* (New York: Humanity Books, 2004), 181–207.

12. C. A. Moore, *Tobit*, AB 40A (New York: Doubleday, 1996), 120: "To bury someone is *the* most important 'charitable act' in Tobit" (Moore's emphasis).

13. F. Zimmermann, *The Book of Tobit: An English Translation with Introduction and Commentary* (Dropsie College Edition: Jewish Apocryphal Literature; New York: Harper & Brothers, 1958), 19–20. Zimmermann (51) rightly rejects the suggestion that the reference to corpses "cast out behind the wall" (Tob 1:17) alludes to Bar Kokhba besieged at Bethar in AD 135 and unwilling to bury the dead within the city. The talmudic discussion of permission eventually granted for the burial of the dead of Bethar (*b. Ta'anit* 31a) hardly provides adequate support the proposed interpretation or date.

"to make a cemetery" of Jerusalem and had regarded the Jews not "worthy even of a grave [ταφῆς ἀξιῶσαι] but had planned to throw (them) out with their children for the wild animals and for the birds to eat." Similarly we are told in 5:10 that Jason, a priestly contender (cf. 2 Macc 4:7, 13), "had cast out many unburied [πλῆθος ἀτάφων ἐκρίψας]" (cf. 1 Macc 7:16–17, where scribes are murdered through treachery and left unburied).

Zimmermann's suggestion is interesting but ultimately unpersuasive. Although one text (i.e., 2 Macc 9:15) makes reference to the king's refusal to allow burial of slain Jews, 1 and 2 Maccabees do not in fact narrate one example of the king preventing burials. The words placed on the mouth of the pagan tyrant is probably no more than literary license, not history. Moreover, the one narrated incident of denying burial involved Jason, the Jewish priest. Had the book of Tobit been written in the 160s BC (or a bit later), we should expect to find evidence of hatred of gentiles, including references to being persecuted for being Jewish, for refusing to worship pagan Gods, and the like.[14] Tobit's only offence is his stubborn efforts in providing burial for those cast out unburied, and even then the focus is on the explicitly named Sennacherib.[15] The book of Tobit was probably composed sometime in the third century BC.

It is hard to determine why the author of the book of Tobit was so deeply concerned with burial. It is possible that the author reacted to Alexander's conquest of the Middle East a generation or so before he wrote. In Alexander's wars, thousands were crucified and left unburied. Perhaps the most infamous example was the king's order to have two thousand survivors of Tyre — the city that had long withstood

---

14. Moore, *Tobit*, 41: "All things considered, then, the book's attitude toward Gentiles clearly suggests a date prior to the ethnic and religious hatred of the Maccabean period"; cf. J. A. Fitzmyer, *Tobit* (Commentaries on Early Jewish Literature; Berlin: de Gruyter, 2003), 53. Fitzmyer also finds the Maccabean date problematic.

15. The Assyrian king who persecutes Tobit for burying Jews is, appropriately, Sennacherib (Tob 1:18). I say "appropriately" because refusing proper burial to his enemies is something the oppressive tyrant, who dies in 681 BC, actually boasts about: "I tore out the tongues of those whose slanderous mouths had uttered blasphemies against my god Ashur and had plotted against me ... others I smashed alive with the very idols ... I fed their corpses, cut into small pieces, to dogs, pigs, birds, vultures ... and fish of the ocean ... I removed the corpses of those whom the pestilence had felled, whose leftovers the dogs and pigs had fed on ..." Translation based on J. B. Pritchard, *Ancient Near Eastern Texts Relating to the Old Testament* (Princeton: Princeton University Press, 1969), 288. After the assassination of Sennacherib (Tob 1:21; cf. 2 King 19:37; Isa 37:38), Tobit is able to return home.

Alexander's siege—crucified along the coast (cf. Curtius Rufus, *De rebus gestis Alexandri Magni* 4.4.17). After Alexander's death, crucifixions continued under Greek rule (cf. Diodorus Siculus, *Bibliothēkē* 19.67.2; 20.103.6). The author of Tobit may also have known of Persia's practice of crucifixion prior to the time of Alexander.

Whatever provided his motivation, either a specific event or a more general awareness of execution and lack of burial under certain pagan despots, the author of Tobit not inappropriately read his concern back into the Assyrian period, the ostensible historical setting of the book of Tobit. In doing so, he created the backdrop against which the piety and courage of Tobit, the book's protagonist, could be more fully appreciated. That the book of Tobit remained popular right on into the time of Jesus and the early church is attested by its several Aramaic and Hebrew copies found among the Dead Sea Scrolls, as well as its survival in two Greek recensions and Latin translation.[16]

The great importance of burial is dramatically expressed in Philo's tractate on the patriarch Joseph. Jacob, thinking his son Joseph had been killed and devoured by wild animals, laments that his son's remains were left unburied.

> Child, it is not your death which grieves me, but the manner of it. If you had been buried in your own land, I should have ... closed your eyes, wept over the body as it lay there, given it a costly funeral and left none of the customary rites undone. ... And, indeed, if it was necessary that you died by violence or premeditation, it would have been a lighter ill to me, slain as you would have been by human beings, who would have pitied their dead victim, gathered some dust and covered the corpse [ἐπαμήσασθαι κόνιν καὶ τὸ σῶμα συγκρύψαι].[17] (Philo, *De Iosepho* 23–25)

Philo goes on to have Jacob say that even if murderers of his son had been the "cruellest of men" and left his corpse unburied, another

---

16. In all, four fragmentary Aramaic copies of Tobit have been identified, and one fragmentary Hebrew copy (= 4Q196–200). For the *editio princeps* of these texts, see J. A. Fitzmyer, "Tobit," in *Qumran Cave 4.XIV: Parabiblical Texts, Part 2* (DJD 19; Oxford: Clarendon Press, 1995), 1–76 + plates I–X. For an overview of all surviving ancient texts of Tobit, see Fitzmyer, *Tobit*, 3–17. As it so happens, the Aramaic and Hebrew texts from Qumran support the long Greek recension.

17. Translation based on F. H. Colson, *Philo VI* LCL 289 (London: Heinemann; Cambridge, MA; Harvard University Press, 1935), 153.

passing by would have taken pity and provided burial. But because Joseph was eaten by animals and there is nothing left to bury, Jacob's grief is beyond measure (*De Iosepho* 26–27). The nonburial of Joseph is worse than the death itself ("it is not your death which grieves me, but the manner of it").

There are two other texts that should also be mentioned. The first, supposedly authored by Philo, is from a text called *Hypothetica* (or *Apologia pro Iudaeis*), two extracts of which are preserved in Eusebius's, *Praeparatio evangelica*. The authorship of the tractate is debated,[18] but for the present purposes it is unimportant. In a section where the author recounts a number of "unwritten customs," including a few that are contained in the laws, he states:

μὴ ταφῆς νεκρὸν ἐξείργειν, ἀλλὰ καὶ γῆς αὐτοῖς ὅσον γε εἰς τὴν ὁσίαν προσεπιβάλλειν· μὴ θήκας, μὴ μνήματα ὅλως κατοιχομένων κινεῖν. (*Hypothetica* 7.7, apud Eusebius, *Praep. ev.* 8.7.7)

He must not prevent a corpse from burial, but throw upon them as much earth as piety demands, nor disturb in any way the resting places and monuments of the departed.[19]

I might note that the command not to interfere with burial is preceded with commands to provide fire, water, and food (*Hypothetica* 7.6), even as we have seen in Josephus, *Ag. Apion* 2.211. This parallel leads some to think that Josephus may have been familiar with the Philonic text. The command to throw earth (γῆ) over the corpse also recalls passages that speak of throwing dust (κόνις) over the corpse (Josephus, *J.W.* 4.332; Philo, *De Iosepho* 23–25). The warning not to disturb "resting places" (θήκας; lit "chests," probably in reference to ossuaries and sarcophagi) and "monuments" (or tombs) brings to mind the imperial ordinance (διάταγμα) that came to light 140 years ago and was first published in 1930. Part of this inscription reads:

---

18. The Philonic authorship of *Hypothetica* is accepted by F. H. Colson, *Philo IX* LCL 363 (London: Heinemann; Cambridge, MA; Harvard University Press, 1941), 408.

19. Translation based on Colson, *Philo IX*, 427, 429. The Greek text is found on 426, 428. See also W. Dindorf, *Praeparationis Evangelicae* libri I–X, *Eusebii Caesariensis Opera*, vol. 1 (Leipzig: Teubner, 1867), 416.

Ordinance of Caesar: It is my pleasure that graves and tombs ... remain unmolested in perpetuity. If any person lay information that another has destroyed them, or has in any other way cast out the bodies which have been buried there [κεκηδευμένους ἐξερριφφότα], or with malicious deception has transferred them to other places ... I command that a trial be instituted .... (SEG VIII 13)[20]

The slab of marble bearing this inscription surfaced in Nazareth in 1878. Franz Cumont, the first to publish it, suggested that Emperor Tiberius had it inscribed and set up in Nazareth as a response to rumors that the body of Jesus of Nazareth had been stolen (as in Matt 28:11–15).[21] This theory is wholly implausible on many fronts. Whatever occasioned the posting of this ordinance,[22] whether by Augustus, Tiberius, or Claudius (all have been suggested), the marble slab likely originated in one of the nearby cities of the Decapolis, such as Scythopolis to the south or Jerash to the east.

The ordinance's reference to κεκηδευμένους ἐξερριφφότα (lit. "[bodies] attended to cast out") recalls what is said in Tobit 1:17, which speaks of the corpse "cast out [ἐρριμμένον] behind the wall" of the city, as well as what is said of Jason the priest, accused of having "cast out [ἐκρίψας] many (corpses) to lie unburied" (2 Macc 5:10), of Antiochus IV, who had planned to "throw out [ἐκρίψειν] (the dead) with their children for the wild animals and for the birds to eat" (9:15), and of the Idumeans who "cast out the corpses without burial [ἀτάφους ῥῖψαι]" (Josephus, J.W. 4.317). Casting out bodies, whether buried or unburied, seems to be stock language that often uses the verb ῥίπτειν/ἐκρίπτειν. Funerary

---

20. Translation based on P. W. van der Horst, *Ancient Jewish Epitaphs: An Introductory Survey of a Millennium of Jewish Funerary Epigraphy (300 BCE–700 CE)* (Kampen: Kok Pharos, 1991), 159. For bibliography and notes, see L. Boffo, *Iscrizioni greche e latine per lo studio della Bibbia* (Brescia: Paideia Editrice, 1994), 319–33.

21. F. Cumont, "Un rescrit impérial sur la violation de sépulture," *Revue historique* 163 (1930): 241–66. Whenever the ordinance of Caesar was inscribed and posted, it reflected the sanctity of sepulture in which it had been held in Mediterranean and Middle Eastern societies for centuries.

22. Violation of sepulture, whether vandalism, theft, or illicit burial, was widespread. It is possible, for example, that the demonized man who lived among the tombs in the vicinity of Jerash (Mark 5:1–14), whom the locals had attempted to restrain but without success (5:3–4), may have damaged some of the tombs.

warnings, including curses, not to disturb the remains of the interred are common in Greek, Latin, and Hebrew.[23]

The second passage is found in the *Sententiae*, pseudonymously attributed to the sixth century BC sage Phocylides:

[99] γαῖαν ἐπιμοιρᾶσθαι ἀταρχύτοις νεκύεσσιν.

[100] μὴ τύμβον φθιμένων ἀνορύξῃς μηδ᾽ ἀθέατα

[101] δείξῃς ἠελίῳ καὶ δαιμόνιον χόλον ὄρσῃς. (Ps.-Phocylides, *Sententiae* 99–101)

[99] Let the unburied dead receive their share of the earth.

[100] Do not dig up the grave of the deceased, nor what may not be seen

[101] expose to the sun and you stir up a demon.[24]

The advice of Ps.-Phocylides coheres with widespread Jewish and non-Jewish piety and superstitution. All agreed that sepulture was to be respected, even without an imperial decree like the one that has already been considered. The mere fact that Ps.-Phocylides cautions against disturbing a grave or casting out of it the corpse within supports the view that grave robbery and vandalism were in fact all too common in late antiquity. The interesting element here is found in sentence 101 and the last part of sentence 100. By exposing the remains of the interred, which often happened in illicit burials (i.e., using someone else's tomb) or in grave robbery, one ran the risk of arousing a demon, which could harm those disturbing the grave. It was widely believed in late antiquity, by Jews and non-Jews alike, that demons were the restless spirits of the dead, which usually lingered in the vicinity of the grave.[25]

---

23. For examples, see J. H. M. Strubbe, "Curses against Violation of the Grave in Jewish Epitaphs from Asia Minor," in *Studies in Early Jewish Epigraphy*, ed. J. W. van Henten and P. W. van der Horst (AGJU 21; Leiden: Brill, 1994), 70–128; R. Hachlili, *Jewish Funerary Customs, Practices, and Rites in the Second Temple Period* (JSJSup 94; Leiden: Brill, 2005), 494–506.

24. Translation based on P. W. van der Horst, "Pseudo-Phocylides," in *The Old Testament Pseudepigrapha*, ed. J. H. Charlesworth (2 vols., New York: Doubleday, 1983–85), 2:577. For Greek text, see the critical edition in E. Diehl and D. Young, *Theognis, Ps.-Pythagoras, Ps.-Phocylides, Chares, Anonymi aulodia, fragmentum teliambicum* (Bibliotheca scriptorum Graecorum et Romanorum Teubneriana; Leipzig: Teubner, 2nd ed., 1971), 103; P. W. van der Horst, *The Sentences of Pseudo-Phocylides: With Introduction and Commentary* (SVTP 4; Leiden: Brill, 1978), 94.

25. P. G. Bolt, "Jesus, the Daimons and the Dead," in *The Unseen World: Christian Reflecctions on Angels, Demons and the Heavenly Realm*, ed. A. N. S. Lane (Grand Rapids: Baker Academic, 1996), 75–102, here 84–86.

Finally, it will be worth briefly reviewing the archaeological evidence relating to the burial of executed persons in the vicinity of Jerusalem. The skeletal remains of at least three victims of execution have been recovered, two of whom were crucified. One suffered beheading;[26] the other two were crucified. The first of these is the well known Yehohanan, whose ossuary is on exhibit in the Israel Museum. The evidence of the man's crucifixion is dramatically witnessed by the presence of an iron spike (11.5 cm. in length) imbedded in his right heel. Those who took Yehohanan down from the cross and placed him in the tomb were unable to remove the spike, which at the sharp end had been bent back. One year later, when Yehohanan's skeletal remains were collected and placed in an ossuary, the heel was still transfixed by the spike. It is only because of this grim find that we know for a fact that Yehohanan had been crucified. It is believed that the man had been executed in the 20s, during the administration of Pontius Pilate.[27]

The remains of a second crucified man were found in the so-called Abba Cave. What makes this find especially intriguing is the presence of a paleo-Hebrew inscription, dated to the 20s or 30s BC, whose seven lines read:

> I am Abba, son of the priest
> Eleazar, son of Aaron the Great. I
> am Abba, the oppressed, the persecuted,
> who was born in Jerusalem
> and went into exile into Babylonia, and carried up Mattathiah,
> son of Judah. I buried him in the cave
> which I purchased by the writ.[28]

The inscription and the ornate ossuary within the cave that contained skeletal remains date to the first century BC. The bones belong to none other than Antigonus son of Aristobulus,[29] the last

---

26. His remains were found in Tomb D on Mount Scopus. For discussion, see J. Zias, "Anthropological Evidence of Interpersonal Violence in First-Century AD Jerusalem," *Current Anthropology* 24 (1983): 233–34. The evidence, however, points to a judicial beheading, not decapitation that took place in a brawl.

27. J. Zias and E. Sekeles, "The Crucified Man from Giv'at ha-Mivtar: A Reappraisal," *IEJ* 35 (1985): 22–27.

28. Translation based on Y. Elitzur, "The Abba Cave: Unpublished Findings and a New Proposal Regarding Abba's Identity," *IEJ* 63 (2013): 83–102.

29. Whose Hebrew name is, as in the Hebrew inscription, Mattathiah son of Judah.

Hasmonean ruler, whom Herod the Great, with Rome's support, defeated in 37 BC. According to Josephus, Marcus Antonius *beheaded* Antigonus in Antioch (Josephus, *Ant.* 15.8–10 [quoting Strabo, *Historica Hypomnemata*]; cf. Plutarch, *Antonius* 36.4). Writing later, Dio Cassius seemingly contradicts Josephus when he specifically refers to *crucifixion*, but his full statement can be harmonized with what Josephus says. The Roman historian says, "Antony bound Antigonus to a cross and flogged him—a punishment no other king had suffered at the hands of the Romans—and afterwards he slew him" (*History* 49.22.6). The slaying "afterwards" probably refers to beheading, which is what Josephus relates. The skeletal remains, which I have personally examined, reveal one stroke across the jaw and neck, a second stroke through the neck, and the metacarpal bones of one hand transfixed with an iron spike. Two other iron spikes, bearing traces of human calcium, were also recovered from the ossuary. The skeletal remains thus confirm the testimony of Josephus and Dio Cassius.

In the eyes of Rome, Antigonus was guilty of high treason for claiming to be king and for allying himself with Rome's archenemies the Parthians. It was likely for this reason that Abba the priest, obligated by the "death commandment" (*met mitzvah*), went to the trouble to transport the skeletal remains of Antigonus from Antioch to Jerusalem and, in secret, we should assume, buried the Hasmonean prince in an unmarked cave. Given his treason, it is possible that the remains of Antigonus were banned from burial in Jerusalem. Abba the priest, perhaps out of loyalty to Antigonus, was himself exiled to the east ("exiled into Babylonia," as the inscription states) and then at a later date managed to return to Jerusalem with the remains of Antigonus and inter them in the cave.[30]

Almost all cultures in late antiquity viewed burial of the dead as important and sacred. Violation of sepulture was regarded as a serious crime against humanity and against the gods. What made Jewish views of sepulture distinctive was the concern to avoid defiling the land by leaving a corpse unburied. It is directly to this concern that the ancient law in Deuteronomy speaks: "And if a man has committed a crime punishable by death and he is put to death, and you hang him on a tree,[23] his body shall not remain all night upon the tree, but you

---

30. I follow the reconstruction offered in Elitzur, "The Abba Cave," 90–91.

shall bury him the same day, for a hanged man is accursed by God; you shall not defile your land which the LORD your God gives you for an inheritance" (Deut 21:22–23 RSV).

The Mosaic law was needed because many cultures in late antiquity did not feel compelled to bury and sometimes did not permit the burial of executed criminals and enemies slain in battle (a grim reality apparently known to the author of the book of Tobit). The law of Deuteronomy required that all be buried, even criminals guilty of the most heinous crimes. One will also observe that the sequence of this law in Deuteronomy 21 is *death* followed by *hanging* followed by *burial*. But in the paraphrase of Deuteronomy 21 as found in the Temple Scroll, the sequence becomes *hanging* followed by *death* followed by *burial* (cf. 11Q19 64:7–13). Most interpreters rightly recognize that the reversal of sequence in the Temple Scroll reflects the practice of crucifixion in the Roman Empire, of which Israel was a part.[31]

Burial of the executed has nothing to do with compassion (as it does in the burial of the righteous); it has everything to do with safeguarding the purity of the land of Israel. It is Deuteronomy's law of burial before sunset to which Josephus alludes when he says, "even malefactors who have been sentenced to crucifixion are taken down and buried before sunset" (*J.W.* 4.317). Elsewhere, Philo and Josephus state that Rome maintained peace in lands like Israel because the local laws and customs were respected (Philo, *Leg. Gaium* 300; Josephus, *Ag. Apion* 2.73, 220). Even Roman law itself permitted the burial of executed criminals (*Digesta* 48.24.1–3).[32] The only exception was in cases of high treason, such as an attempt to assassinate Caesar or raise an army against the Empire (*Digesta* 48.41–11). The case of Antigonus, reviewed above, could well be an example of denial of burial—at least

---

31. I review all the pertinent data in C. A. Evans, "Hanging and Crucifixion in Second Temple Israel: Deuteronomy 21:22–23 in the Light of Archaeology and the Dead Sea Scrolls," in *Qumran und Archäologie: Texte und Kontexte*, eds. J. Frey et al., WUNT 278 (Tübingen: Mohr Siebeck, 2011), 481–501. One should also consult D. W. Chapman and E. J. Schnabel, *The Trial and Crucifixion of Jesus: Texts and Commentary*, WUNT 344 (Tübingen: Mohr Siebeck, 2015). The Temple Scroll dates to approximately 125 BC. Crucifixion was practiced by the Persians, the Greeks/Macedonians, and the Romans, all of whom influenced or controlled Israel in late antiquity.

32. The pertinent laws in the *Digesta* date as early as the time of Augustus. I review the execution and burial laws of the *Digesta* in C. A. Evans, "'He Laid Him in a Tomb' (Mark 15.46): Roman Law and the Burial of Jesus," in *Matthew and Mark across Perspectives: Essays in Honour of Stephen C. Barton and William R. Telford*, eds. K. A. Bendoraitis and N. K. Gupta, LSTS 538 (London and New York: Bloomsbury T&T Clark, 2016), 52–66, here 56–63.

in his home country, which was then contravened by a courageous and sympathetic priest named Abba.

The Gospel accounts of the burial of Jesus should be viewed in the light of what Josephus states in *J.W.* 4.317: during peacetime "even malefactors who have been sentenced to crucifixion are taken down and buried before sunset." There is nothing about the conduct of Jesus in Jerusalem, nothing in the judicial process that overtook him and resulted in his execution, and nothing in the burial narratives themselves that suggest that Jesus and the men executed along with him would have been treated as exceptional and so would have been denied burial according to Jewish law and custom.

The debate surrounding the resurrection of Jesus is admittedly complex and controversial, but attempts to deny it or explain it away on the grounds that no burial took place and therefore no empty tomb could be discovered are not only misguided, in that they fly in the face of a great deal of evidence, but seem to strike a note of desperation. The burial of Jesus is as certain as his crucifixion. Moreover, it is inconceivable in light of Jewish views of sepulture and the sacred duty of burial that the family and disciples of Jesus would have had no idea where Jesus had been buried and would therefore have had no idea where to go to complete the customary seven days of graveside mourning.[33]

---

33. On Jewish burial practices, including ossilegium (bone-gathering), see C. A. Evans, *Jesus and the Ossuaries* (Waco TX: Baylor University Press, 2003), esp. 10–16, 26–30; idem, *Jesus and the Remains of His Day* (Peabody, MA: Hendrickson, 2015), 131–33.

10

NEAR-DEATH EXPERIENCES AND CHRISTIAN THEOLOGY

Dale C. Allison, Jr.

So-called near-death experiences (NDEs) long ago moved into the mainstream of popular Western culture.[1] By now, almost everybody is familiar with the stereotypical sequence related by many individuals who have come close to death. Commonly reported features of NDEs include believing one has left one's body; meeting a being of light (sometimes identified as God, Jesus, or an angel); encountering dead relatives and friends; seeing something like a replay of one's entire life or episodes from it; feeling a strong sense of peace and well-being; being sent back to earthly life or choosing to return.[2] As these features are far from invariant and do not appear in a fixed order, "the NDE is best regarded as a collection of typical sub-experiences: a variable combination of a number of possible elements from an established repertoire, the details of which differ on a case-by-case basis for reasons which remain largely obscure."[3]

---

1. In large part due to Raymond Moody, *Life after Life: The Investigation of a Phenomenon: Survival of Bodily Death* (Atlanta: Mockingbird, 1975). For an introduction to the field, see Janice Miner Holden, Bruce Greyson, and Debbie James, eds., *The Handbook of Near Death Experiences: Thirty Years of Investigation* (Santa Barbara, CA: Praeger Publishers, 2009).

2. I refer here to positive or pleasurable NDEs. Negative and even "hellish" experiences are also attested; see esp. Nancy Evans Bush, *Dancing Past the Dark: Distressing Near-Death Experiences* (Cleveland, TN: Parson's Porch Books, 2012). On the general phenomenology of NDEs see Bruce Greyson, "Defining Near-Death Experiences," *Morality* 4 (1999): 7–19; Pim van Lommel et al., "Near-Death Experience in Survivors of Cardiac Arrest: A Prospective Study in the Netherlands," *The Lancet* 358 (2001): 2039–45; V. Charland-Vervilee, "Near-Death Experiences in Non-Life Threatening Events and Coma of Different Etiologies," *Frontiers in Human Neuroscience* 8 (2014): art. # 203; Charlotte Martial et al., "Temporality of Features in Near-Death Experience Narratives," *Frontiers in Human Neuroscience* 11 (2017): art. # 311.

3. Gregory Shushan, "Near-Death Experiences," in *The Routledge Companion to Death and Dying*, ed. Christopher M. Moreman (New York: Routledge, 2018), 320. One recalls in this connection Wittgenstein's notion of family resemblance.

How have Christian thinkers come to terms with what is now a vast literature on the subject?[4] I think it is fair to urge that they have, by and large, responded in the following eight ways.[5]

1. Some—or rather most[6]—have continued to write about Christian eschatology while completely ignoring NDEs. For example, the famous German biblical scholar and Roman Catholic theologian Gerhard Lohfink has recently given us a large book entitled, *Is This All There Is? On Resurrection and Eternal Life*.[7] It is an informed, far-ranging Christian discussion and defense of life after death. And it has nothing at all to say about NDEs. The implication seemingly is that they are unimportant, or at least of scant significance for deciding whether there might be life after death or for determining what a Christian might believe on that score.[8]

2. A second option is for the Christian to dismiss NDEs, not by ignoring them, but by explaining them away. This is the strategy of Michael Marsh. In his book on NDEs and out-of-body experiences, he joins the materialists who regard NDEs as subjective hallucinations explicable in terms of contemporary neurophysiological knowledge.[9] Marsh is not just a physician but holds a PhD in theology, and part of his argument is that Christianity, properly understood, teaches the resurrection of the dead, not the immortality of the soul; and since NDEs, if they contain veridical elements, suggest the latter rather than

---

4. Herein I treat only Christian responses to NDEs. One could also discuss Buddhist responses, Mormon responses, etc.

5. I make no attempt here to be exhaustive but only to list what, in my reading, seem to be the most common responses.

6. Mark Fox, *Religion, Spirituality, and the Near-Death Experience* (London/New York: Routledge, 2003), 62, quotes Michael Perry as saying that the theologians' response to NDEs has been a "deafening silence."

7. Gerhard Lohfink, *Is This All There Is? On Resurrection and Eternal Life* (Collegeville, MN: Liturgical Press, 2018).

8. Others who have written about eschatology without reflecting upon NDEs include Anthony Kelly, *Eschatology and Hope* (Maryknoll, NY: Orbis, 2006) and N. T. Wright, *Surprised by Hope: Rethinking Heaven, the Resurrection, and the Mission of the Church* (New York: HarperOne, 2008). Stephen T. Davis, *After We Die: Theology, Philosophy, and the Question of Life after Death* (Waco, TX: Baylor University Press, 2015), briefly discusses NDEs in a scant two pages (29–30), comes to no firm conclusions, and subsequently ignores them.

9. Michael N. Marsh, *Out-of-Body and Near-Death Experiences: Brain-State Phenomena or Glimpses of Immortality?* (Oxford: Oxford University Press, 2010). For an instructive critical review see Edward F. Kelly in the *Journal of Scientific Exploration* 24 (2010): 729–37.

the former, they fail the doctrinal test of truth. Marsh is, then, committed to branding NDEs as purely subjective.[10]

John Haldane has been only a little less critical.[11] In his judgment, NDEs cannot be what they seem to be because human beings are material organisms. This follows not only from Christian theology, which teaches the resurrection of the body as opposed to the immortality of the soul, but also from modern philosophy and science, which have falsified the dualist's notion of a soul capable of surviving in a disembodied state. It is, then, simply impossible that, for instance, those who have NDEs ever actually encounter dead individuals.[12] Haldane does, however, leave open the possibility that, in the dream-like NDE state, God sometimes vouchsafes "previews" of the world to come. "That world does not yet exist, and so these 'meetings' are not real ones but can only be images of how life will be following the resurrection of the dead."[13]

3. Some Christian theologians have judged that, while NDEs are interesting and may in time and with further study become evidence of something significant, at this point it is too soon to render a verdict. This was the strategy that Hans Kung adopted in his well-known book *Eternal Life?*[14] In making his case that the theologian should carry on without paying much attention to NDEs, Kung asserted that (a) the remarkable phenomena associated with NDEs occur not just near death but in multiple mental states, including states induced by dreams, meditation, drugs; (b) some people experience dying not as a blissful NDE but as terrifying; (c) "it is possible that a scientific or

10. For similar arguments, see Richard Abanes, *Journey into the Light: Exploring Near-Death Experiences* (Grand Rapids: Baker, 1996) and H. Leon Greene, *If I Should Wake Before I Die: The Biblical and Medical Truth about Near-Death Experiences* (Wheaton, IL: Crossway Books, 1997). Greene urges that "NDEs seem to be overwhelmingly counterfeit" because they contradict Scripture (296); further, they are most likely "the result of the synthesis of unfamiliar sensory experiences (supported by the maintenance of minimal profusion of the brain) in the background of a particular religious framework, augmented by the memories of what has been heard about the process of dying and near-death from popular media" (114). For effective critical commentary, see Gary Habermas and J. P. Moreland, *Beyond Death: Exploring the Evidence for Immortality* (Wheaton, IL: Crossway Books, 1998), 200–206.

11. John Haldane, "A Glimpse of Eternity? Near Death Experiences and the Hope of Future Life," *The Modern Churchman* 30 (1988), 20–28.

12. Cf. the similar argument of Richard Swinburne, *The Evolution of the Soul*, rev. ed. (Oxford: Clarendon, 1997), 303–305.

13. Haldane, "Glimpse of Eternity," 27.

14. Hans Kung, *Eternal Life? Life after Death as Medical, Philosophical, and Theological Problem* (Garden City, NY: Doubleday & Co., 1984), 8–21.

medical explanation may be found for all the phenomena associated with dying";[15] and (d) none of the relevant reports come from the dead but from the living. "What, then, do these experiences of dying imply for life after death? To put it briefly, nothing!"[16] With this allegedly established, Kung returns to theological business as usual.

4. The next option is to see some limited value in NDEs. They may not only help in the religious battle against reductive materialism but may also offer glimpses into the early stages of what happens at death.[17] This is the view of the Protestant theologian Hans Schwarz in his year 2000 volume *Eschatology*. According to Schwarz, while NDEs do not prove immortality, they may legitimately give some people assurance and encourage them to believe "that our present existence is but a necessary prelude to a larger entity—life eternal."[18] The discussion of NDEs, however occupies very few pages of his volume. On the whole, Schwarz sticks to traditional theological topoi and traditional ways of handling Christian eschatology (through, for example, the citation of biblical texts).

The Eastern Orthodox theologian Constantine Cavarnos takes a similar approach. In his view, NDEs

> constitute a confirmation of Orthodox teaching on the follow-ing points: 1) that death does not constitute an annihilation of the human person, since, besides the visible man, the body, there is the invisible man, the soul, which continues to exist beyond death; 2) that the soul, separated from the body, main-tains self-consciousness and does not fall into a state of sleep

---

15. Kung, *Eternal Life?*, 17.

16. Kung, *Eternal Life?*, 20.

17. This, it seems to me, captures the main point of Gary's work with J. P. Moreland in *Beyond Death*, 155–218. For similar voices, see Terence Nichols, *Death and Afterlife: A Theological Introduction* (Grand Rapids: Brazos Press, 2010), 91–112, and Paul Badham, *Making Sense of Death and Immortality* (London: SPCK, 2013), 47–57. Particularly interesting in this connection is Jerry L. Walls, *Heaven: The Logic of Eternal Joy* (Oxford: Oxford University Press, 2002), 133–60. Walls draws upon the work of Alvin Plantinga and William Alston on the epistemic justification of religious claims to argue that NDEs provide "at least prima facie evidence for life after death" and further that "there are no convincing overriders from either Christian theology or other sources to warrant rejecting the beliefs produced by NDEs"; indeed, "unless and until the naturalistic account of NDEs is prove to be true, they deserve serious consideration as positive evidence for the Christian doctrine of heaven" (160).

18. Hans Schwarz, *Eschatology* (Grand Rapids: Eerdmans, 2000), esp. 263–69. See further his earlier book, *Beyond the Gates of Death: A Biblical Examination of Evidence for Life after Death* (Minneapolis: Augsburg, 1981), esp. 37–54.

or unconsciousness; 3) that the soul, separated from and outside the body, continues to think—and, in fact, clearly—to have feelings, such as fear and serenity, sorrow and joy, etc.; 4) that after death the soul maintains its memory intact, remembering all of its deeds, all thoughts, all the words it spoke, and so on, from its childhood years forth; 5) that the soul has senses that correspond to the bodily senses of sight and hearing, so that, separated from the body, it can see and hear.[19]

What we have here is the use of NDEs, not as independent sources of knowledge for what happens in the afterlife, but as an apologetical prop for, or confirmation of, theological convictions already firmly in place. To the extent that there are parallels between Cavarnos's Orthodox eschatology and modern NDEs, he finds them useful.[20]

5. Not all Orthodox theologians think like this. Father Seraphim Rose associates modern NDEs with what he calls "Occultism," as well as with the "Spiritualism" of the nineteenth century.[21] He contrasts such modern reports with accounts of the afterlife that appear in the lives of the saints. For him, the Orthodox "Christian experience is of the genuinely other world of heaven and hell, while the spiritistic experience is only of the aerial part of this world, the 'astral plane' of the fallen spirits."[22] Indeed, "today's experiences, far from confirming the truths of Christianity are proving to be a subtle pointer to deception and false teaching, a preparation for the coming reign of Antichrist."[23] On this interpretation, NDEs are real experiences that Protestants and new agers have misconstrued. As a result, they have become captive to teachings "literally devised by demons with the single clear intention

19. Constantine Cavarnos, *The Future Life according to Orthodox Teaching* (Etna, CA: Center for Traditionalist Orthodox Studies, 1985), 16–17.

20. Much the same might be said of Jerry Walls, *Heaven: The Logic of Eternal Joy* (Oxford: Oxford University Press, 2002), 133–60. Although Walls admits that reductionistic accounts might turn out to be true in the long run, he nonetheless regards NDEs as "prima facie evidence for life after death," urges that they may offer "a glimpse" of "realities we know about from the revelation of Scripture and Christian tradition," and holds that "there are no convincing overriders from either Christian theology or other sources to warrant rejecting the beliefs produced by NDEs" (160).

21. Seraphim Rose, *The Soul after Death: Contemporary "After-Death" Experiences in the Light of the Orthodox Teachings on the Afterlife* (Plantina, CA: Saint Herman of Alaska Brotherhood, 1993).

22. Rose, *Soul after Death*, 153.

23. Rose, *Soul after Death*, 165.

of overthrowing the traditional Christian teaching on life after death and changing mankind's whole outlook on religion."[24]

Some conservative Protestants have had similar thoughts. In his autobiography, Raymond Moody reports on fundamentalist Christians who have insisted that NDEs are or can be "the work of the devil."[25] Francis Bulle offers just this polemical take on NDEs in her book *The Many Faces of Deception*.[26] She is not alone.[27]

6. At the opposite end of the spectrum from Bulle is the Episcopal priest John Price's book *Revealing Heaven*.[28] He confesses: "I believe these experiences are central to our Christian faith. Each account verifies for the Christian community God's love and promise of eternal life in a literal heaven. As Christians, we should celebrate these near-death experiences as living testaments of this promise."[29] Price argues at length that the lessons of NDEs largely cohere with what the Bible has to say about the world to come. He recognizes, however, that some returnees are confused because what they experienced conflicts with what they had hitherto believed. His explanation, as a liberal Christian, is that their notion of a "remote, wrathful, and vengeful" God needs to be replaced by a theology that puts unconditional divine love at the center, a theology he thinks belongs to the phenomenology of the NDE.[30]

24. Rose, *Soul after Death*, 162.

25. Raymond Moody and Paul Perry, *Paranormal: My Life in Pursuit of the Afterlife* (New York: HarperCollins, 2012), 107. Cf. Raymond A. Moody, *Reflections on Life after Life* (Covington, GA: Mockingbird Books, 1997), 58–60. For critical discussion of this point of view, see Habermas and Moreland, *Beyond Death*, 182–83.

26. Florence Bulle, *The Many Faces of Deception* (Minneapolis, MN: Bethany House, 2001), 172–85. According to Bulle, while the being of light in an NDE is sometimes Jesus Christ, in other experiences the light is "the Master Deceiver" disguised as an angel of light.

27. E.g., Tim LaHaye, *Life in the Afterlife* (Wheaton, IL: Tyndale House, 1980) and Doug Groothuis, *Deceived by the Light* (Eugene, OR: Harvest House, 1995). Cf. Elizabeth L. Hillstrom, *Testing the Spirits* (Downers Grove, IL: InterVarsity Press, 1995), 103: "the two most likely explanations ..." of NDEs "... are that they are self-generated ... or that they are visionary experiences that are initiated and/or shaped by spiritual forces ... very likely demonic."

28. John W. Price, *Revealing Heaven: The Christian Case for Near-Death Experiences* (New York: HarperCollins, 2013).

29. Price, *Revealing Heaven*, vi–vii.

30. Price, *Revealing Heaven*, 145–52. Cf. the argument of Ken R. Vincent, "The Near-Death Experience and Christian Universalism," *Journal of Near-Death Studies* 22 (2003): 57–71, that NDEs harmonize with the notion of universal salvation, although this does not exclude the possibility of judgment. For a positive use of NDEs by a conservative Roman Catholic, see Michael H. Brown, *The Other Side* (Palm Coast, FL: Spirit Daily Publishing, 2008). He seamlessly weaves NDEs from

Although far more theologically conservative, the Protestant devotional writer Rita Bennett—also an Episcopalian—takes a similar approach.[31] Her strategy is to recount NDEs that support her evangelical theology and her (crassly literal) understanding of the Bible. She neglects serious discussion of accounts that would not easily harmonize with her version of a Christian afterlife. This explains why her appended list of recommended reading includes books by Maurice Rawlings and Michael Sabom—both traditional Christians—but nothing by Raymond Moody or Kenneth Ring, whom some Christians have disparaged as new agers.[32]

7. The polar opposite of Bennett is John Gibbs.[33] The latter contends that NDEs offer authentic perceptions of a spiritual reality, and that those perceptions suggest a theology at odds with traditional Christian orthodoxy. Gibbs takes NDEs to be evidence that humanity is "continuous with the all-encompassing, loving light of God."[34] In line with this, he believes that the phenomenology of NDEs harmonizes with John Shelby Spong's controversial theology, one that promotes panentheism rather than "the supernatural theism of antiquity."[35] For Gibbs, NDEs are a significant ingredient in forging a modern liberal theology.

8. The Catholic historian of religion Carol Zaleski, in her well-known 1988 book on NDEs, offers a much more nuanced and cautious take on them.[36] She emphasizes the central role of imagination, language, and culture in both experiencing and then recording NDEs. Her historical orientation moves her to emphasize the relativity of experiences in various times and places and so to recognize the

---

a variety of sources with Roman Catholic stories and doctrine (although on p. 169 he warns that "the spirits" must be tested by Scripture).

31. Rita Bennett, *To Heaven and Back: True Stories of Those Who Have Made the Journey* (Grand Rapids: Zondervan, 1997).

32. Also belonging to this category are books that recount at length a single NDE from a Christian perspective and refrain from engaging other NDE accounts; see e.g. Mary C. Neal, *To Heaven and Back: A Doctor's Extraordinary Account of Her Death, Heaven, Angels, and Life Again* (Colorado Springs, CO: WaterBrook Press, 2012).

33. John C. Gibbs, "What Do Near-Death Experiences and Jesus Have in Common? The Near-Death Experience and Spong's New Christianity," *Journal of Near-Death Studies* 24 (2005): 61–95.

34. Gibbs, "Near-Death Experiences and Jesus," 78.

35. Gibbs, "Near-Death Experiences and Jesus," 86.

36. Carol Zaleski, *Otherworld Journeys: Accounts of Near-Death Experiences in Medieval and Modern Times,* rev. ed. (New York: Oxford University Press, 1988).

difficulty of finding cross-cultural and cross-temporal constants. In her hands, reports of NDEs become mostly expressions of the religious culture in which individuals are immersed. This is not, she insists, to dismiss them in a reductionist fashion, because first-hand accounts can invigorate the theological symbol system of a religious tradition. Moreover, she holds that "in the context of a fully realized religious worldview," an NDE "may provide far-reaching consolation. Under such conditions, naturalistic explanations of near-death experiences have no purchase."[37]

I do not have space here to review these eight different ways of thinking about NDEs, although perhaps it is not out of place to record my opinion that view 1, which altogether bypasses the subject, is uninformed and—as I shall argue below—imprudent; that view 2, which denies any veridical elements to NDEs, has been, to the open-minded, empirically falsified;[38] that view 3, which holds that the data are too thin to say anything much, is outdated;[39] and that view 5, which attributes to the devil experiences that do not smoothly fit one's preconceived theology, is recklessly presumptuous and theologically perilous.[40] It also stigmatizes a phenomenon in such a way that some people in certain circles will be inhibited from being honest—with themselves and others—about what has happened to them.[41] However, rather

---

37. Carol Zaleski, "Near-Death Experiences," in *The Oxford Handbook of Eschatology*, ed. Jerry L. Walls (Oxford: Oxford University Press, 2008), 625. Her remark is occasioned by the firsthand account of Richard John Neuhaus in *As I Lay Dying: Meditations upon Returning* (New York: Basic Books, 2012). Cf. her comment on 62: "By themselves, near-death experiences prove nothing about the prospect for the survival of death; but if there are other grounds for believing in a future life, near-death experiences may be a source of justified beliefs about that life." For critical discussion of Zaleski see, Walls, *Heaven*, 140–45.

38. Reductionist accounts, such as John Martin Fischer and Benjamin Mitchell-Yellin, *Near-Death Experiences: Understanding Visions of the Afterlife* (Oxford: Oxford University Press, 2016), are obliged to explain away all reports of veridical elements during NDEs. In the light of the fully-documented collection of testimony in Titus Rivas, Anny Dirven, and Rudolf H. Smith, *The Self Does Not Die: Verified Paranormal Phenomena from Near-Death Experiences* (Durham, NC: IANDS Publications, 2016), this seems to me to be an increasingly desperate maneuver. See also Bruce Greyson, "Seeing Dead People Not Known to Have Died: 'Peak in Darien' Experiences," *Anthropology and Humanism* 35, no. 2 (2010): 159–71.

39. Kung was writing in the 1980s, and since then our knowledge of NDEs has grown exceedingly.

40. It is worth remembering that some of Jesus' opponents adopted exactly the same strategy when criticizing him: they ascribed his activities to the devil (Mark 3:22). One may further recall, given the positive outcomes strongly associated with most NDEs, that part of his response was that a kingdom divided against itself cannot stand.

41. Cf. Laurin Bellg, *Near Death in the ICU: Stories from Patients Near Death and Why We Should Listen to Them* (Appleton, WI: Sloan Press, 2016), 171: "I often wonder about the power

than criticize others, I wish in the following pages to offer my own suggestions as to how Christians might think about NDEs.

How Christians Might Think about NDEs

Let me begin by emphasizing that, forty years after Moody's first book, it is irresponsible for theologians to ignore NDEs. One reason is that, no matter how one accounts for them, the implications are momentous. On the one hand, if it turns out that NDEs are (whatever the mechanism) purely endogenous, that is, brain-generated hallucinations, then a widespread, cross-cultural human experience,[42] one that commonly moves people to become more loving and less selfish,[43] an experience that feels wholly real—or, as often reported, even "more real than real"—an experience that even small children have reported,[44] is, at bottom, wholly illusory. And if such an experience is nothing but a phantom, then human experience and human testimony, including religious experience and religious testimony, whether past or present, are well-nigh worthless. Would not the consequences of this be far-reaching?

Let me put a face on this, or rather three faces. Several years ago, a woman working in a Methodist church, after relating to me her NDE of a decade ago, told me two things. First, I was the only person besides her husband with whom she had ever shared her story. Second, her NDE was not only truly real but the most important thing that had ever happened to her. Similarly, a while back, a Christian minister, when

---

of limiting beliefs to obscure our ability to see things a different way. So firmly rooted are our tightly knit convictions that sometimes, when something occurs that is beyond our understanding of reality, we instinctively set about gathering up those bits that have escaped the confines of what we think is possible and try to neatly tuck them back into the framework we recognize and are comfortable with."

42. See Gregory Shushan, *Conceptions of the Afterlife in Early Civilizations: Universalism, Constructivism and Near-Death Experiences* (London/New York: Continuum, 2009), and Ornella Corazza and K.A.L.A. Kuruppuarachchi, "Dealing with Diversity: Cross-Cultural Aspects of Near-Death Experiences," in *Making Sense of Near-Death Experiences: A Handbook for Clinicians*, eds. Karuppiah Jagadheesan, Anthony Peake, and Mahendra Perera (London/Philadelphia: Jessica Kingsley, 2012), 51–62.

43. See Bruce Greyson, "Near-Death Experiences and Spirituality," *Zygon* 41 (2006): 401–5; and Russell Noyes, Jr., Peter Fenwick, Janice Miner Holden, and Sandra Rozan Christian, "Aftereffects of Pleasurable Western Adult Near-Death Experiences," in *Handbook of Near Death Experiences*, Holden et al., 41–62; and Penny Sartori, *The Wisdom of Near-Death Experiences: How Brushes with Death Teach Us to Live* (London: Watkins, 1893), 24–53.

44. See Cherie Sutherland, "Near-Death Experiences of Children," in *Making Sense of Near-Death Experiences*, Perera et al., 63–78; and Sartori, *Wisdom*, 53–69.

dying of cancer, confided to me that, not long before, he was sure that NDEs were "bunk." Then, however, after having his own NDE in the hospital, he had learned otherwise: these things happen, they are not hallucinations, and now he knew it. More recently, I was on a panel with the coauthor of a book that regards NDEs as purely subjective. Following the discussion, a young man from the audience strolled up and spoke to my fellow panelist, then to me. When he informed me that he himself had had an NDE, I asked him what he made of my skeptical counterpart's assessment of NDEs. He laughed and said that he knew, from first-hand experience, that the guy did not know what he was talking about.

Now if these three people, who represent a multitude, were wholly deluded, if their experiences were hallucinations through and through, akin to childhood dreams of monsters, it arguably follows that people being utterly certain about their experiences is of no account, even if it is a group of hundreds of thousands who are bearing witness.[45] The implication, I submit, would be that this world, which God created, is more than profoundly deceitful.[46]

On the other hand, if NDEs are not purely subjective, if they include veridical elements, then the apparent implications are equally far-reaching. NDEs may suggest, against a number of influential theologians and biblical scholars,[47] the existence of something like a tra-

---

45. Given what we now know, NDEs are not rare; hundreds of thousands of people now living have had NDEs. On the problem of determining incidence see Bruce Greyson, "The Incidence of Near-Death Experiences," *Medicine Psychiatry* 1 (1998), 92–99, and Nancy L. Zingrone and Carlos S. Alvarado, "Pleasurable Western Adult Near-Death Experiences: Features, Circumstances, and Incidence," in *Handbook*, Holden et al., 38–39.

46. A certain kind of Protestant can, of course, retort that there is no problem because we learn about religious subjects from the Bible alone. But the truth is that, whatever theology we profess, none of us can ignore his or her own religious experiences and sentiments. Beyond that, the Bible is full of extraordinary religious experiences, such as dreams, visions, and auditions; and one might well wonder whether, if human testimony to exceptional experiences is so misleading today, things can have been altogether different in biblical times. I am sympathetic to the position of Walls, *Heaven*, 147–48: "Why would God design us in such a way that many people would form strong convictions that they had encountered him, had experienced his love and the like, when in fact they had not really done so? Would the positive psychological benefits outweigh the apparent deception required to achieve this? I am inclined to think they would not, so I judge it unlikely that God would deceive us in this fashion ... It seems highly unlikely that such experiences could be unintended byproducts when the designer involved is perfectly wise and good."

47. Note, e.g., Wolfhart Pannenberg, *What Is Man? Contemporary Anthropology in Theological Perspective* (Philadelphia: Fortress, 1970); Nancey C. Murphy, *Bodies and Souls, or Spirited Bodies?* (New York: Cambridge University Press, 2006); Joel Green, *Body, Soul, and Human Life: The Nature of Humanity in the Bible* (Grand Rapids: Baker Academic, 2008). For how one might develop my

ditional soul.[48] Moreover, NDEs probably entail that worldviews built upon modern materialism and reductionism are false, and that modern neuroscience does not encompass everything about us.[49] Those are no small things. Indeed, in our cultural context they are revolutionary. Can theologians really be apathetic about this?

Theological indifference towards NDEs also makes little sense given that so many people who have NDEs end up using the word "God" when recounting their stories. In this connection I can refer to Jeffrey Long's book *God and the Afterlife*.[50] There are issues with this volume, above all its failure to discuss the different conceptions of "God" that are embedded in the various NDE reports. Nonetheless, Long makes the empirical claim, for which he offers strong support, that NDEs are correlated with "increased belief in God." Furthermore, NDEs are, in his judgment, correlated with such belief more than with any other—to use his words—"specific life event."[51] It is dumbfounding that a theologian would not sit up and take notice at such a claim. For many, NDEs function just like—or rather are—experiences of profound religious conversion, whose effects can be transformative and lifelong. How can this be theologically of no account?

There is at least one more reason why theologians should pay serious attention to NDEs. Even if theologians are not interested, countless people, including countless religious people, are interested. Raymond Moody's *Life after Life* sold millions of copies, and it has been translated into a dozen languages. Related books, such as Melvin Morse's *Closer to the Light*, Betty Eadie's *Embraced by the*

---

argument here, see Johann Christoph Hampe, *To Die is Gain: The Experience of One's Own Death* (Atlanta: John Knox, 1979), esp. 101–14. Cf. Carol Zaleski, *The Life of the World to Come: Near Death-Experiences and Christian Hope* (New York: Oxford University Press, 1996), 59: "the study of near-death testimony has convinced me that Christian eschatology must inevitably resort to some form of soul-body dualism."

48. I use the words "may" and "suggest" here and in the following sentences because the notion of "proof" seems, at this point in time at least, inappropriate. See on this esp. Michael Sudduth, *A Philosophical Critique of Empirical Arguments for Postmortem Survival* (New York: Palgrave Macmillan, 2016). In my judgment, NDEs are suggestive in and of themselves; depending upon the worldview one otherwise holds, they can become more than that.

49. Here NDEs do not stand alone; for additional reasons to reject modern reductionistic materialism see esp. Edward F. Kelly, Emily Williams Kelly, et al., *Irreducible Mind: Toward a Psychology for the 21st Century* (Lanham, MD: Rowman & Littlefield, 2007).

50. Jeffrey Long with Paul Perry, *God and the Afterlife: The Ground-Breaking New Evidence for God and Near-Death Experience* (New York: HarperOne, 2016).

51. Long and Perry, *God and the Afterlife*, 40–41.

Light, Dannion Brinkley's *Saved by the Light*, Jeffrey Long's *Evidence of the Afterlife*, Mary Neal's *To Heaven and Back*, and Eben Alexander's *Proof of Heaven*, have also made bestseller lists.[52] Clearly, NDEs have captured the public's imagination, a fact further evident in the large number of TV shows, movies, documentaries, and YouTube videos that, in one way or another, deal with NDEs. My guess is that most people today in the American pews, even in conservative pews, when they think about their own deaths and what might lie beyond, now entertain first the standard scenario first popularized by Moody. Moreover, many of these folks must wonder how they should put together what they have heard about NDEs with what they otherwise have believed about death from reading their Bibles and listening to sermons. If, then, the professional theologians ignore NDEs, they are implicitly confessing that they do not care about the pew-sitters, that they have no interest in helping churchgoers with a matter many of them deem to be of crucial existential importance, a matter—death and what lies beyond—that theologians have, historically, cared about deeply.

Having, I hope, made my point that theologians should pay attention to NDEs, the remaining question is, what should they make of them? They need, in my view, to face the real possibility that critical study of NDEs will, after all is said and done, allow us to catch a glimpse of the first stages of what likely lies beyond our death.[53] After we take full account of the cultural codes and predispositions of experiencers,[54] of the influence of expectation and imagination upon

---

52. Melvin Morse and Paul Perry, *Closer to the Light: Learning from the Near-Death Experiences of Children* (New York: Ivy Books, 1990); Betty J. Eadie, *Embraced by the Light* (Carson City, NV: Gold Leaf Press, 1992); Dannion Brinkley with Paul Perry, *Saved by the Light: The True Story of a Man Who Died Twice and the Profound Revelations He Received* (New York: Villard, 1994); Don Piper and Cecil Murphy, *90 Minutes in Heaven: A True Story of Life and Death* (Grand Rapids: Revell, 2004); Jeffery Long with Paul Perry, *Evidence of the Afterlife: The Science of Near-Death Experiences* (New York: HarperOne, 2010); Neal, *To Heaven and Back*; Eben Alexander, *Proof of Heaven: A Neurosurgeon's Journey into the Afterlife* (New York: Simon & Schuster, 2012).

53. See the succinct overview of the relevant arguments in Imants Barušs and Julia Mossbridge, *Transcendent Mind: Rethinking the Science of Consciousness* (Washington, DC: American Psychological Association, 2017), 107–23.

54. Here the work of Zaleski is helpful even if, in the end, too skeptical. See also Allan Kellehear, *Experiences Near Death: Beyond Medicine and Religion* (Oxford: Oxford University Press, 1996), and John Belanti, Mahendra Perera, and Karuppiah Jagadheesan, "Phenomenology of Near-Death Experiences: A Cross-Cultural Perspective," *Transcultural Psychology* 45 (2008): 121–33.

perception,[55] of the frailties of human memory,[56] and of the biases of interviewers,[57] some things begin to suggest themselves. Here I can refer to Mark Fox's important work on the so-called "being of light" that often appears in stories from people with NDEs.[58] His study is, to my mind, exemplary in showing how we can, through critical analysis and broad comparison, begin to make some plausible generalizations about the cross-cultural and cross-temporal phenomenology of NDEs and even, if I may be so bold, the "extra-linguistic" experiences underlining NDEs.[59] While there may be no such thing as experience without interpretation, the two are not identical. Just as Samuel Johnson's life cannot be equated with Boswell's *Life of Johnson*, so, too, NDEs and their interpretations remain distinct, even if the two cannot be wholly disentangled. "Accepting that experience is culturally mediated is not the same as accepting that it is entirely culturally fabricated."[60]

Christian theologians should, I contend, be utterly open-minded here. One reason is that our tradition has, at its best, been exceedingly cautious about what it has termed the "interim state," that is, the state between death and the final consummation. It would be easy to fill page after page with quotations from theologians who have recognized that they have no detailed knowledge of what lies immediately beyond death. Here is a sampling:

---

55. See, e.g., Joel Pearson, Colin W. G. Clifford, and Frank Tong, "The Functional Impact of Mental Imagery on Conscious Perception," *Current Biology* 18, no. 13 (2008): 982–86; Timea R. Partos, Simon J. Cropper, and David Rawlings, "You Don't See What I See: Individual Differences in the Perception of Meaning from Visual Stimuli," *PLOS ONE* 11, no. 3 (2016): 1–26.

56. Daniel L. Schacter, *The Seven Sins of Memory: How the Mind Forgets and Remembers* (Boston/New York: Houghton Mifflin, 2001). The question of how memories of NDEs may differ from ordinary, everyday memories, is both important and fascinating. For data suggesting that "memories of near-death experiences are recalled as 'realer' than real events or imagined events," see Lauren E. Moore and Bruce Greyson, "Characteristics of Memories for Near-Death Experiences," *Consciousness and Cognition* 51 (2017): 116–24.

57. Helpful for understanding ways in which researchers can color reports and affect interpretation is Michael Sabom, *Light & Death: One Doctor's Fascinating Account of Near-Death Experiences* (Grand Rapids: Zondervan, 1998), 131–41.

58. Fox, *Religion*, 98–141.

59. I am fully cognizant of the philosophical issues involved here. All I can do here is refer readers to Fox, *Near-Death Experiences*, 98–141, and Gregory Shusham, "Extraordinary Experiences and Religious Beliefs: Deconstructing Some Contemporary Philosophical Axioms," *Method and Theory in the Study of Religion* 26 (2014): 384–416.

60. Shusham, "Extraordinary Experiences," 391.

- William Whitaker: "Although we generally know that the saints in heaven are blessed, yet we know not their particular state, their actions, the manner and degree of their happiness. ... Christ revealed to the saints on earth, heavenly things, but not what was done in heaven."[61]

- John Rogers: heaven is "transcendent, infinite, ineffable, incomprehensible, and remote from our weak senses."[62]

- Francis Turretin: "Whatever symbols are used, drawn from earthly things to adumbrate" the happiness of heaven, "it must always be recollected that they are employed allegorically and ought to be understood mystically."[63]

- A. E. Taylor: the church "affirms the permanence of human personality, and the continuity of the soul's life hereafter with its now; on all else she has nothing to say."[64]

- Harry Emerson Fosdick: "A wise agnosticism chastens our speech about the detailed meanings of life eternal."[65]

- John Baillie: "This is a region in which agnosticism is assuredly the better part of wisdom"; "many questions may be asked but none can be answered."[66]

- Carl E. Braaten and Robert W. Jenson: "Anything beyond this world can never be in strict analogy to things in this world. This means that the concepts we use to talk about

61. William Whitaker, *An Answere to the Ten Reasons of Edmund Campian the Iesuit: In Confidence wherof he offered Disputation to the Ministers of the Church of England, in the Controversie of Faith* (London: Felix Kyngston, 1606), 106.

62. John Rogers, *A Discourse of Christian Watchfulnesse: Preparing how to Liue, how to Die, and to be Discharged at the Day of Iudgement, and so Enioy Life Eternall* (London: William Iones, 1620), 356.

63. Francis Turretin, *Institutes of Elenctic Theology*, vol. 3: *Eighteenth through Twentieth Topics* (Phillipsburg, NJ: P&R Publishing, 1997 [1685]), 617.

64. A. E. Taylor, "The Belief in Immortality," in *The Faith and the War: A Series of Essays by Members of the Churchmen's Union and Others on the Religious Difficulties aroused by the Present Condition of the World*, ed. F. J. Foakes-Jackson (London: Macmillan & Co., 1915), 155.

65. Harry Emerson Fosdick, *Spiritual Values and Eternal Life* (Cambridge, MA: Harvard University Press, 1927), 36.

66. John Baillie, *And the Life Everlasting* (New York: Charles Scribner's Sons, 1933), 236, 302.

eternal 'things' are always somehow inadequate. We have a choice between mystical silence and inadequacy."[67]

Such eschatological caution, I submit, goes back all the way to the New Testament. Jesus himself preferred parables about the eschatological kingdom of God over prosaic description. It was his habit to say "The kingdom of God is like ..." or "will be like ..." He was not wont to say, "Here is how the future will literally be." Paul showed himself to be of like inclination when he confessed, "eye has not seen nor ear heard, what God has laid up for those who love God" (1 Corinthians 2:9). Similarly, the author of 1 John wrote, "What we will be has not yet been made known" (3:2).

Christian theologians should take this tradition of eschatological ignorance seriously. With regard to what immediately follows death, the New Testament says next to nothing other than that Christians will be "with Christ."[68] And that is scarcely a concrete description, especially when one recalls that, in the New Testament, Christ is, even now, "with" Christians, just as they are "with" him in their current, earthly lives.[69] The New Testament says so little about the interim state that some have been able to argue that it teaches "soul sleep." I think they are wrong about this. But they can make their case only because the New Testament is so reserved regarding this subject.

Biblically based, descriptive details of the interim state are unavailable,[70] so using alleged conflicts between the Bible and NDEs to urge, as have some, that the latter cannot give us a glimpse of life after death is hermeneutically out of bounds.[71] The "bosom of Abraham"

---

67. Carl E. Braaten and Robert W. Jenson, eds., *Christian Dogmatics, Vol. 2: The Content of Christian Hope* (Philadelphia: Fortress, 1984), 574.

68. Luke 23:43; Phil 1:23; Rev 20:4.

69. Note, e.g., Matt 18:20 ("where two or three are gathered in my name, there I am among them"); 28:20 ("I am with you always"); Eph 2:5 ("made us alive together with Christ"); Col 3:1 ("you have been raised with Christ"); 3:3 ("your life is hid with Christ in God").

70. I have made the case for this at length in my book, *Night Comes: Death, Imagination, and the Last Things* (Grand Rapids: Eerdmans, 2016), 69–92.

71. Here I disagree with Sabom, *Light & Death*. He contends that NDEs are real "spiritual experiences" that occur when the soul is beginning to separate from the body; yet NDEs do not tell us anything about the afterlife. As justification, he appeals to several biblical texts. He infers, for instance, from Heb 9:27 ("it is appointed for people to die once") and 2 Sam 14:14 ("We must all die, we are like water spilt on the ground, which cannot be gathered up again" RSV) that people cannot return from death, so NDErs cannot have died. This, however, has become an empirical question that depends upon how we define death; it cannot be settled by appeal to two verses

(Luke 16:22–23) is a metaphor. John's vision of souls under God's throne (Rev 6:9) is no more literal than the beast who rises out of the sea with ten horns and seven heads (Rev 13:1). And so it goes.

Another reason for theologians to be open-minded about NDEs is that the end may very well turn out to be like the beginning. There was a time, when it came to archaic history, human origins, and the creation of the world, when theologians, with Bible in hand, were the sole source of knowledge. That, however, has changed radically over recent centuries. When looking into the dim, primeval past, Christian theologians of whatever stripe have learned that they cannot blithely ignore what cosmologists, geologists, anthropologists, and ancient historians have uncovered. To ignore or dismiss what they have to teach us because we need only the Bible would be irrational. What, then, if we are at the beginning of learning truly some things about the process of death? And what if, at some point, the evidence that NDEs offer a glimpse into the earliest stages or transition to post-mortem existence becomes compelling? In such a situation, the theologian who claims to know everything important ahead of time would be an obscurantist, and as foolish as the fundamentalists who insist that, because of their interpretation of Genesis, the world must be around six thousand years old, despite all the scientific indices to the contrary. This is the danger when the Southern Baptist Convention issues a declaration "On the Sufficiency of Scripture Regarding the Afterlife,"[72] or

---

taken out of their original contexts. Furthermore, Sabom ignores the story of the witch of Endor (1 Sam 28:3–25), he turns a simile (2 Sam 14:14) into dogma, and he treats a generalization (Heb 9:27) as an absolute even though Scripture itself, in the stories of Elisha, Jesus, and Paul raising the dead, offers exceptions. Again, Sabom draws inferences from Luke 16:26–31, the story of the rich man and Lazarus. This, however, is a parable, not a prosaic description of the world to come. It presupposes a life beyond this one, and that is all; the rest is a warning or exhortation in story form. Like the other parables, it is fiction. Mining it for facts about the afterlife makes no more sense than seeking agricultural advice from the parable of the sower. Even worse, Sabom remarks that no one who is raised from the dead in the Bible returns "from the grave with afterlife details. Accordingly, I conclude that modern-day descriptions of NDEs are not accounts of life after death" (198). This argument from silence has no force at all. We simply have no records of what Lazarus or anyone else purportedly raised from the dead in the Bible said about anything. Finally, Sabom urges that, because the Bible teaches that no one can see God and live (Exod 33:20; cf. 1 Tim 6:16), claims by NDErs to have seen God should be rejected. But one could (in theory) just as easily argue that, given the eschatological promises that the saints will see God (Matt 5:8), NDErs must have been dead when they saw what they claim to have seen! That Sabom can do no better than he does with Scripture proves my point, which is simply that it has very little to say on the subject of what happens immediately upon death.

72. For this text, issued in 2014, a text which, in response to "books and movies purporting to explain or describe the afterlife," affirms "the sufficiency of biblical revelation over

when a Roman Catholic theologian baldly asserts, "We do not judge the Catholic teaching by reports of after-life experiences; rather, we judge these reports by Catholic teaching."[73]

The theologian's task is not to dispute empirical facts but to study them and explore their meaning. Here Sam Parnia is right: "Although the subject of death and what happens when we die has traditionally been perceived as a religious or philosophical question, it is clear that it is a field of knowledge that requires the objectivity of science. We should remain impartial and be willing to accept whatever our inquiries bring up without being fixed to what we have been conditioned to perceive as reality."[74]

Conclusion

Three final notes. First, the study of NDEs is still in its initial stages, and it is not yet clear what we should make of the various and often conflicting interpretations that come from NDErs, as well as from the experts who study them. My own view is that evangelicals should be just as circumspect regarding evangelical NDErs and their evangelical interpretations of NDEs as they are of non-evangelical NDErs and their non-evangelical interpretations. We know that NDEs are subjectively real, but we are still learning how we might determine the extent to which experiences and memories of them have been effected by the percipients themselves. In everyday life, our perceptions are heavily colored by our linguistic framework, our expectations, our desires, and much else; and our memories are far from one hundred percent reliable.

Two, many theologians will not welcome the possibility that NDEs are important. Traditionally, Christians have said much about death and the afterlife without reference to NDEs. Once, however, you become persuaded that some NDEs can have some veridical elements, you may have to rethink some things, and you may have to

---

subjective experiential explanations to guide one's understanding of the truth about heaven and hell," see "On the Sufficiency Of Scripture Regarding the Afterlife" (Baltimore, MD, 2014), *Southern Baptist Convention*, obtained online June 3, 2020, http://www.sbc.net/resolutions/2247/on-the-sufficiency-of-scripture-regarding-the-afterlife.

73. Albert Hebert, *Saints Who Raised the Dead: True Stories of 400 Resurrection Miracles* (Charlotte, NC: TAN Books, 2004), 255.

74. Sam Parnia with Josh Young, *Erasing Death: The Science that is Rewriting the Boundaries between Life and Death* (New York: HarperOne, 2013), 174–75.

acknowledge that what was once an exclusively religious provenance has been invaded by others. That may not be an easy step to take. Some will want rather to stick to their own realm of discourse, to maintain an independent epistemology, to operate with something like Stephen J. Gould's idea of "nonoverlapping magisteria." But NDEs, if not wholly subjective, may destroy the truce between worlds.

Here are the words of a theologian, an Anglican writing about a hundred years ago, when spiritualism still mattered and the Society for Psychical Research and its studies of apparitions were important cultural facts: "The reduction of immortality to a fact of science means … the transference of the subject from the sphere of faith to the sphere of experiment. It would make the matter impossible to deny. Would that be beneficial? I believe on the contrary that there is a high moral value in an undemonstrated immortality."[75] This theologian wanted immortality to remain in the realm of the sermon, in the universe of faith and exhortation, in the exclusive jurisdiction of theology. To quote the same theologian again: it is better that belief in immortality be "left unprovided with any scientific foundation; better left … individually appropriated, according to individual earnestness, by moral effort, rather than forced by experimental evidence of a purely external kind, upon all alike, indiscriminately, and apart from the question whether the fact would be to their spiritual gain or loss."[76]

To me, this is not an argument but an inconvenience. The words quoted reflect a desire to keep theology cordoned off, so that theologians and pastors can go about their business as usual, without troubling too much about other areas of knowledge. Ultimately, however, truth will win out, whether welcome or not. And if life after death becomes probable on empirical, non-religious grounds, and if, further, at some point we can plausibly utter a few stammering words about what may be its initial stages, the theologians will just have to make their peace with it. My suggestion is that they should recall past battles lost to empirical science and embrace the Methodist quadrilateral, which teaches that, in addition to the Bible and tradition, theology has to pay keen attention to reason and experience.

---

75. W. J. Sparrow Simpson, *The Resurrection and Modern Thought* (New York: Longmans, Green, 1911), 437.

76. Sparrow Simpson, *Resurrection*, 440.

Finally, some conservative Christians seem to be upset that more NDEs are not of the hellish variety, and further that people outside the fold often report blissful experiences that lack any specifically Christian elements. My theology is such that I not only do not share this concern but also find such an attitude ungracious in the extreme. The conversation, however, breaks down here, for such people will inevitably see any theological line of reasoning that I might develop as coming from someone too liberal to be taken seriously. So rather than vainly mount such an argument, let me close by asking what one might make of Matthew 5:45, which declares that the Father who is in heaven "makes his sun rise on the evil and on the good, and sends rain on the just and on the unjust." Whence comes the knowledge that these words can have nothing to do with people who are not in one's religious fold and yet report positive NDEs?

11

THE DEATHS OF THE APOSTLES AND BELIEF IN JESUS' RESURRECTION

Sean McDowell

The deaths of the apostles for their belief in the risen Jesus is one of the most popular arguments in favor of the resurrection. Yet until recent times, this claim has not been carefully scrutinized. In this chapter, we are going to consider two important questions: What is the evidence the apostles actually died for their belief in Jesus' resurrection? And to what extent would their sufferings and martyrdoms count as evidence for the reliability of their testimonies regarding the risen Christ?

First, we need to consider the argument carefully. Bart Ehrman describes how popular apologists often make their case:

> All the apostles were martyred for their faith, because they believed Jesus had been raised from the dead; you can see why someone might be willing to die for the truth; but no one would die for a lie; and therefore, the disciples—all of them—clearly believed that Jesus was raised from the dead. And if they all believed it, then it almost certainly is true.[1]

Ehrman proceeds to dismiss the argument because of the lack of "reliable information about what happened to Jesus' disciples after he died"[2] as well as the legendary nature of later traditions. Insofar as the argument depends upon establishing the deaths of *all* the apostles, Ehrman

---

1. Bart Ehrman, "Were the Disciples Martyred for Believing the Resurrection? A Blast from the Past," The Bart Ehrman Blog: The History and Literature of Early Christianity (Oct 13, 2017): https://ehrmanblog.org/were-the-disciples-martyred-for-believing-the-resurrection-a-blast-from-the-past/.

2. Ehrman, "Were the Disciples Martyred for Believing the Resurrection?"

is right to dismiss it. He is correct that we don't know how *most* of the apostles died. Well-meaning apologists have often overstated the evidence regarding the deaths of the apostles and the significance of what follows for the historicity of the resurrection.

But can the argument be salvaged in a manner that offers corroborative support for the resurrection of Jesus? The answer is yes, if we state it more carefully. Here is a more judicious rendition: *Because of their sincere belief that Jesus had risen and appeared to them after his death, the apostles willingly suffered and were prepared to die for their public proclamation of the risen Christ. They did not invent the stories but willingly suffered because of the depth of their sincerity.* As Gary Habermas has noted, virtually all scholars who research in this area accept that the apostles had experiences they believed were actual appearances of the risen Jesus, which transformed their lives, and for which they were willing to die.[3]

A few important points emerge when the argument is stated in this manner. First, it does not depend upon proving that all the apostles, or even any, died as martyrs. The key is that they were *willing* to suffer for their belief in the risen Christ. If it can be shown that at least some of the apostles did die as martyrs, as we will see below, then the argument is strengthened. But strictly speaking, the argument does not depend upon the historical demonstration of their actual martyrdoms. If there is good reason to believe the apostles were willing to face persecution for their resurrection faith, then even if Ehrman is right about the unreliability of later traditions, we still have reason to trust their sincere conviction that Jesus appeared to them.

Second, the argument does not establish the truth of the resurrection, nor does it defeat all naturalistic accounts, such as the hallucination hypothesis.[4] Rather, it merely demonstrates the sincerity of the apostles. Ancients recognized that willingness to die for convictions establishes sincerity and undermines fabrication.[5] Thus, if the apostles

---

3. Gary Habermas, *Risen Jesus & Future Hope* (Lanham, MD: Rowman & Littlefield, 2003), 9, 26–27.

4. For a careful response to the hallucination hypothesis, see Gary R. Habermas, "Explaining Away Jesus' Resurrection: The Recent Revival of Hallucination Theories," *Christian Research Journal* 23, no. 4 (2001). This essay is available online: http://www.garyhabermas.com/articles/crj_explainingaway/crj_explainingaway.htm.

5. Craig Keener, *The Historical Jesus of the Gospels* (Grand Rapids: Eerdmans, 2009), 342.

were willing to suffer for their convictions regarding Jesus, we can fairly conclude that they were not liars. They did not conspire together to proclaim a story they knew was false. The willingness of the apostles to die for their beliefs helps establish the reliability of their testimony, which is one piece in a larger case that can be made for the resurrection.

Third, the argument does not depend upon the belief that only Christians have martyrs, as Candida Moss has suggested.[6] Maccabean heroes were willing to suffer and die for their commitment to the law.[7] And there was a pagan tradition in the first two centuries AD of people willingly dying in defiance of an unjust ruler.[8] While it is widely acknowledged that people are willing to die for a cause they believe in, the apostles suffered for the cause that Jesus had risen from the dead in accordance with the Old Testament Scriptures (See 1 Cor. 15:3–7). If Jesus had not risen, there would not have been a cause for the disciples to die for.

Preliminary Considerations

Before considering the evidence for the martyrdom of the apostles, we need to address two key issues. First, did the apostles have a resurrection faith? We can count the sufferings of the apostles as evidence for the sincerity of their convictions about the risen Jesus only if the apostles had a *resurrection* faith. Second, is there reason to believe Christians were persecuted in the first century? Establishing the persecution of Christians in the first century provides a helpful backdrop for evaluating the likelihood of the suffering and martyrdom of the apostles.

---

6. Candida Moss suggests that Christians tend to view their martyrs as unique and that many people have died for religions that no longer exist. See Candida Moss, *The Myth of Persecution: How Early Christians Invented a Story of Martyrdom* (New York: HarperOne, 2013), 17. Yet this misses the point. The question is not *if* other groups have martyrs but *what* those martyrs uniquely died for. In the case of the apostles of Jesus, their sufferings cannot be separated from their belief that Jesus rose from the dead. Their cause was that Jesus had defeated death and offers forgiveness. They were willing to suffer and die for a cause that was inextricably linked to their belief that they had seen the risen Jesus.

7. See 2 Maccabees 7:30b–32 (KJV), "I will not obey the king's commandment: but I will obey the commandment of the law that was given unto our fathers by Moses. And thou, that hast been the author of all mischief against the Hebrews, shalt not escape the hands of God. For we suffer because of our sins."

8. W. H. C. Frend, "Martyrdom and Political Oppression," in *The Early Christian World*, ed. Philip F. Esler, vols. 1–2 (New York: Routledge, 2000), 818.

The Centrality of the Resurrection

While some critics doubt the centrality of the resurrection, the majority of scholars accept that Christianity was a resurrection faith since its inception.[9] There is no credible evidence for an early Christian faith apart from belief in the resurrection. The basis for this confidence begins with an analysis of Christological creeds, our earliest sources regarding Christian belief.

Early Christian Creeds

Early christological creeds, verbal proclamations of the faith that circulated before their inclusion in various New Testament books, are often considered the most promising glimpse into the earliest Christian beliefs before the composition of the New Testament writings.[10] These creeds provide a window into the earliest known Christian beliefs that motivated the proclamation of their faith, the most common elements of which were the death and resurrection of Jesus, which demonstrates the present lordship of Christ.

There are many passages that scholars consider christological creeds,[11] yet the most crucial is arguably 1 Corinthians 15:3–7, which is dated roughly twenty-five years after the death of Jesus. This creed offers a glimpse of a pre-Pauline tradition even earlier than the writing of 1 Corinthians (AD 54–55):

> For I delivered to you as of first importance what I also received: that Christ died for our sins in accordance with the Scriptures, that he was buried, that he was raised on the third day in accordance with the Scriptures, and that he appeared to Cephas, then to the twelve. Then he appeared to more than five hundred brothers at one time, most of whom are still alive, though some have fallen asleep. Then he appeared to James, then to all the apostles.[12]

---

9. In *The Resurrection of the Messiah*, New Testament scholar Christopher Bryan begins his inquiry with the assumption that three established facts can be considered "historical certainties," one of which is the centrality of the resurrection in the earliest Christian self-definition. See Christopher Bryan, *The Resurrection of the Messiah* (Oxford: Oxford University Press, 2011), 3–4.

10. Gary Habermas has made a massive contribution to the importance of early creeds in his book *The Historical Jesus: Ancient Evidence for the Life of Christ* (Joplin, MO: College Press, 1997), 143–70. I credit him for many of the insights that guide the formulation of this section.

11. For example, Rom 1:3–4; 4:24b–25; 1 Thess 4:14; and 1 Pet 3:18.

12. Unless otherwise noted, Scripture citations in this chapter are from the ESV.

Gary Habermas offers five reasons why the creedal nature of this passage is accepted by the vast majority of scholars. First, Paul uses the words "delivered" (*paradidōmi*) and "received" (*paralambanō*), which are technical terms for the transmission of tradition. Second, many of the words in the creed are non-Pauline, indicating a distinct origin. Third, the creed is likely organized in a stylized, oral form. Fourth, there are internal indications of a Semitic source, such as the reference to Peter with the Aramaic "Cephas." Finally, the triple usage of "and that" as well as the reference to the fulfillment of Scripture indicate ancient Hebraic narration.[13]

Scholars debate when Paul received this creed. He could have received it during his stay with Ananias and other disciples after his conversion (Acts 9:19), during his first visit to Jerusalem three years later (Acts 9:26–28; Gal 1:18), or during a later visit before writing his first letter (Acts 11:27; 15:2; Gal 2:1–10). We may not have certainty when he received it, but we do know that he had ample opportunity to interact with leading Jerusalem figures and had both the incentive and ability to pass on the earliest teachings of the disciples on the resurrection of Jesus. The important point for our study is that the earliest record of Christian belief, which predates the writing of the New Testament, is grounded in the claim that Jesus rose from the grave and appeared to his followers.

Resurrection in the New Testament

The centrality of the resurrection can also be seen in the apostolic preaching in Acts. Speeches in Acts make up approximately one-third of the book's content. The resurrection of Jesus is mentioned in most evangelistic speeches in Acts, to both Jews and Gentiles, as well as in other passages in Acts.[14] In his Pentecost speech, the apostle Peter describes how God appointed Jesus to do wonders but he was killed by lawless men, and yet "God raised him up, loosing the pangs of death, because it was not possible for him to be held by it" (Acts 2:24). James Dunn concludes:

---

13. Habermas, *Historical Jesus*, 153–54.

14. Acts 1:21; 2:24, 31–32; 3:15; 4:2, 10–11, 33; 5:30; 10:40; 13:30, 33–34; 17:3, 18, 31; 23:6; 24:15, 21; 25:19; 26:8, 23.

The claim that Jesus had been raised from the dead is the central and principal message of the preaching in Acts. ... We can be quite confident, then, that Jesus' resurrection was from the first a prominent and distinctive feature of earliest Christian belief and functioned as a defining identity marker of the new sect which gathered round his name.[15]

The centrality of resurrection is not limited to Acts. With the exception of Hebrews, all the major books of the New Testament make resurrection a central focus.[16] This focus continues into the writings of church leaders shortly after the apostles, known as the Apostolic Fathers.[17] Thus, the resurrection was central to Christian proclamation from the inception of the church to *at least* the generation after the apostles. All the earliest sources reveal that the apostles believed in and preached the risen Christ.

Persecution in the Early Church

Biblical Record

According to the biblical record, starting shortly after the death of Jesus, Christians were persecuted in Judea, Syria, Arabia, Rome, Asia, Asia Minor, and southeastern Europe. This persecution included verbal harassment, public denunciation, court challenges, physical beatings, flogging, exile from a city, execution, and mob killings. In his analysis of the various biblical accounts, Eckhard J. Schnabel concludes,

The survey of all instances of the persecution of the earliest followers of Jesus demonstrates the pervasiveness of verbal and physical attacks against Christians. The only provinces of the Roman empire for which no persecution is reported are Cyprus, Cilicia, and Pamphylia (as well as Spain and Egypt,

---

15. James D. G. Dunn, *Beginning from Jerusalem: Christianity in the Making* (Grand Rapids: Eerdmans, 2009), 2:212–13.

16. N. T. Wright, *Resurrection of the Son of God* (Minneapolis: Fortress Press, 2003), 476.

17. See Sean McDowell, *The Fate of the Apostles: Examining the Martyrdom Accounts of the Closest Followers of Jesus* (New York: Routledge, 2015), 22–23.

provinces for which we have no explicit record of missionary activity in the first century).[18]

The biblical account is consistent and clear that the first Christians were persecuted for their proclamation of the faith. This kind of mistreatment should not have surprised the first followers of Jesus. The forerunner of Christ, John the Baptist, was imprisoned and beheaded. Jesus of Nazareth was himself crucified. By choosing to follow Christ, the first believers were identifying with a crucified enemy of the Roman state. Jesus had also instructed them to expect such treatment specifically because of their proclamation of his name.[19] Jesus taught his disciples to be prepared to lose their lives for the sake of saving it.[20] And he instructed his followers to deny themselves and pick up their crosses and follow him.[21] To pick up one's cross was to sacrifice one's entire life and allegiance to the cause of Christ. This saying has clear martyrological connotations.[22]

The expectation and importance of suffering and persecution is not unique to the Gospels. It is a central theme throughout the rest of the New Testament. Paul discusses suffering and persecution in six of his seven undisputed letters, and it is a central theme in some of his disputed letters as well.[23] The book of Hebrews is written as an encouragement for believers undergoing trials to follow the example of Jesus, who suffered profoundly for his faith (13:12–13). James teaches that the righteous will suffer for their faith (1:2, 12). Peter encourages believers to stand strong in their faith even as they face the same kind of

---

18. Eckhard J. Schnabel, "The Persecution of Christians in the First Century," *JETS* 61.3 (2018): 545–46.

19. For instance, see Matt 10:16–23; Mark 13:9; John 15:18–27; Luke 21:12–13, 17.

20. If parallel passages are considered, this teaching occurs six times in the four Gospels (Mark 8:35; Matt 10:39, 16:25; Luke 17:33, 9:24; John 12:25). John Meier concludes that such a saying has a good chance of going back to the historical Jesus. See John Meier, *A Marginal Jew* (New York: Doubleday, 2001), 3:63.

21. Meier, *A Marginal Jew*, 3:65. Multiple attestation for this teaching occurs in Mark 8:34; Matt 16:24; Luke 9:23; and Q (Matt 10:38 and Luke 14:27). A similar saying also occurs in *The Gospel of Thomas* 55.

22. Thomas J. Wespetal, "Martyrdom and the Furtherance of God's Plan: The Value of Dying for the Christian Faith" (PhD diss., Trinity Evangelical Divinity School, 2005), 83.

23. Passages that discuss suffering in Paul's undisputed letters are Rom 5:3–4, 8:18, 35, 12:12, 14, 14:8, 15:31; 1 Cor 4:9–13; 2 Cor 1:3–10, 4:8, 6:4–9, 7:5, 11:24–27, 12:10; Gal 4:29, 5:11; Phil 1:29; 1 Thess 2:1–2, 2:14–15, 3:3–4. Passages from his disputed letters are Eph 3:1; Col 1:24; 2 Thess 1:4–9; 2 Tim 1:8, 12, 2:3, 8, 10–12, 3:12.

"fiery trial" Jesus faced, which included being beaten, insulted, reviled, and even killed (4:12–16). Suffering is also a key theme in 1 John and Revelation.[24] The writings of the New Testament are clear: suffering and persecution are to be accepted as part and parcel of following Jesus.

Extrabiblical Record

Nero was the first emperor (AD 54–68) to persecute Christians. He used Christians as a scapegoat in order to squelch rumors that he set fire to Rome. The Roman historian Tacitus reports the details (AD 115):

> Therefore to eliminate this rumor he falsely produced defendants and inflicted the most extraordinary punishments upon those whom, hated for their crimes, the people called Christians. The origin of this name was Christ, whom the procurator Pontius Pilate put to death in the reign of Tiberius; crushed for a while, the deadly superstition burst forth again not only throughout Judea, the source of this evil, but even throughout Rome, to which all horrible and shameful things flow from everywhere and are celebrated. Therefore the first persons arrested were those who confessed; then on their information, a great multitude was convicted not so much on the charge of setting fire as on hatred of the human race. Mockeries were added to their deaths, so that wrapped in the skins of wild animals they might die torn to pieces by dogs, or nailed to crosses they were burned to death to furnish light at night when day had ended. Nero made his own gardens available for this spectacle and put on circus games, mingling with the people while dressed in a charioteer's uniform or standing in his chariot. As a result there arose compassion toward those who were guilty and who deserved the most extraordinary punishments, on the grounds that they were being destroyed not for the public good but for the savagery of one man (*The Annals* 15.44.2–5).[25]

Several observations are worth noting. First, the reliability of this account is widely accepted by scholars. One reason is that negative

---

24. See McDowell, *Fate of the Apostles*, 43.

25. Herbert W. Benario, "The Annals," in *A Companion to Tacitus*, ed. Victoria Emma Pagán, Blackwell Companions to the Ancient World (Malden, MA: Wiley-Blackwell, 2012), 114–15.

descriptions of Christians—"hated for their crimes," "deadly superstition," "evil"—are unlikely to be Christian inventions. Further, Suetonius also mentions a persecution by Nero that is consistent with the Tacitus account (*Nero* 16.2).

Second, it appears the official persecution was confined to Rome, since there is no mention of persecution elsewhere. However, nothing was done to revoke the laws Nero had put in place against Christians. Consequently, these laws provided sanction and precedent for Christian persecution beyond Rome.

Third, Tacitus reports that Christians were killed for confessing the *name* of Christ, which is consistent with the New Testament account (e.g., 1 Pet 4:14). Once Nero officially condemned Christians for confessing the name of Christ, nothing prevented other provincial governors from persecuting those involved, by definition, with the same deviant and potentially treasonous religion. Professing the name of Christ could officially be treated as a crime throughout the Roman Empire.[26]

The authenticity of the account in Tacitus has recently been called into question.[27] Candida Moss suggests we ought to "exercise some caution when it comes to dealing with Tacitus" because he wrote fifty years after the events he describes and because he used the term "Christian," which followers of Jesus did not appear to utilize as a self-designation until the end of the first century.[28] While Moss is right that caution should be observed, many accounts are written over fifty years after the events they record, including the writings of Moss herself. Further, while Jesus' followers may have started using the term "Christian" at the end of the first century (popular use emerged more prominently in the latter half of the second century), outsiders were using it much earlier. In the New Testament, the name "Christian" first appears in Acts 11:26 as a popular term used to describe followers of Christ in

---

26. Herbert B. Workman, *Persecution in the Early Church* (Cincinnati: Jennings & Graham, 1906; reprint, Oxford: Oxford University Press, 1980), 42.

27. For recent rejection of the entire Neronian persecution of Christians, see Brent D. Shaw, "The Myth of Neronian Persecution" in *Journal of Roman Studies* 105 (Nov 2017): 73–100. Earlier scholars have noted that Tacitus is the only source that blames Christians for the Great Fire, and thus some have argued that Tacitus combined two separate accounts. Shaw rejects the Neronian persecution altogether. For an extensive response to Shaw, see Jan N. Bremmer, "Tacitus and the Persecution of the Christians: An Invention of Tradition?" in *Eirene: Studia Graeca Et Latina*, LIII (Prague, Czech Republic: Institute of Philosophy of the Czech Academy of Sciences, 2017), 324.

28. Moss, *The Myth of Persecution*, 139.

public. In fact, the term "Christian" was likely invented by Roman authorities and only later adopted by Christians themselves.[29] Moss is right that believers popularly used the term "Christian" much later than in the events recorded by Tacitus, but this provides no reason to reject the authenticity of his account that there was a group of followers of Jesus who were persecuted by Nero for their beliefs.

Christians who minded their own affairs and focused on living moral lives before outsiders were often spared persecution from the state (cf. 1 Thess 4:11). Outspoken leaders of the faith, however, such as the apostles, were much more likely to come into conflict with the general public, religious leaders, and state officials. They preached a message that not only undermined Jewish authority but offended Graeco-Roman sensibilities. Since the gods were understood as protectors of Rome, the Christian message that proclaimed Jesus as Lord was viewed as undermining the welfare and safety of the state.[30] In preaching the risen Christ, the apostles put themselves in genuine danger of facing persecution and martyrdom. And, as we will see below, we have reason to believe that at least a handful of them experienced such a fate.

Deaths of the Apostles

While there are a few sources in the second to fourth centuries that comment on the fate of the apostles, they offer minimal historical support.[31] The most promising approach is to analyze the historical evidence for the likelihood of the martyrdom of the individual apostles of Jesus.

Peter

The traditional view is that Peter was crucified in Rome during the reign of Nero between AD 64–67. There are nearly a dozen sources from the first two centuries that help with our investigation.[32] We will consider a few of the most important passages here.

---

29. See Jan N. Bremmer, "Tacitus and the Persecution of the Christians: An Invention of Tradition?" in *Eirene: Studia Graeca Et Latina*, LIII (Prague, Czech Republic: Institute of Philosophy of the Czech Academy of Sciences, 2017), 324.

30. Craig de Vos, "Popular Graeco-Roman Responses to Christianity," in *The Early Christian World*, ed. Philip F. Esler, vols. 1–2 (New York: Routledge, 2000), 871.

31. See Josh McDowell and Sean McDowell, *Evidence that Demands A Verdict* (Nashville: Thomas Nelson, 2017), 262–63.

32. For an in-depth analysis of each source, see McDowell, *Fate of the Apostles*, 60–92.

John 21:18-19. The earliest reference to the death of Peter is found on Jesus' lips in John 21:18-19:

> "Truly, truly I say to you, when you were young, you used to dress yourself and walk wherever you wanted, but when you are old, you will stretch out your hands, and another will dress you and carry you where you do not want to go." (This he said to show by what kind of death he was to glorify God). And after saying this he said to him, "Follow me."

The cryptic nature of this passage makes it likely an authentic saying of Jesus.[33] A solid case can be made that John 21 is part of the original Gospel and not a later addition, as some critics have suggested.[34] The context of this passage makes it clear that Jesus is calling Peter to become the new shepherd of his people, and that he will lay down his life for the flock, just as Jesus had done. Commentators unilaterally agree that this passage predicts the martyrdom of Peter, even though there is disagreement over *how* Peter would die.[35] Bart Ehrman concludes, "It is clear that Peter is being told that he will be executed (he won't die of natural causes) and that this will be the death of a martyr."[36] Even though the passage offers no indication of when or where Peter would die, John 21:18-19 is a first-century reference to the martyrdom of Peter, written within three decades of his death, when there would still be eyewitnesses present to confirm or deny such a report.

First Clement 5:1-4. *First Clement* is the first non-canonical document that refers to the martyrdom of Peter. It is typically dated AD 95-96 and so is a valuable first-century source. Clement writes:

---

33. Craig L. Blomberg, *The Historical Reliability of John's Gospel* (Downers Grove, IL: InterVarsity Press, 2001), 278.

34. Gilbert Van Belle, "Peter as Martyr in the Fourth Gospel," *Martyrdom and Persecution in Late Antique Christianity, Festschrift for Boudewijn Dehandschutter*, ed. J. Leemans (Leuven, Belgium: Peters, 2010), 288-89.

35. Most commentators agree that John incorporates a veiled reference to crucifixion, although a significant minority are skeptical. For a discussion of the reasons for and against crucifixion, see McDowell, *Fate of the Apostles*, 62-64. Thomas Barnes has argued that the account in John's Gospel cannot refer to crucifixion because it describes Peter as dying clothed, not naked. He believes Peter was likely burned to death during the reign of Nero. See Timothy Barnes, "Another Shall Gird Thee," in *Peter in Early Christianity*, ed. Helen K. Bond and Larry W. Hurtado (Grand Rapids: Eerdmans, 2015), 76-95.

36. Bart Ehrman, *Peter, Paul, & Mary Magdalene: The Followers of Jesus in History and Legend* (Oxford: Oxford University Press, 2006), 84.

But to stop giving ancient examples, let us come to those who became athletic contenders in quite recent times. We should consider the noble examples of our own generation. Because of jealousy and envy the greatest and most upright pillars were persecuted, and they struggled in the contest even to death. We should set before our eyes the good apostles. There is Peter, who because of unjust jealousy bore up under hardships not just once or twice, but many times; and having thus borne his witness he went to the place of glory that he deserved (5.1–4).[37]

In this passage, Clement describes how Peter and Paul were persecuted and struggled "even to death," which may be a term for martyrdom.[38] He also describes that Peter bore his "witness," which was a term on its way to becoming a technical term for martyrdom.[39] Nevertheless, while a grammatical analysis of this passage is favorable to the martyrdom of Peter, it is insufficient.

On the other hand, the context strongly implies Clement was referring to the martyrdom of Peter. *First Clement* 5 is part of the catalogue of examples in chapters 4–6. Clement provides seven examples of jealousy from the Old Testament in chapter 4 and then seven contemporary examples in chapters 5–6. Of the final list, Peter and Paul are introduced as individuals, jointly in that order. Each example in 5–6 emphasizes the evil conclusions that come from jealousy among the people of God and lead to division, violence, and the threat of death. The latter "contemporary" examples are distinguished from the first by their martyrological theme.[40] Clement indicates that a significant number of other persecuted Christians also became examples because

---

37. Bart D. Ehrman, ed. and trans., *The Apostolic Fathers* (Cambridge, MA: Harvard University Press, 2004), 1:43–45.

38. See Michael Licona, *The Resurrection of Jesus: A New Historiographical Approach* (Downers Grove, IL: InterVarsity Press, 210), 366–68. Licona observes that "unto death" appears sixteen times in the LXX and can mean dying or being on the verge of death. Jesus said, "My soul is very sorrowful, even to death" (Mark 14:34; Matt 26:38), yet he did not die from this intense grief. A generation later, Polycarp used the same phrase in a manner that undeniably referred to the death of Jesus: "He persevered to the point of death on behalf of our sins" (Polycarp *Letter to the Philippians* 1.2).

39. Theodor Zahn, *Introduction to the New Testament*, trans. Melancthon Jacobus, vols. 2–3 (Edinburgh: T&T Clark, 1909), 71.

40. Regarding the women Danaids and Dircae (6.2), Michael Holmes observes, "In ancient mythology, the daughters of Danaus were given as prizes to the winners of a race; thus it is likely that *Danaids* is a reference to Christian women being raped prior to being martyred. Dirce died

of their faithful witness through suffering. It seems highly doubtful Clement would have included Peter and Paul in this list if they were not martyred. Thus, Bart Ehrman appropriately concludes, "By the end of the first century and into the second it was widely known among Christians that Peter had suffered a martyr's death. The tradition is alluded to in the book of 1 Clement."[41] 1 Clement 5:1–4 is a second first-century passage that affirms the martyrdom of Peter.

The Ascension of Isaiah. Another reference to the martyrdom of Peter can be found in the early second-century Old Testament pseudepigraphical text *The Ascension of Isaiah* (c. AD 112–138). The passage referencing the fate of Peter is 4:2–3:

> Then will arise Beliar, the great prince, the king of this world, who has ruled it since its origin; and he will descend from his firmament in human form, king of wickedness, murderer of his mother, who himself is king of the world; and he will persecute the plant which the Twelve Apostles of the Beloved shall have planted; one of the Twelve will be delivered into his hands.[42]

In this passage, "Beliar" likely refers to Nero, the one who descends in human form. "Murderer" is a reference to the matricide committed by Nero, which confirms his identification. The "one of the twelve" is most likely Peter,[43] who was persecuted and "delivered into the hands" of Beliar (Nero). The most natural interpretation of this passage is that it refers to the martyrdom of Peter during the reign of Nero. This passage is admittedly not as strong as the first two, but it is an early attestation that contributes to the cumulative case that Peter died as a martyr.

Other early textual evidence for the martyrdom of Peter can be found in writings such as Ignatius (*Letter to the Smyrneans* 3:1–2, *Letter to the Romans* 4:3), *The Apocalypse of Peter*, *The Acts of Peter*, *The Apocryphon of James*, Dionysius of Corinth (Eusebius, *Ecclesiastical*

---

by being tied to the horns of a bull and then dragged to death." Michael W. Holmes, *The Apostolic Fathers: Greek Texts and English Translation*, 3rd ed. (Grand Rapids: Baker, 2007), 53.

41. Bart Ehrman, *Peter, Paul & Mary: The Followers of Jesus in History and Legend* (New York: Oxford, 2006), 84. Ehrman also says *1 Clement* "refers to the martyrdoms of Peter and Paul" (Ehrman, *The Apostolic Fathers*, 24).

42. Robert Henry Charles, *The Ascension of Isaiah* (London: A & C Black, 1900), 95.

43. There are parallels for the expression "one of the twelve" referring to Peter. See Jan N. Bremmer, "Tacitus and the Persecution of Christians," 314.

History 2.25.4), *Muratorian Canon*, Irenaeus (*Against Heresies* 3.1.1), and Tertullian (*Scorpiace* 15, *Prescription Against Heresies* 36). The early, consistent, and unanimous testimony is that Peter died as a martyr.

Paul

The traditional view is that Paul was beheaded as a martyr in Rome sometime during the latter part of the reign of Nero (AD 54–68). There are roughly ten relevant sources from the first two centuries.[44] The New Testament does not directly state Paul's fate, which is to be expected, since it covers material before his death. While there are significant Scriptural hints that Paul was about to experience martyrdom,[45] the strongest evidence comes from extrabiblical sources.

First Clement 5:5–7. First Clement is the first passage that refers to the martyrdom of Paul. This passage is both an early extrabiblical account of the death of Paul *and* was written in Rome, which is the traditional site of his execution in the AD 60s. Thus, Clement would have been in a unique position to assess the historicity of such a tradition firsthand. Given that Clement only refers to Paul by name twice, it is significant that one of them references his martyrdom. While the manner of his fate is lacking, the context (as with Peter) strongly implies that Paul died as a martyr:

> Because of jealousy and strife Paul pointed the way to the prize for endurance. Seven times he bore chains; he was sent into exile and stoned; he served as a herald in both the East and the West; and he received the noble reputation for his faith. He taught righteousness to the whole world, and came to the limits of the West, bearing his witness before the rulers. And so he was set free from this world and transported up to the holy place, having become the greatest example of endurance (1 Clement 5:5–7).[46]

---

44. For an in-depth analysis of each source, see McDowell, *Fate of the Apostles*, 99–114.

45. 2 Timothy 4:6–8 portrays Paul in prison for preaching the risen Christ (1:11) and anticipating his own death (4:6–8). He has stayed faithful to his mission to the end and expects his life to be "poured out as a drink offering," which is a reference to his looming martyrdom. Also, arguably the book of Acts depicts Paul traveling through Jerusalem on his way to martyrdom. See Udo Schnelle, *Apostle Paul: His Life and Theology*, trans. M. Eugene Boring (Grand Rapids: Baker, 2003), 81.

46. Ehrman, *The Apostolic Fathers*, 1:45.

Clearly, the author of 1 Clement wants to reveal Paul as a model of endurance for others to imitate. Paul, then, is given considerably more space than Peter, indicating he is the prominent person in this text.[47] Even though both Peter and Paul are among the pillars of the faith, Paul is the greatest example of endurance—he faced considerable persecution, yet continued to preach the gospel throughout the world, and was ultimately executed for his faith.

Ignatius, Letter to the Ephesians 12:2. In his letter to the Ephesians, Ignatius writes:

> I know who I am and to whom I am writing. I am condemned, you have been shown mercy; I am in danger, you are secure. You are a passageway for those slain for God; you are fellow initiates with Paul, the holy one who received a testimony and proved worthy of all fortune. When I attain to God, may I be found in his footsteps, this one who mentions you in every epistle in Christ Jesus (12:2).[48]

In this passage, Ignatius may be referring to Paul's meeting with the Ephesian elders when they sent him off to imprisonment and eventual martyrdom (Acts 20:17–38), such that Ignatius sees his own impending martyrdom as following Paul's example. Ignatius clearly aims to imitate Jesus,[49] but practically he is following in the footsteps of Paul. Since Ignatius aimed to face martyrdom in Rome courageously, it would make no sense for him to hold up Paul as a model of someone who "proved worthy of all fortune" if he had not died as a martyr in Rome. Ignatius was likely aware of an early tradition of the martyrdom of Paul.

Polycarp, Letter to the Philippians 9:1–2. Polycarp wrote this letter to the church at Philippi to encourage them to stay faithful to the core tenets of the faith (7:1), to live out the Christian faith (5:1), and to endure suffering as Christ, Paul, and the other apostles had (1:1; 2:3; 8:2; 9:2; 12:3). Polycarp encourages the church to follow the faith "that was delivered to us from the beginning" (7:2; cf. 3:1–3). Thus, Polycarp links the message he is delivering to the faith as taught by Jesus, Paul, and the first apostles.

47. Andreas Lindemann, "Paul in the Writings of the Apostolic Fathers," in *Paul and the Legacies of Paul*, ed. W. S. Babcock (Dallas: Southern Methodist University Press, 1990), 29.

48. Ehrman, *The Apostolic Fathers*, 1:233.

49. Ignatius, *Letter to the Ephesians*, 10:3.

Polycarp knew Paul and the other apostles had been martyred:

> Therefore I urge all of you to obey the word of righteousness
> and to practice all endurance, which you also observed with
> your own eyes not only in the most fortunate Ignatius, Zosimus,
> and Rufus, but also in others who lived among you, and in Paul
> himself and the other apostles. You should be convinced that
> none of them acted in vain, but in faith and righteousness, and
> that they are in the place they deserved, with the Lord, with
> whom they also suffered. For they did not love the present age;
> they loved the one who died for us and who was raised by God
> for our sakes. (*Letter to the Philippians* 9:1–2)[50]

The wider context of this passage portrays Polycarp guiding Christians
to imitate the model of Christ, even if they suffer for his name. The
example of Paul is in the wider context of Jesus, who was crucified
(8:1), and Ignatius, who died as a martyr (9:2). Then Polycarp refers to
Paul and the other apostles who "are in the place they deserved, with
the Lord, with whom they also suffered" (9:2). The clear implication is
that Paul suffered and faced a martyr's death as Jesus and Ignatius did.
Polycarp links their examples together as models for the Philippian
Christians to imitate. Bart Ehrman agrees that Polycarp was aware of
a tradition in which Paul and other apostles were in fact martyred.[51]

Other early textual evidence for the martyrdom of Paul can be
found in writings such as Ignatius (*Letter to the Romans* 4:3), Dionysius
of Corinth (Eusebius, *Ecclesiastical History* 2.25.4), Irenaeus (*Against
Heresies* 3.1.1), *The Acts of Paul*, and Tertullian (*Scorpiace* 15:5–6;
Prescriptions Against Heresies 24). The early, consistent, and unanimous
testimony is that Paul died as a martyr.

James, the Son of Zebedee

Along with Peter, James the son of Zebedee is the only other apostle whose fate is specifically mentioned in the New Testament (Acts
12:2). Compared to the other apostles, apocryphal accounts are rare for

---

50. Ehrman, *The Apostolic Fathers*, 1:345.

51. Ehrman, *The Apostolic Fathers*, 1:327. Polycarp specifically mentions Paul as an apostle,
so he must be using the term more broadly than one who is a member of the Twelve. Thus,
beyond the martyrdom of Paul, it is difficult to know what other apostles Polycarp refers to as
facing a similar fate.

James.[52] The most likely reason was because his martyrdom in Judea (AD 44) was so firmly entrenched in the early church and limited the trajectory of such stories.

Acts 12:2 reports the death of James by King Agrippa: "About that time Herod the king laid violent hands on some who belonged to the church. He killed James the brother of John with the sword" (Acts 12:1–2). The brevity of this account is quite unexpected in Acts, especially give the amount of space dedicated to the martyrdom of Stephen (6:8–7:58). And yet this brevity gives it the ring of authenticity. No parallels are drawn between his death and Jesus. No legendary details creep into the narrative. In fact, quite the opposite is true. The account reads like an official execution.[53]

Not only is the tradition of the martyrdom of James the son of Zebedee emphasized in the biblical record (Acts 12:2; Mark 10:39), it is also consistently affirmed by later church fathers from the second century onwards.[54] While the evidence for the martyrdom of James is not as strong as for Peter and Paul, and Gary Habermas would not include it in his list of minimal facts, given the historical reliability of the book of Acts[55] and the consistent testimony of the church fathers, there is good reason to believe Luke reliably records the martyrdom of James, the son of Zebedee.

James, the Brother of Jesus

Jewish historian Josephus provides the earliest account of the death of James in *Antiquities* 20.197–203 (c. 93/94). Unlike the Testimonium Flavianum, this passage is largely undisputed. In the wider context, Josephus offers a discussion about the difficulties Rome was having with its residents, which led to the invasion and destruction of Jerusalem in AD 70. The specific passage regarding James allows the

---

52. *The Apostolic History of Abdias* (sixth-seventh century) tells a story of James and his interaction with two pagan magicians who eventually confess Christ. *The Acts of Saint James in India* reports a tradition that he went to India along with Peter. See E.A. Wallis Budge, *The Contendings of the Apostles: Being the Histories and the Lives and Martyrdoms and Deaths of the Twelve Apostles and Evangelists* (Oxford: Oxford University Press, 1935), 246–52.

53. Dunn, *Beginning from Jerusalem*, 2:209.

54. Clement of Alexandria, *Outlines* Book 7; Eusebius, *Ecclesiastical History* 2.9.1; Chrysostom, *Homilies on the Acts of the Apostles* 26; Gregory of Nyssa, *Homily 2: On Stephen*; Philip of Side, *Christian History*; *The Apostolic Acts of Abdias* (Latin text).

55. See Craig S. Keener, *Acts: An Exegetical Commentary: Introduction and 1:1–2:14* (Grand Rapids: Baker, 2012), 90–220.

dating of his execution to be AD 62, since Josephus places his death between two Roman procurators, Festus and Albinus. Upon the death of Festus, Nero appointed Albinus as the next procurator, but during the brief transition period, Ananus, who was appointed high priest by Herod Agrippa II, seized the opportunity provided by the vacancy in the procuratorial government, to have James, the brother of Jesus, and others with him, stoned to death.

A later account occurs in Book 5 of the *Memoirs* of Hegesippus (c. AD 170, preserved by Eusebius, *Ecclesiastical History* 2.23.8–18). In this more detailed account, the scribes and Pharisees place James on the pinnacle of the temple and accuse him of leading the people astray through his proclamation of Christ. They throw him down, stone him, and then beat him with a club. This account is almost certainly filled with some legendary material, but it does affirm the charges raised against him and his death by stoning.

Other early traditions regarding the fate of James can be found in Clement of Alexandria (*Hypotyposes* Book 7) and *Pseudo-Clementines*.[56] There is also a gnostic source, the *Second Apocalypse of James* (62.7), that reports the stoning death of James.[57] For the martyrdom of James to be proclaimed by at least three early sects—Jews, Gnostics, and Christians—the tradition had to be early, widespread, and consistent.

The tradition that James was put to death by stoning is on solid historical ground. But some critics have claimed he was put to death for political reasons rather than religious reasons, and so James does not qualify as a martyr. Yet this is a false dichotomy. Like Jesus, James was put to death for political *and* religious reasons.

The key factor for determining the nature of James's crime is the penalty of stoning. Religious leaders attempted to stone Jesus on multiple occasions for blasphemy (John 8:58–59, 10:30–39, 11:8; cf. Luke 4:16–30). Darrell Bock rightly draws attention to this fact:

---

56. In final form, the Pseudo-Clementines were written before the end of the third and the beginning of the fourth centuries. Yet most scholars agree that both *Recognitions* and *Homilies* rely upon an earlier Jewish Christian source written in Syria in the third century. See Robert E. Van Voorst, *The Ascents of James: History and Theology of a Jewish-Christian Community*, Society of Biblical Literature Dissertation Series 112 (Atlanta, GA: Scholars Press, 1989), 2.

57. The *Second Apocalypse of James* is notoriously difficult to date accurately. Estimates range from AD 400, when the manuscripts at Nag Hammadi were buried, and AD 62, when James was killed.

What Law was it James broke, given his reputation within Christian circles as a Jewish Christian leader who was careful about keeping the Law? It would seem likely that the Law had to relate to his Christological allegiances and a charge of blasphemy. This would fit the fact that he was stoned, which was the penalty for such a crime, and parallels how Stephen was handled as well.[58]

James willingly put himself in danger as the leader of the Christian church in Jerusalem, which was based on the identity of its executed leader—his brother—as an enemy of Rome, and where many of the original leaders were persecuted for their faith. James was well aware of the cost of following Jesus, yet he continued in public leadership of the church, and it ultimately cost him his life.

Remaining Apostles

There is solid historical evidence for the martyrdoms of the four apostles above. There are moderately early traditions for the martyrdoms of Andrew and Thomas that cannot be simply dismissed as legend.[59] Some even believe John the son of Zebedee died as a martyr, but I remain unconvinced.[60] What about the rest of the apostles? The reality is that we simply do not know what happened to most of them, as Ehrman has observed. The first account of the skinning of Bartholomew appears around AD 500, and there are also reports he died by drowning, beating, and crucifixion. One of these accounts could be true, but we simply do not know. The historical record is inconclusive regarding the fate of most of the apostles of Jesus.

Yet there is also not a shred of evidence that any of the apostles recanted their faith. This is not merely an argument from silence that can be glibly dismissed. When discussions arose in the early church about how to handle believers who faltered under persecution, if there was any tradition of any of the apostles recanting, people would have certainly used it in their defense. And early critics of the Christian

---

58. Darrell L. Bock, *Blasphemy and Exaltation in Judaism: The Charge against Jesus in Mark 14:53–65* (Grand Rapids: Baker, 2000), 196 n. 30.

59. See McDowell, *Fate of the Apostles*, 157–85.

60. McDowell, *Fate of the Apostles*, 135–56.

faith, such as Celsus, Lucian, and Porphyry of Tyre, would have been eager to cite the tradition of an apostle who recanted his faith, if such a tradition had existed. The silence of history is revealing.

Two Key Objections

Before offering some concluding thoughts, it will be helpful to address two common objections.

Objection #1: The Apostles Were Not Given the Chance to Recant

According to Candida Moss, there is no evidence the apostles were given the chance to recant their beliefs and preserve their lives. As a result, we cannot prove they died *for* Christ, and so their deaths are evidentially meaningless.

Moss is right that there is not an early record of the apostles being offered the opportunity to recant. But this point does not have the force she thinks it does. They ministered in threatening environments with full awareness of the possible ramifications of following a leader crucified as an enemy of the Roman state. Jesus had warned his disciples that the world would hate and even persecute them, as they did him (John 15:18–25). They were aware of the fates of John the Baptist, Stephen, and even Jesus himself. Every time the apostles proclaimed the name of Christ, then, they knowingly risked suffering and death *for* Christ. Even so, they continued to teach and proclaim the risen Jesus.

Objection #2: Others Have Died for Their Beliefs

As noted previously, many people throughout history have died for their beliefs. This is true for Muslim radicals today. Should their claims be considered reliable as well?

This objection misses a key difference between modern martyrs and the apostles. Modern martyrs die for what they sincerely believe is true, but their knowledge comes secondhand (at best) from others. For instance, the Muslim terrorists who attacked the Twin Towers on 9/11 were not eyewitnesses of any events of the life of Mohammed.[61]

---

61. Technically, terrorists who kill for their faith are not martyrs. Rather than dying at the hands of others, they actively kill others in the name of their God. They are murderers, not martyrs.

They lived over thirteen centuries later and were willing to die for a tradition passed down to them from others. Yet the beliefs of the apostles, in contrast, stemmed from their personal experiences with Jesus, not stories received from others (Acts 1:3; 2:22–24). As noted earlier, virtually all scholars acknowledge that the apostles had experiences they believed were of the risen Jesus. There is a massive difference between willingly dying for the sake of religious ideas accepted from the testimony of others and willingly dying for the proclamation of a faith based upon one's own personal experience.

Conclusion

Popular apologists have often overstated both the evidence and significance of the deaths of the apostles for the truth of Christianity. Yet when carefully construed, the argument provides one important piece of a larger case that can be made for the resurrection. The willingness of the apostles to suffer and die for their faith does not prove Christianity is true. But it does show that they really believed it. They were not liars. They staked their lives on the belief that Jesus had risen from the grave and personally appeared to them. It is difficult to imagine what a group of ancient witnesses could have done to show greater depth of sincerity and commitment to the truth.

12

THE HISTORY AND CURRENT STATE
OF MODERN SHROUD RESEARCH

Barrie M. Schwortz

In 2018, we celebrated the fortieth anniversary of the historic, 1978 scientific examination of the Shroud of Turin performed by a team of American scientists known as the Shroud of Turin Research Project, or STURP.[1] Their examination marked the first time in the history of that venerated yet controversial relic that science was permitted to perform an in-depth battery of non-destructive tests directly on the cloth. Their purpose was simply to try and determine what formed the faint and enigmatic image that it bears. The team did NOT set out to prove that the image was that of Jesus or confirm the Resurrection. At the time, most people believed the image on the Shroud to be a painting or an artwork of some sort, or a scorch or even possibly a photographic image. The STURP team was formed to try and answer that one question, and their tests were designed for that specific purpose. Of course, many people in the world also believed that the cloth was the actual burial shroud of Jesus.

After conducting a nonstop, 120-hour series of carefully controlled experiments and nondestructive tests designed to collect as much data as possible, the team returned to the US and began the real work. They spent the next three years analyzing and evaluating their data and writing their methods, observations, and conclusions into more than twenty papers that were published in highly regarded peer-reviewed scientific

---

1. I have written this essay in narrative form to make it easier to read and more interesting. To that end, I have attempted to minimize footnotes and references. However, all the information discussed or referenced in this essay was taken directly from the Shroud of Turin Website (Shroud .com), most notably the Shroud History, Shroud Library, and Scientific Papers & Articles pages.

journals. In essence, they created the first real scientific database of Shroud science that still forms the foundation of all the Shroud research conducted to this day.

I have a unique perspective on the STURP project, since I was privileged to serve as the official documenting photographer for the team. That gave me a front row seat to everything that happened. My primary responsibility was to photographically document the team members throughout the planning stages and, ultimately, during the five days and nights of the testing in Turin, as well as documenting where on the Shroud they took their various samples from. This last responsibility resulted in my creating eight maps of the sample sites from where four of the major experiments took their data. These were also published in a scientific journal.

I was asked to write this article to address and summarize the current state of Shroud research, now that four decades have passed since we collected our data in 1978. As the founder and editor of The Shroud of Turin Website (www.shroud.com), which celebrated its twenty-fourth anniversary on the internet on January 21, 2020, I am in a rather unique position to do so. Over the years, I have stayed in constant touch with Shroud researchers and scholars around the world and have sometimes participated with them in new research. We have also archived online, in their entirety, some of the most important English language Shroud publications ever produced and have just started the archiving of the first Spanish language journal on our website. In the end, the website has become the oldest, largest, and most extensive Shroud resource on the internet, and it has allowed me to stay in close touch with the research still being done.

To properly understand the current state of Shroud research, we first have to go back and take a look at the founding of the STURP team, whose data formed the foundation of twentieth-century Shroud science. Without the history of the events between then and now, it will be difficult to understand where we currently stand. I should first acknowledge that some excellent Shroud science was done in the earlier part of the twentieth century by such pioneers as Paul Vignon and Pierre Barbet in the 1930s and Leo Vala and Giovanni Battista Judica-Cordiglia in the 1960s. By the time the STURP team had formed in 1977, there was an active research community in Turin being led by the International Center of Sindonology (the study of the Shroud). I am starting this article with the story of the STURP team, since I was a firsthand observer and participant in the events and can speak as an eyewitness to everything that occurred.

The Story of the STURP Team

I think it is best to start by reviewing how an independent, multi-disciplinary group of thirty-three scientists and researchers representing twenty different scientific or professional organizations came together as a team to perform an unprecedented series of non-destructive tests on the Shroud of Turin. Here is my firsthand account of what took place.

In 1976, a group of scientists from the Air Force Academy were working on a project with researchers at Los Alamos National Laboratory and its sister facility, Sandia Laboratories. On February 19, 1976, at Sandia Laboratories, John Jackson, Eric Jumper, Don Devan, Ken Stevenson, and Bill Mottern viewed the Shroud's so-called three-dimensional properties on the screen of a VP-8 Image Analyzer for the first time. Mottern was using the analog device to evaluate x-rays in his other work at the lab. The VP-8 basically took the density (lights and darks) of an image and converted it proportionately into vertical relief on a green screen display monitor similar to an oscilloscope.

The researchers used a 1931 Giuseppe Enrie photograph of the Shroud and input it into the VP-8 using a black and white video camera. They could then change the gain, rotate the image, and tilt it at different angles in 3D space. The results were nothing less than astounding! The Shroud image apparently had spatial (or distance or topographical) data encoded into its density that yielded an accurate, *natural relief of a human form* on the VP-8 screen, a result virtually unobtainable using any type of normal artwork or photographic image. Although this property had been suggested by Shroud scholars as far back as the early 1900s, this moment marked the first time that this property was visualized using a scientific instrument.

I should note again that at around this very same time in Turin, professors Giovanni Tamburelli and Nello Balossino were achieving similar results with the Shroud's image using computers and software they developed at their university.

Although the VP-8 Image Analyzer is completely obsolete by today's standards, it remains the catalyst that caused John Jackson and Eric Jumper to form the STURP team. It also provided us with the first important piece of scientific evidence that showed the Shroud image to have properties unlike any other known image.

Jackson and Jumper began looking for researchers with the required skills and talents that would be willing to volunteer their time and expertise and participate in a team project to study the Shroud's image. That is where I came into the picture. At the time, I was operating a commercial photographic studio in Santa Barbara, California, specializing in scientific and technical photography and had just completed a seven-month stint as a photographic consultant on an imaging project for Los Alamos National Laboratory. I was working with a local scientific imaging company (Oceanographic Services Inc.) that was a contractor to Los Alamos. The imaging scientist I worked with on that project was Don Devan, who also happened to be present at the VP-8 experiment!

Shortly after we completed the Los Alamos project, Don called me again and asked me what I knew about the Shroud of Turin. I reminded him that I am Jewish (and he reminded me that he was, too) and told him I had no knowledge or interest in the Shroud. He explained in rather technical terms that the VP-8 had revealed a new image property on the Shroud, stating, "There seems to be a correlation between image density and cloth-body distance." That got my attention, since I understood that it would be nearly impossible to encode such data into an image using photography or art mediums. To me, it seemed totally unlikely that such an image could have been created intentionally in the medieval era, but I firmly remained skeptical about the Shroud in general.

He then explained that a team was forming up to study the Shroud and perhaps get permission to examine it in person. They would need a photographer, and was I interested? I immediately said, "No!" I didn't want to get involved in a religious project. At that point, I was not aware of just how deeply scientific this project would be. In the end, the unique properties of the Shroud image are what finally convinced me to participate, but, to be totally honest, I was also thinking, "Free trip to Italy!"

As new needs were determined, new members were added to the team that were experts in the disciplines necessary to perform the tests that would be proposed. They represented prestigious scientific or academic organizations, including Los Alamos National Laboratory, Sandia Laboratory, Jet Propulsion Laboratory, Brooks Institute of Photography, the New England Institute, the Air Force Weapons Laboratory, and many others. In that manner, a multi-disciplinary team was formed with the sole purpose of studying the Shroud and its image. To that end, they began drafting a formal test plan that would outline the intended non-destructive experiments in great detail. After nearly seventeen months of intense team effort, the test plan was completed and STURP was officially formed. Our purpose was very clear: develop a battery of appropriate non-destructive scientific experiments and seek permission to physically examine the Shroud itself so we could characterize it chemically and physically and try to determine how the image was formed.

That plan was submitted to the legal owner of the Shroud at that time, King Umberto II, Duke of Savoy, whose family had owned the Shroud for over five centuries. Most people are unaware that the church was only the custodian of the Shroud in those days, and the Savoy family were the legal owners. Our permission came from the King, not from the church. I personally believe that if it were up to the church alone, we probably never would have been granted permission to examine it. To assist us in our liaison with the King, the church, and the Turin custodians, we worked closely with the late Fathers Peter Rinaldi, Francis Filas, and Adam Otterbein of the Holy Shroud Guild in Esopus, New York, who provided us with much needed support and assistance.

After working in smaller regional groups for over sixteen months, STURP came together in September 1978, one month before the team was scheduled to leave for Turin, at a meeting called the "Dry Run." It was there that all the team members met each other (many for the first time), tested their instruments and equipment, some of which was custom designed and fabricated for the project, and rehearsed the procedures they intended to use on the Shroud.

It was the culmination of a massive amount of work and planning, and it resulted in the formation of an amazing team of multi-disciplinary researchers working together with a single goal. After having my doubts at the beginning of the process, I was very happy to have ultimately agreed and joined the team. I was surrounded by a group of scientists that were dedicated, serious, disciplined, and empirical. They taught me that to do good science, you do an experiment and follow the data. They also represented around twenty different laboratories and scientific or professional organizations, which had the added benefit of eliminating any possibility of this turning into an agenda-driven project, since there was no single organization that had any more influence or control than any other. In the end, it allowed us to work together as a team and focus completely on our single goal in a truly honest and unbiased scientific manner. It was a great learning experience for me.

It has been my observation that just when you think that everything is settled, a new obstacle appears. That trend seemed to run consistently throughout every step during the first seventeen months of the project, and at every step we overcame the obstacles and moved forward. Then, late on the evening of September 28, 1978, the night before we were scheduled to fly to Italy, we received the shocking news that Pope John Paul I had died suddenly in Rome. What impact might this have on our examination?

At that moment in history, there were no faxes, texts, or emails. It was either postal mail or the telephone, so the team members found themselves on the phone until well past midnight that evening, discussing the ramifications of the Pope's death and what impact that might have on our examination of the Shroud. In the end, it was decided we would proceed as planned, not knowing for sure whether our permission to examine the cloth would still be honored. We had already purchased airline tickets, made the hotel reservations, and shipped around eighty wooden crates of equipment and instruments to Turin. The die was cast. The next day, September 29, 1978, the team met at Kennedy International Airport, boarded the plane, and we were off!

STURP arrived in Turin on September 30, 1978, four weeks into the five-week public exhibition commemorating the Shroud's four-hundredth anniversary in Turin. We were immediately notified upon arrival that all eighty crates of the equipment we shipped to Italy in advance had been seized and was being held by Italian customs. After a very stressful five day delay, days that were originally scheduled for setting up and calibrating our equipment and instruments, the equipment was finally released, and the team members loaded it all into the Royal Palace, where the examination would take place. Having lost most of our originally scheduled time for setup, we had to spend the next day and a half working around the clock to unpack, set up, and calibrate everything before the Shroud was taken off public display and brought to us for the examination. It was a hectic thirty-six hours, and nobody slept.

On October 8, 1978, at around 10:45 p.m., and slightly ahead of schedule, the Shroud was brought from the Cathedral, where it had been publicly displayed, through the Guarini Chapel and into the rooms in the Royal Palace where STURP would examine the cloth.

The first twelve hours were reserved for Swiss criminalist Max Frei and Professors Baima Bollone and Giovanni Riggi and their respective teams of Italian researchers. When they had finished their experiments, STURP began executing their detailed test plan, which consisted of a battery of non-destructive tests and data collecting. They spent the next 108 hours working virtually around the clock to complete their battery of tests in a variety of important disciplines.

These tests consisted of multiple types of photography, including photomosaic, macro and micro photography, spectrally resolved quad-mosaics, ultraviolet reflectance and fluorescence photography, transmitted light photography, and documentation photography. Other testing included x-ray radiography and x-ray fluorescence, as well as infrared reflectance and fluorescence spectroscopy, surface adhesive tape sampling, and ultra-violet and visible spectroscopy. I will not go into further detail in this essay, since the STURP materials are all now available online at Shroud.com, where you can read them for yourself.

Upon completion of their data collection efforts in Turin, STURP returned to the US and spent the next three years reducing and evaluating their data, writing their results into formal scientific papers and submitting them to the finest scientific journals of the day. A total of twenty-four papers were published between 1980 and 1984, most of them in highly respected peer-reviewed publications.

STURP held annual meetings during these years, at which the team gathered to review and refine their data. Their final formal meeting was held at Connecticut College in New London, Connecticut, on October 10 and 11, 1981, at an invitation-only symposium closed to the public. It was at this meeting that they issued a summary of their final report. Here is an excerpt:

> The basic problem from a scientific point of view is that some explanations which might be tenable from a chemical point of view, are precluded by physics. Contrariwise, certain physical explanations which may be attractive are completely precluded by the chemistry ... there are no chemical or physical methods known which can account for the totality of the image, nor can any combination of physical, chemical, biological or medical circumstances explain the image adequately. Thus, the answer to the question of how the image was produced or what produced the image remains, now, as it has in the past, a mystery.
>
> We can conclude for now that the Shroud image is that of a real human form of a scourged, crucified man. It is not the product of an artist. The blood stains are composed of hemoglobin and also give a positive test for serum albumin. The image is an ongoing mystery and until further chemical studies are made, perhaps by this group of scientists, or perhaps by some scientists in the future, the problem remains unsolved.[2]

In the end, the STURP team could not answer the primary question their research was designed to resolve, "How was the image formed?" We could tell you what it is not—not a painting, not a scorch, not a photograph—but we could not determine any mechanism that could account for both the chemical and physical properties of the image. In addition to the scientific papers published by the team, they also received some very positive media coverage in several major publications, including an article in *Life Magazine* in December 1979 and a large spread in *National Geographic* in 1980. For the next ten years, many people around the world reasonably believed that the Shroud of Turin was indeed the burial cloth of Jesus of Nazareth.

---

2. "A Summary of STURP's Conclusions," accessed June 12, 2020, https://www.shroud .com/78conclu.htm.

Of course, the story of Shroud science in the twentieth century does not begin or end with STURP, but I have not quite finished their story yet. When STURP's work formally came to an end in October 1981, many of the researchers wanted to continue their research. They understood that the massive amount of data they collected in 1978 helped to answer some questions about the Shroud and its image (proving it was not the product of an artist) and characterized it chemically and physically, but they also knew that their data raised a whole new set of additional questions that would require further examination of the cloth. They decided that a new team, STURP II, should be formed, in part to deepen the research and answer the many new questions that were raised in 1978, and, in part, to explore new facets of Shroud research that had been suggested by the data.

To that end, in 1984 a new group of researchers was gathered, including some who had been members of the original STURP team along with a number of new colleagues, all of them representing important disciplines critical to a further examination of the Shroud. Again, they developed a test plan and protocols for twenty-six different nondestructive experiments, and, interestingly, experiment number twenty-six on their list was radiocarbon dating.

They submitted their test plan and proposal to (then) Cardinal Ratzinger (later Pope Benedict), who reviewed it, approved it, and forwarded it to Pope John Paul II. Sadly, here is where this part of the story comes to an abrupt end. Apparently, several of the Pope's advisors from the Pontifical Scientific Academy convinced him that STURP II would cause harm to the Shroud. This is rather ironic, since the original STURP team showed more care with the Shroud than some of the Italian researchers did in 1978 and had proven themselves to be very careful in their handling of the cloth during their entire examination. They had gone so far as to design and have fabricated a full-size custom steel table on which the Shroud could be fastened by magnets to avoid any harm to the cloth during their examination. Sadly, it appears that politics of some form was at the root of the denial, but the STURP II protocol was, in fact, denied. Unfortunately, only one part of the protocol was retained: the radiocarbon dating. Although STURP II continued their efforts until 1988, the next part of the story ended the STURP involvement forever.

I think the real sadness in this story (so far) is that an important opportunity to gather additional information directly from the Shroud was lost, leaving only the original STURP data as a basis for all the science over the next forty years. STURP never intended that their preliminary work would mark both the beginning and the end of its scientific examinations of the Shroud. Yet sadly, it was, and no in-depth study has been permitted since. When you think about it, a lot of questions remain unanswered because we never had that second opportunity.

So what exactly were STURP's contributions and achievements, considering that, in the end, they really could not answer their primary question? Here are my suggestions:

1. In an unprecedented series of tests, they performed the first-ever direct, in-depth scientific examination of the Shroud of Turin using a comprehensive array of then state-of-the-art non-destructive technologies.

2. They documented and characterized the chemistry and physics of the image and published more than twenty-four multi-disciplinary papers in credible scientific journals.

3. Their collective work still constitutes a major portion of the scientific database of published Shroud science and remains the basis for much of Shroud research to this day.

4. STURP demonstrated that modern science could investigate an emotionally charged, enigmatic, and highly controversial relic and do so in a truly professional, respectful, and unbiased manner. Most importantly, STURP set the example and formed the solid foundation upon which future Shroud science will be based.

Their legacy was secure, but from that point forward, STURP was completely and officially out of the picture, and for all practical purposes, their era of dominating Shroud research came to an end. For better or for worse, that is exactly what happened.

Unfortunately, what happened next was even worse.

In 1983, King Umberto II died and, in his will, left the Shroud to the living pope rather than to one of his heirs or the institution of the Roman Catholic Church. He must have realized that leaving it to the Church would mean that the 130 cardinals would have to vote each time a decision was needed regarding the Shroud. After consulting with his scientific advisors, he decided that such decisions should not be made by committee, but rather by a single person, the living pope. In 1985, the king's will was probated, and Pope John Paul II became the first legal owner of the Shroud of Turin outside of the Savoy family in over five centuries. Ownership would now pass in succession from pope to pope. The king made only one stipulation: the Shroud must remain in Turin forever.

When the pope rejected the STURP II proposal, he decided to keep just one of their recommended tests, radiocarbon dating. To that end, the word was sent out to a number of established radiocarbon dating laboratories to prepare specific proposals for dating the Shroud. This set off a rather unusual series of events that drew great concern from those Shroud scholars who were paying close attention. Frankly, the story is a rather long and complicated one, but it is critically important for you to know what took place so you can better understand and evaluate the validity of the radiocarbon dating results. I will do my best to summarize it here.

For three days, between September 29 and October 1, 1986, representatives of several radiocarbon dating laboratories met in Turin under the chairmanship of professor Carlos Chagas (president of the Pontifical Academy of Sciences) and held a workshop to develop the best protocol for radiocarbon dating of the Shroud. They agreed upon a protocol in which seven laboratories (five Accelerator Mass Spectrometry [AMS], two small counter) would participate. This was then submitted to both the pope and the Cardinal of Turin, and a few days later, on October 6, 1986, news of the meeting was released to the world's press.

What was not mentioned was the fact that Hong Kong-based field archaeologist and American Shroud scholar William Meacham had come all the way to Turin to participate in the meeting, since he had years of hands-on experience in using the C-14 dating method to date ancient Chinese archaeological materials. In 1983 and 1986, Meacham had written two important papers on the topic of dating the Shroud of Turin, well before any of the dating labs came on the scene. Sadly, since Meacham did not represent a major dating laboratory, he was not permitted to speak. That was too bad, since his knowledge and experience would certainly have been useful. As it turned out, many of the issues he raised and problems he predicted in his papers became reality just a few years later. Things were not getting off to a great start.

Then, about six months later, an article appeared in the Turin newspaper *La Stampa* that publicly quoted professor Luigi Gonella, the scientific advisor to Cardinal Ballestrero, the Archbishop of Turin, as saying that only two or three laboratories would be involved in the testing. This marked a rather dramatic change in the protocol developed at the Turin meeting, which had apparently been approved by the pope, and it prompted a response from representatives of the seven laboratories, who wrote a letter to Cardinal Ballestrero advising, "As participants in the workshop who devoted considerable effort to achieve our goal, we would be irresponsible if we were not to advise you that this fundamental modification in the proposed procedures may lead to failure."[3]

A few months later, Cardinal Ballestrero responded to the seven radiocarbon laboratories and informed them that on the advice of his scientific advisor, Professor Gonella, only three of their number, the Oxford, Arizona, and Zurich laboratories, had been chosen to perform the testing. Ballestrero's letter also stated that "experience in the field of archaeological radiocarbon dating" was their criterion (rather ironic considering their treatment of William Meacham the year before).[4] The cardinal also advised that certain other details of the 1986 protocol had been scrapped, including any further involvement of the Pontifical Academy of Sciences in the exercise.

Sadly, that last statement turned out to be false, although it took years before anyone found out. Based on the cardinal's letter, many people blamed professor Gonella for many of the questionable decisions made regarding the C-14 dating of the Shroud. Not until years later was it revealed that most of the actual decisions were still being

---

3. "Shroud History," accessed June 12, 2020, https://shroud.com/history.htm.

4. "Shroud History," accessed June 12, 2020, https://shroud.com/history.htm.

made clandestinely by professor Chagas and others at the Pontifical Academy of Sciences and that Gonella was just following their instructions. Although Gonella certainly made some mistakes (he was a professor, not a politician), he does not deserve all the blame for the poor decisions that were made.

The Turin authorities, on the advice of the Pontifical Scientific Academy and the Secretary of State of the Vatican, appointed Michael Tite, then director of research at the British Museum, as the person to act as supervisor of the three laboratories and to oversee certification of the samples. Shortly thereafter, the directors of the three chosen laboratories warned Cardinal Ballestrero: "As you are aware, there are many critics in the world who will scrutinize these measurements in great detail. The abandonment of the original protocol and the decision to proceed with only three laboratories will certainly enhance the skepticism of these critics." The chosen three declared themselves "hesitant to proceed" and requested the matter be given "further consideration." [5]

Everything seemed to be unraveling, and it appeared that the situation could not get any worse. Unfortunately, it did.

On January 13, 1988, the Turin newspaper *La Stampa* disclosed that Harry Gove (the inventor of the AMS radiocarbon dating method used by the three laboratories) and Garman Harbottle (of the Brookhaven C-14 lab in Upton, New York, where Gove was affiliated) wrote an open letter to the pope, as well as to *Nature* and the director of the British Museum, deploring the rejection of the seven-laboratory protocol. They claimed that the pope had been "badly advised" and "that he is making a mistake if he approves a limited or reduced version of the research whose outcome will be, to say the least, questionable."[6]

Two days later in a press release, Gove and Harbottle concluded, "The Archbishop's plan, disregarding the protocol, does not seem capable of producing a result that will meet the test of credibility and scientific rigor" and that "it is probably better to do nothing than to proceed with a scaled-down experiment."[7]

5. "Shroud History," accessed June 12, 2020, https://shroud.com/history.htm.

6. "Shroud History," accessed June 12, 2020, https://shroud.com/history.htm.

7. "Shroud History," accessed June 12, 2020, https://shroud.com/history.htm.

When asked, professor Gonella declined to explain the specific reasons for his choice of laboratories, terming it a private matter. Gove promptly became *persona non grata* and was totally eliminated from the proceedings. Writing open letters to the pope and having them published in the Italian press is obviously a bad idea. A few months later, he wrote directly to the pope outlining all that had transpired and appealed to him to persuade Cardinal Ballestrero to revert to the original protocol. His letter was ignored. Remember, this is the very same scientist who developed the AMS radiocarbon dating method that was ultimately used by the three laboratories to date the cloth, and he was a Shroud skeptic himself. In the end, Gove only got to be an observer to the testing, courtesy of the Arizona laboratory. These circumstances did not instill much confidence in the eyes of those following the proceedings.

In February 1988, Tite tried unsuccessfully to find control samples of a weave identical to the Shroud. This was critically important, since the testing was supposed to be a "blind study," in which case none of the researchers would know specifically which samples came from the Shroud. This lack of controls was just one issue that would help to foster skepticism when the results of the dating were finally released.

At 5 a.m. on April 21, the Shroud was secretly taken out of its casket, and at 6:30 a.m., Tite and the representatives of the three laboratories assembled at the cathedral. In the cathedral sacristy, the Shroud was unrolled and shown to the assembled representatives of the three chosen radiocarbon dating laboratories. Giovanni Riggi (who had participated in the 1978 examination alongside STURP) and Gonella reportedly spent two hours arguing about the exact location on the Shroud from which the sample should be taken. Compare this to the thoroughly detailed test plan that STURP prepared long before they ever arrived in Turin and you can understand why there was great concern in the Shroud world.

At 9:45 a.m., with a video camera recording his every move, Riggi cut a sliver from one edge and divided this into two, then divided one of the halves into thirds. In a separate room, and now unrecorded by any camera, the cardinal and Tite placed these three latter samples in sealed, opaque metal canisters for the respective laboratories to take away with them. At 1 p.m., the sample-taking for carbon-dating purposes was formally completed, and the laboratory representatives departed. The next day, on April 22, the news of the taking of the samples was released to the world's press.

It is interesting to note that on April 24, having safely arrived back in Tucson with their Shroud sample, Damon and Donahue of the Arizona laboratory informally opened the containers, immediately recognizing the characteristic weave of the Shroud on opening sample A1. No surprise there, and so much for a "blind study."

During the next few months, the three laboratories ran their procedures and calculated their results. On May 6, in the presence of Harry Gove, who had been invited to be present, the Shroud sample was run through the Arizona system. With the calibration applied, the date concluded was AD 1350. The laboratories completed their work a month later. Tite received the Zurich laboratory's findings in July, and the results from the Oxford laboratory a few weeks later.

Much to everyone's shock, on August 26, the *London Evening Standard* carried banner headlines declaring the Shroud to be a fake made in 1350. The source, Cambridge librarian Stephen Luckett, had no known previous connection with the Shroud or with the carbon dating work, but in this article declared that scientific laboratories are "leaky institutions."[8] The story was picked up around the world. Without quoting its source, on September 18, the *Sunday Times* publishes a front-page story headlined: "Official: The Turin Shroud is a Fake." Teddy Hall of the Oxford lab and Tite firmly denied any responsibility for this story or the obvious leaks to the media that have revealed their results months before the publication of their data in the scientific literature.

Then, on October 13, at a press conference held in Turin, Cardinal Ballestrero, Archbishop of Turin, made an official announcement that the results of the three laboratories performing the carbon dating of the Shroud have determined an approximate 1325 date for the cloth.

At a similar press conference held at the British Museum in London, it was announced that the Shroud dated between AD 1260 and 1390. The moment was immortalized in a now-famous photograph of Hall, Tite, and Robert Hedges sitting in front of a blackboard with

---

8. "Shroud History," accessed June 12, 2020, https://shroud.com/history.htm.

"1260–1390!" written boldly in chalk behind them. There seemed to be an arrogance to their presentation, perhaps best demonstrated by the exclamation point after the dates. Perhaps this was a new form of scientific notation! Of course, newspaper headlines immediately branded the Shroud a fake and declared that the Catholic Church had accepted the results. Things had truly gone from bad to worse.

Finally, on February 16, 1989, the official results of the Shroud radiocarbon dating were published in the prestigious scientific journal *Nature*. This had twenty-one signatories and declared that the results "provide conclusive evidence that the linen of the Shroud of Turin is medieval."[9] Game over!

As the rest of the world accepted the C-14 dating results and moved on, many scholars in the Shroud world were left stunned and wondering what happened. There was a considerable amount of credible historical evidence that pointed to the existence of the Shroud well before 1260, the earliest possible date given by the C-14 labs. And of course, much of the published STURP science pointed towards authenticity and against the possibility of it being any form of artwork.

However, all of this evidence was now being totally disregarded by just about everyone in favor of that single C-14 test that garnered banner headlines around the world. It was both frustrating and disheartening. In the real world of science, when you perform one hundred tests and ninety-nine point in one direction and one points in the other direction, that single one is labeled an "outlier" and is typically discarded. In the case of the Shroud, just the opposite occurred. They threw away the ninety-nine in favor of the one that claimed the Shroud was a fake.

If that wasn't bad enough, on March 25, 1989, an article in the *Daily Telegraph* in London announced that forty-five anonymous businessmen and rich friends had donated one million pounds sterling to create a chair of archaeological sciences at Oxford in order to perpetuate the radiocarbon-dating laboratory created by Professor Edward Hall. The first recipient to hold this chair was the British Museum's Michael Tite, who left the museum to become the new director of the Oxford University Research Laboratory!

---

9. "Shroud History," accessed June 12, 2020, https://shroud.com/history.htm.

I hate to think that money might have been an issue in any of this, but radiocarbon dating has become a very profitable business around the globe. It would appear that, if nothing else, debunking the Shroud was very good for business.

For the next twelve years, most Shroud research came to a halt, and many Shroud scholars simply accepted the dating results and walked away. The few remaining researchers proposed a number of different theories, all attempting to explain what went wrong with the C-14 dating. Some theories were very scientific, others less so, but each was examined, discussed, and debated in great detail. In the end, all were ultimately rejected or discarded. To this day, there is still not agreement amongst pro-authenticity researchers on this question.

For those of us familiar with the science and history of the cloth, the C-14 dating results seemed unexplainable and contrary to all the other evidence. Many of us continued to study the Shroud, but we did not have an explanation either. In the eyes of the world, however, we were like flat-earthers.

That all started to change in 2000.

In the years after the radiocarbon dating, Shroud researchers focused mainly on what might have gone wrong with the dating process itself, or what external event might have occurred to modify or skew the age of the linen. However, at the Sindone 2000 Worldwide Congress held in Orvieto, Italy, in August 2000, independent Shroud researchers Joseph Marino and Sue Benford presented a paper that dealt with the C-14 issue from a new perspective. Titled, "Evidence for the Skewing of the C-14 Dating of the Shroud of Turin Due to Repairs," it suggested that the corner where the C-14 sample had been taken from had undergone an earlier, undocumented repair; did not represent the main body of the cloth since new material had been interwoven with the old; and was thus anomalous and invalid for accurately dating the Shroud.[10]

During the course of their research, they had consulted three different independent textile experts and showed each of them close-up photographs of the Shroud C-14 samples (without revealing they were from the Shroud). All the experts independently reported that they

---

10. Joseph G. Marino and M. Sue Benford, "Evidence for the Skewing of the C-14 Dating of the Shroud of Turin Due to Repairs," https://www.shroud.com/pdfs/marben.pdf.

saw evidence of very skillful reweaving in the samples. This came as a surprise to Benford and Marino, so they deepened their research and discovered that a technique known as *French invisible reweaving* had been developed and perfected by the French court, in part to repair tapestries that were imaged on both sides. It also happened that the Shroud itself was in France at that moment in its history.

I was sitting in the front row at Sindone 2000 when Benford and Marino presented that paper, and I was dumbfounded. What they were suggesting was actually very simple and plausible compared to the many complex theories that had been proposed since the 1988 dating. Since only one sample was taken for the testing, and that site was selected at the very last moment, was it possible that the site itself was the problem? There were no other samples taken from elsewhere on the cloth to use as a control, so there was nothing to compare the results to. In essence, Benford and Marino were saying that the C-14 dating was correct but that the real problem was actually the poor choice of the sample site. One did not need to be a nuclear physicist to understand that theory!

Sir Arthur Conan Doyle once wrote through the lips of Sherlock Holmes, "When you have eliminated the impossible, whatever remains, *however improbable*, must be the truth."[11] And the principle of Ockham's razor states (paraphrasing) that the simplest answer requiring the fewest assumptions is most likely the correct one. In the case of the C-14 dating of the Shroud, I realized that Benford and Marino's research may have stumbled onto something that everyone else had missed and that needed to be taken seriously.

As they exited the stage after their presentation, I approached them and asked if I could reprint their paper on Shroud.com. They agreed, and I did. Within a day or two of posting their paper on the site, I received a rare and angry phone call from Ray Rogers, the lead chemist on the STURP team from Los Alamos National Laboratory, who chastised me for publishing it. He was upset that I was willing to include it on Shroud.com, since it had been written by non-scientists that he typically referred to as the "lunatic fringe."

---

11. Doyl, *The Sign of Four* (London: Spencer Blackett, 1890), 111. https://www.gutenberg.org/files/2097/2097-h/2097-h.htm#chap06.

I explained why I felt their work was valid (it had followed proper scientific method and provided a novel but viable explanation for the dating results) and why I thought the public should at least hear about it. In my mind, it was no less feasible than some of the other theories that had been proposed, and was far simpler and more plausible than most of them. He then said he still had some Shroud samples in his safe, and he was going to examine them again and prove Marino and Benford were wrong.

Several hours later, he called back and simply said, "I can't believe it, but I think they are right!" He had found evidence in his own samples that corroborated their results. He also reviewed all of the STURP data and found additional corroboration there.

What Rogers actually had in his safe were Shroud samples given to him by professor Gilbert Raes, the Belgian textile expert who was permitted to perform a basic textile analysis of the Shroud in 1973. He had removed a small, triangular section from one corner of the Shroud for his analysis and in 1979 gave Rogers some of the threads and fibers from that sample. Rogers had not used them for any other research, so they were still basically intact. He also knew that the Raes sample site was located directly adjacent to the C-14 sample site and that some threads from the Raes sample were common to both.

Rogers's microscopic and chemical examination revealed cotton interwoven with the linen and an end-to-end splice in one of the samples. He also found evidence of gum Arabic and rose madder dye that had been intentionally applied to the surface of the fibers in an apparent attempt to match the color of the rewoven area to the rest of the cloth. Rogers realized these observations were very controversial and enlisted the aid of another, independent scientist, John Brown, to review his work.

Brown was a materials scientist and expert microscopist in Atlanta, Georgia, and made a detailed examination of Rogers's samples, methods, observations, and conclusions and corroborated all of his findings. He documented everything photographically and compiled his results into an article titled "Microscopical Investigation of Selected Raes Threads from the Shroud of Turin," which I ultimately published on Shroud.com in January 2005.

Rogers wanted to formalize his results but realized he would first have to obtain a portion of the actual C-14 Reserve Sample for analysis. You might recall that they cut a long strip for the C-14 sampling, divided it in half, divided one-half into thirds for distribution to the three labs, and set aside the other half as the official Reserve Sample. Rogers understood that the provenance of the Raes samples he used as the basis for his primary research had been in his safe for twenty-five years and could easily be challenged.

He then contacted Thomas D'Muhala, former STURP President, who had previously received a small part of the Reserve Sample from Professor Luigi Gonella (the Scientific Advisor to Archbishop Ballestrero during the 1978 STURP examination and the 1988 C-14 dating). The sample had an unbroken, documented chain of custody, and D'Muhala had already allowed Doctor Alan Adler, STURP blood chemist, to examine it.

D'Muhala provided Rogers with this same Reserve Sample for his analysis and direct examination. Based on his analyses of this documented sample, Rogers found exactly the same properties that he had observed on the Raes samples. He then compiled all his data into an article that he submitted to the peer-reviewed journal *Thermochimica Acta*. After a seven-month review process (twice the normal review time) in which many corrections and revisions were made, the paper was finally accepted for publication and appeared in the January 20, 2005 issue.[12] Here is what it concluded:

1. Preliminary estimates of the kinetics constants for the loss of vanillin from lignin indicate a much older age for the cloth than the radiocarbon analyses propose.

2. The radiocarbon sampling area is uniquely coated with a yellow-brown plant gum containing dye lakes.

3. Pyrolysis-mass-spectrometry results from the sample area, coupled with microscopic and microchemical observations, prove that the radiocarbon sample was not part of the original cloth of the Shroud of Turin.

---

12. Raymond N. Rogers, "Studies on the Radiocarbon Sample from the Shroud of Turin," *Thermochimica Acta* 425 (2005): 189–94, http://www.shroud.it/ROGERS-3.PDF.

4. The radiocarbon date was thus not valid for determining the true age of the Shroud.

The above list of conclusions is a bit technical, but the only one you really need to remember is item four. Rogers's paper became the first paper published in the peer-reviewed scientific literature to directly challenge the 1988 radiocarbon dating results. Although he initially set out to prove Benford and Marino wrong, in the end his detailed analysis wound up proving that they were right. Sadly, Rogers died about six weeks after the paper was published, on March 8, 2005.

In July 2008, a new paper by Benford and Marino was published in the peer-reviewed scientific journal *Chemistry Today*.[13] Their new research further supported the earlier data and provided additional evidence for an anomalous sample. It was also the second paper to be published in the refereed scientific literature that challenged the 1988 dating results. Sadly, less than a year later, Sue Benford died unexpectedly after a brief illness.

As a final note to the Rogers and Benford-Marino theory, a group of nine researchers from Los Alamos National Laboratory, headed by the late physicist Robert Villarreal, performed a battery of tests on some of the Raes samples Rogers gave them just before his death. Their results corroborated all of Rogers's earlier observations and findings and were presented at a Shroud conference in Columbus, Ohio, in August 2008. I could go on and quote a lot more material, but this is getting very long, and the details are all available on shroud.com.

In spite of all the evidence to the contrary, most people in the world simply accepted the C-14 dating results and moved on. To this day, much of the public has never heard about the credible scientific and historical evidence challenging the dating results. Apparently, "Shroud Is a Fake" makes a much better headline than, "Scientific Evidence May Prove the Shroud is Authentic." Even many pro-authenticity Shroud scholars rejected Rogers's and Benford and Marino's work for a variety of reasons. I often say that if agreement were necessary for friendship in the Shroud world, *no one* would have *any* friends!

---

13. M. Sue Benford and Joseph G. Marino, "Discrepancies in the Radiocarbon Dating Area of the Turin Shroud," *Chemistry Today* 26:4 (2008): 4–12, https://www.shroud.com/pdfs/benfordmarino2008.pdf.

Personally, I believe that the most credible body of evidence we have regarding the C-14 dating results, from both a scientific and historical perspective, points to the anomalous nature of the sample used for dating the Shroud as the primary reason for the medieval result. Since much of this data appeared in respected, peer-reviewed scientific journals, I will continue to consider this the best answer we have until new research comes along that provides a better explanation, or until another *properly conducted* radiocarbon dating is permitted.

After the 1988 dating, most pro-authenticity science was generally disregarded, and very few credible scientific journals would even consider publishing any new research if the words "Shroud of Turin" appeared anywhere in the text. Fortunately, over the ensuing years, in great part because of the internet and the growing availability of most of the science, there has been a resurgence of interest on the part of both Shroud scholars and the general public.

I realize that so far, this article discusses only the 1978 STURP research and the 1988 radiocarbon dating, but these two events truly dominated the last forty years of Shroud science and have greatly influenced the current status of Shroud research. Of course, throughout the bleak years after the dating results were released, there was always an active core group of Shroud researchers that continued their work, and that work continues to this day.

The Current State of Shroud Research

I would love to report that Shroud research has made great progress in recent years, but that would be grossly overstating the case. There is still research being conducted in the United States by STURP cofounder John Jackson and his research group at the Turin Shroud Center in Colorado Springs. Some excellent work is being done in Italy by Paolo Di Lazzaro and his research team at the ENEA Center in Frascati, and they have published a long list of scientific papers in recent years. Giulio Fanti in Padua also continues to conduct experiments and publish on various aspects of the Shroud.

There is also the private, international online Shroud Science Group (SSG) with around 120 members composed of Shroud scholars from around the world. Unfortunately, they are primarily a discussion group, and aside from one paper coauthored jointly by around twenty of their members ten years ago, they have not really advanced the science in any significant way as a group. I should note that all the individual researchers I mentioned above are also members of the SSG.

Of course, there is the International Study Center on the Shroud (CISS) in Turin, the oldest Shroud research organization in the world. They continue to study the Shroud and work closely with the Ateneo Pontificio Regina Apostolorum (Pontifical University) in Rome to educate new Shroud scholars and researchers by offering accredited courses onsite and online in both Italian and English. The CISS holds annual meetings where scholars come together to share information and evaluate new research.

There are still many other international Shroud research organizations, in Spain, France, Portugal, England, Norway, Poland, Mexico, Panama, Peru, etc., and many dedicated Shroud researchers around the world. Every few years, a Shroud conference is held somewhere in the world where scholars can attend and share their latest work with each other. Researchers continue to study various aspects of the Shroud's science and history, but, again, without making any truly significant progress.

All of these researchers, and Shroud studies in general, suffer from the same problem. No new data has been made available in forty years, and there is a real limit to how much more can be extracted from the forty-year-old data STURP collected. The fact that it has been used by so many for so long certainly attests to the quality of their original work, but everything has its limits. In the realm of Shroud science, that limit has been reached, which results in a lot of repetition and rehashing of earlier research without much real forward progress being made.

To make matters worse, countless theories are now posted online in blogs and videos by unqualified researchers that are mostly expressing their personal opinions without any credible scientific basis, adding to the already vast, often confusing, and frequently erroneous information that is available to the public. I have written several editorials warning people not to use YouTube videos, blog sites, and television documentaries as their basis for Shroud studies, but to little avail. Television is primarily an entertainment medium. Real science is still published in credible, peer-reviewed journals.

Sadly, if I had to choose one word to describe the current state of Shroud research (the purpose of this essay), I would have to choose "stagnant." I believe it is virtually impossible to make any further significant scientific progress in our understanding of the Shroud of Turin until new data can be collected using modern, twenty-first-century technology. Without additional testing, very little progress can be made. Remember, there was already enough scientific evidence to convince even me, a non-Christian (and a total skeptic back in 1978), that the most plausible explanation for the Shroud of Turin is that it is the cloth that wrapped the crucified body of Jesus of Nazareth. In the end, with all the credible evidence we have to support that view, I challenge the skeptics to prove it untrue.

13

RACING TOWARD THE TOMB: PURITY AND SACRIFICE IN THE FOURTH GOSPEL

Beth M. Sheppard

In a 2014 article, Kent Brower rightly observes that the topic of purity in the Fourth Gospel has largely escaped scholarly attention.[1] Brower is clearly throwing down a gauntlet. Unable to resist the challenge to explore this overlooked dimension, what follows is an investigation into how the threads of Christology, sacrifice, and purity are deftly interwoven in John's portrait of Jesus.[2] In his own work, Brower studies three passages where, even if the word "purity" itself might not be present, the idea of cleansing or sanctification in those pericopes implies it. His attention is specifically drawn to the wedding of Cana/temple expulsion sequence, the foot-washing prior to the meal that was shared before

---

1. Kent Brower, "Purity in the Gospel of John," in *Purity: Essay in Bible and Theology*, ed. Arseny Ermakov and Andrew Brower Latz (Eugene, OR: Pickwick Publications, 2014), 114. Brower clearly means the purification system within Judaism in particular. Themes related to cleansing in a more general sense have occasionally been recognized in the Fourth Gospel. For example, Barnabas Lindars links the water from John 9:34 to spiritual cleansing. Barnabas Lindars, *The Gospel of John* (Grand Rapids: Wm. B. Eerdmans, 1972), 583.

2. This is a different program than is represented in the literature of the Third Quest with regard to purity. There, discussion often turns on whether or not the historical Jesus abrogated the purity laws, was indifferent to them, or observed them. For instance, Tom Holmén takes the last position, writing, "Jesus did not oppose the ritual purity paradigm, nor did he aim at devaluing it. Instead, he can be said to have had a positive and appreciative disposition to it. The paradigm was of relevance to him." Tom Holmén, "Jesus and the Purity Paradigm" in *Handbook for the Study of the Historical Jesus*, eds. T. Holmén and S. E. Porter, vol. 3 (Leiden: Brill, 2011), 2739.

Passover, and Jesus' prayer immediately prior to his arrest.[3] This particular project takes up where Brower lets off: the empty tomb.

To be sure, when it comes to issues related to purity, there are several burning questions that might be raised about the aftermath of Jesus' death. For instance, if Jesus' death on the cross is sacrificial, is there a particular level of purity required for him to serve as the victim? Then, following his execution, do the resurrected Jesus and his empty grave function as sources of corpse defilement that impart ritual impurity to his disciples and other mourners? The answers to these questions affect how one might interpret passages such as John 20:3–8, where Peter and the Beloved Disciple race to the burial site when they learn that Jesus' body is missing (20:3–8).

Actually, it seems as though the Evangelist may have wrestled with these same issues. Indeed, despite the fact that Jesus undergoes a criminal's death at Golgotha and interment in a tomb, it is possible to read the text in a way that John's Jesus, who also has an intimate relationship with God as the pre-existent *logos*, the Lamb of God, the only born of the Father, and Savior of the world, is scrupulous about ritual cleanliness and almost completely escapes any sort of defilement, including corpse impurity.

Blood and Water

Before diving into a discussion of purity and sacrifice in the Gospel, however, it is important to acknowledge that this study was actually inspired by reading the works on the resurrection by Gary Habermas. Indeed, this interest in purity is the result of Habermas pulling my attention again and again to John 19:34–35.[4] In that passage, the Beloved Disciple, who was by his own account a witness to events, records that a spear was thrust into Jesus' side on the cross. This vicious assault on Jesus' body with the Roman weapon resulted, as the Evangelist tells us, in a wound from which spilled both water and

---

3. In regard to the prayer, Brower maintains that Jesus uses the term "sanctify" to indicate that the disciples have been previously cleansed (purified) through Jesus' word (15:3) and are now to be consecrated for service (17:17). Brower, "Purity in the Gospel of John," 128–30.

4. Gary R. Habermas and Michael R Licona, *The Case for the Resurrection of Jesus* (Grand Rapids: Kregel, 2004), 102; Antony Flew and Gary R. Habermas, *Did the Resurrection Happen? A Conversation with Gary Habermas and Antony Flew,* ed. David Baggett (Downers Grove, IL: IVP Books, 2009), 26; Gary Habermas, *Historical Jesus: Ancient Evidence for the Life of Christ* (Joplin, MO: College Press, 1996), 74.

blood, both elements of which are connected with purity, as will be explicated below.

Now, Habermas seized on the presence of water and blood, not because he himself was interested in the issue of ritual cleanliness, but in order to marshal it as evidence that the type of wound Jesus received was lethal; it would have ended Jesus' life had he not already perished from hanging on the cross.[5] If Jesus' death can be proven incontrovertibly, Habermas clearly reasons, then the empty tomb cannot be

---

5. Habermas's own explanation for the presence of both water and blood in 19:34–35 owes much to his understanding of modern medicine. He asserts that the presence of the two fluids likely indicates that the spear thrust pierced the pericardial sac that surrounds the heart. The second-century AD physician Galen, who lived two generations after Jesus, is aware of the existence of the pericardium and references it when giving advice on how to study the heart and circulatory system when conducting a vivisection. See Galen, *De Anatomicis Administrationibus*, trans. Charles Singer (Oxford: Oxford University Press, 1956), 190–91. Not every sect of medical practitioners in the Greco-Roman world, however, viewed dissection and anatomy favorably, and many held firm to the theory of the four humours, a hypothesis which persisted through the Middle Ages. See Hippocrates, "On the Nature of Man," in *Hippocratic Writings*, trans. J. Chadwick and W. N. Mann (London and NY: Penguin Books, 1950), 261–62. While Plato did ascribe to the four elements of air, earth, fire, and water as related to health, Aristotle and his contemporaries emphasized the humoral theory of phlegm, black bile, yellow bile, and blood. On humoral theory, see Vivian Nutton, *Ancient Medicine* (London and NY: Routledge, 2013), 117. In biblical medicine, the heart, *lev*, is viewed as the seat of the emotions, and the many citations to this effect have been gathered by Fred Rosner. See Fred Rosner, *Medicine in the Bible & The Talmud*, augmented ed. (Hoboken NJ: KTAV Publishing/Yeshiva University Press, 1955), 93.

Regarding modern anatomy, Habermas's linking the wound in 19:34–35 with the pericardial sac may be problematic. Although he references an article by William D. Edwards, Wesley J. Gabel, et al., "On the Physical Death of Jesus Christ," (JAMA 255.11 [March 1986]: 1455-63), that article itself set off a furor that was reflected in the letters to the editor that appeared in the subsequent issue. (See JAMA May 255.20 [May 1986]: 2752–60 for those letters. Some were concerned about anti-Semitism related to the piece, others about the use of the Gospels as sources for history, and one medical doctor, Howard S. Rubenstein, questioned the speculative nature of the medical findings, writing, "one simply cannot do an autopsy without a corpse" [2755].) Leaving aside the question of how visible the "water" from a pericardial breach would have been to a casual observer, given that pericardial fluid is generally not present in copious amounts in a healthy heart, it is not clear that a witness might describe pericardial fluid as water. It is a serous fluid, which is often a pale yellow color. Further, in a healthy heart it does not appear to be present in great quantity. In fact, the sac of a healthy heart may only contain a "few drops." For this description, see the entry "Pericardium" in *Mosby's Dictionary of Medicine, Nursing, & Health Professions*, 7th ed. (St. Louis: Elsevier, 2006), 1433. According to the entry in the Merck Manual of Diagnosis and Therapy, the amount of pericardial fluid in a healthy heart runs between 25 to 50 mL, or roughly one eighth to a quarter of a cup. To be sure, in a heart that is damaged, there may be several mL of fluid (mostly blood, pus, or chyle) that builds up. In modern surgery, the excess fluid can be aspirated out with a syringe in a procedure known as *pericardiocentesis*. See "Pericarditis" in *The Merck Manual of Diagnosis and Therapy*, 19th ed., eds. Justin L. Kaplan and Robert S. Porter (Whitehouse Station, NJ: Merck & Company, 2011), 2201. By contrast, liquid in the lungs, known as a *pleural effusion*, might involve copious amounts of liquid that could be as much as 4 L (Merck, "Pleural Effusion," 1998), and might be a better explanation for the phenomenon if an appeal is being made to modern anatomy and medical knowledge of the possible effects of crucifixion on a bodily organ.

attributed to Jesus simply wandering off after a temporary state of unconsciousness. In short, Habermas's argument owes much to his role as an apologist; to get to the resurrection, one must first pass a cross where Jesus truly died and find a tomb that is inexplicably empty, leaving the miracle of the resurrection as the only explanation for the events recorded in the Gospel.[6] For Habermas, the sword thrust provides support for the first link in this chain.

It is unlikely, though, that the Evangelist included the piercing merely to prove that Jesus' death was an irrefutable fact. In the first century, when knowledge of anatomy was not advanced and it was thought that the body was composed of four humors, none of which was water, recording the flow of two liquids may have served other purposes instead.[7] Perhaps it was to confirm that Jesus was, even physically, something more than a normal human being.[8] The mention of water and blood may have even had some other symbolic significance. For instance, a popular interpretation in commentaries is that the blood calls to mind the Eucharist, while the water is evocative of the sacrament of baptism.[9]

---

6. Habermas, *Historical Jesus*, 129; Flew and Habermas, *Resurrection*, 31. The position taken by some of Habermas's opponents that Jesus only seemed to die and that the tomb was empty because he subsequently regained consciousness and wandered away from his resting place is a position held by some skeptics of the Christian tradition and which Habermas colorfully calls the "swoon theory" (*Historical Jesus*, 69–72). Essentially, Habermas marshals what he terms the "heart wound" passage in John 19:34–35 as the ultimate counter to the swoon theory.

7. Granted, the LXX Greek of 4 Maccabees 19:20 mentions that in the death of the Jewish martyr, blood is spread on a torture device, and bodily fluids (the word ichor is used) drip down onto the embers of the fire that had been lit underneath. See the summary of the discussion on ichor in Pamela E. Kinlaw, *The Christ Is Jesus: Metamorphosis, Possession, and Johannine Christology* (Atlanta: Society of Biblical Literature, 2005), 164 n. 206. It is uncertain whether blood and water were synonyms, though more work would have to be done on this issue. Aristotle used the word "ichor" rather than "hydor" for amniotic fluid. See *Historia Animalium* 586.32. It seems that ichor (rather than water) was also used for what we know of today as serous fluid. If ichor was a well-known concept in antiquity for any non-blood bodily fluid, and a non-blood substance was indeed intended here in John, the word "water" instead of "ichor" seems to be a deliberate choice.

8. For instance, Andreas Köstenberger, *John* (Grand Rapids: Baker, 2004). William Loader maintains that the focus is on the human side of the equation in order to combat those early Christians with a docetic understanding of Christology who might assert Jesus was only divine or a "non-human." William Loader, *Jesus in John's Gospel: Structure and Issues in Johannine Christology* (Grand Rapids: William B. Eerdmans, 2017), 186.

9. Edward W. Klink III asserts that the image of blood and water can function both on the historical level and the symbolic level simultaneously; *John: Exegetical Commentary on the New Testament.*(Grand Rapids: Zondervan, 2016), 814. Andrew Lincoln provides one example of a symbolic interpretation. He maintains the verse references rabbinic interpretive traditions for Numbers 2:11 and Exodus 17, in which Moses struck the rock in the wilderness twice, the first time resulting in blood and the second in water. If that is the background for the allusion, then

In fact, the two fluids suggest the concepts of purity and sacrifice because both water and blood play a role in the purificatory rituals and sacrificial system of Judaism.[10] For instance, immersing oneself in water, whether living water in the form of a river or lake or in specially constructed ritual baths known as *mikva'ot*, was widespread and was accomplished, in particular, before engaging in a ritual in the temple. As Jonathan Klawans writes, "In Leviticus, it becomes clear that ritual purity is a prerequisite for those who came to the sanctuary to offer sacrifices, for those priests who regularly officiate at sacrifices, and for any animals that are to be offered as sacrifices."[11] The aim of the cleansing was to ensure that one was not bringing impurities into contact with the sacred, since the temple was the dwelling place of God. Achieving a state of holiness when approaching the deity was required.[12]

Blood, for its part, was an element of the sacrificial system that was used for purificatory rituals related to atonement, but sometimes it was also applied as a purifying agent, even when sin in an ethical sense was not necessarily involved. For example, the blood of a sacrificed lamb was rubbed on the ear, thumb, and foot of a leper as part of the cleansing ritual (Lev 14:13–14) he or she would undergo once the skin disease had cleared up.[13] Moses also demonstrated that sin and atonement were not prerequisites for the need to apply blood when, during the consecration of the tabernacle, he dabbed this vital fluid of

---

the theme evoked here is that of life; Andrew Lincoln, *The Gospel According to Saint John* (Peabody, MA: Hendrickson, 2005), 479. It is also possible to link the water and blood to the giving of the Holy Spirit by referencing John 7:37–39 and 1 John 5:6, as maintained by Demetrius R. Dumm, *A Mystical Portrait of Jesus: New Perspectives on John's Gospel* (Collegeville MN: The Liturgical Press, 2001), 33–34. A sacramental interpretation, in which the blood points to the Eucharist and the water to baptism, was advanced by Rudolph Bultmann, *The Gospel of John*, trans. G. Trans. Beasley-Murray, R. W. N. Hoare, and J. K. Riches (Philadelphia: Westminster Press, 1971), 677–78.

10. Contra Jennifer Glancy, who maintains that "John specifies no truth beyond the piercing itself," in "Torture, Flesh, Truth, and the Fourth Gospel," *Biblical Interpretation* 13, no. 2 (January, 2005): 131.

11. Jonathan Klawans, *Purity, Sacrifice and the Temple: Symbolism and Supersessionism in the Study of Ancient Judaism.* (Oxford: Oxford University Press, 2006), 4.

12. Morten Hørning Jensen hypothesizes that the use of the Sea of Galilee itself as a source of living water might be one explanation for oddities in the distribution of constructed ritual baths throughout the Galilee region. See "Purity and Politics in Herod Antipas's Galilee: The Case for Religious Motivation," *Journal for the Study of the Historical Jesus* 11 (2013): 18.

13. On the *hattat* offering for purposes of purification (in addition to expiation), see N. Kiuchi, *The Purification Offering in the Priestly Literature: Its Meaning and Function*, JSOT SS 56 (Sheffield: Sheffield Academic Press, 1987), 161. See also Thomas Kazen, *Jesus and the Purity Halakhah: Was Jesus Indifferent to Impurity?*, rev. ed., Coniectanea Biblica NT Series 38 (Winona Lake, IN: Eisenbrauns, 2010), 211–14.

ritually slaughtered animals on the altar to purify it. He also applied it to the priests themselves when he ordained Aaron and his sons (Lev 8: 14–15, 18–19, 23–24). Later, in Leviticus 14:49–52, we find that water and blood together were used to purify not just people but also the homes of persons cured of leprosy. According to the instructions provided in that passage, the priest was to hold a bird over living or fresh water and kill it. Then he was to dip a brush of hyssop, cedarwood, and red twine into the resulting mix of avian blood and watersprinkle the house.

Clearly, it is possible to associate both the elements of water and blood with cleansing rituals. Although the water and blood together in John 19: 34 are not usually viewed, in commentaries, in light of Jesus' own purity as a perfect sacrifice, exploring whether or not that verse can be read as part of such a motif that occurs elsewhere in the Fourth Gospel and has its climax in the empty tomb, is worthwhile—especially given that such a theme may be obscured to modern readers due to distance from the purity practice of first-century Judaism.[14]

Purity in John

In John's Gospel, purity isn't an obvious topic that can be easily discovered by keeping an eye peeled for the repetition of a particular word or phrase in the narrative. So it doesn't jump out at the twenty-first century reader like, say, John's use of the concept of witnessing does. In that motif, the word "testify" is used numerous times in the text.[15] The idea of purity is not even as blatant in the Gospel as the image that Jesus is one who is God's emissary, a theme linked to the repetition of the word "sent" in the text.[16] Even the Synoptics are more obvious in portraying Jesus in relation to questions of purity. Matthew (15:2) and

---

14. See note 9 above for some other interpretations of the water and blood. Oddly, the idea of ritual cleansing and sacrifice are sometimes mentioned in passing, but not necessarily linked to Jesus' own purity as a sacrifice. For instance, C.K. Barret, in listing other mentions of water in John's Gospel, does acknowledge that the foot washing in 13:5 is an instance where "water is the means by which men are cleansed," and that there are allusions in the blood at the cross to sacrifice. He then goes on, however, to assert that the water and blood were likely "those living streams by which men are quickened and the church lives." In essence, he stops short of linking the water and blood with purification related to the person of Jesus and his ritual death. C. K. Barrett, *The Gospel According to St. John*, 2nd ed. (London: SPCK, 1978), 556–57.

15. 1:19, 32; 3:26; 4:39; 12:17; 19:35.

16. Peder Borgen, "God's Agent in the Fourth Gospel" in *The Interpretation of John*, ed. John Ashton (Philadelphia, PA: Fortress Press, 1986), 67–78.

Mark (7:2–20), for instance, record a debate with religious authorities related to handwashing and the purity *halakhah,* or customs, some of which may have had legally binding force in a given group and developed from interpretation of Scripture. By contrast, John's Jesus doesn't engage in verbal sparring with the authorities on this topic.[17]

This lack of either prominent, repetitively used keywords or a specific conversation focused on some element related to purity in the Fourth Gospel has the effect of masking any purity concerns the Evangelist might have had, making discovery of issues related to the Johannine Jesus and cleanliness, including questions related to corpse defilement and impurity associated with the empty tomb, challenging. This is only exacerbated by what Adele Reinhartz aptly observes is a cultural gap between our own Western Christian culture, which has little to say about religious purity, and the Judaism of antiquity, where the notion was deeply intertwined with the concepts of holiness, priesthood, and temple.[18]

The Purity System in Brief

It was Jonathan Kalwans who, after expanding on the thought of his predecessors, described a basic structure for understanding the purification system of Judaism that is often referenced in the literature today.[19] In his formulation, the scheme centers on two types of defilement: ritual impurity and moral impurity.[20] The former, as summarized by Hannah K. Harrington, "can be mechanically purified ... by the action of the priest

---

17. Kazen maintains that the debate in Mark 7 is unlikely from the historical Jesus, but rather originates in early Christian polemics. Kazen, "Less Halakic Jesus," 120, 134.

18. Adele Reinhartz, Introduction and Acknowledgments in *'They Shall Purify Themselves': Essays on Purity in Early Judaism,* by Susan Haber, ed. Adele Reinhartz (Atlanta: Society of Biblical Literature, 2008), 1. Purity was not just a concern of Judaism. Walter Burkert observes that the ancient Greeks were sensitive to the boundaries between the sacred and profane, and, consequently, various groups and communities employed rituals to restore or ensure purity. These might involve elements like blood, water, and sacrifice, and possibly community expulsions in rituals that would have looked not unlike those described in the Hebrew Bible. Walter Burkert, *Greek Religion* (Cambridge, MA: Harvard, 1985), 77, 83.

19. For a literature review of those who contributed to the field prior to Klawans, see Susan Haber, *'They Shall Purify Themselves': Essays on Purity in Early Judaism,* ed. Adele Reinhartz (Atlanta: Society of Biblical Literature, 2008), 9–28.

20. Jonathan Klawans, *Purity, Sacrifice and the Temple: Symbolism and Supersessionism in the Study of Ancient Judaism* (Oxford: Oxford University Press, 2006), 53. A third type of impurity, genealogical, is sometimes also adduced from the Jewish tradition and relates to questions of intermarriage and the conversion of gentiles. See the summary presented in Wil Rogan, "Purity in Early Judaism: Current Issues and Questions," *Currents in Biblical Research* 16, no. 3 (2018): 322.

and the prescribed ritual. Indeed, it is not a sin to become ritually impure. Most of the impurities requiring ablutions are inevitable in the normal course of life. However, failure to perform the necessary purifications is considered sin and will contaminate the sanctuary."[21]

Another point about this type of defilement is that, although it is an impermeant state, it is nonetheless contagious. The impure status coved by ritual defilement can be transferred to other Israelites, including the priests, and even to nearby objects, through contact or proximity.[22] Those persons or things infected by, say, a leper or a woman who is menstruating, must themselves in turn be purified. The remedies deemed appropriate for ameliorating ritual uncleanliness include ritual immersions in living water, such as the water contained in specially built ritual baths (*miqwa'ot*) like the one pictured; the passing of a specified period of time; and in some cases, sacrifices. These are

One of the immersion pools at Qumran. Author photo.

21. Hannah K. Harrington, *The Impurity Systems of Qumran and the Rabbis: Biblical Foundations* (Atlanta, GA: Scholars Press, 1993), 31–32.

22. Klawans, *Purity, Sacrifice, Temple,* 54. Gentiles do not contract ritual impurity (Paula Fredriksen, "Did Jesus Oppose the Purity Laws?" *Bible Review* 11, no. 3 [June 1995]: 25). See the discussion of this topic by Hyam Maccoby, who draws extensively on Rabbinic sources in his analysis. Hyam Maccoby, *Ritual & Morality: The Ritual Purity System and Its Place in Judaism* (Cambridge: Cambridge University Press, 1999), 8–12.

even applied in combination with regard to some particular sources of impurity.

Corpse defilement, by contrast, is a kind of pollution that requires several steps to eliminate. One of the Mishnah's so-called "fathers of uncleanliness," corpses cause ritual uncleanliness for persons and objects through touch or proximity. [23] Then that contaminated person or object has the potential to convey an additional round of contagion to still other items or individuals. There is a difference, however, between the first person who actually touches the corpse and those whom he or she subsequently infects with impurity. Direct contact with the corpse results in impurity for a full week, while someone exposed to a cadaver through an intermediary is only unclean for a day.

Although one comes in contact with corpse pollution by caring for the body of the deceased, it was a task that was valued in society. In the book of Tobit, for instance, although Tobit lives in the diaspora, he is depicted as virtuous because he takes the initiative to properly bury his fellow countrymen, whose bodies had been left ignominiously exposed or for whom there does not appear to be a family member available to arrange for a burial within the preferred timeframe for doing so (Tobit, 1:17 -20, 2:3–10). With regard to Judea proper, Tikva Frymer-Kensky observes that "even priests may attend the deceased of their immediate family and then remain in limbo until their corpse contamination is over (Lev. 21:1–6). Only the High Priest (Lev 21:10–11) and the Nazarite (Num 6:6–7) must avoid all corpses." [24]

Corpse defilement also requires extensive interventions. These are described in Numbers 19:11–22. Indeed, while the passing of time and the observance of general ablutions are usually sufficient to ameliorate many forms of contamination, exposure to corpses, and even to graves, calls for the extra measure of sprinkling the one who is contaminated with the ashes of a red heifer. In a nutshell, the individual who is defiled by contact with the deceased:

---

23. *m. Kelim*, 1.1.

24. Tikva Frymer-Kensky, "Pollution, Purification and Purgation in Biblical Israel" in *The Word of the Lord Shall Go Forth: Essays in Honor of David Noel Freedman*, eds. Carol L. Meyers and M. O'Connor (Winona Lake, IN: Eisenbrauns, 1988), 403.

1. is unclean for a period of seven days,

2. undergoes immersion on the third and seventh days,

3. washes their clothes on the seventh day, and

4. receives a sprinkling of the ashes of the red heifer mixed with living water on the third and seventh days.

During the Second Temple period, it appears that this regimen was slightly modified in some quarters. The discovery of several *miqwa'ot* in cemeteries, along with references to immediate immersions in literature from the period, has led Klawans to the conclusion that a person could undertake an ablution on the first day as well.[25] The practice of immersion directly after exposure, which is known as gradual purification, would provide a sufficient state of cleanliness to allow resumption of some regular routines of daily life during the period of uncleanliness.[26] This means that the impure person would not face what would essentially be a quarantine period outside of settlements, but could return to their home within the city and also eat in purity.[27] This additional bath, however, would not supplant the mandatory rituals. Progress through the full regimen would still be necessary for resumption of activity in the Temple.

While corpse defilement is an example of ritual impurity, it is important to remember that there is a second category: moral impurity. This type involves uncleanliness that disrupts one's relationship with the sacred, stemming from sins like murder, idolatry, or adultery. Unlike ritual impurity, which accrues to an individual through the routines of everyday life, many of which are viewed as noble and quite desirable (such as attending to burying a family member or birthing a child), the uncleanliness associated with sin cannot be removed by

---

25. Klawans, "4Q274 Fragment 1 Revisited—or Who Touched Whom? Further Evidence for Ideas of Graded Impurity and Graded Purification," *Dead Sea Discoveries* 17 (2010): 77, 80. Also, Yonatan Adler, "Ritual Baths Adjacent to Tombs: An Analysis of the Archaeological Evidence in Light of Halakhic Sources," *Journal for the Study of Judaism* 50 (2009), who lists the locations of tombs with *miqwa'ot* on pages 57–60.

26. In rabbinic literature, this state of partial cleanliness until sunset after an initial immersion is known as *Tebul Yom*. See the detailed commentary by Jacob Neusner in *A History of the Mishnaic Law of Purities. Part 19 Tebul Yom ad Yadayim* (Eugene, OR: Wipf & Stock, 1977), 3–11.

27. Frymer-Kensky, "Pollution, Purification and Purgation," 400, observes that Numbers 19 indicates that any individual who had contact with the dead was in limbo outside of the camp for the seven-day period required before rejoining the group.

rites of purification. It can only be ameliorated through atonement or punishment, including exile.[28] Even the Yom Kippur ceremonies are of limited use against moral impurity. On the Day of Atonement, the sanctuary is cleansed and there is some atonement for the people, but the ritual, according to Klawans, "does not appear to purify grave sinners" who continue to exist "in a degraded state."[29]

Klawans identifies several other ways in which moral and ritual impurity differ. These are presented in table 1. For instance, those who are defiled with ritual impurities are excluded from the temple during the period of their impurity. By contrast, those with moral impurity are not.[30] This would explain, perhaps, why in the pericope of the woman caught in adultery, the woman is being interrogated in the temple itself, despite being accused of a sinful act (John 8:2–11).[31]

In addition, just as was the case with ritual impurity, there was no static understanding of moral purity. For example, in addition to sexual impropriety, adultery, and murder, within the Qumran community bribery was considered to be morally defiling.[32] Despite the elasticity of interpretation concerning the finer implications of moral impurity, however, both moral and ritual defilement were recognized by those who lived in the context of Second Temple Judaism.

The Ubiquity of Purification in Second Temple Judaism

That the Johannine Jesus would have been at least as knowledgeable as any other Jew of his day about the requirements of the purity system may be assumed. After all, he frequented the temple on several occasions both to confront the trade done there by those providing sacrificial animals to the moneychangers (2:13–16) and also to teach or converse (5:14, 7:14, 8:20, 10:23; 18:20). In addition, he was also present

---

28. Klawans, *Purity, Sacrifice, Temple*, 56. At Qumran, it seems that the distinction between the two types of defilement is not at all sharp, and both carried the idea of contagion and the need for purifications. Thomas Kazen in *Jesus and Purity Halakhah: Was Jesus Indifferent to Purity?* Coniectanea Biblica NT Series 38 (Winona Lake, IN: Eisenbrauns, 2010): 209–10, provides some other examples where moral and ritual purity appear to overlap.

29. Joseph Klawans, *Impurity and Sin in Ancient Judaism* (Oxford: Oxford University Press, 2000), 30.

30. Klawans, *Impurity and Sin*, 29.

31. Disagreements between the textual evidence make it uncertain that this pericope was original to the Fourth Gospel.

32. Klawans, *Impurity and Sin*, 51.

	Duration	Transmission to Others	Removal	Vocabulary for Source in Hebrew	Regarded as a Sin	Excluded from Sanctuary While Impure
Ritual Impurity	Impermanent, often temporary	Contagious	Rites of purification (lustrations, sacrifices, passage of time)	Impure	No	Yes
Moral Impurity	Long lasting	Noncommunicable	Atonement, punishment	Impure, abomination, pollutes	Yes	No

Table 1: Differences in Types of Impurity

Summary based on material presented in Jonathan Klawanns, *Impurity and Sin in Ancient Jerusalem* (Oxford: Oxford University Press, 2000), 26, 29, 30.

in Jerusalem for several religious festivals.[33] One might infer that he attended the ceremonies held in the temple during those holidays (2:13; 2:23; 5:1; 7:2–14, 37; 10:22; 12:12). In fact, Paula Fredriksen speculates that when Jesus encounters the man with the protracted illness at the pool by the Sheep Gate (5:2–5) at the time of an unnamed festival (5:1), it was because they were both waiting to immerse, though this is by no means made explicit in the text and is, as will become clearer as the discussion about purity unfolds, an unlikely inference that the Evangelist would have intended, given his Christology.[34]

Even apart from the times when worshipers might be in Jerusalem to attend events in the temple in the decades before its destruction, knowledge of the sacrificial and purification rituals as sketched in the Pentateuch was widespread and, as James D. G. Dunn puts it, "It cannot be doubted that purity was a major preoccupation in the Judaism of Jesus' time."[35] Certainly, different groups such as the Essenes and Pharisees promulgated varying interpretations concerning the degree that ritual purity should be observed outside of the temple, but still, the period is one in which there was widespread interest in non-priestly purity amongst the laity broadly. This is supported by an ever-growing body of archeological evidence as cities like Sepphoris are excavated. For instance, there are more than 850 *miqwa'ot*, or baths for immersion, which were typically used for attaining ritual cleansing, that have been discovered throughout Jewish territories in Jerusalem and beyond, with many of the recent discoveries occurring in private homes or shared courtyards.[36] The existence of such baths implies that purification that involved washing or immersion was a "widely subscribed practice in Second Temple Judaism."[37]

For his part, Eyal Regev links attentiveness to personal purification beyond the temple precincts in the first century to the fact that

---

33. For an attempt to sequence the festivals within the context of the Jewish liturgical calendar, see Michael A. Daise, *Feasts in John*, WUNT2 Reihe 229 (Tübingen: Mohr Siebeck, 2007).

34. Fredriksen, "Did Jesus Oppose the Purity Laws?": 42.

35. James D. G. Dunn, "Jesus and Purity: An Ongoing Debate," *New Testament Studies* 48, no. 4 (October 2002): 450.

36. Yonatan Adler, "Between Priestly Cult and Common Culture: The Material Evidence of Ritual Purity Observance in Early Roman Jerusalem Reassessed," *Journal of Ancient Judaism* 7 (November 1, 2016): 233.

37. John C. Poirier, "Purity beyond the Temple in the Second Temple Era," *Journal of Biblical Literature* 122, no. 2 (2003): 252.

The archaeological site at Sepphoris. Author photo.

limestone vessels for eating and serving, such as cups, are in evidence far and wide, even in small towns and rural settlements.[38] The existence of stone serving ware is significant because even though some forms of impurity were contagious, meaning the person who became ritually unclean could contaminate other objects or persons through touch, the use of limestone vessels for daily meals would inhibit the rapid spread of the contagion. Stone would keep impurities from infecting other objects and persons in a household, even when individuals were using the same service items and sharing the same food. In essence, according to Regev, employing chalkstone vessels for daily meals would assist laypersons in maintaining a certain level of purity and "achieving personal sanctity which accompanies a religious experience."[39] Though,

---

38. Regev Eyal, "Pure Individualism: The Idea of Non-Priestly Purity in Ancient Judaism," *Journal for the Study of Judaism* 31, no. 2 (2000): 182.

39. Regev, 191. He maintains that observation of purity was not restricted to particular segments of Jewish society, such as rabbis or Pharisees, but were a feature of common Judaism due to ubiquity of the archeological evidence (187). Along these same lines, Thomas Kazen, "A Perhaps Less Halakic Jesus and Purity" *Journal for the Study of the Historical Jesus* 14 (2016): 125–27. Others, however, such as Roland Deines, assert that the practices of a very influential segment of religious society, such as the Pharisees, might inspire their sympathizers to emulate their purity observances to some extent. "The Pharisees between 'Judaisms' and Common Judaism" in *The Complexities of Second Temple Judaism*, WUNT 2.52, ed. D. A. Carson, P. T. O'Brien, and M.

to be fair, Jürgen K. Zangenberg rightly cautions that not every instance of a stone vessel is an indication that those who owned or used it did so for reasons of purity.[40] While Zangenberg's warning to be vigilant about generalizing interpretations based on the presence of material evidence is sound, nonetheless, Kazen's observation that "there is no way to explain the present state of these material finds except for a *wide-spread* and *general* observance of purity practices, including frequent, probably daily, purifications, far from the temple" has merit.[41]

Purity in the Text of the Gospel

Given widespread interest in purification during the first century, it is no surprise that there are several allusions in the text of the Fourth Gospel that reflect notions of purity. First, during the foot-washing prior to Passover, the act of washing (νίπτω) is linked to the idea that one becomes clean (καθαρός).[42] As John Christopher Thomas observes, however, scholars who interpret this passage in light of forgiveness of sins or cleansing often associate it with removing post-baptismal

---

A. Seifrid (Tübingen: Mohr Siebeck, 1993), 443–504. For a fuller summary of the two differing perspectives, see Jürgen K. Zangenberg. "Pure Stone: Archaeological Evidence for Jewish Purity Practices in Late Second Temple Judaism (Miqwa'ot and Stone Vessels)" in *Purity and the Forming of Religious Traditions in the Ancient Mediterranean World and Ancient Judaism,* eds. Christian Frevel and Christophe Nihan, Dynamics in the History of Religion, vol. 3 (Leiden: Brill, 2013), 538–9. The observation is often made that the differences in perspective can be traced back to Jacob Neusner, who favored limited circles for purity observance, and E. P Sanders, who was a proponent of wider observance throughout Jewish society. See Neusner, *From Politics to Piety: The Emergence of Pharisaic Judaism,* 2nd ed. (NY: Ktav, 1979), 14.

40. Zagenberg points out that given that other limestone objects, such as ossuaries, tabletops, and sundials that are unaffiliated with uses related to purity also exist, it may be the case that some of the smaller stone objects for eating and drinking simply reflect new fashions for luxury goods at a time of relative prosperity for Palestine, rather than a "common quest for purity" throughout Judaism as a whole (569, 553–54). Other aspects of his argument, though, are unconvincing. For instance, he hypothesizes that if limestone vessels were intended for purity, it would be logical to expect cooking pots, casseroles, jugs, jars, and lamps of stone (553). Yet, he seems to overlook basic chemistry and the inherent properties of various stone materials themselves. For instance, the relative weight of stone vs. fired clay, not to mention its conductivity, may have rendered stone implements impractical for some applications. As for limestone, when heated over an open flame it will break down into carbon dioxide and calcium oxide (quicklime). When water is added to quicklime, which is extraordinarily exothermic when it comes in contact with water, it simply pops apart.

41. Kazen, "Less Halakic Jesus," 127 (emphasis original).

42. The idea of cleansing also appears in Jesus' use of the image of the true vine in 15:2–3. The pericope includes a word play between pruning (cleansing) a branch and a comment that the disciples have been cleansed through a word that Jesus had previously addressed to them. The focus in the wider context of the passage, however, does not appear to be purification per se, as much as it is the cohesiveness of a community that remains (abides) faithful and fruitful.

sin and/or as a preliminary step for receiving the Eucharist.[43] These views, however, are difficult to reconcile with the Jewish purity system as outlined by Klawans. On the one hand, unless repentance was also somehow involved, it is unlikely that ablutions would remediate sins associated with moral impurity. [44] On the other, if the concern was eating in purity, which, granted, would be within the bounds of the purity *halakhah* observed in some segments of Judaism, it would be more likely that the hands would be rinsed as opposed to the feet. After all, there is a greater chance to come in contact with impure objects or people by touching them than by walking.[45]

These trepidations about linking the footwashings at the Last Supper with either moral impurity post-Baptism or ritual defilement vis-à-vis the Eucharist do not even address the issue of whether or not the washing might be intended for some other purpose, such as to demonstrate humility or hospitality.[46] It is important to say, however, that the Evangelist does nonetheless have an interest in moral defilement, given that sin (άμαρτία) serves as a framework against which Jesus' life plays out. Almost immediately after the sweeping grandeur of the prologue, Jesus is identified by John as the one who removes the sins of the world (1:29). Then, near the very end of the Gospel, the resurrected Jesus endows the disciples with the Holy Spirit and notifies them that they have the power to forgive sins (20:22–23). In John, sin tends to have a particular cast to it. As laid out in 15:22–24 Jesus links sin to rejection of the revelation that he shared during his ministry via his works and his words.[47] While this is not one of the traditional

---

43. John Christopher Thomas, *Footwashing in John 13 and the Johannine Community*, 2nd ed. (Cleveland, TN: CPT Press, 2014), 4–5.

44. Craig Keener does cite some examples where the concepts of cleansing and sin are linked, such as Sir 38:10. In the case of Sirach, as verse 11 confirms, the cleansing of one who is ill, a state of health that was presumably the result of being sinful, is accomplished through sacrifice, not ablutions. Craig Keener, *The Gospel of John*, vol. 2 (Peabody, MA: Hendrickson, 2003), 996. While Keener himself does not speculate on what type of "sin" necessitated the disciple's cleansing, Craig R. Koester provides a helpful definition of "sin" as understood by the Evangelist. Sin is "unbelief or estrangement from God" that is "replaced by faith," per Craig R. Koester, *Symbolism in the Fourth Gospel: Meaning, Mystery, Community*, 2nd ed. (Minneapolis: Fortress, 2003), 245.

45. Kazen, *Jesus and Purity*, 67–72. Kazen does indicate that at Qumran, immersion was prerequisite for participation in community meals (237). Since corpse impurity travels vertically, it is theoretically possible that one might inadvertently incur corpse defilement by walking over a grave.

46. Other interpretations of this pericope are surveyed by Thomas, *Footwashing in John 13*, 1–8.

47. Also 8:21–24.

sources of moral impurity, given that there was no single moribund understanding of what might constitute a grave sin amongst various communities within Judaism, the Johannine-formulation understanding would likely not be out of bounds.

In any case, within John's Gospel there are actually three instances where the words καθαρισμός ("purity/purification") or ἁγνίζω ("purify") casually appear in the text. Two relate to ritual impurities, and the third is a bit more ambiguous and may indicate some blurring of the lines between ritual and ethical impurity.

The first use of the word "purify," which clearly evokes defilement of the ritual sort, was subjected to analysis by Brower himself. It occurs when the narrator reveals in a seemingly offhanded way that the stone vessels containing the water that Jesus turned to wine in Galilee were intended as part of the typical Jewish purification rites (2:6).[48] Then, in John 3:25, we have the reference to purity that is difficult to categorize. Readers are informed that in the Judean town of Aenon, the Baptist's disciples were engaging in a debate with one or more Jews about purification.[49] Although, as Kazen notes, John's Gospel does not include references to forgiveness and repentance in connection with the work of the Baptist, nonetheless, it likely had "an additional function which goes beyond that of mere bodily purification."[50] Finally, the narrator is firmly thinking of ritual cleanliness when he adds the small detail that just prior to Passover, many Jews were heading to Jerusalem in advance of the festival to purify themselves (11:55), no doubt to take advantage of the various public ritual immersion pools that surrounded the Temple complex for use by pilgrims. Taken together, these three mentions of purification are spread throughout the public ministry portion of the Gospel and occur across the full range of the territory represented in Jesus' travels, save Samaria. The geographic settings of these verses within the Gospel attest to the idea that in the Johannine frame of reference, purity was of equal importance to both rural and urban populations and from northern locations to Jerusalem itself. Surely, these incidental mentions of the practice of ablutions, which appear

---

48. Brower, "Purity in the Gospel of John," 118–19.

49. The singular "Jew" appears in some manuscripts.

50. Kazen, *Jesus and Purity*, 234. Note that Kazen is here drawing a portrait of the work of the Baptist based on all of the Gospels, not just the Fourth.

without elaboration or definition, are a clear indication that the ministry of the Johannine Jesus is firmly situated in the context where it is thought that concept of the purity could be taken for granted.

Purity and the Johannine Jesus

Locating Jesus within the context of a Judaism that is attuned to issues related to purity is a slightly different matter than trying to understand how the Evangelist thinks about purity in relation to Jesus' person. This is particularly true given that Jesus and God are bonded together in a special relationship. The unity between Father and Son is apparent in the controversies in John 10: 25–30 and 5:17, 19–21, in which the Son's claims of a link between what he and the Father do serves as a point of contention between Jesus and his detractors. Unity is also an aspect of the "I am" statements, since they imply that the Johannine Jesus is concomitant with the God of Moses. In addition, the intimate connection between Jesus and God in the text is indicated by the ideas that Jesus is sent by God, essentially serving as an agent, and that he is the only-born Son of God (1:18). These are just a few examples.[51]

Given that Jesus is intimately and constantly interrelated with God, the issue of his purity cannot be avoided. After all, "since the impure can defile the sacred, the sacred must be protected."[52] Logically, the author of the text would have three options to pursue in order to determine how the historical Jesus could be in constant contact with God:

1. Jesus himself would have to maintain a pure state without ceasing.

2. The purity laws would be suspended or superseded by Jesus' work on earth, and/or Jesus would outright oppose the purity system.

3. The purity laws would stand, but the divine portion of his nature would ensure they are fulfilled in a unique way, or that Jesus was indifferent to them.

---

51. See, for instance, the detailed analysis of Adesola Joan Akala, *The Son-Father Relationship and Christological Symbolism in the Gospel of John*, LNTS 505 (London: Bloomsbury, 2014), 193–211.

52. Frymer-Kensky, "Pollution, Purification and Purgation," 403.

Although the second and third options have been suggested in the literature related to Jesus and purity, most of which is focused on interpreting episodes from the Synoptics, rather than from John, a close reading of the Fourth Gospel shows that the Evangelist is at pains to craft his narrative and select its content so that in his portrait, Jesus is not in situations where he would be subjected to ritual impurity—even when it comes to corpses and resurrection, be it his own or that of others.[53]

During Jesus' public ministry, as the narrative rolls toward its inevitable climax with Jesus' trial and death, the Johannine Jesus and the disciples are indeed depicted as generally adhering to Jewish religious customs and practices.[54] Festival attendance, for instance, has already been mentioned, as has Jesus' presence in the temple to teach. The Evangelist does not go out of his way, however, to depict Jesus as participating in rituals related to ameliorating defilement. The implication is that, at least for the Evangelist, Jesus is already complete and perfectly sanctified.

---

53. For instance, Thomas Kazen, whose focus was the historical Jesus rather than the portrait of Jesus in John, asserts that Jesus was indifferent to various aspects of the Jewish Purity *Halakhah*, or at least set different priorities that provided an exemption from its strict observance. Kazen reaches this conclusion with regard to corpse-impurity in particular by focusing on the stories of Jesus' blithely touching Jarius' daughter (Mark 5:21–24, 35–43) and approaching the bier of the widow's son (Luke 7:11–18). Thomas Kazen, *Jesus and Purity Halakhah: Was Jesus Indifferent to Impurity?* Coniectanea Biblica NT Series 38 (Winona Lake, IN: Eisenbrauns, 2010), 169–177, 196, 344. Fredriksen surveys the views of several scholars on the issue of purity and Jesus (20–22). Holmén maintains that Jesus' divine nature enables him to "conquer impurity," or to essentially heal their uncleanliness rather than become impure himself when he touches others (2722–23).

54. At first glance, two incidents in the Gospel seem to contradict this statement. Regarding Jesus' seeming disregard of the Sabbath (John 5; 9:1–10:21), Martin Asiedu-Peprah maintains that the purpose of the Sabbath controversy scenes is to lead the reader to an understanding of Jesus' identity as the Son of God (Martin Asiedu-Peprah, *Johannine Sabbath Conflicts as Juridical Controversy*, WUNT2 Reihe 132 [Tübingen: Mohr Siebeck, 2001], 11, 240). Jesus' failure to observe the Sabbath is due to Jesus' identity as God's Son, which means he has obligations related to the Sabbath that are not the same as would be expected of the Jewish population in general. In this Gospel, his followers are never remembered as complicit in disregarding expectations for a day of rest, unlike in others (see Matt 12:1–8; Luke 6:1–5).

A similar argument might be made about the temple incident. Nothing in the pericope itself, however, indicates an explicit concern with the purity of the religious complex, but instead focuses on economic inequality related to the sales taking place (Klawans, *Purity, Sacrifice, and the Temple*, 224). In support of this point, he notes that in the Fourth Gospel, Jesus' miracles of superabundance, such as turning the water to wine, the miraculous catch of fish, and feeding the five-thousand, would demonstrate God's providence and benefit those without substantial means. To Klawans's point, the very fact that Jesus chases the money changers from the temple with a whip at the beginning of his public ministry, rather than at its end (as recorded in the other Gospels), and yet continues to worship and work in that sanctuary up until his arrest implies that he does not view the temple itself to be impure—God, his Father, still dwells in it. In the Synoptics, the temple expulsion is a contributing factor to Jesus' arrest (Matt 21:12–17, Mark 11:15–19, Luke 19:45–56).

One of the first examples of this relates to Jesus' encounter with John the Baptist (1:29–34). Baptism by John undoubtedly is intended to effect a cleansing, whether it be from ritual impurity or sin. Regardless, unlike scenes in the Synoptics, the Johannine Jesus is never truly baptized. He does not enter the water or actually receive purification in any form from the man who self-identifies as one who is unworthy to untie the straps of Jesus' sandals (John 1:27). It might be said that Jesus receives nothing in particular from John except testimony on his behalf. He does, however, obtain divine endorsement at the Jordan when the Spirit descends on Jesus in the form of a dove, which subsequently remains on him rather than fluttering away (1:32). Let us reiterate the heart of the matter: instead of enacting a purifying ritual, the Baptist's primary service to Jesus is to testify that while he himself baptizes with water, Jesus is greater than he. Furthermore, John's testimony links sacrificial theology and Christology by declaring that Jesus is the Lamb by which the sin of the world will be abrogated (John 1:29–30). With this statement, the Baptist provides a lens through which subsequent references in the Gospel to Jesus' death and its culmination on the cross might be interpreted.[55]

Similar to Jesus' avoidance of actual baptism by John, the Johannine Jesus is not, in fact, depicted as making use of the vessels for ritual purification that are present at the wedding of Cana in Galilee (2:6). He simply repurposes the containers so they become the repository of copious amounts of wine. Perhaps one might go so far as to theorize that Jesus' presence at the event, and his own level of purity, conveyed a similar state of purity to the partygoers, making the need to have recourse to the water in the jars unnecessary, consequently freeing them to serve as makeshift wine amphorae.

Yet one more example of Jesus being seemingly exempt from a need for purification is recounted by the Evangelist. According to details in the narrative, it was customary for those who lived outside of Jerusalem to travel to the city a few days prior to the Passover festival in order to purify themselves immediately prior to the religious celebration (11:55). The narrative suggests that Jesus foregoes this opportunity for

---

55. William R. G. Loader, "Tensions in Matthean and Johannine Soteriology Viewed in Their Jewish Context" in *John and Judaism: A Contested Relationship in Context*, ed. R. Alan Culpepper and Paul N. Anderson (Atlanta: Society of Biblical Literature, 2017), 176.

cleansing. Rather than joining the early crowds who seek to become ritually clean prior to the celebration, six days prior to Passover, Jesus is in Bethany, sitting at a table with Lazarus, whom he had raised from the dead, and having his feet anointed by Mary. Taken together, these anecdotes seem to imply that Jesus himself has no need of purification because he is already, by virtue of his identity as God's Son, pure. Which reminds us that earlier in this piece we had mentioned Fredriksen's speculation that Jesus, like the man he encountered at the Sheep Gate (5:2–5), was present at the pool for purification himself. In the context of these other Johannine scenes, we now see that her interpretation is unlikely. The cosmic Christ, the *logos*, is already perpetually in the presence of the divine and fully sanctified. Purity rituals are not necessary.

That is not to say, however, that one can conclude that Jesus is impervious to accumulating impurity, should he be exposed to it. He is, after all, human as well as God's Son. Presumably he interacts with followers and opponents who both are likely occasionally in states of ritual impurity through menstruation, discharges of bodily fluids like semen, and exposure to death. In any case, just as the Johannine Jesus moves in a world where rituals for purification are available, but he is not portrayed as explicitly taking advantage of them, the Evangelist is very circumspect when it comes to scenes where Jesus touches others. In fact, John's Jesus rarely does so, thereby limiting exposure to persons and liquids that might transfer impurity to him.[56]

Healings and Resurrection Miracles

There are only four miracles relating to healing or resurrection in John, and in each, the story unfolds in ways that any possible taint of impurity through contact is either sidestepped or, if it occurs, there are hints in the text that any impurity contagion is mitigated. First, Jesus heals an official's son sight unseen simply by declaring the youngster would live (4:46–53). No contact is involved. In a similar fashion he uses words alone in order to cure the man who had the prolonged illness—the one whom he met by the pool at the Sheep Gate (5:1–16).

---

56. For a description of sources of impurity and modes of transference, see Harrington, *Impurity Systems of Qumran,* 41.

By not touching him, Jesus avoids any chance of encountering impurity in that scene, too.

In regard to the third healing, that of the man born blind (9:1–14), Jesus changes up his healing technique a bit by spitting and creating a mud poultice, which he then applies to the man's eyes. That the sightless man was already free of at least moral impurity is established at the outset of the pericope. As soon as the disciples see the sightless man, in fact, they wonder whether the man's blindness was caused by sins he committed in the womb or, because it was the case that he was blind from birth, by his parents' sins. Jesus' students were no doubt voicing the perception that infirmity was a punishment from God. The idea that transgressions resulted in punishments, including sickness, is already at work in the Pentateuch. A key example occurs when Miriam is afflicted with a skin aliment (leprosy) after slandering her brother (Num 12:1–15).[57] In the case of the man born blind, however, Jesus assures his disciples that sin was not part of the picture at all; the man's blindness only served to highlight God's works (John 9:3). Although free of moral uncleanliness, this still leaves the question of whether the man might have nonetheless possessed some sort of ritual impurity that could have been transferred to Jesus through the application of the mud. After all, Jesus sends the man to the pool of Siloam to wash (9:7), which looks like a ritual ablution. As point of fact, this particular pool may not have functioned as a *miqwa'ot* at all, but was likely a community bath or even swimming pool, due to its very large size and elaborate ornamentation.[58] To be specific, it is probably the case that the command to wash had the more practical goal of enabling the man to remove the grime from his eyes.

The final miracle is that of the raising of Lazarus from the dead (11:1–44). The situation in which the Johannine Jesus finds himself upon traveling to Bethany is one in which it would seem that exposure to corpse impurity would be inevitable—through contact with the corpse, the grave, a mourner, the defiled home in which the deceased likely breathed his last before interment, or any objects that had been

---

57. Kazen comments on Miriam's illness in *Jesus and Purity*, 209.

58. Yoel Elitzur takes this position and even observes that if this is the pool described by Josephus, the vocabulary for swimming and diving that the historian employs suggests that the pool was used for leisure. Yoel Elitzur, "The Siloam Pool—'Solomon's Pool'—Was a Swimming Pool," *Palestine Exploration Quarterly* 140, no. 1 (2008): 22.

in the home. Amazingly, though, Jesus skates through this veritable minefield of sources of impurity without any contact with persons or objects that might carry the contagion.

First, he never enters the home or, for that matter, even the town of his grieving friends. Instead, Martha heads out to meet him while her sister stays in their house (11:20). After they finish conversing, Martha calls Mary to come and speak with Jesus; he doesn't walk back with Martha to see her in the residence where she has been hosting other mourners. So at this point in the narrative, Jesus is still lingering outside the village—more than a safe distance from any potential defilement that might be conveyed by stepping into their dwelling. Jesus also appears to skirt any one-day contamination, since he does not comfort either of the sisters by touching them. In fact, Mary kneels at his feet, making it difficult for him to hug her, even if he wished to do so (11:32). To this point in the scene, it almost appears as though Mary and Martha are intentionally working together to preserve Jesus' purity at a time when one might have expected them to be consumed by their loss. This does not mean, however, that Jesus is detached from their sorrow and the loss of his friend. On the contrary, he is deeply sympathetic when he sees Mary crying, and soon begins to weep himself (11:34–35).

Within short order he accepts an invitation to travel to Lazarus' gravesite, a point in the narrative where Jesus seems most at risk to compromise his own purity. After all, graves were a source of defilement, too.[59] Yet, Jesus neither enters the cave nor touches the stone that sealed its entrance. Rather, from a safe distance away he directs others to move it (11:39, 41) before he calls out to Lazarus. Even here the Evangelist inserts a significant detail. By pointing out that Jesus uses a booming voice ($\phi\omega\nu\tilde{\eta}$ $\mu\epsilon\gamma\acute{\alpha}\lambda\eta$), the implication is that he is standing at some distance, likely far enough to avoid any likelihood of contracting impurity.[60] Then, when Lazarus does emerge from the tomb, Jesus still avoids contamination, since he does not touch his reanimated friend.

---

59. Even the tombs at Qumran are situated a little over 4 yards outside of the community walls, providing evidence that the sectarians were attuned to corpse impurity. Hannah K. Harrington, *The Impurity Systems of Qumran and the Rabbis: Biblical Foundations* (Atlanta, GA: Scholars Press, 1993), 69–70.

60. The volume he employs here to call Lazarus stands in significant contrast with what was presumably the normal conversational level he uses to address his Father, emphasizing that his relationship with God is very close.

He simply adjures others to remove the burial bindings with which he had been confined.[61] At this point, Jesus disappears from the scene, presumably without having compromised his purity in the slightest. It is only after quite some period of time and a sojourn in Ephriam, where he lingered with his disciples (11:54), that he finally returns to Bethany and enters the home of his friends in order to dine with them (12:1–2). No doubt by this point, the week-long period during which corpse impurity was contagious had long passed.[62]

John's christologically driven agenda to assert Jesus' inherently pure nature is set in vivid relief when compared to some of the accounts of healings and resurrection miracles in the Synoptics. For instance, in the narrative world created by John, it would be unimaginable for Jesus to take the hand of Peter's feverish mother (Matt 8:14–15),[63] touch a leper (Matt 8:1–3; Mark 1:40–45; Luke 5:12–16), or put his fingers into the ears of someone who is unable to hear (Mark 7:31–37).

In the episode with Lazarus, Jesus' ability to avoid touching a grave or even the person of Lazarus, one of his close friends, offers marked contrast to the pericope in Luke 7:11–17, in which Jesus grabs hold of the pallet carrying the deceased son of a widow before bringing him back to life, or even the passage when he enters Jairus' recently corpse-defiled home and grasps the hand of his dead daughter (Mark 5:22–24, 35–43) before resurrecting her. It is not surprising that these stories of healings and resurrections involving bodily contact, and others besides, are missing from the Fourth Gospel, given John's concerns to portray Jesus' as possessing a constant state of purity.

Further, the Evangelist is consistent in downplaying or skirting other episodes from Jesus' life that would involve Jesus coming into physical contact with impurity. For instance, a prologue that is

---

61. Kazen recognizes that Jesus does not touch the grave or the corpse, yet for some reason is reluctant to claim that Jesus is respecting purity regulations in this case, presumably because Kazen's focus is the historical Jesus and the purity concerns are a result of Christological concerns. Kazen, *Jesus and Purity*, 167.

62. This is not to say that Jesus is modeling behavior where everyone should avoid corpse defilement. In the Lazarus story, the various mourners who are present in the home, Lazarus' sisters, and even those who assist with the stone and unbinding incur impurity and are not upbraided for doing so. It is only Jesus who appears to need to maintain his status, presumably so he might continue his close association with his Father and, ultimately, to serve as an unblemished sacrifice on the cross. In short, one cannot imagine the Johannine Jesus suggesting to one of his disciples that he should not bury a family member (Matt 8:21–22).

63. Mark 1:29–31; Luke 4:38–39.

concerned about the cosmos and asserts the Son's unity with the Father and emphasizes preexistence takes the place of a birth story in which Mary would have been impure for seven days after delivering a male child (Lev 12:1–8). Then, while ministering in proximity to the Baptist, Jesus' group began to offer baptisms of their own (3:22), but the narrator is careful to offer an editorial aside that Jesus himself was not performing the lustrations but was leaving it up to his disciples (4:2). Thus, Jesus never touches those coming to seek cleansing through the ritual.[64]

Soon after this event in the narrative, Jesus travels to Samaria, where he asks a woman whom he meets at a well for a drink. It seems, however, that this was merely an icebreaker that paved a way for the two of them to engage in a theological discussion. Jesus does not actually imbibe any water drawn by the women. Surely this is one more instance where he maintains his personal purity. At the close of their conversation, the woman even leaves her own water jug behind (4:28). This, too, has purity overtones, since, unlike limestone vessels (very few of which have been discovered by archeologists in Samaria), a jug made with fired clay could transmit uncleanliness.[65] What seems to be a practice of abandoning lamps or even perfume bottles at gravesites since they had acquired corpse impurity would fit well with a scenario in which a polluted water jug would be discarded after a woman learns about the pure living water available through Jesus.[66]

On top of these examples, in the run-up to the passion, John's Jesus gives Judas a piece of bread (13:26, 30), which occurs before the act of betrayal, but receives no kiss from this disloyal follower in the garden (contrast Matt 26: 47–49; Mark 15:43–45; also Luke 22:48). Given that Jesus is in some way intertwined with his Father, it is not surprising that in the Fourth Gospel the betrayer, whose actions would be considered a moral sin, nevertheless completes his work without touching Jesus.[67]

---

64. Regev notes that early Christians believed that the Baptist called for two sorts of purification: a ritual or symbolic purification that involved immersion and repentance of sins. Regev, "Moral Impurity," 390.

65. Jensen, "Purity and Politics in Herod Antipas's Galilee," 13.

66. On the abandonment of *unguentaria* and lamps, see Byron R. McCane, *Roll Back the Stone: Death and Burial in the World of Jesus* (Harrisburg, PA: Trinity Press International, 2005), 48–49.

67. The fact that Jesus travels throughout Galilee but the Evangelist does not include a visit to Tiberias may be linked to the purity theme, since that city was built on a burial ground. See Kazen,

At this point in the narrative, Jesus is arrested and bound, constrained while led to the examinations preceding his crucifixion. As Kathleen Troost-Cramer notes, the binding calls to mind the sacrifice of Isaac, who was bound when he was to be sacrificed by his father (Gen 22). She also finds links with the twice daily *tamîd,* or offering of a lamb on the temple altar (Exod 29:38–42).[68] From this point in the narrative until his death, Jesus is clearly serving as a sacrificial victim. In this context, the Johannine concern with preserving Jesus' purity makes sense, since it was expected that those animals that were selected for sacrifice should be blemish free (Lev 1:3; 22:17–28). Klawans, in discussing the requirement concerning sacrificial victims, writes,

> It is commonly pointed out that it is fitting for animals offered on the holy altar to be perfect and whole. It is equally important to recognize, however, that this stipulation does not only concern the animal: it requires the offerer to carefully examine the animal destined for sacrifice. These regulations, moreover, don't only apply at the moment of sacrifice. Prudent shepherds will properly care for their flocks, watching for blemishes that have appeared, trying to prevent others from coming about.[69]

It is almost as though the Evangelist had these exact precepts in mind when portraying Jesus arriving at the cross without so much as a speck of impurity to blemish his sacrificial act. At this point, one might object that Jesus was exposed to impurity during his interrogation by Pilate. Indeed, while Jesus is ushered inside Pilate's *praetorium,* those who delivered him to that space eschewed entering so that they themselves could avoid defilement prior to eating the Passover meal (John 18:28). In actuality, this verse is an example of Johannine irony. Since the building was occupied by a Roman administrator and likely contained leavened bread and perhaps even pork, the Jewish officials were demonstrating a voluntary, supererogatory act of piety that could be

---

"Concern, Custom and Common Sense: Discharge, Hand Washing and Graded Purification," *Journal for the Study of the Historical Jesus,* 13 (2015): 153.

68. Kathleen Troost-Cramer, *Jesus as Means and Locus of Worship in the Fourth Gospel* (Eugene, OR: Pickwick, 2017), 7, 72. While Troost-Cramer mentions that there are sources that link the *tamîd* and atonement, Klawans asserts that expiation is not a goal of these daily sacrifices, which were instead to provide a pleasing odor to encourage God's continued presence in the sanctuary. Klawans, *Purity, Sacrifice,* 72.

69. Klawans, *Purity, Sacrifice,* 62.

contrasted with their willingness to seek Jesus' death. Although eating or handling unclean foods would result in defilement, as is clear in 1 Maccabees 1:62–63, Jesus himself was a bound prisoner and not a guest who would be invited to dine. Therefore, he would not be sullied.[70] To that end, given that the Evangelist has set the timing of Jesus' death to coincide with the sacrifice of the lambs for Passover, and that the religious leadership has essentially already fulfilled its duties with regard to selecting a sacrificial victim (Exod 12:6) when Caiaphas declares that Jesus will die on behalf of the nation and all believers in the diaspora (John 11:45–53), all that remains, if one is following the steps of sacrificial rituals, is the death of the victim and the disposal of its remains. With Jesus, the Son, it should be no surprise that there will be a twist to these elements, too.

Purity in Death and Resurrection

Here is where we return to the fact that blood and water flow from Jesus side when he is pierced by the spear. The expulsion of water and blood from Jesus, who in the Gospel is the source of living water (4:10–15; 7:37–39), not only serves as a symbol of the purification that Jesus' expiatory death accomplishes, a point recognized by Brower, but also and at the same time affects self-purification of Jesus' corpse.[71] Even in death, Jesus is clean.

Just as the author was scrupulous to show that purity was maintained during the raising of Lazarus and at the cross, so, too, is care taken to ensure that no taint of corpse defilement trickles into the time period that follows the death to contaminate either the corpse of Jesus (perhaps by exposure to some other corpse or source of ritual

---

70. Keener asserts that dwellings of gentiles were impure and that the *Praetorium* was Pilate's residence (1099). He references *M. Ohal.* 18:7 in making his case. That same passage states that gentiles must be in residence for forty days for the home to be considered unclean. Given that Pilate's primary dwelling would have been in the administrative capital of the province, Caesarea Maritima, and he likely was in Jerusalem only on a temporary basis, such as while undertaking an assize, it is not clear his presence would have met the forty day requirement. If the *Praetorium* was one of Herod the Great's palaces and continued also to serve as a residence for his descendants, its identification as a gentile residence is even further complicated. Looking at another possibility, if the *Praetorium* was located in the Antonia Fortress, which also housed a legion, *M Ohal* 18:10 would exempt it from laws related to dwellings of gentiles. Even apart from *M. Ohal.* 18:7, Acts implies that a key issue related to gentile dwellings revolved around acts of hospitality and eating unclean foods served by non-Jews (Acts 11:3).

71. Brower is primarily referencing and interacting with a doctoral dissertation by Rhonda Crutcher. See Brower, "Purity in the Gospel of John," 126–27.

impurity) or his closest associates. The first way this is accomplished involves the actions of Joseph of Arimathea and Nicodemus. These are, by all accounts, relatively minor players in the narrative. Nicodemus stepped on stage just briefly early in Jesus' public ministry (3:1–10), but this is the first time Joseph is introduced in the text. That they retrieve Jesus' body, treat it with a generous supply of spices, and subsequently ensure that it is properly entombed, accomplishes two things. First their act of a prompt burial would have guaranteed that corpse impurity, if present at all, would have had only a minimal chance to spread to the wider population. Of course, if indeed Jesus corpse was self-purifying, this would be redundant, since impurity would not exist. It would, however, prevent any recontamination of Jesus' corpse by other sources of defilement.

Second, it seems that generally it was the case that women tended to take on the task of wrapping the body and applying the spices, an activity that took place in the home.[72] With Joseph and Nicodemus' intervention, however, even if some sort of impurity associated with the corpse might be present, the women and their house would remain undefiled. It seems that the Evangelist was covering all bases and exercising an excess of caution. For readers who might have missed the self-purifying action of the mix of water and blood on the cross, the spread of contamination to Jesus' closest friends and family by his body would have been negligible, if it occurred at all. On the other hand, the quick interment of what might ironically be described as a "pure corpse" is an anomaly, to be sure.

There is one more detail regarding Jesus' entombment that is important not to overlook: Jesus' body is placed in a grave in which no one else had ever been interred. Family tombs were the norm, and while the Essenes chose the method of individual burials rather than committals with kin, this might be attributed to a sense that primary ties were to the community rather than to one's family.[73] Although it is sometimes suggested that the new tomb was a mark of dishonor because criminals, the status society might accord to anyone who was executed through crucifixion, would not normally be accorded the

---

72. InHee C. Berg, "The Gospel Traditions Inferring to Jesus' Proper Burial through Depictions of Female Funerary Kinship Roles," *Biblical Theology Bulletin* 47, no. 4 (2017): 219.

73. Markus Bockmuehl, "'Let the Dead Bury Their Dead' (Matt 8:22/Luke 9:60): Jesus and the Halakah," *Journal of Theological Studies* NS 49, no. 2 (October 1998): 560.

privilege of being buried with family, awareness of the purity motif in John provides an alternate interpretation.[74] Since the new tomb would not already be contaminated by other corpses, it is, in a word, pure. Consequently, those who visit the tomb would not incur defilement.

If this interpretation of the tomb is plausible, when Mary Magdalene approaches but does not enter the grave on Sunday (20:1, 11), she would not incur impurity. Likewise when Peter and the Beloved Disciple race each other to the burial chamber in order to confirm that it is empty, they would not be subjected to corpse contagion either, even when they take it a step further and actually enter into the small space.[75] Nonetheless, the Evangelist does evidence the same abundance of caution related to purity when it comes to touching the resurrected Jesus that was a characteristic of the earlier part of the Gospel. For instance, when Mary Magdalene finally does see and recognize the resurrected Jesus in the garden later that same Sunday (20:14–17), she is warned not to throw her arms around him. This makes sense. If she had lingered in the cemetery for almost a full day, it would not be a stretch to infer that she might have somehow incurred a mild one-day impurity. Since it was not yet evening at the time of their conversation (20:19), such a defilement would not yet have been completely ame-liorated. Yet, the sun had already set by the time Jesus passes through a locked door and convenes with the disciples to bestow the Sprit on them with a breath. Associating with them at that point in the day was a safer bet, given that some potential one-day impurities they may have accumulated in the daytime would have expired. Along these same lines, it turns out that Thomas' absence on that evening is fortuitous. It is not until an entire week passes (20:26) that he is invited to put his fingers into the holes in Jesus' hands and insert his fist into the wound in Jesus' side (20:27–28). Given that timeframe, there would have been ample opportunity for Thomas to complete the regimen for even the most severe form of corpse defilement, had he somehow contracted it.

---

74. Berg, "The Gospel Traditions," 224.

75. Holmén writes, "If a human corpse regains its life, its purity is the same as if it had lived the whole time, i.e., it is no longer unclean." In support of this assertion, he cites private com-munications with Jacob Neusner and his personal rabbi. He also references 1 Kings 17:17–24 and 2 Kings 4:18–37. He does concede to some uncertainty concerning whether or not this interpretation might be anachronistic when applied to Jesus' time period. (See Holmén, 2718.)

Before closing, there is one last observation to make. The final stages of sacrificial rituals, which, given the Johannine emphasis on maintaining Jesus' purity as victim, his crucifixion appears to be, include the disposition of the remains of the sacrifice. Certainly Nicodemus and Joseph of Arimathea assist in this regard with their role in burying Jesus. Further, the resurrection certainly eliminates the need for additional concern with a body. Yet, as Klawans points out, a typical element that closes a sacrificial ritual involves a meal, whether God "consumes" the victim when it is burned or it is dissected (butchered) by the officiating priests and distributed to some or all of those taking part in the ritual, whether the priests themselves or the individual or group on whose behalf the offering was made.[76] There are some examples in Jewish tradition. The Passover lamb is consumed by the people after it is killed, and Leviticus 7:11-38 provides descriptions of some other types of sacrifices that are eaten, at least in part, by either the priests or the one(s) making the offering.

It is unsurprising, then, that the resurrected Jesus provides the disciples with a miraculous and super-abundant catch of fish (21:4-6). In addition, a few fish are cooked over a fire and shared in a breakfast meal (21:9, 12).[77] These acts bring the sacrificial rite to its natural end.

Conclusion

A decade ago, David Baggett asserted that Gary Habermas "is arguably the world's leading expert on the historicity of the resurrection of Jesus."[78] He recognized Habermas's tremendous contribution to that topic through the esteemed scholar's copious and, by Baggett's

---

76. Klawans, *Purity, Sacrifice*, 65.

77. With the command to feed Jesus' sheep (21:15–17), it seems as though Peter is being charged to take on a priestly role. This is not farfetched. Already during the footwashing in John 13, Jesus effectively ordained Peter. Rinsing one's feet was required of the priests who officiated at sacrifices in the tent of meeting (Exod 30:17–21; 40:30–32). John Christopher Thomas confirms that this ablution was also mentioned by Josephus and practiced in the Second Temple period (*Footwashing in John 13*, 19). Although Peter is not from one of the traditional priestly lineages, and might not be a logical choice for priestly duties as a result, the Evangelist is not overly concerned with issues of human genealogy—even for Jesus himself, as the question of Jesus' human lineage in 8:39–47 and fatherhood indicates. It is the relationship with God and his Son that takes priority. That Jesus would ordain just as Moses did would also flow from the Moses typology that is prevalent elsewhere in the Gospel, such as the Bread of Heaven discourse in John 6.

78. Habermas and Flew, *Resurrection*, 13.

evaluation, successful debates with skeptics and non-believers, along with a mountain of publications on that subject.

Habermas inspired this particular exploration of the interweaving of Christology, purity, and sacrifice in the Fourth Gospel. By and large, this study is rooted in the work of Jonathan Klawans. For his part, Klawans makes the observation that sacrifice and purity are closely related; in Leviticus, the two concepts are juxtaposed, and sacrifice begins with the process of purification. Thus he asserts that "an integrated approach to purity and sacrifice is a desideratum."[79] Exploring the concept of purity in the Fourth Gospel, which Kent Brower maintains is a relatively unplumbed area, reveals that purity is a thread that is wound through the entirety of the narrative and is related to the cross. For the Evangelist, Jesus' personal purity is anchored to the Christological issue of Jesus' identity as God's son. In addition, the Johannine Jesus is portrayed in such a way that this purity is scrupulously maintained throughout the Jesus' public ministry. In fact, this purity serves to justify Jesus' role as a perfect, blemish-free, sacrificial victim on the cross.

Finally, this constant state of purity is also reflected in scenes related to Jesus' burial and resurrection. There is no corpse impurity to remove with Jesus' death. Instead, when the disciples race toward the empty tomb, they are running to life and a renewed relationship with God.

---

79. Klawans, "Pure Violence," 134.

14

A NOTE ON WOMEN AS WITNESSES AND THE EMPTY TOMB RESURRECTION ACCOUNTS

Darrell L. Bock

It is often said that women could not be witnesses in the Jewish ancient world. This point is applied to the resurrection empty tomb accounts and the kerygmatic event tied to them. The claim is that these accounts are not fabricated. One would not choose to have as witnesses a group that does not culturally count as witnesses for a controversial event. One difficult cultural hurdle (physical resurrection) should not be supported by yet another cultural hurdle (women witnesses) in a battle to argue for the credibility of something. The women are in the story because they were a part of the original event. This use of the criterion of embarrassment has been an important argument in making the case that there was an empty tomb and a concrete event behind resurrection claims.[1]

The argument of women as non-witnesses needs a closer look. Carefully examining ancient texts, Robert Maccini has sought to qualify this argument, contending that there are a few cases where women were allowed to be witnesses.[2] So a look at the nature of such claims

---

1. I made a version of this argument in Darrell L. Bock and Benjamin I. Simpson, *Jesus according to Scripture,* 2nd ed. (Grand Rapids: Baker Academic, 2017), 503. The resurrection accounts are a key concern to the work of Gary Habermas, so this topic honors him in ways that connect to his significant labors.

2. Robert Gordon Maccini, *Her Testimony Is True: Women as Witnesses according to John,* JSNTSS 125 (Sheffield: Sheffield Academic Press, 1996), esp. 77–79, 161–71, 225–33.

and the dates of those resources needs attention. It raises the question whether this broader witness argument has validity or needs refining.

Women as Witnesses

Fair questions to ask in a discussion about witnesses is what kind of witness we have and how women were seen for such a role. There is formal testimony in essentially legal situations tied to things like an oath. There also is broader, general testimony about events. A question to pursue is how the culture saw such general testimony.

There is no explicit text on women giving or not giving legal evidence in the Pentateuch. Perhaps the perspective is best seen in that ten men were required for a synagogue to be formed. This inherently suggests that the presence of a woman does not matter in larger social affairs. This fits the general patriarchal character of ancient Jewish society. A woman *may* be able to corroborate a man's testimony, but in most cases such testimony does not count when given on her own. For example, Deuterony 21:18–21 and 22:13–21 point to the same conclusion. In the first example, both parents are to testify about a troublesome son. In the second, parents can bring evidence to defend the virginity of a daughter by bringing tokens of virginity, such as blood-stained garments or bedding.[3]

By the time we get to the Jewish rabbis, the prohibition on women testifying is strong. Women are not to take an oath. The text *m. Šebuoth* 4.1 declares, "An oath of testimony applies to men but not to women." Another Mishnaic text, *Rosh haShana* 1.8, says, "Any evidence a woman is not able to bring." The absence of a listing of women in *m. Sanhedrin* 3.4 as relatives who can be witnesses assumes women are not in the mix. Only a much later text, *Sifre Deut* 190, notes that some regard women to be fit to testify. However, the way that view is cited means most rejected it. In fact, a portion of that text reads,

> Is it possible to say that a *woman* could also be qualified to testify? "Two (*shnei*) witnesses" (Dt. 19:15) is stated here, and "Two (*shnayim*) witnesses" (Dt. 17:6) is stated elsewhere. Just as the *two* stated here specifies male witnesses, rather than women

---

3. Maccini, *Her Testimony Is True*, 66.

[*shnei* being gendered masculine], so, the *shnayim* stated else-where specifies male witnesses, rather than women.[4]

The same passage also stresses that Deuteronomy 19 refers to men. The later Talmud makes the same point in *Baba Qamma* 88a, reading, "a woman ... is disqualified from giving evidence." Josephus explains in *Antiquities* 4.219 that a woman's testimony is not to be permitted because of "levity and the boldness of their sex." The idea is that women lack the serious substance of character that a witness requires. In ancient Jewish settings, women are seen in a very limited light, very different from modern views. This is an important ancient cultural script that informs how surprising their appearance as key players in the empty tomb account becomes.

Some texts that portray events also have relevance. The book of Susanna tells the story of a woman accused of adultery. Two versions exist. In each, she defends her innocence in a way that suggests she is appealing to God. In the first version in the LXX, she is looking upward as she appeals directly to God, since she does not testify to her condition. In Theodotion, she saves her appeal until the testimony against her has come from elders and judges. Here she cries out in a loud voice (to God) and says directly that their testimony is false. Only Daniel's withering cross-examination saves her, as he exposes their false testimony. Daniel serves in the account as an elder equal in status to her accusers. Susanna never testifies, nor is she asked to do so. Her only recourse is an appeal to God. The case pictures the reality of the limited cultural position of women. There is debate whether this is merely because she is a woman or because of skepticism about self-testimony in general.

At elite levels, there might be exceptions. Josephus notes a few such examples in *Antiquities* 15.82–84 (with an oath), 16.213–19, 16.328–31, and 17.121. However, in one of the examples, Josephus' aside reveals the attitude. He says that Antipater's mother "prattled like a woman" (17.121). In all the cases, it is issues involving men as principals that are in view.

---

4. *Sifre Deut* 190, found at https://jewishstudies.washington.edu/book/sifre-devarim/chapter/pisqa-190.

The Mishnah also shows that there are some limited examples of woman being allowed to testify. These include cases of challenged virginity (*m. Ket* 1.6–7), a witness to a man's death (*m. Yeb* 15.1–2), and some property cases (*m. Ket* 9.4). Even with such limited use, the point remains that women were at best second-tier witnesses. You do not go here for help to decide a matter unless it is absolutely required.

Application to the Empty Tomb Scene

So what do we say about the empty tomb scene? The point emerges that although it is false to claim that women were never allowed to be witnesses, it was rarely the case, taking place only in very limited situations. When it did take place? It was only for certain kinds of cases, where there might be no other way to know. In the case of the empty tomb, it might be that the question about a person being dead or not may be in play as the women testify that Jesus is alive. That might be the door into which this scene can be brought forward as general testimony. However, despite this qualification, the larger point remains. A fabricated event would be unlikely to create a story using a set of second-tier witnesses to make a point about a controversial idea.

An interesting corroboration of this reality might be the traditional list on appearances in 1 Corinthians 15. It does not mention women at all. Of course, this list is about who Jesus appeared to, not about witnesses to an empty tomb. Still this list does not note the appearance to Mary Magdalene that John 20 describes. The 1 Corinthians 15 list is limited to men, with only the possible exception of the mention of the five hundred that may be both male and female.

So our brief note on women as witnesses shows that in a Jewish context, they were at best second-tier witnesses. You might call on them to corroborate certain things tied to sexual status issues. You also might call on them for certain facts, such as the death of someone. You might call on them when there was no other choice. When male witnesses exist, they are unnecessary. Corroboration as a parent or as an elite might also make for other exceptions.

In the Gospel accounts, women are the lone witnesses to the initial awareness of an empty tomb. They alone hear an angelic announcement that God had raised Jesus from the dead. There is no reason to expect a fabricated story to go there unless it took place this way. The tradition shows a certain care in how it presents the sequence that runs counter to the cultural customs. Since we are not in an environment that pushed in a feminist direction (such being a modern reality, not an ancient one), there is no reason to think such a tradition was intended to make a point about women and that such a goal alone can explain its presence. The point stands that the role of the women in this story exists because it was part of the account tied to the event from the beginning, not to some later fabrication. A fabricated story about the empty tomb would have a very different character, given the cultural hurdles already existing in the claim of resurrection. The women are in the story because they were at the event.

15

HISTORICAL EPISTEMOLOGY AND DIVINE ACTION

Benjamin C. F. Shaw

I first met Gary Habermas when I was walking on campus with another player on the ice hockey team who knew him. Rather than being introduced to me as one of the leading experts on Jesus' resurrection, he was introduced to me as the former head coach of the men's ice hockey team. It was not until I later read *The Case for the Resurrection* that I discovered Habermas was known for more than just coaching! A few years later I was fortunate enough to begin working with him. I have been especially impressed by his tremendous work ethic as well as his heart for academics and ministry. Despite having many professional engagements, he is still very mindful to make time for those who come to him with various needs. In fact, prior to working with him, I was one of those very people he took time to help. It is a wonderful honor to be able to contribute a chapter in this book celebrating his career.

Historians and Miracles

In this chapter I will discuss an issue that has important implications to Habermas's research on Jesus' resurrection, namely the question of whether a historian *qua* historian can conclude that a miracle has occurred. The question itself has been undergoing a reevaluation among scholars in recent years.[1] Interestingly, where one falls on this question

---

1. For example, Graham Twelftree's recent book presents several different scholars who examine the historian's responsibility to miracle claims, specifically Jesus' nature miracles. The book, Twelftree argues, "seeks to discuss the problem with the view to seeing whether there is the possibility of greater consensus." Graham H. Twelftree, ed., *The Nature Miracles of Jesus: Problems, Perspectives, and Prospects* (Eugene, OR: Cascade Books, 2017), xi. David Basinger has recently noted

does not appear to be guided directly by the question of whether God exists.[2] There are skeptics who believe historians should, in principle, be able to investigate miracle claims, and there are theists who think they are beyond the historian's grasp.[3] This does not mean that there are not theological or atheological factors that may contribute to how one answers this question. It is simply to point out that presently this issue does not seem to inherently place believers and skeptics at odds with one another.

I will present an argument that outlines why historical epistemology allows for a historian to, in principle, conclude whether a miracle has occurred. To do this I will briefly address the concept of a miracle in general. Then I will examine how our epistemic access to the past allows for the possibility to recognize divine acts. Lastly, I will briefly address two common objections. The goal, then, is not to argue for any specific miracle in particular, but to explain why historians have the epistemological tools to investigate alleged divine acts.

Defining a Miracle

Scholars have had a surprising difficulty in defining a miracle.[4] It is important to examine and define the concept because our definition could affect whether we believe a historian can investigate miracle claims.[5] I also want clarity regarding what sort of events I am referring

---

that the interest of philosophers on the question of the miraculous has not diminished. David Basinger, *Miracles* (Cambridge: Cambridge University Press, 2018), 69.

2. Philosopher Raymond Martin similarly does not find this to be a partisan issue. Raymond Martin, *The Elusive Messiah: A Philosophical Overview of the Quest for the Historical Jesus* (Boulder, CO: Westview Press, 1999), 50.

3. For example, Gerd Lüdemann is a skeptic who maintains that the question of Jesus' resurrection must be asked historically. Gerd Lüdemann, *The Resurrection of Christ: A Historical Inquiry* (Amherst, NY: Prometheus Books, 2004), 11–21. On the other side of the spectrum is the late Anglican bishop Peter Carnley, who believed that those who spoke about the resurrection (and even the "certainty" of the disciples' belief) were not doing so *qua* historians. Peter Carnley, *The Structure of Resurrection Belief* (Oxford: Clarendon Press, 1993), 89.

4. Michael Licona, for example, lists around two dozen different definitions that have been offered in an attempt to define a miraculous event. Michael R. Licona, *The Resurrection of Jesus: A New Historiographical Approach* (Downers Grove, IL: IVP Academic, 2010), 134–35n. 3. See also Robert A. Larmer, *The Legitimacy of Miracle* (Lanham, MD: Lexington Books, 2014), 27–52.

5. Bart Ehrman exemplifies such a problematic definition of miracles. For him, because miracles are events that "defy all probability, [they] create an inescapable dilemma for historians. Since historians can only establish what probably happened in the past, and the chances of a miracle happening, by definition, are infinitesimally remote, historians can never demonstrate that a miracle *probably* happened." Bart D. Ehrman, *The New Testament: A Historical Introduction to the Early Christian Writings*, 3rd ed. (New York: Oxford University Press, 2004), 228–29 (emphasis

to in this chapter. It will thus be helpful to briefly consider the concept of a miracle so that we can better understand why historians would be within their epistemological rights to evaluate them.

David Hume's (d. 1776) well-known definition of miracles as "violation[s] of the laws of nature" is a helpful place to begin.[6] The late Antony Flew, a supporter of Hume, noted that this definition demonstrated some challenges for the believer in miracles. One in particular is the difficulty, if not the impossibility, for one to reasonably conclude a miracle occurred a posteriori. He writes,

> The natural scientist, confronted with some occurrence inconsistent with a proposition previously believed to express a law of nature, can find in this disturbing inconsistency no ground whatever for proclaiming that a particular law of nature has been supernaturally overridden. ... On the contrary, the new discovery is simply a reason for his conceding that he had previously been wrong in thinking that the proposition, thus confuted, did indeed express a true law; it is also a reason for his resolving to search again for the law which really does obtain.[7]

In short, any observed violation of a law of nature will simply cause a revision of the laws of nature rather than the acceptance of a miracle. Additionally, appeals to supernatural intervention due to a violation of a natural law *alone* would also seem to require faulty God-of-the-gaps reasoning since God is used to explain a gap in our knowledge.[8]

---

in original). Licona also rightly objects to those who define *history* in such a way that it a priori excludes inquiries into miracle claims. Michael R. Licona, "Historians and Miracle Claims," *Journal for the Study of the Historical Jesus* 12 (2014): 106–29.

6. David Hume, *An Enquiry Concerning Human Understanding*, 2nd ed., ed. Eric Steinberg (Indianapolis, IN: Hackett Publishing, 1993), 76. For a recent discussion on the decline of Hume's influence, see Timothy J. McGrew, "Of Miracles," in *The Nature Miracles of Jesus: Problems, Perspectives, and Prospects*, ed. Graham H. Twelftree (Eugene, OR: Cascade Books, 2017), 152–73.

7. Antony Flew, "Miracles," in *Encyclopedia of Philosophy*, ed. Paul Edwards (New York: Macmillan, 1967), 349.

8. Philosopher Larry Shapiro also appears to require the believer in miracles to accept God-of-the-gaps reasoning by his definition of miracle. For him, miracles are events that are so incredibly improbable that we simply infer God must have been the cause. Lawrence Shapiro, *The Miracle Myth: Why Belief in the Resurrection and the Supernatural Is Unjustified* (New York: Columbia University Press, 2016), 19–20, 21, 58–61, 78–81. Bart Ehrman gets close to this position as well (Ehrman, *The New Testament*, 226–27). As we will see below, he also incorporates notions of "faith" into his assessment of miracle claims.

Flew makes a fair point. We should not believe that a miracle has occurred merely because of an apparent violation of a natural law or the normal course of nature *alone*. Perhaps a new discovery was rightly observed and our understanding of the world needs to be modified (e.g., the change from Newton's interpretation of physics to Einstein's view). While an odd event could possibly be evidence of a divine agent, it could also be evidence of new discovery. Without *positive reasons* to believe a divine agent was involved, one would be perfectly reasonable to believe a new discovery has been observed.

However, rather than identifying a problem for the believer, Flew's observation actually identifies limitations in Hume's concept of a miracle. The definition as it stands is too narrow since it seems to limit miracles to anomalous events, something many would reject as accurately reflecting their understanding of a miracle.[9] It also appears to conflate scientific discoveries and divine action since there is no way to distinguish between the two. If a miracle is simply a violation of a natural law, then it could be argued there is no room for science to make new discoveries since any new discovery would be considered a miracle.[10] This also places the believer of a miracle in the uncomfortable position of using God-of-the-gaps reasoning to explain the apparent violation. Thus, we see some internal problems with this definition that should lead us to think it needs to be expanded in order to properly capture what is meant by the term *miracle*.[11]

A second reason to expand this definition is, as Craig Keener points out, that Hume neglects to consider purported miracles that do not violate natural laws. Keener argues that "many biblical accounts of miracles portray God working through nature, merely in extraordinary ways. For example, the formulation of 'miracle' against which Hume directs his case fails to cover many of Jesus' works treated as 'signs'

---

9. Even those in the ancient world recognized that a miracle was more than just an experience contrary to the normal workings of nature. Colin Brown, *Miracles and the Critical Mind* (Grand Rapids: Eerdmans, 1984), 5, 7–8.

10. Interestingly, Flew critiques Hume's dogmatic refusal to accept events simply because they are reported as miraculous as detrimental to the sciences. Flew, "Miracles," 351. Flew was referring to what he believes were psychosomatic healings, which Hume had dismissed a priori.

11. Bart Ehrman notes that "scientists today are less confident" of the phrase "natural law" and prefer to think in terms of the "normal workings of nature." Ehrman, *The New Testament*, 226.

or 'miracles' in the Gospels."[12] Thus, for Keener, God could perform incredible acts through, for example, a "powerful wind," as described in Exodus 14:21 or Numbers 11:31.[13] Similarly, "providence" or answers to certain prayers (e.g., healing via natural means) could be described as miraculous without any violations of the laws of nature. The point here is that miracles should not be limited to only violations of natural law but need to include the possibility of God acting through nature itself.[14]

The Super/Natural Distinction

Not only might our definition affect our conceptualization of a miracle, but so could our understanding of the relationship between the natural world and the supernatural world. For example, our beliefs about God's relationship to the world can subsequently impact how we view God's ability to then interact with the world.[15] I will thus briefly contrast two different paradigms that attempt to describe the relationship between supernatural and natural. Although the paradigms below are admittedly broad generalizations, they nevertheless provide a helpful heuristic for highlighting how each paradigm can potentially impact our understanding and knowledge of miracles.

Paradigm one places a hard line between the super/natural worlds. It views the supernatural and natural realms as wholly distinct and separate. Paradigm one has become more prevalent since the Enlightenment and can often be associated with a mechanistic understanding of the natural world.[16]

---

12. Craig S. Keener, *Miracles: The Credibility of the New Testament Accounts* (Grand Rapids: Baker Academic, 2011), 1:133. Adding, "Likewise, most Muslims claim that the Qur'an is a miracle but not that it violates a law of nature."

13. Keener, 181. See also 180–85. Similarly, Stephen T. Davis, *Risen Indeed: Making Sense of the Resurrection* (Grand Rapids: Eerdmans, 1993), 28.

14. As will be discussed below, God working through nature could be understood as analogous to other agents (e.g. humans) who act through nature.

15. As Millard Erickson notes, "The position taken on one doctrine greatly affects our conclusions about other doctrines as well." Millard J. Erickson, *God the Father Almighty: A Contemporary Exploration of the Divine Attributes* (Grand Rapids: Baker Academic, 2003), 14.

16. Wright notes this paradigm is primarily due to Enlightenment assumptions. N. T. Wright, *The New Testament and the People of God*, Christian Origins and the Question of God 1 (Minneapolis: Fortress Press, 1992), 97. Ehrman similarly recognizes the influence of the Enlightenment with respect to our understanding of natural laws. Ehrman, *The New Testament*, 226.

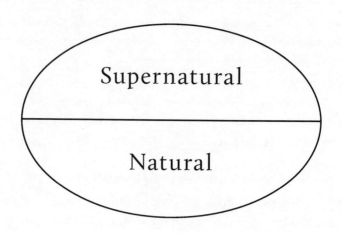

Paradigm One

The second paradigm is one where the dividing line is erased. In this paradigm there is no hard distinction between the super/natural. This does not necessarily imply a form of monism or pantheism, but rather expresses the point that both the supernatural and natural are part of reality.[17]

Undoubtedly other paradigms could be presented, but these two provide a helpful contrast with respect to the ontology and epistemology of miracles.[18] Paradigm one, for example, is foreign to many in the distant past who have claimed that a miracle occurred. Bart Ehrman reminds us that for those in the ancient world, a miracle "did not involve an intrusion from outside of the natural world into the established nexus of cause and effect. ... For ancient people there *was* no ... natural world set apart from a supernatural realm."[19] For Ehrman, then, not only would they seem to reject paradigm one, but they would be at home in paradigm two.

---

17. Similarly, Michael Cantrell observes that the "believer perceives the sacred as quite a natural reality." Michael A. Cantrell, "Must a Scholar of Religion Be Methodologically Atheistic or Agnostic?" *Journal of the American Academy of Religion* 84, no. 2 (June 2016): 378.

18. Another example would be to add the nuance that the line dividing the two may be conceived of in a more porous manner (thus enabling more interaction). Paul Rhodes Eddy and Gregory A. Boyd, *The Jesus Legend: A Case for the Historical Reliability of the Synoptic Jesus Tradition* (Grand Rapids: Baker Academic, 2007), 39 n. 1.

19. Ehrman, *The New Testament*, 226 (emphasis in original).

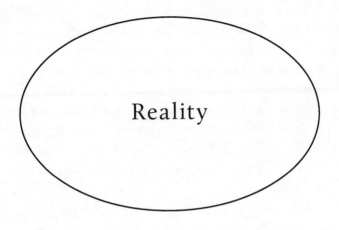

Paradigm Two

Of course, this is not just an ancient viewpoint. N. T. Wright similarly dismisses paradigm one when he writes, "I reject the nature/supernature distinction. ... It seems to me ... that ontologies based on a nature/supernature distinction simply will not do. ... [It is an] untenable ontological dualism."[20] For Wright, part of the problem seems to be, at least in part, how we distinguish between the two worlds.[21] Paradigm one makes it difficult, if not impossible, for the supernatural to interact with the natural because if it does, then it, by definition, becomes part of the natural (similar to Flew's point above), or because it cannot cross the dividing line at all.

Contrarily, paradigm two eliminates one from asking whether something is natural or supernatural (or how we even distinguish between the two).[22] One could argue that Ockham's razor could be

---

20. Wright, *New Testament*, 97; see also 10. For Wright, other false dichotomies that should be abandoned are theology/history and subjectivity/objectivity (24–25, 34, 93, 95). Thomas F. Torrance also argues strongly against dualisms of ontology (Newton), epistemology (Kant), etc. For a summary, see John D. Morrison, *Knowledge of the Self Revealing God in the Thought of Thomas Forsyth Torrance* (Eugene, OR: Wipf & Stock, 1997), 48–60.

21. Wright notes a concern that such dualisms may be used in such a way that collapses one side into the other. Wright, *New Testament*, 25. Similarly Oxford philosopher Steven Clarke has noted the challenges of defining the dividing line between these two worlds. Steve Clarke, "Naturalism, Science and the Supernatural," *Sophia* 48, no. 2 (May 2009): 130, 138–39.

22. Wright holds to a form of critical realism which seeks to inquire into reality while also acknowledging the limitations of the observer. Wright, *New Testament*, 35. He also presents a general outline of his understanding of reality (97–98).

employed here to simplify our understanding. Thus, the difficulty, or possibly the impropriety, of distinguishing between these two realms might be dismissed due to the unnecessary complexity it creates.

For example, let us think about the implications of Wright's argument regarding "heaven" (i.e., "life after life after death").[23] Consider for the moment that Wright is right and that followers of Jesus have been resurrected bodily into an incorruptible new life and world. While it would seem appropriate for one who holds to paradigm two to consider heaven simply a part of reality, how is one to understand this reality on paradigm one? It seems that an implication of Flew's point would be that heaven is part of the natural world, since life in heaven would be a revised set of natural laws. Included in this revised set of natural laws would include things such as eternal life. While it may be true that a rose by any other name would still smell as sweet, it would certainly seem odd for someone who holds to paradigm one to suggest that heaven is part of the natural world.

Conversely, perhaps those who hold to paradigm one might say that heaven in this case is a part of the supernatural world and not the natural world. In this case, one would be left questioning what it means for (resurrected) humans to be a part of the supernatural world and no longer part of the natural world. It would seem odd to consider humans, even resurrected humans, to not be part of the natural world. One would be left wondering what it is that makes these humans part of the supernatural. Is it just that they have eternal life? Are there some set of traits or laws that making something supernatural? However one answers the question, the answers illustrate the concern of Wright and others regarding how one precisely distinguishes the supernatural and the natural worlds.

One might also consider Habermas's research on *evidential* near-death experiences (NDEs).[24] Evidential NDEs refer to a specific type of NDE whereby a person has been "dead" (or almost dead), later revives, and then is able to report empirical data from experiences he or she

---

23. N. T. Wright, *Surprised by Hope: Rethinking Heaven, the Resurrection, and the Mission of the Church* (NY: HarperOne, 2008), 148–52.

24. Recently, Habermas has provided five different categories of corroborated NDEs. Gary R. Habermas, "Evidential Near-Death Experiences," in *The Blackwell Companion to Substance Dualism*, eds. Jonathan J. Loose, Angus J. L. Menuge, and J. P. Moreland (Hoboken, NJ: Wiley-Blackwell, 2018), 227–46.

had while "dead," which are subsequently corroborated by physical evidence, testimony, and so on.[25] Are these evidential cases demonstrative of the natural or supernatural? How is one to classify the reality they experience if these reports are accurate? Again, it seems odd to suggest that such experiences are what we typically mean when we speak of the natural world.[26] Moreover, the distinction between the supernatural and natural worlds becomes more and more blurred.

Although I cannot pursue these issues further here, my goal was simply to explore the different implications of these two different paradigms. Importantly, I have not argued in favor of a specific paradigm but only highlighted how paradigms can affect one's understanding of miracles and their relationship to the world.[27] I will end this section with my own tentative definition. The definition will seek to limit inappropriate a priori considerations while trying to remain open to the possibilities of the different paradigms above. For my purposes, I am seeking to be purposefully broad. A miracle, then, may be defined

---

25. In Habermas's earlier work he provided a categorized list of evidential NDEs according to one's level of death. Gary R. Habermas and J. P. Moreland, *Immortality: The Other Side of Death*, 1st ed. (Nashville: Thomas Nelson, 1992), 74–78. For an entire book dedicated to these types of verified and corroborated cases, see Titus Rivas, Anny Dirven, and Rudolf H. Smit, *The Self Does Not Die: Verified Paranormal Phenomena from Near-Death Experiences*, ed. Robert G. Mays and Janice Miner Holden, trans. Wanda J. Boeke (Durham, NC: International Association for Near-Death Studies [IANDS], 2016). One example of an evidential NDE from the book describes a patient who was undergoing surgery (and properly connected to the medical monitoring equipment). The patient's heart activity ceased for about twenty minutes. The patient was being prepped for an autopsy when suddenly the monitoring equipment began to detect heart activity and other vitals. The patient recovered and later reported various details from this world that should have been unknown to him. His reports were later confirmed (71–78, case 3.11).

26. Another contribution of Habermas might also be used as an example, namely the Shroud of Turin. If this is the burial cloth of Jesus and represents a piece of remaining empirical evidence of the resurrection, the differing paradigms are going to understand the Shroud differently. Kenneth E. Stevenson and Gary R. Habermas, *Verdict on the Shroud: Evidence for the Death and Resurrection of Jesus Christ* (Ann Arbor, MI: Servant Books, 1981). For a minimal facts approach to the Shroud, see Tristan Casabianca, "The Shroud of Turin: A Historiographical Approach," *Heythrop Journal* 54, no. 3 (May 2013): 414–23.

27. Another reason I have not sought to engage these issues more fully here is that to do so would border on the type of metaphysical discussions David Hackett Fischer warns about (see below). The reason I have pointed out these paradigms is that they, particularly paradigm one, frequently do get imposed into historical investigation. It was thus important to evaluate these two interpretive models to see how they might affect one's interpretation. I will be suggesting below that, as part of the normal workings of history, historians should not allow the differing paradigms to wholly interpret data, such as a miracle claim, but that the data should be able to inform the observer how to formulate their paradigm via a dialogical relationship between the two. Wright, *New Testament*, 35.

as *a dynamic event in space/time whereby a divine agent has acted in such a way as to communicate or reveal something intelligible.*[28]

Historical Epistemology and the Miraculous

We now turn to historical epistemology with respect to miracle claims. There are generally two ways scholars have suggested we could proceed. The first is that a historian could say that event X has occurred, without arguing for its cause(s).[29] The second is that one can conclude that X has occurred *and* argue for a specific cause(s). Although the first approach is more modest, as Flew rightly noted, the "essential aim of the historian is to get as near as he can to a full knowledge of what actually happened."[30] Among other things, historians seek to describe past events and, when possible, their cause(s).[31] Thus, I will be arguing that a historian *qua* historian can investigate the event *and* the cause of purported miracles in ways analogous to other historical claims. First, we must briefly look at how historians approach and investigate the past.

Investigating the Past: A Brief Overview of Fundamental Principles

The very first section of David Hackett Fischer's *Historians Fallacies* is dedicated to highlighting fallacies of question framing.[32] One of the fallacies historians ought to avoid is asking metaphysical questions that seek to answer a "nonempirical problem by empirical means."[33] Fischer argues that historians should abandon metaphysical questions raised by determinism and voluntarism, materialism and idealism, and

---

28. This definition does not consider whether the divine agent is benevolent or malicious. Generally benevolent beings are considered to have performed miracles. Our broad definition seeks to avoid these (and other) issues in order to stay focused upon whether a historian can investigate the activity of the divine agent (good or bad).

29. Licona notes that this is a more modest approach and one that is compatible with methodological naturalism. Licona, "Historians," 122–25. Dale Allison appears to make comments sympathetic to such an approach. Dale C. Allison, *Resurrecting Jesus: The Earliest Christian Tradition and Its Interpreters* (New York: T&T Clark, 2005), 298.

30. Flew, "Miracles," 352.

31. Fischer writes, "A historian is someone (anyone) who asks an open-ended question about past events and answers it with selected facts which are arranged in the form of an explanatory paradigm." David Hackett Fischer, *Historians' Fallacies: Toward a Logic of Historical Thought* (New York: Harper & Row, 1970), xv. See also James D. G. Dunn, *Jesus Remembered*, vol. 1 (Grand Rapids: Eerdmans, 2003), 101; Davis, *Risen Indeed*, 24.

32. Fischer, *Historians' Fallacies*, 3–39.

33. Fischer, *Historians' Fallacies*, 13.

"all manner of other monism and dualisms. *The progress of an empirical science of history squarely depends upon a sense of the possible*"[34] This does not mean historians operate from a neutral position on these topics.[35] The point is, however, that although one may have their own metaphysical preferences, these should not be inappropriately imposed on the historical data, because to do so would mistakenly limit what is possible based upon a metaphysical commitments (see below). Fischer suggests that to avoid this and other fallacies, historians should ask questions that are open, flexible, and that can be revised throughout the process of research.[36]

History must not only be open regarding the questions it asks, but also regarding its conclusions. Historians cannot restrict, a priori, the answers to an open historical question.[37] The nature of history is such that many things are possible, but evidence directs us to what is most probable.[38] Since so many things are possible, the historian must remain open to them when beginning their inquiry and allow the data to guide their inquiry towards what is probable.[39] Historical conclusions need to be made on the basis of the available evidence and held provisionally, such that if new evidence should arise, one can revise their initial conclusions.

It is also vital to point out that all historians approach evidence from some perspective, worldview, or paradigm. Just as photos provide true and objective knowledge of what they capture, they too are limited by their vantage point.[40] The historian must keep a constant

---

34. Fischer, *Historians' Fallacies*, 13, emphasis added.

35. Fischer calls this the "Baconian Fallacy." Fischer, *Historians' Fallacies*, 5–6. For a list of metaphysical beliefs held by historians, see Licona, *The Resurrection of Jesus*, 156.

36. As well as operational (empirical), analytical, explicit and precise, and testable. Fischer, *Historians' Fallacies*, 38–39, 160–61.

37. As will be seen below, closed minds of this sort are damaging to scholarship. Wright, *New Testament*, 92–93.

38. For those concerned about history only being able to provide probabilistic conclusions, the words of James D. G. Dunn are helpful: "Probability, we now realize, is *much more integral to daily living* than was previously understood." James D. G. Dunn, "Response to Darrell L. Bock," in *The Historical Jesus: Five Views*, ed. James K. Beilby and Paul R. Eddy (Downers Grove, IL: IVP Academic, 2009), 299 (emphasis added).

39. For one who argues strongly for following after the data, see Thomas F. Torrance, *Space, Time and Resurrection* (Edinburgh: T&T Clark, 2000), 5.

40. Wright, *Surprised by Hope*, 61.

dialogue between the evidence and their interpretive model.[41] Significantly, evidence is not wholly interpreted and can potentially change one's perspective.[42] "The important thing for a historian," writes historian Carl Trueman, "is that a balance be maintained between an *a priori* model that allows an identification and interrogation of the evidence, and an acknowledgement that the evidence itself may require a modification or even an ultimate rejection of the model."[43] Thus, if evidence is obscured from one vantage point, another one can be adopted. Indeed, a plurality of worldviews can enable historians to see events from a variety of angles and better determine which ones are better and why.[44]

In order to examine these different angles, historians must be willing to bracket their own worldviews and consider different vantage points.[45] Wright helpfully notes that in some situations, one should, based upon publicly available evidence, reexamine their worldview and consider other alternatives. He writes,

> If events are public, they can be discussed; evidence can be amassed; and some worldviews become progressively harder and harder to retain, needing more and more conspiracy theories in order to stay in place, until they (sometimes) collapse under their own weight. ... worldviews, though normally hidden from sight like the foundations of a house, can themselves in principle

---

41. Richard J. Evans, *In Defense of History* (NY: W. W. Norton & Company, 2000), 188; Wright, *New Testament*, 1:35, 44; Ben F. Meyer, *Critical Realism and the New Testament* (Allison Park, PA: Wipf & Stock, 1989), 92; Thomas F. Torrance, *Theological Science* (London: Oxford University Press, 1969), 341.

42. "The simple point is that, for all the postmodern rhetoric, there is a referentiality in the historical task that is intimately connected to evidence." Carl R. Trueman, *Histories and Fallacies: Problems Faced in the Writing of History* (Wheaton, IL: Crossway, 2010), 56.

43. Trueman, *Histories*, 107. See also 73. Allison points out that we "have the magical ability to be self-aware and so self-critical." Dale C. Allison, *The Historical Christ and the Theological Jesus* (Grand Rapids: Eerdmans, 2009), 19.

44. Benjamin C. F. Shaw, "What's Good for the Goose Is Good for the Gander: Historiography and the Historical Jesus," *Journal for the Study of the Historical Jesus* 15, nos. 2–3 (December 11, 2017): 300–1.

45. Licona has rightly stressed the need to bracket worldviews, while Eddy and Boyd have correctly noted that worldviews need to be open to critical evaluation. Licona, *Resurrection of Jesus*, 58–62; Eddy and Boyd, *The Jesus Legend*, 81, 83–84.

be dug out and inspected. ... Dialogue is possible. People can change their beliefs; they can even change their worldviews.[46] Differing worldviews, horizons, or explanations can be challenged or supported by the evidence.[47] Unless one maintains a rigid dogmatism, they are not impenetrable fortresses to which all data must conform in order to be accepted.[48]

The basic principles for historians, then, when investigating the past, begin with open questions that can be answered based on evidence. Although we all approach the evidence from a certain perspective, this does not inhibit our ability to know the past.[49] We have the ability to bracket our worldviews, consider alternatives, and judge whether any revisions or changes are needed. As we approach the data, we allow it to inform us of its own structure. We then begin to reconstruct this model and test it against the data, whereby our conceptual frameworks are in dialogue with the evidence.

Methodological Naturalism

While there are several types of inappropriate a prioris that could negatively affect one's investigation of the past (e.g., worldviews, assumptions, etc.), methodological naturalism (MN) is frequently used to negate the historian's ability to discuss miracles.[50] MN requires that historians examine the world *etsi Deus non daretur* (as if there were no God).[51] Such a methodology, imposed a priori, dogmatically restricts

---

46. Wright, *New Testament*, 117. See also 92, 95, 97–99; Davis, *Risen Indeed*, 24–25. For the argument that we may not just read anything we like into the evidence, see Evans, *In Defense of History*, 188.

47. This is precisely Flew's point above with respect to the scientist who comes across evidence that violates the natural law of a current scientific interpretation. The evidence forces the scientist to search for a new interpretive model.

48. Larmer is correct when writing, "Historians can scarcely escape the influence of interpretive horizons based on assumptions they bring to their work, but to the degree that such assumptions cannot be challenged or overthrown by actual evidence, they cease to function as genuine historians and become merely dogmatists." Larmer, *The Legitimacy of Miracle*, 181.

49. Notably pointed out in Thomas L. Haskell, "Objectivity Is Not Neutrality: Rhetoric vs. Practice in Peter Novick's That Noble Dream," *History & Theory* 29, no. 2 (May 1990): 129–57.

50. For examples outside of the issue of methodological naturalism, see Evans, *In Defense of History*, 168, 188. See also Trueman, *Histories and Fallacies*, 87–107; Margaret MacMillan, *Dangerous Games: The Uses and Abuses of History* (New York: Modern Library, 2010), 114.

51. Roland Deines provides a helpful discussion on the origins of this phrase (which is attributed to Hugo Grotius). Roland Deines, *Acts of God in History: Studies Towards Recovering a Theological Historiography*, ed. Christoph Ochs and Peter Watts, Wissenschaftliche Untersuchungen Zum Neuen Testament 317 (Tübingen: Mohr Siebeck, 2013), 2–3. See also

what can be concluded by not allowing one to examine the past with open inquiry.[52] By refusing to allow the evidence of the past to be examined freely, history is undermined, because an open questioning of the past, which is crucial to historical study, is impossible.[53] It is antithetical to the discipline of history for MN to prescribe what questions and answers are acceptable.[54]

Given these issues, it is understandable that discontent for MN has been growing in recent years.[55] In his book *Acts of God in History*, Roland Deines argued that dogmatic MN "*coerces* those who desire to talk intelligibly and rationally about God acting in history, and in their own lives, to *convert* first to a worldview where the very thing they seek to communicate is already assigned to the non-real."[56] Michael Cantrell has similarly contested against such dogmatism. For him it not only "prejudices the integrity of a scholar's work" but can actually lead scholars to do worse in their research.[57] Church historian Brad Gregory highlights the circularity of methodological naturalism in that it unsurprisingly yields only naturalistic conclusions.[58] Even more damaging is when proponents of MN acknowledge these limitations.

Gregory Dawes, "In Defense of Naturalism," *International Journal for Philosophy of Religion* 70, no. 1 (2011): 6.

52. I am *not* arguing against those who hold to MN in an a posteriori manner. Those who hold to MN in such a manner do so provisionally and are open to revising their view in light of new evidence. An example of this would be Dawes, "In Defense of Naturalism."

53. Some scholars refer to the dogmatic imposition of MN as a form of intellectual imperialism. Davis, *Risen Indeed*, 33; Martin, *The Elusive Messiah*, 193–200; Eddy and Boyd, *The Jesus Legend*, 70–71.

54. Eddy and Boyd, *The Jesus Legend*, 48–51, 55, 70–73, 80.

55. A recent series was featured in *History Compass*. See, for example, Luke Clossey et al., "The Unbelieved and Historians, Part I: A Challenge," *History Compass* 14, no. 12 (December 1, 2016): 595, 598–600.

56. Deines, *Acts of God in History*, 26 (emphasis in original). He adds, "[To stay silent about truth] is against the ethos of the university and the practice of good scholarship."

57. Adding, "It is not going too far to say that, by using methodological atheism, a scholar may actually fabricate the data of experience—an action that, in any other circumstance would raise serious concerns about the shirking of proper scholarly conduct." Cantrell, "Must a Scholar of Religion Be Methodologically Atheistic or Agnostic?," 384. See also 379–386. Similarly, Licona, "Historians and Miracle Claims," 112–13.

58. Adding that this "goes on unrecognized to the extent that such metaphysical beliefs [e.g. naturalism] are widely but wrongly considered to be undeniable truths." Brad S. Gregory, "The Other Confessional History: On Secular Bias in the Study of Religion," *History and Theory* 45, no. 4 (2006): 146; Eddy and Boyd, *The Jesus Legend*, 48. More skeptical thinkers have also recognized this point. Maarten Boudry, Stefaan Blancke, and Johan Braeckman, "Grist to the Mill of Anti-Evolutionism: The Failed Strategy of Ruling the Supernatural Out of Science by Philosophical Fiat," *Science & Education* 21, no. 8 (February 22, 2012): 1155.

Robert Webb, for example, concludes that MN is "less satisfying, for its conclusions may be more tentative and explanations are incomplete in certain cases."[59] Rather than settle for an admittedly limited epistemological method, we should strive to examine the past openly, critically, and with a more robust methodology.

Interestingly, much of MN has stemmed from the Enlightenment, which itself sought to undue the dogmatisms of its day. It is ironic that MN is now used to dogmatically deny inquiry into certain questions.[60] Wright rightly calls attention to this inconsistency:

> The underlying rationale of the Enlightenment was, after all, that the grandiose dogmatic claims of the church ... needed to be challenged by the fearless, unfettered examination of historical evidence. *It will not do*, after two hundred years of this, for historians in that tradition to turn round and rule out, a priori, certain types of answer to questions that remain naggingly insistent.[61]

A dogmatic acceptance of MN, then, makes one vulnerable to significant and avoidable objections.[62] In order to sidestep these problems, one simply need not be dogmatic and a priori impose methodological naturalism that artificially limits our knowledge of the past.

Inquirers of the past must remain open and allow the evidence to direct them while refusing to allow arbitrary (or potentially tyrannical) assumptions to be forced upon them. Philosopher of history Aviezer Tucker provides a good reminder that there "are *no a priori* shortcuts. To reach any reasoned conclusion about miracles or any other past event, it is necessary to examine hypothesis about the past in competition with one another over the best explanation that increases most

---

59. Robert L. Webb, "The Rules of the Game: History and Historical Method in the Context of Faith: The Via Media of Methodological Naturalism," *Journal for the Study of the Historical Jesus* 9, no. 1 (January 2011): 83.

60. Eddy and Boyd note that such a method is exemplified when it opens one to investigate the supernatural activity. Eddy and Boyd, *The Jesus Legend*, 16–17, 51–53, 58, 82–90. Adding that dogmatic methodological naturalism claims to be the truly critical method but, ironically, refuses to be critical of itself (55, 75, 78, 80).

61. N. T. Wright, *The Resurrection of the Son of God*, vol. 3 (Minneapolis: Fortress Press, 2003), 713 (emphasis added). See also Wright, *New Testament*, 93 n. 26.

62. Shaw, "What's Good for the Goose," 305–8.

the likelihood of the broadest scope of evidence."[63] There are no short-cuts to good scholarship, let alone excellent scholarship.[64]

Agency and Context

Richard Taylor has helpfully identified two kinds of explanation. For example, one could refer to a *match* starting a fire or a *man* starting a fire.[65] These two kinds of explanations refer to different aspects of the same past event (scientific and agency). The important explanation for our present purposes is agent explanation.[66] Agent explanations can generally be identified by a *telos* or intentionality. Taylor writes that "any true assertion that something *does* occur *in order that* some result may be achieved does seem to entail that the event in question is not merely an event, but the act of some agent."[67] While history is concerned with a multitude of topics, one form of explanation that historians will frequently appeal to is that of agency. As Wright notes, history is "the study of aims, intentions and motivations."[68] Historians frequently seek to know what caused certain people (or groups) to act in certain ways in order to achieve certain goals.[69]

Of course, agency is a broad category and need not apply exclusively to human agency.[70] Historian Christopher Pearson has argued that although many historians believe agency to be a uniquely human characteristic, animals should be recognized as agents who are also capable

---

63. Aviezer Tucker, "Miracles, Historical Testimonies, and Probabilities," *History and Theory* 44, no. 3 (October 1, 2005), 73–390 (390). See also 381, 385.

64. "[T]he freer the historian from alien intrusions, the more demanding his task becomes. He cannot loftily dismiss whole complexes of material as *a priori* unhistorical, nor even begin with the supposition that non-historicity holds until proved otherwise." Meyer, *Critical Realism*, 151.

65. Richard Taylor, "Two Kinds of Explanation," in *Miracles*, ed. Richard Swinburne (NY: Macmillan, 1989), 103. See also Richard Swinburne, *The Concept of Miracle* (London: Palgrave Macmillan, 1970), 53–57.

66. Hume's definition above appeared to be more concerned with the scientific component rather than agency.

67. Taylor, "Two Kinds of Explanation," 107 (emphasis in original). Taylor rightly adds that even if an agent's "actions were quite unprecedented, they would nevertheless be understood, intelligible, and in that sense explained, if they did satisfy these conditions—that is, if they could be truly represented as an appropriate means to some end" (112).

68. Wright, *New Testament*, 111. See also 91, 95. Cf. Trueman, *Histories and Fallacies*, 119.

69. This is especially true in court cases when considering the motive of an alleged perpetrator.

70. Human agency may be the most interesting and popular (thus a reason for studying it and writing it), but that would in no way diminish the fact that there are other forms of agency whereby intentional acts are performed.

of acting intentionally.[71] For Pearson, militarized dogs, although not having the same caliber of agency as humans, nevertheless exhibit the ability to act with forms of intentionality that can, and have been, discussed historically.[72] Thus, historians already examine the past actions of non-human agents with lesser degrees of agency than humans.

Divine agents with potentially greater degrees of agency should similarly be open to historical investigation.[73] Since historians already discuss agency in both humans and non-humans, it would seem odd to refuse to address divine agency (a category of non-human agency). If we can recognize intentional actions in other agents, we should also be able to recognize, at least to some extent, intentionality in divine agents (should they so choose to act).[74]

Agent explanation is important because it provides the type of explanation proper to understanding miraculous events as something different from natural laws (and avoids God-of-the-gaps accusations that merely consider the oddness of an event) and more about intentionality, will, and purpose.[75] But for agents to act with intentionality, a context is necessary.[76] Cutting someone with a knife could be a good thing or a bad thing; it depends on the context. If the context

---

71. Chris Pearson, "Dogs, History, and Agency," *History and Theory* 52, no. 4 (December 1, 2013): 128–45.

72. Licona has made a similar suggestion (using the term "persons" instead of "agents"), but more unique in that he refers to the *possibility* of alien interaction with humans in order to demonstrate that agency could exist beyond humanity. Licona, "Historians and Miracle Claims," 112–13. The overall point here would still apply even to those who suggest that history is a study of the *human* past since the types of events described here would involve human interaction with non-humans (be it dogs, aliens, or the divine).

73. We must add the nuance of the potential immateriality of some divine agents (Eddy and Boyd, *The Jesus Legend*, 59). Regarding the ability of a divine immaterial agent to act causally within the physical world, see Larmer, *The Legitimacy of Miracle*, 105–8. J. P. Moreland also notes the similarity between human and divine agency in J. P. Moreland, "Science, Miracles, Agency Theory and God-of-the-Gaps," in *In Defense of Miracles: A Comprehensive Case for God's Action in History*, ed. R. Douglas Geivett and Gary R. Habermas (Downers Grove, IL: IVP Academic, 1997), 143.

74. "One can definitely speak of a 'plan' here, if this is understood as a purposeful undertaking directed towards a goal." Deines, *Acts of God*, 334 n. 60. Ehrman notes that when apparent miraculous events occurred, "the only questions for most ancient persons were (a) who was able to perform these deeds and (b) what was the source of their power? Was a person like Jesus, for example empowered by a god or by black magic?" Ehrman, *The New Testament*, 226.

75. Gary R. Habermas, *The Risen Jesus and Future Hope* (Lanham, MD: Rowman & Littlefield, 2003), 64–66, 89.

76. An agent cannot act towards a desired goal if they do not know what actions will help achieve this goal. The context of the agent's situation will help reveal which actions will assist in achieving their goals and which ones will not.

is a surgery, then it is good, but it would be bad if the context were a robbery. Without knowing the context, one is unable to move towards a desirable goal because they do not know which actions will help them achieve their goals (in this case, whether to save a life or take it). Context is absolutely crucial to understanding the actions of agents, including the possible actions of divine agents.[77]

How would this apply to divine agents? Skeptical philosopher Larry Shapiro has questioned our epistemic ability to know that God was the causal agent in Exodus when Moses confronts Pharaoh (even if one grants the events occurred as described). He sees no reason to think that God would express himself through might and that to do so is just speculation.[78] Perhaps God's nature is one that prefers to turn the other cheek instead? For Shapiro, we do not have access to God's intentions or desires, so any comment about God's actions (e.g., using might) is conjecture. If one considers this event without a context, then it is indeed difficult to know how God might act.[79]

However, the Exodus account, which Shapiro grants for the sake of the argument, does provide a context for which understanding of the actions of the agents involved makes sense, including God's actions.[80] Among other factors, there is a clear challenging of power occurring whereby God informs Moses that Pharaoh will not let Israel go unless a "strong hand" is used (Ex. 3:19–20; 6:1). Thus, the context enables us to understand why God would use might in this situation (Israel's release), while in other situations He may act differently (just as human agents act differently in different situations).[81]

---

77. This includes unique (possibly divine) actions. Even if such actions, as Taylor notes, "were quite unprecedented, they would nevertheless be understood, intelligible, and in that sense explained if they satisfied these conditions—that is, if they could be truly represented as an appropriate means to some end." He also points out that this is what is done routinely in law courts when trying to determine motive. Taylor, "Two Kinds of Explanation," 112.

78. Shapiro, *The Miracle Myth*, 44.

79. Gregory offers a humorous anecdote that reminds us of the ambiguity of trying to identify the actions of an agent when the agent has not revealed their motivations for acting in a certain way. Gregory, "The Other Confessional History," 132–33.

80. For more details, see Benjamin C. F. Shaw and Gary R. Habermas, "Miracles, Evidence, and Agent Causation: A Review Article," *Philosophia Christi* 20, no. 1 (January 2018): 189–91.

81. On the importance of context, see Larmer, *The Legitimacy of Miracle*, 148–62, 187–88; Habermas, *Risen Jesus*, 63, 66; Davis, *Risen Indeed*, 8, 28. For Licona, context is a criterion for identifying a miracle. Licona, "Historians and Miracle Claims," 119ff.; Licona, *The Resurrection of Jesus*, 163–66.

While it is true that Shapiro grants the evidence for the sake of the discussion, the point I am highlighting is that when the evidence is considered within the context where it occurred, a historian could recognize the intentions of the divine agent. The historian would be using publicly available evidence in order to ascertain what occurred and in a specific context. If this information suggests that a divine agent has acted, then a historian would not be violating any rule in concluding that such an event has occurred.

In summary, I have suggested that miracles are the intentional actions of divine agents. History is a discipline that requires the freedom to be able to openly inquire into the past. I also highlighted that historical methods should be abandoned if they artificially restrict what can be studied a priori, because such methods improperly impose epistemic restraints that distort our knowledge of the past. Additionally, history is frequently concerned with explaining the actions of agents. The intentions of agents are best understood by considering the context in which their actions occurred and should not be neglected. Thus, historians can quite properly investigate the important and significant questions regarding alleged actions of divine agents and draw conclusions on the basis of positive and publicly available evidence, as they would with human agents.

Historical Concerns: "What About..."

As should be clear, I am advocating for an open historical methodology. While there are limitations to such a method, I have sought to take these into account and integrate them into them method above. However, it will be helpful to briefly address two common concerns directly.

History and Faith

A common objection to the historian's ability to access miracles has to do with faith and evidence. Many presume belief in miracles to be known through (subjective) faith and apart from publicly available (or objective) evidence.[82] Ehrman provides a helpful illustration of this response:

---

82. Deines notes that the assumption of religious truths being equated with subjective truths is pervasive in academia. Deines, *Acts of God in History*, 7–9.

> Faith in a miracle is a matter of faith, not of objectively established knowledge. That is why some historians believe that Jesus was raised and other equally good historians do not believe he was. Both sets of historians have the same historical data available to them, but it is not the historical data that make a person a believer. Faith is not historical knowledge, and historical knowledge is not faith.[83]

This objection, although common, has a number of significant problems to overcome if it is to be sustained.

First, historians come to different historical conclusions on all sorts of topics despite also having the "same historical data" available to them.[84] In these situations, scholars (including Ehrman) do not typically accuse their opponents of having some generalized notion of faith.[85] One is left wondering why those who conclude a miracle claim are being treated differently.

It appears one reason is because it is assumed that miracles can only be known by faith. While it is unclear how Ehrman understands faith as an epistemology that can reveal that a miracle has occurred, it would still need to be demonstrated that those who argue for the historical occurrence of a miracle are actually *doing* history differently rather than assuming they are doing so.[86] Contrarily, if they are doing history and providing the relevant data and arguments, then these must be engaged.[87]

---

83. Bart D. Ehrman, *How Jesus Became God: The Exaltation of a Jewish Preacher from Galilee* (NY: HarperOne, 2014), 173. This comment appears to explain why Ehrman's understanding of "canons of historical evidence" cannot demonstrate a miracle. Ehrman, *The New Testament*, 226.

84. Ehrman writes, for example, that historical Jesus research is a "hotly debated area of research" and that he is therefore only able to present what he believes to be the "most compelling" position. Ehrman, *The New Testament*, 231. For an example outside of Jesus research, different interpretations of the French Revolution are mentioned in introductory works on the subject. William Doyle, *The French Revolution: A Very Short Introduction* (Oxford: Oxford University Press, 2001), 98–108. Licona makes a similar observation. Licona, *The Resurrection of Jesus*, 156.

85. Ehrman does not think, for example, Jesus was a cynic philosopher, but he (rightly) does not accuse those who do as acting on some undefined notion of faith (or as a believer). Ehrman, *The New Testament*, 259. Cf. 229. As has been noted, historians do not approach the data from a neutral position, and there are certainly cases where scholars have imposed certain worldviews or assumptions into their historical work, which affects interpretations. For a fascinating discussion on differing interpretations of data, see Michael Polanyi, *Personal Knowledge: Towards a Post-Critical Philosophy* (Chicago, IL: University Of Chicago Press, 1974), 150–60, 286–94.

86. For example, Licona rightly notes that it is hard to read Wright's *The Resurrection and the Son of God* as the product of mere blind faith. Licona, "Historians and Miracle Claims," 111.

87. Philosopher Tiddy Smith makes the distinction between those who use faith as appeals to "supernatural methods of justification" (which are private) and his version of methodological

Second, the notion of faith being used here appears to assume a form of blind or entirely subjective faith. This understanding of faith is problematic both for the historian and the Christian. The problem for the historian is that it is only one understanding of faith among others and thus should not be used as the only interpretive grid for evaluating miracles. As noted above, historians can, and should, conceptualize other models of faith (as they do with different worldviews) rather than ones that make miracles impervious to investigation a priori.

The problem for the believer is that some people appeal to this notion of faith precisely to safeguard their faith from being less than certain or potentially being falsified.[88] The effect of this is that miracles (among other claims) are immune from inquiry. Wright has correctly warned that "without historical enquiry there is no check on Christianity's propensity to remake Jesus, never mind the Christian god, in its own image."[89] It is important that "faith" is distinguished from some sort of Gnosticism whereby secret or hidden knowledge is paramount; this is all the more important when taking the doctrine of original sin into account.[90] Historical evidence is thus important for divine action as well as doctrine.[91] As Davis rightly reminds us, "The

---

naturalism (which relies on publicly available evidence). On his version of methodological naturalism, which appears to be provisional, one could, in theory, investigate miracle claims so long as the evidence is publicly available for analysis. Tiddy Smith, "Methodological Naturalism and Its Misconceptions," *International Journal for Philosophy of Religion* 82:3 (February 2, 2017): 1–16. Additionally, I am not arguing that one may come to know a miracle because of an existential private encounter with God. Such events would only be evidential to the individual who had the experience and if a transformation occurs in that individual, then that transformation could be considered *indirect* evidence to others.

88. "Much Christianity is afraid of history, frightened that if we really find out what happened in the first century our faith will collapse." Wright, *New Testament*, 10. See also 93–94. Similarly, Deines, *Acts of God in History*, 4 ("Committed Christians within Biblical Studies sometimes try to bracket out a supra-historical core from historical examination to leave their central beliefs unthreatened"). See also 344. Dunn offers the following reminder: "The Liberal flight from history was also a search for an 'invulnerable area' for faith. ... But a crucial question was too little asked: whether we should expect *certainty* in matters of *faith*, whether an invulnerable 'certainty' is the appropriate language for faith, whether faith is an 'absolute.' ... The language of faith uses words like 'confidence' and 'assurance' rather than 'certainty.' Faith deals in trust. ... Faith is commitment, not just conviction." Dunn, *Jesus Remembered*, 1:104 (emphasis in original).

89. Wright, *New Testament*, 10. One need not understand this comment as making history and the help of the Holy Spirit mutually exclusive.

90. Deines reminds us that "the authority of the sentence, 'God wills it' is a dangerous weapon in the hands of religious leaders, and even more so, from a theological perspective, *within the reality of a fallen humanity*, for which 'will to power' is one of the most disastrous sins." Deines, *Acts of God in History*, 2 (emphasis added).

91. "Theology does not rule out history; in several theologies, not only some Christian varieties, it actually requires it." Wright, *New Testament*, 95.

only rational way to show that a given event occurred is by historical evidence."[92]

Moreover, knowledge of a miracle alone does not appear to equal faith in the Biblical sense. The Bible recognizes that miracles have and will occur in other traditions (e.g., Deut 13; Mark 13:22 [cf. Matt 7:21–23]) and that these miraculous acts can (and should) be recognized without any subsequent faith or following after the divine agent who performed them. Similarly, but from an inverted perspective, in the New Testament we find examples of people who believe that a miracle occurred but are without committing themselves to following Jesus (Mark 3:22; Matt 11:16–19). Even some more recent scholars have accepted Jesus' resurrection while refraining from commitment (i.e., faith) to Jesus as Messiah.[93] Knowledge alone does not yield faithfulness.

Third, those who argue that historians are unable identify a miracle because it is an act of faith can be the very ones who provide hypothetical examples where a miracle is expected to be identified by their readers *apart from faith*. In other words, they presume their readers will recognize a miracle given the *right constellation of evidence* and not by faith. By presenting a hypothetical example of a miracle occurring in the world, they have simultaneously provided an example of how one could identify a miracle apart from faith. The hypothetical example, then, also provides an example of how a historian could recognize a miracle.

For instance, in addition to Ehrman's comments above, he also argues against the historian's ability to discuss miracles when he writes, "Many historians, for example, committed Christians, observant Jews, and practicing Muslims, believe that they [miracles] have in fact happened. When they think or say this, however, they do so not in the capacity of the historian but in the capacity of the believer."[94] Yet without acting in the capacity of a believer or appealing to faith, Ehrman then goes on to suggest that it would be a miracle "if a preacher prayed

---

92. Davis, *Risen Indeed*, 31.

93. One well-known scholar who takes this view is the late Pinchas Lapide in *The Resurrection of Jesus: A Jewish Perspective* (Eugene, OR: Wipf & Stock, 2002). In his recent work on Jewish research on Jesus' resurrection, David Mishkin notes other Jewish scholars who accepted Jesus' resurrection but remained Jewish. He notes, "A belief in the historicity of the resurrection does not necessarily lead to a personal faith." David Mishkin, *Jewish Scholarship on the Resurrection of Jesus* (Eugene, OR: Pickwick, 2017), 212.

94. Ehrman, *The New Testament*, 229.

over a bar of iron and thereby made it float."[95] The reader is *expected* to be able to envision such an event occurring and recognize it as miraculous despite not having faith or acting in the capacity of a believer.

The reason readers can recognize the event as a miracle is because the right constellation of events have occurred that provide positive evidence that a divine agent has acted in that context. Ehrman appears to be aware of this, which explains why he is able to use it as an example of what a miracle would look like.[96] Yet, if, according to the objection, we can only conclude that a miracle occurred by faith or as a believer, it is not clear how this is so. In his hypothetical situation, if there was, in fact, evidence of a priest who prayed over a bar of iron and evidence that the bar of iron floated, then historical evidence could be used to demonstrate that a miracle has occurred. It seems that the reason the reader would understand the example given by Ehrman is because, and consistent with our contention, they would be able to identify the miracle because of our epistemological access to the past (i.e., history), which enables us to evaluate the evidence of events. Ultimately, then, it is not merely a matter of faith, but simply the right evidence in the right context.

Philosophers, Worldviews, and Faith

Another objection is that historians should pass the question of miracles to other disciplines. The objection suggests that historians do not have the right tools to adjudicate on miracle claims. We might wonder what exactly are these tools, who has them, and, most importantly,

---

95. Ehrman, *The New Testament*, 227. See also 229. More fully, Ehrman presents this example in the context of the natural sciences, whereby one could perform a number of tests and see that the iron bars will sink in every instance. Interestingly, it is not just that the iron bar floats contrary to the normal working of nature that makes the event a miracle, but when the preacher prays over an iron bar and it floats—that's when it becomes a miracle. Thus, we see Ehrman incorporating, at least to some degree, an element of context and agency whereby God is answering the preacher's prayer in his hypothetical example.

96. Ehrman contends that his example is how the natural sciences could possibly identify a miracle, but history could not do so since it "cannot operate through repeated experimentation." Ehrman, 227. Yet this overlooks the fact that in Ehrman's example, he is performing the role of a historian by describing the past experiments in which the iron bars sank every time with the exception being when a preacher prayed over a bar and it floated. Moreover, as noted above, what helps historians (or anyone) identify a miracle is the evidence, context, and agency involved, not whether we can conduct repeated experiments, since a divine agent could possibly work through nature.

why is the historian unable to use them? The general sentiment is that philosophers (and theologians) have these tools.

Noted historian Dale Allison provides an interesting example of this point. Although he used to think these sorts of questions could be answered historically, he has changed his mind. He now thinks the

> discussion has to be handed over to the philosophers and theologians, among whose lofty company I am not privileged to dwell. They, not me, are the ones who can address the heart of the matter, the problem of justifying—if such a thing is possible—a worldview, the thing that makes the resurrection of Jesus welcome or unwelcome, plausible or implausible, important or unimportant.[97]

This comment raises several considerations worth noting.

First, and perhaps most important, philosophers do believe historians can conclude a miracle has occurred. Leon Pearl argued in the *American Philosophical Quarterly* that "*This matter is best left to historians* and archaeologists; *all that philosophical inquiry can do is clear the path for them.*"[98] Skeptical philosopher Evan Fales contends that he "cannot find any principled reason why, *if* supernatural causation is metaphysically possible, its presence could not be detected."[99] While the Christian philosopher Stephen Davis writes, "Could a historian *as a historian* affirm that Jesus was raised from the dead? ... Could a historian *as a historian* affirm that *God* raised Jesus from the dead? ... I believe the answer to both questions ought to be Yes."[100]

---

97. Allison, *Resurrecting Jesus*, 351; Carnley, *The Structure of Resurrection Belief*, 89; Ehrman, *The New Testament*, 226. Despite their arguing for "supernatural occurrences," Eddy and Boyd raise a similar concern in Eddy and Boyd, *The Jesus Legend*, 40, 87–89. A *slightly* different shift appears in Allison, *The Historical Christ and the Theological Jesus*, 66–78.

98. Leon Pearl, "Miracles: The Case for Theism," *American Philosophical Quarterly* 25, no. 4 (1988): 336 (emphasis added). See also Martin, *The Elusive Messiah*, 116–17, 188–89. He also notes the need for criteria in this discussion (110, 115, esp. 116, 119, 189). For one list of critical criteria, see Deines, *Acts of God in History*, 24–26.

99. Evan Fales, "Reformed Epistemology and Biblical Hermeneutics," *Philo* 4, no. 2 (2001): 176 (emphasis in original). See also the skeptical Smith, "Methodological Naturalism and Its Misconceptions." The noted theologian Wolfhart Pannenberg makes a similar argument. Wolfhart Pannenberg, *Jesus: God and Man*, trans. D. A. Priebe and L. L. Wilkins (Philadelphia, PA: Westminster Press, 1975), 109.

100. Davis, *Risen Indeed*, 27. See also 26–34. Similarly, C. Stephen Evans, *The Historical Christ and the Jesus of Faith: The Incarnational Narrative as History* (Oxford: Oxford University Press, 1996), 203.

Second, suppose we grant the point that historians, by the nature of their discipline, do not have the tools to examine miracles, why should we think that they could not obtain these tools and apply them historically? Historians frequently cross-discipline in order to better understand the past.[101] For example, without being a psychologist, a historian could legitimately appropriate knowledge from the field of psychology in order to try to better understand the past.[102] Similarly, one could, as a historian, become familiar with various issues related to miracles in order to better understand the past.[103]

Conclusion

When we consider the historian's epistemic access to the past, we find that there do not appear to be any reasons a priori that a historian could not, in principle, investigate the actions of divine agents. Moreover, given the nature of the discipline as an open inquiry into the past, examining the alleged actions of divine agents is similar to historical investigation into human or non-human agents. This also means that claims of miracles, like other claims about past events, should be critically assessed.[104] Historians should not shy away from these investigations. In fact, given their training, investigating such claims can be incredibly helpful in the discussion. While some

---

101. Licona argues that historians should cross discipline and take into account the doctrine of God as it relates to a historical question (particularly miracles). Licona, *The Resurrection of Jesus*, 155–60, 166–67. Cf. Craig S. Keener, *Miracles: The Credibility of the New Testament Accounts*, vol. 2 (Grand Rapids: Baker Academic, 2011), 665–66. Deines highlights the inverse relationship, that divine acts could potentially impact other disciplines. Deines, *Acts of God in History*, 26.

102. Allison draws from psychology in analyzing disciples' experiences of the risen Jesus in order to draw comparisons and contrasts with bereavement visions. Allison, *Resurrecting Jesus*, 269–99, 364–75. "Allison builds an impressive case for the ontological authenticity of some apparitions [bereavement visions]." Licona, *The Resurrection of Jesus*, 626.

103. One might object to this last response by saying that we argued above that the historian cannot address metaphysical questions. To clarify, we did not say that historians cannot address metaphysical questions (or that historical questions *might* have metaphysical ramifications). Historians can entertain a variety of metaphysical beliefs (Licona, *The Resurrection of Jesus*, 156). The point we were making is that these must be held tentatively and bracketed when appropriate. This maintains the balance between an open approach to history while also recognizing that we cannot help but approach the data from some perspective.

104. Deines rightly notes, the teachings of various religious traditions warn against believing false claims to the miraculous. Deines, *Acts of God in History*, 23. Adding, "But the critical task for a theistically motivated historiography remains to discern whether God's involvement should indeed be seen or heard in an event ... or whether revelatory claims function as an attempt to embellish someone or something for some particular reason" (24). See also Luke Clossey et al., "The Unbelieved and Historians, Part II: Proposals and Solutions," *History Compass* 15, no. 1 (January 1, 2017): 1–9.

historians have already begun doing this, it would be great to see others likewise enter the dialogue.

16

THE PRIMACY OF PAUL IN DISCUSSIONS ON JESUS' RESURRECTION

Michael R. Licona

It is difficult to overstate the importance Jesus' resurrection had among his early followers. The apostle Paul wrote that our hope of eternal life is worthless if Jesus did not rise from the dead: "And if Christ has not been raised, your faith is futile, you are still in your sins. In that case, those who have died as Christians have been lost. If our hope in Christ is for this life only, we are to be pitied more than all others" (1 Cor 15:17–19).[1] Why should followers of Jesus subject themselves to scorn and persecution if following Jesus provides benefits for this life only? In that case, let us eat and drink. For tomorrow we die (1 Cor 15:29–32). If Jesus did not rise from the dead, one might still choose to admire him, or at least some of his teachings. However, there would be little reason for enduring great suffering for his cause or for maintaining any hope of his promise of eternal life being fulfilled for following him.

Given the crucial nature of the question pertaining to whether Jesus actually rose from the dead, we should not be surprised to learn that the question is given a prime place of attention by many New Testament scholars. Pieter Craffert writes, "There is probably no other topic in Jesus research that creates such controversy and inspires more seminars than that of Jesus' resurrection."[2] In reference to the question of what "led certain of the disciples and St. Paul to believe that Jesus had survived in

---

1. All translations and paraphrases in this chapter are mine unless otherwise stated. Italics in translations and paraphrases indicate my added emphasis.

2. Pieter F. Craffert, *The Life of a Galilean Shaman: Jesus of Nazareth in Anthropological-Historical Perspective* (Cambridge: James Clarke, 2008), 383.

some supernatural way," Dale Allison writes, "The question holds its proud place as the prize puzzle of New Testament research."[3]

I know of no one who has spent as much time as Gary Habermas researching matters related to the topic of Jesus' resurrection. His knowledge on the subject matter is encyclopedic. Habermas has no peer.

Since historians must begin with assessing the pool of sources from which they will draw, in what follows, I offer five reasons for viewing the apostle Paul as our best ancient source for answering the most important questions related to Jesus' resurrection.

1. Paul's Letters Are Early

Of the thirteen letters in the New Testament attributed to Paul, there is a nearly unanimous consensus among scholars that seven are genuinely written by Paul (Romans, 1 Corinthians, 2 Corinthians, Galatians, Philippians, 1 Thessalonians, Philemon). A slight majority think Paul wrote two others (Colossians, 2 Thessalonians), and a majority think the remaining four were not written by Paul (Ephesians, 1 Timothy, 2 Timothy, Titus). In order to make my points as strongly as possible, I will confine my discussion to letters that were undisputedly written by him.

Since it is believed that Paul was martyred no later than AD 65, we have a *terminus ad quem* of AD 65 for his letters. Since Jesus' crucifixion is usually dated to either April AD 30 or April AD 33, there is a maximum amount of time of thirty-five years that elapsed between Jesus' death and Paul's letters. And most scholars date at least some of these letters earlier, with all but Philippians and Philemon having been written between AD 48 and 58, which is only fifteen to twenty-eight years after Jesus' crucifixion.[4]

---

3. Dale C. Allison, *Resurrection Jesus: The Earliest Christian Tradition and Its Interpreters* (New York: T&T Clark, 2005), 200.

4. For Romans, see, for example:

AD 57	M. Eugene Boring, *An Introduction to the New Testament: History, Literature, Theology* (Louisville: Westminster John Know, 2012), 317.
AD 57–58	Raymond E. Brown, *An Introduction to the New Testament* (New York: Doubleday, 1996), 560.
Probably AD 57	Douglas J. Moo, *Romans*, New International Commentary on the New Testament (Grand Rapids: Eerdmans, 1996), 3.
AD 57–58	Mark Allan Powell, *Introducing the New Testament: A Historical, Literary, and Theological Survey* (Grand Rapids: Baker Academic, 2009), 258.

But we can trace the traditions about Jesus' resurrection in some of Paul's letters to an even earlier period. For example, virtually all

---

For 1 Corinthians, see, for example,

AD 53–54	Paul J. Achtemeier, Joel B. Green, and Marianne Meye Thompson, *Introducing the New Testament: Its Literature and Theology* (Grand Rapids: Eerdmans, 2001), 336.
AD 54–55	Boring, *An Introduction*, 317.
AD 56–57	Brown, *An Introduction*, 512.
AD 55	D. A. Carson and Douglas J. Moo, *An Introduction to the New Testament*, 2nd ed. (Grand Rapids: Zondervan, 2005), 448.
AD 53–57	Powell, *Introducing*, 279.

For 2 Corinthians, see, for example,

AD 55–56	Achtemeier, Green, and Thompson, *Introducing*, 347.
AD 56	Boring, *An Introduction*, 317.
AD 57	Brown, *An Introduction*, 542.
AD 56–58	Carson and Moo, *An Introduction*, 448.

For Galatians, see, for example,

Mid-50s	Brown, *An Introduction*, 477.
AD 51	Martinus C. de Boer, *Galatians: A Commentary*, New Testament Library (Louisville: Westminster John Knox, 2011), 11.
Before the Jerusalem Council	David A. DeSilva, *An Introduction to the New Testament: Contexts, Methods and Ministry Formation* (Downers Grove, IL: InterVarsity Press, 2004), 496.
AD 48	Carson and Moo, *An Introduction*, 464.
AD 50–52	Craig S. Keener, *Galatians: A Commentary* (Grand Rapids: Baker Academic, 2019), 13

For Philippians, see, for example,

Mid-50s	Achtemeier, Green, and Thompson, *Introducing*, 403.
AD 52–53	Boring, *An Introduction*, 317.
AD 54–56	Brown, *An Introduction*, 495–96.
Mid-50s to early 60s	Carson and Moo, *An Introduction*, 507.
AD 54–63	Powell, *Introducing*, 348.

For 1 Thessalonians, see, for example,

AD 50	Boring, *An Introduction*, 317.
AD 51	Brown, *An Introduction*, 464–65.
About AD 50	F. F. Bruce, *1 & 2 Thessalonians*, Word Biblical Commentary, vol. 45 (Dallas: Word Books, 1982), xxxiv.
AD 50	Carson and Moo, *An Introduction*, 543.
Early 50s	Carl R. Holladay, *A Critical Introduction to the New Testament: Interpreting the Message and Meaning of Jesus Christ* (Nashville: Abingdon Press, 2005), 301 n. 10.
AD 49–52	Powell, *Introducing*, 376.
AD 51	Ben Witherington III, *1 and 2 Thessalonians: A Socio-Rhetorical Commentary* (Grand Rapids: Eerdmans, 2006), 10.

For Philemon, see, for example,

AD 56	Brown, *An Introduction,* 508.
Early 60s	Carson and Moo, *An Introduction*, 592.
AD 54–61	Powell, *Introducing*, 421.

scholars who opine on 1 Corinthians 15:3–7 agree that these verses contain oral tradition(s) that predate the letter. In 15:1, Paul tells the Corinthians that he will remind them of the gospel message he had preached while with them in AD 51–52. In 15:3–7 he writes,

> ³ For I delivered to you of primary importance what I also received: that Christ died for our sins according to the Scriptures ⁴ and that he was buried and that he was raised on the third day according to the Scriptures ⁵ and that he appeared to Cephas, then to the Twelve, ⁶ then he appeared to more than five hundred brothers at one time—from whom most remain alive until now, but some have fallen asleep, ⁷ then he appeared to James, then to all the apostles.

Although scholars differ on whether we are reading remnants of one or two oral traditions, there are items that suggest Paul has embedded oral tradition here in his letter. For example, the terms for "delivered" and "received" suggest the imparting of oral tradition. There is also the presence of parallelism where the lines alternate in length (long-short-long-short), which suggests it may have been arranged in this manner to assist in memorization:

> Christ died for our sins according to the Scriptures
> and that he was buried
> and that he was raised on the third day according to the Scriptures
> and that he appeared

Paul delivered this message to the Corinthians in AD 51–52, so the tradition must be even earlier. How early? There are good reasons for concluding that this tradition probably came from Jerusalem. Paul's letter to the Galatian believers and references in Acts indicate that the early church was headquartered in Jerusalem. It was there when Paul was persecuting the church. It was there three years after Paul's conversion (Gal 1:18). It was there fourteen years later when Paul met with church leadership (Gal 2:1–10). The Jerusalem leadership held supreme authority for adjudicating on doctrine and praxis to which even Paul submitted. Decisions made by the Jerusalem leadership held equally for the church outside of the city (Acts 15:1–29).

Paul could have received the tradition(s) encapsulated in 1 Corinthians 15:3–7 in Damascus after his conversion experience. He could have received it three years later when he spent time with Peter in Jerusalem or fourteen years later when he visited again with the Jerusalem leadership. Likewise, he could have received it from Silas or Barnabas when they traveled with him. Although it is impossible to know when Paul received it and from whom, what can be said is that the tradition(s) about Jesus' resurrection embedded in 1 Corinthians 15:3–7 predates Paul's founding of the church in Corinth in AD 51 and could go back to the very earliest period of the post-Easter church.

2. Paul Had Been an Enemy of the Early Christians

Far from being an overt disciple of Jesus or even a secret one like Joseph of Arimathea (John 19:38), Saul of Tarsus knew enough about Jesus' message that he believed Jesus had been a false prophet and failed Messiah. For Saul, the movement Jesus had started was a danger-ous one that was leading Jews away from the authentic Jewish faith. Therefore, it needed to be crushed, and Saul was happy to help accom-plish the task. He wrote,

> For you heard of my former conduct in Judaism, how I exces-sively persecuted the church of God and tried to destroy it. And I was advancing in Judaism beyond many of my contemporaries among my people, being abundantly zealous for the traditions of my fathers. (Gal 1:13–14)

> [The churches in Judea were hearing], "The one who formerly persecuted us is now proclaiming the faith he once tried to destroy." (Gal 1:23)

> For I am the least of the apostles, not worthy to be called an apostle because I persecuted the church of God. (1 Cor 15:9)

> Circumcised on the eighth day, of the people of Israel, of the tribe of Benjamin, a Hebrew of Hebrews; as to the Law, a Pharisee; as to zeal, a persecutor of the church; as to the righ-teousness in the Law, I was blameless. (Phil 3:5–6)

Luke also reports Saul's persecutory activities. In Acts 7:58, the Jews who stoned the Christian Stephen laid their outer clothing at the feet of Saul before proceeding. Many commentators refrain from guessing what this gesture meant. Fitzmyer writes, "The piling of cloaks at the feet of someone seems to have been a symbolic act, whose meaning escapes us today."[5] If Acts 4:35–36 and 5:1–2 provide insights on the matter, the act may imply the person before whose feet something is laid has some degree of authority or oversight.[6]

In Acts 9:1–2, 22:3–5, and 26:9–12, Luke reports that Saul uttered threats even of death to Christians and secured letters from the high priest, the body of elders, and chief priests, which authorized him to identify and arrest any Jews attending the synagogues in Damascus, men and women alike, who identified themselves as followers of Jesus. He compelled them to blaspheme Christ, then cast his vote against them as they were being led off to their execution.

Therefore, we have Paul's own testimony that he had zealously persecuted members of the Christian movement. This is supported by Luke's narrative in Acts, which has a reasonable chance of being accurate, since Luke probably knew Paul and had traveled with him.[7]

3. Paul Believed He Was an Eyewitness of the Risen Jesus

At some point, Saul had an experience that convinced him Jesus had been raised from the dead and had appeared to him. From then on, he assumed his Greek name, "Paul." He wrote,

> Am I not free? Am I not an apostle? Have I not seen Jesus our Lord? Are you not my work in the Lord? (1 Cor 9:1)

> And last of all as to one abnormally born, he even appeared to me. (1 Cor 15:8)

> [3] Now as he was traveling, he came near Damascus. And, suddenly, a light from heaven flashed brightly around him. [4] And he fell to the ground and heard a voice saying to him, "Saul, Saul,

---

5. Joseph A. Fitzmyer, *The Acts of the Apostles: A New Translation with Introduction and Commentary*, Anchor Bible (New York: Doubleday, 1998), 394.

6. Acts 22:20 is ambiguous: "And when the blood of your witness Stephen was being poured out and I myself standing there and approving and guarding the clothes of those killing him." Was Saul's approval suggesting his authority or merely that he agreed with those stoning Stephen?

7. See Fitzmyer, *Acts*, 50; Craig S. Keener, *Acts: An Exegetical Commentary*, 4 vols. (Grand Rapids: Baker Academic, 2012), 1:407–9.

why are you persecuting me?"⁵ And he said, "Who are you, Lord?" And he answered, "I am Jesus whom you are persecuting. ⁶ But get up and enter the city and you will be told what you must do."⁷ And the men traveling with him had been standing speechless, hearing the voice but seeing no one. ⁸ And Paul rose up from the ground and, although his eyes were open, he could see nothing. And leading him by the hand, they brought him into Damascus. ⁹ And he was without sight for three days and he did not eat or drink. ¹⁰ Now there was a certain disciple in Damascus named Ananias. And the Lord spoke to him in a vision. And he said, "Here I am, Lord." ¹¹ And the Lord said to him, "Arise. Go to Straight Street and seek a Tarsian named Saul in the house of Judas. For, behold, he is praying. ¹² And he saw [in a vision] a man named Ananias come and lay hands on him in order that he may receive sight." ¹³ But Ananias answered, "Lord, I have heard from many concerning this man, how much evil he did to your saints in Jerusalem. ¹⁴ And here he has authority from the chief priests to bind everyone calling on your name." ¹⁵ But the Lord said to him, "Go, because he is my chosen instrument. This one is to bear my name before the gentiles and kings and the people of Israel. ¹⁶ For I myself will make known to him how much he must suffer for my name." ¹⁷ Ananias went away and came into the house, and laying his hands upon him he said, "Brother Saul, the Lord has sent me, [that is,] Jesus who appeared to you on the road on which you were coming, in order that you may receive your sight and may be filled with the Holy Spirit." ¹⁸ And immediately, something like scales fell from his eyes, he received his sight, rose up and was baptized. ¹⁹ He took food and was strengthened. And he was with the disciples in Damascus for several days. ²⁰ And immediately, he began preaching in the synagogues, "This one is the Son of God." (Acts 9:3–20)

The account of Jesus' appearance to Paul and the immediate aftermath is also reported in Acts 22:6–16 and 26:12–18. Although there are some differences in minor details when all three accounts are examined carefully, these should not concern us, since all three accounts were written at the same time by the same author in the same book. Moreover, most of the differences can be easily reconciled.[8]

It is important to go one step further. Paul not only claimed to have been an eyewitness of the risen Jesus, but his willingness to suffer continually and eventually experience martyrdom for his proclamation of the message of Jesus demonstrates his sincere belief in what he was preaching.[9]

4. Paul provides a link to the preaching of the Jerusalem apostles.

Paul wrote the following:

> [18] Then after three years, I went up to Jerusalem to meet with Cephas [i.e., Peter] and stayed with him for fifteen days. [19] And I did not see any other of the apostles except James the brother of the Lord. (Gal 1:18–19)

> [1] Then after fourteen years, I went up again to Jerusalem with Barnabas, taking Titus along, too. [2] I went up because of a revelation and presented to them the gospel that I preach among the Gentiles, but privately to those who seemed influential to ensure I was not running or had run in vain. [3] And Titus who was with me, being a Greek, was not compelled to be circumcised. ... [6] And from those who seemed to be somebody—what they were makes no difference to me; God shows no favoritism—those who seemed influential added nothing to my message. [7] On the contrary, having seen that I had been entrusted with the gospel to the uncircumcised just as Peter has been to the circumcised— [8] for the one who had empowered Peter for his apostleship to the circumcised also empowered me to the

---

8. I have provided a detailed analysis of all three accounts and their differences in Michael R. Licona, *The Resurrection of Jesus: A New Historiographical Approach* (Downers Grove, IL: IVP Academic, 2010), 382–97.

9. See 2 Cor 1:5–11; 4:8–14, 17; 6:4–5; 7:4–5; 11:23–28; Eph 6:20; Phil 1:7, 13, 14, 17, 29–30; 3:10; Col 1:24; 4:3, 18; 1 Thess 1:3–4, 7; 2:2; 3:4; 2 Tim 1:8, 12, 16; 2:3, 9; 3:11; and Phlm 10, 13. His sufferings are also reported in Acts 14:19; 16:19–24; 17:5, 13–15; 18:12–13; and 21:27–36. Paul's sufferings and martyrdom are also reported by Clement of Rome (1 Clem. 5:2–7), Polycarp (Pol. *Phil.* 9:2), Tertullian (*Scorp.* 15; cited in Eusebius *Hist. eccl.* 2.25.8), Dionysius of Corinth (cited in Eusebius, *Hist. eccl.* 2.25.8), and Origen (*Comm. Gen.*; cited in Eusebius, *Hist. eccl.* 3.1). Tertullian reports that Paul was beheaded, whereas Origen and Dionysius do not specify the mode by which he was executed.

Gentiles— [9] and recognizing the grace that had been given to me, James and Cephas and John, those reputed to be pillars, gave the right hand of fellowship to me and Barnabas, in order that we may go to the Gentiles and they to the circumcised. (Gal 2:1–3, 6–9)

From his letter to the Galatians, we learn that on a first visit to Jerusalem, Paul spent time with Peter, who was Jesus' lead disciple. This is an instance when one may rightly infer that the visit involved more than shaking hands and then moving on. Paul spent fifteen days with Peter. Birger Gerhardsson opines that Paul would not go up to visit Peter merely to talk about the weather, as C. H. Dodd had observed, and, as head of the church, Peter would not waste two weeks talking about trivial matters with Paul.[10] Each felt a calling from God to which they were committed to the death. Paul also reports that he only saw one other apostle during that first visit: Jesus' brother James.

During the second visit, Paul says he met privately with Peter, James, and John (almost certainly the son of Zebedee) for the purpose of presenting before them the gospel message he had been preaching to the gentiles to ensure he was on message and had been acting appropriately by sharing that message with gentiles. This was a second meeting with Peter, a time during which he became better acquainted with James, and a first meeting with John—the foremost Jerusalem apostles whom he refers to as "those reputed to be pillars." Paul claims that they verified that his gospel message was aligned with their own. As we observed above in relation to 1 Corinthians 15:1–7, Paul's gospel message included Jesus' resurrection and his appearances to others.

The book of Acts describes at least three and probably four visits by Paul with the apostles in Jerusalem.

[26] Having now come to Jerusalem, he was attempting to join the disciples. And all were fearful of him, not believing that he was a disciple. [27] And Barnabas took him and brought him to the apostles and explained to them how he saw the Lord on the

---

10. Birger Gerhardsson, *Memory and Manuscript: Oral Tradition and Written Transmission in Rabbinic Judaism and Early Christianity with Tradition and Transmission in Early Christianity*, trans. Eric J. Sharpe, Bible Resource Series (2 vols., 1961, 1964; repr. in 1 vol., Grand Rapids: Eerdmans; Livonia, MI: Dove, 1998), 298; C. H. Dodd, *The Apostolic Preaching and Its Developments* (New York: Harper & Row, 1964), 16.

road and that he spoke to him and how in Damascus he boldly preached in the name of Jesus. (Acts 9:26–27)

[27] Now during these days, some prophets from Jerusalem came down to Antioch. [28] And one of them named Agabus stood up and, by the Holy Spirit, indicated that a great famine was about to come over the whole world. (This happened during the reign of Claudius.) [29] So, of the disciples, as each had means, each of them determined to send financial help to the brothers living in Judea. [30] And they did, sending funds to the elders by the hand of Barnabas and Saul. (Acts 11:27–30)

[1] And having come down from Judea, some were teaching the brothers that you cannot be saved if you were not circumcised in the custom of Moses. [2] And when Paul and Barnabas had a major argument and debate with them, Paul and Barnabas and some of the others from them arranged to go up to the apostles and elders in Jerusalem concerning this issue. … [4] And having arrived in Jerusalem, they were welcomed by the church, and the apostles, and the elders. And they reported everything God did with them. … [12] And the whole group became silent and were listening to Barnabas and Paul describe all the signs and wonders God did through them among the gentiles. [13] And after they finished speaking, James answered saying, "Men! Brothers! Listen to me." (Acts 15:1–2, 4, 12–13)

[18] And on the following day, Paul went in with us to James. And all the elders were present. [19] And having greeted them, he explained one by one the things God did among the gentiles through his ministry. (Acts 21:18–19)

Acts reports that Barnabas presented Paul to the apostles in Jerusalem. Paul and Barnabas would return to Jerusalem from Antioch sometime later and deliver a financial gift to help believers during a famine. Although it is probable that he met with the apostles during that visit, it is not clear, since Acts 15:4 may distinguish the apostles from the elders. At a still later date, Paul and Barnabas would depart again from Antioch and go to Jerusalem in order to discuss their dispute with the Judaizers and to share what God was doing through them among the gentiles. During this third visit, Paul saw no less than two of the apostles: Peter and James. Then, at a later time, Paul conversed again with James in Jerusalem.

Scholars differ on how Luke's accounts of Paul's Jerusalem visits may be reconciled with Paul's own accounts in Galatians. For our purposes, however, it is sufficient to observe that Paul and Luke both report that Paul had met with the Jerusalem apostles on several occasions, that he was acquainted with them, that they certified his gospel message as aligned with their own, and that they approved his ministry to the gentiles.

But were Paul and Luke accurately reporting that the Jerusalem apostles had given their stamp of approval on the content and scope of Paul's gospel message? It is likely that Luke had been one of Paul's traveling companions during certain portions of Paul's travels. This is suggested by passages in which the author of Acts uses the plural pronouns "we" and "us" to include himself in the narrative during those periods (16:10–17; 20:5–15; 21:1–18; 27:1–28:16). Scholars disagree on whether Luke was truly a traveling companion of Paul. Yet, according to Craig Keener, "A large number (probably the majority) of English-speaking commentators believe that the author was a companion of Paul, as the 'we' narratives suggest."[11] If those scholars are correct, Luke provides an eyewitness report of the fourth meeting reported in Acts between Paul and the leadership of the Jerusalem church, which, at minimum, included Jesus' brother James (21:17–18).

We may also find some corroboration of Paul's claim from two of the apostolic fathers, Clement of Rome and Polycarp, each of whom have a reasonable chance of having been an associate of one of Jesus' apostles. *First Clement* is a letter written to the church at Corinth from the church at Rome. It is about the same size as 1 Corinthians and is usually dated c. AD 95–97, although a number of scholars prefer a time between the late 60s and 70s.[12] Although the letter has been attributed to Clement of Rome, it is technically anonymous in the same sense as our four canonical Gospels, since Clement's name appears nowhere in the text. Who was Clement of Rome, and should we think he was the author of this letter?

---

11. See Keener, *Acts*, 407.

12. See Licona, *The Resurrection of Jesus*, 250–55.

Sometime between AD 174–189, Irenaeus wrote of a Clement who had seen and conversed with the apostles. While Clement served as the third bishop of Rome to succeed the apostles, the church in Rome wrote a letter to the church in Corinth.[13] This is the first affiliation of 1 Clement to the bishop of Rome named Clement. Within a few decades, Clement of Alexandria attributed the text of 1 Clement to the "apostle Clement," counting him as an associate of those who had known Jesus, and provided numerous quotations from it.[14] In the early fourth century, Eusebius cited a portion of a letter written by Dionysius the bishop of Corinth to Soter the bishop of Rome (AD 166–174) in which Dionysius tells Soter that he believes Soter's letter to the church in Corinth will be helpful as was Clement's earlier letter.[15]

Several early church fathers link Clement the bishop of Rome to Peter. Tertullian wrote of a Clement ordained by Peter for the church in Rome.[16] In the long recension of Ignatius's letter to the Trallians, a Clement is mentioned as being a helper of Peter.[17] It is possible that this Clement is the same person Paul mentions in Philippians 4:3, since Eusebius reports that this same Clement became the bishop of Rome in AD 92.[18] There are no competing traditions.

Unfortunately, the early church fathers are often not as careful with the facts as we would like. Therefore, when speaking of the authorship of 1 Clement and whether Clement of Rome was personally acquainted with the apostle Peter, certainty eludes us. That said, with the absence of good reasons to doubt all of the reports, there is enough here to suggest that a man named Clement who had at least had some contact with the apostle Peter was probably involved in writing the letter we now call 1 Clement.

Polycarp was the bishop of Smyrna (present-day Izmir, Turkey) when he wrote a letter to the church in Philippi. Although scholars debate whether Polycarp's letter to the Philippians that is in our possession is one letter or two that were subsequently combined, most, if

---

13. Irenaeus, *Haer.* 3.3.3.

14. Clement of Alexandria, *Strom.* 4.17.

15. Eusebius, *Hist. eccl.* 4.23.11.

16. Tertullian, *Praescr.* 32.

17. Ign. *Trall.* 7:3 (long version).

18. Eusebius, *Hist. eccl.* 3.4.10; 3.15.1.

not all, believe that Polycarp is the author.[19] We have more information about Polycarp than we have for any of the other apostolic fathers.
Bart Ehrman notes that "[a]mong the writings of the Apostolic Fathers,
there is one text written *to* him (by Ignatius), another written *about*
him (the Martyrdom *of Polycarp*), and yet another written *by* him."[20]

Unlike the author of 1 Clement, Polycarp identifies himself as the
author of this letter. Irenaeus asserts that Polycarp was instructed by
the apostles, especially John, with whom he had interacted, and also
spoke with a number of others who had seen Jesus. Elsewhere, Irenaeus
claims that in his early youth he had seen Polycarp and heard him
tell about Jesus' miracles and teachings, which he had learned from
the apostles.[21] Similar to 1 Clement, Polycarp's letter is quite valuable, since he may have known the apostles, even one of Jesus' closest
disciples, John. However, with only Irenaeus linking Polycarp to John,
although Eusebius knows of Irenaeus's claim and does not dispute it,
certainty again eludes us. Notwithstanding, with the absence of good
reasons for doubting Irenaeus on the matter, probability weighs in
favor of Polycarp's association with the apostles.

Some have strong hesitations toward assigning much weight to
Irenaeus's claim about the affiliation of Clement and Polycarp with
the apostles. Although modern historians must avoid the uncritical
acceptance of what the early church fathers report, they should likewise avoid an inveterate skepticism toward them. A comparison may
be helpful in the matter.

Irenaeus stated that he was writing when Eleutherius held the
twelfth episcopate, which spanned AD 174–189.[22] Clement's letter to
the Corinthians is typically dated c. AD 95–97, and Polycarp's letter to
the Philippians at c. AD 110–125.[23] If these dates are correct, Irenaeus
was writing between seventy-seven and ninety-four years after
Clement's letter and between only forty-nine and seventy-nine years
after Polycarp's letter.

---

19. Clayton N. Jefford, *The Apostolic Fathers and the New Testament* (Peabody, MA:
Hendrickson, 2006), 13.

20. Bart D. Ehrman, ed. and trans. *The Apostolic Fathers*, 2 vols. (Cambridge: Harvard
University Press, 2003), 1:324.

21. Irenaeus, *Haer.* 3.3.4; cf. Eusebius, *Hist. eccl.* 5.20.5–8.

22. Irenaeus, *Haer.* 3.3.3.

23. See Licona, *The Resurrection of Jesus*, 249–56.

Let us compare these with two important Greco-Roman authors from that same era. Sallust is regarded as one of Rome's greatest historians. Addressing students of rhetoric, Quintilian wrote,

> I think the best should come both first and always, but among the best the most straightforward and accessible: for example, Livy for boys rather than Sallust. (Sallust indeed is the greater historian, but one needs further progress to understand him.) (Quintilian, *Inst.* 2.5.19)[24]

Sallust wrote the *Historiae* (of which only fragments remain), the *War with Catiline*, and the *War with Jugurtha*, both of which have been preserved in their entirety. Sallust died c. 35 BC and probably published his literature prior to 40 BC. The earliest mention of the *Historiae* is found in Elder Seneca's *Controversiae* 9.13, which was written c. AD 35, seventy-five years or a little longer after Sallust published the *Historiae*.[25] There, he quotes Sallust by name as saying, "Success is a wonderful screen for vice."[26] This is a quote from Sallust's *Histories*.[27] The earliest source to attribute the *War with Catiline* and *War with Jugurtha* is Quintilian, who wrote c. AD 95,[28] 135 years or a little longer after Sallust wrote. No classicist questions the authorship of the *War with Catiline*, the *War with Jugurtha*, and the *Historiae*.

Plutarch is regarded as the greatest ancient biographer. Ronald Mellor refers to Plutarch as "the greatest of all ancient biographers," while J. L. Moles opines that Plutarch is "the greatest Greek writer of the post-Classical era."[29] He died shortly after AD 120. His extant writings include a compilation of more than seventy short works called

---

24. Quintilian, *Quintilian: The Orator's Education, Books 1–2*, eds. and trans. Donald A. Russell, Loeb Classical Library 124 (Cambridge: Harvard University Press, 2001), 308–9.

25. Winterbottom says, "Seneca can hardly have started writing his book of controversiae much before AD 37." Seneca the Elder, *Declamations*, Volume I, "Controversiae," Books 1–6, trans. M. Winterbottom, Loeb Classical Library 463 (Cambridge, MA: Harvard University Press, 1974), xx.

26. Seneca the Elder, *Declamations*, Volume II, "Controversiae, Books 7–10, Suasoriae, Fragments," trans. M. Winterbottom, Loeb Classical Library 464 (Cambridge, MA: Harvard University Press, 1974), 230–31.

27. Sallust, *Hist.* 1.49.24. See Sallust, *Fragments of the Histories, Letters to Caesar*, ed. and trans. John T. Ramsey, Loeb Classical Library 522 (Cambridge, MA: Harvard University Press, 2015), 48–9.

28. Quintilian, *Inst.* 3.8.9.

29. Ronald Mellor, *The Roman Historian* (London: Routledge, 1999), 133; J. L. Moles, *Plutarch: Life of Cicero*, trans. J. L. Moles (Warminster, Wiltshire: Aris & Phillips, 1988), 5.

Moralia and *Lives*, which consists of forty-eight biographies. The earliest source attributing authorship of these writings to Plutarch is probably the *Lamprias Catalogue*, which is usually dated one hundred to two hundred years or more after Plutarch's death, and is pseudonymously attributed to Plutarch's son, for which this is the only occasion where he is ever mentioned. Moreover, the *Lamprias Catalogue* omits some books written by Plutarch while including some known to be spurious. For example, it includes "Aristotle's *Topics*, which no one in his right mind can have thought Plutarch's."[30] Close to that are a few occasions where Plutarch is quoted by Eusebius in the first half of the fourth century, and by Stobaeus in the fifth century. Finally, we have manuscripts of literature attributed to Plutarch dated to the end of the thirteenth and beginning of the fourteenth centuries. These also include some spurious works attributed to Plutarch.[31] A few of the works in the *Moralia* are known to be spurious.[32] And there is some debate among classicists pertaining to the authorship of a few others. However, the authorship of *Lives* is not doubted by classicists.

Classicists do not question the authorship of most of the literature attributed to Sallust and Plutarch, even though the earliest sources attesting to their authorship were written at a minimum of seventy-five and one hundred years later, respectively, and are far from perfect, especially in the case of Plutarch. Irenaeus is not a perfect source, either. But he is probably better than most of the sources reporting the authorship of Sallust and Plutarch. Moreover, he wrote closer to the composition of 1 Clement (seventy-seven to ninety-four years) and Polycarp's *To the Philippians* (forty-nine to seventy-nine years) than the earliest sources who attributed authorship to the writings of Sallust (seventy-five to 135 years) and Plutarch (one hundred to two hundred years or even longer). This is not to suggest there are no reasons to give pause to Irenaeus's reports. And it may be that classicists are too quick to accept the testimonies of the Elder Seneca, Quintilian, and especially the *Lamprias Catalogue* pertaining to the authorship of certain literature written by Sallust and Plutarch. Yet, it may likewise

---

30. D. A. Russell, *Plutarch*, 2nd ed. (London: Bristol Classical Press, 2001), 19.

31. Russell, *Plutarch*, 18.

32. See Russell, *Plutarch*, Appendix. I am in debt to Christopher Pelling for informing me of this source.

be that some scholars of the New Testament and early Christianity are too quick to dismiss the testimonies of Irenaeus and other early church fathers.

We should likewise keep the immediate matter before us in perspective, which is not whether Jesus had actually risen from the dead. It is whether Clement and Polycarp had actual ties to some of the Jerusalem apostles. Scholars having strong reservations about Jesus' resurrection should be careful not to allow those reservations to bleed over unnecessarily into relatively mundane matters—in this instance, whether Clement and Polycarp knew some of the apostles who had been with Jesus. It is certain that several Christian leaders had known the Jerusalem apostles and had been appointed by them to positions of leadership in the early church. And even if we were to speculate that Irenaeus claimed more about his firsthand hearing of Polycarp than what had actually occurred, it can be accepted that Polycarp was affiliated with the apostles, since Irenaeus would not have exaggerated his claim had Polycarp been an insignificant or even fictive figure. Moreover, Irenaeus's letter to Florinus suggests he actually believed Polycarp had been associated with the apostles, since he again mentions Polycarp's affiliation with John and tells Florinus he had seen him (i.e., Florinus) in Polycarp's house.[33] Accordingly, although caution remains, we can have a reasonable amount of confidence that the authors of 1 Clement and Polycarp's *Philippians* had affiliations with the leading apostles.

What do Clement and Polycarp say about Paul? Clement refers to him as the "blessed Paul the apostle" (1 Clem. 47:1) and places him on par with his mentor Peter, referring to both as "noble examples" (5:1), "the greatest and most righteous pillars" (5:2), "good apostles" (5:3), "a great example of endurance" (5:7, said only of Paul), and "these men who had lived in a holy manner" (6:1). Polycarp states that Paul "taught the word of truth accurately and reliably" (Pol. *Phil.* 3:2).[34]

---

33. Eusebius, *Hist. eccl.* 5.20.5.

34. In Pol. *Phil.*, Polycarp quotes from Ps 4:4, "Be angry and do not sin," and Eph 4:26, "Do not let the sun set on your anger," and refers to them as "sacred Scriptures." Although Polycarp does not attribute the latter text to Paul's letter to the Ephesians, it is the only source to which it may be rightfully attributed. A few decades after Ephesians was written, Plutarch wrote something similar: "We should next pattern ourselves after the Pythagoreans, who, though related not at all by birth, yet sharing a common discipline, if ever they were led by anger into recrimination, never let the sun go down before they joined right hands, embraced each other, and were reconciled"

Since Clement and Polycarp likely had affiliations with the apostles Peter and John, respectively, their opinions on Paul are of great value to us, since Paul claimed that Peter, James, and John had certified that the gospel Paul was preaching was aligned with their own (Gal 2:1–10). And Paul's gospel message included Jesus' resurrection and appearances to others (1 Cor 15:1–7). We have observed that Clement and Polycarp both use laudatory terms in their letters when writing of Paul, terms that are entirely consistent with and even provide some support to Paul's claim that the apostles with whom Clement and Polycarp had been affiliated had approved Paul's message and ministry. Accordingly, when we are reading Paul on the gospel message, it is very likely that we are also hearing the voice of the Jerusalem apostles.

5. Paul's Teachings on Jesus' Resurrection Are Consistent with the Resurrection Narratives

In all four canonical Gospels, the resurrection of Jesus is narrated as an event in which Jesus' corpse returns to life. All four Gospels contain an empty tomb. Jesus can eat and fix meals (Luke 24:41–43; John 21:9–13). He can be touched (Matt 28:9; Luke 24:39; John 20:17, 27). He is seen by groups and converses with the percipients (Matt 28:9–10, 16–20; Luke 24:13–34, 35–51; John 20:19–23, 26–29; 21:4–13). Therefore, the Gospels portray Jesus' resurrection as a historical event that occurred in space and time.

Paul is not as clear as the Gospels. However, he is clear enough. Although he mentions Jesus' resurrection on numerous occasions, he neither narrates nor describes it. However, we can learn what Paul believed about Jesus' resurrection by entering through the back door. Paul says believers will be raised as Jesus was raised. He writes, "But now, Christ has been raised from the dead, the firstfruits of those sleeping" (1 Cor 15:20). All others will be raised at the parousia: "But each in his own order: Christ the firstfruits,[35] then those belonging to Christ at

---

(Plutarch, "On Brotherly Love," *Moralia*, 488c, in Plutarch, *Moralia*, Volume VI, trans. W. C. Helmbold, Loeb Classical Library 337 [Cambridge, MA: Harvard University Press, 1939], 302–3).

35. "Firstfruits" (*aparche*) is here in the singular and can refer to a singular (Rom 16:5; 1 Cor 15:20, 23) or plural (1 Cor 16:15; Jas 1:18; Rev 14:4) noun. In the New Testament, the term always appears in the singular. Josephus uses the terms in both the singular (*Ant.* 3.35; 5.26; 7.378) and plural (*Ant.* 3.250–51; 4.70–71, 226; 9.273; 12.50; 16.172; *J.W.* 5.21)

his coming" (15:23).[36] Paul goes on in the same chapter and elsewhere to describe how believers will be raised. So by learning Paul's thoughts pertaining to the nature of the resurrection of believers, we can likewise learn his thoughts pertaining to the nature of Jesus' resurrection.

Paul seems to think of life after death in two stages. The first is a state of disembodied existence in the presence of Christ for believers who die prior to the parousia. Paul writes, "Therefore, we are always courageous, knowing that being at home in the body we are absent from the Lord. For we walk by faith, not by sight. And we are courageous and content rather to be absent from the body and to be at home with the Lord" (2 Cor 5:6–8). When in prison and facing possible execution, Paul wrote the following to the church at Philippi, "For to me, to live is Christ and to die is gain. Now if I am to live in the flesh, this will mean fruitful labor for me. And what I will choose I cannot tell. For I am torn between the two, having the desire to leave and be with Christ, which is far better. But to remain in the flesh is more necessary for you" (Phil 1:21–24). In Paul's mind, there are two options: die and be with Christ or continue his ministry here. He desires the former but knows the Philippian believers still need him. Had Paul imagined entering a "soul sleep" upon death in which he would remain until the parousia, that would have been the option to contrast with remaining in the flesh, rather than with dying and being with Christ.

Paul's statements elsewhere support this conclusion. Encouraging those who have believing loved ones who have died, Paul writes the following:

> Now we do not want for you to be ignorant, brothers, concerning those who sleep, in order that you may not grieve as the rest who have no hope. For since we believe that Jesus died and rose again, we also believe that, through Jesus, *God will bring with him those who sleep*. For we tell you this by the word of the Lord that we who are alive and remain until the coming of the Lord will not go ahead of those who are asleep. For the Lord himself will come down from heaven with a loud command, with the voice of an archangel, and with God's trumpet, and *the dead*

---

36. See also Rom 8:11, "But if the Spirit of the one who raised Jesus from the dead dwells in you, the one who raised Christ from the dead will also give life to your mortal bodies through his Spirit dwelling in you."

in Christ will be raised first. Then, we who are alive and remain, will be snatched up together with them in the clouds to meet the Lord in the air. And so we will always be with the Lord. (1 Thess 4:13–17)

Note the progression: At the parousia, God is going to bring with him those who sleep. They are with him now. Then they are raised. But how can this be, if they are already with him? It is the spirits of disembodied believers whose bodies have died and whose spirits now exist in Christ's presence that God will bring with him. Those spirits will be returned to their corpses, which will then be raised and transformed into bodies that are incorruptible, glorious, powerful, and empowered by the Holy Spirit.[37] Therefore, it is *bodily* resurrection, an event that involves corpses. This is fairly similar to the process described in 2 Baruch 49–51, which I summarize here: (49) How are the dead raised? (50) The earth will return the dead as it received them. (51) The dead will then be changed and will shine like the stars.

There are a few texts in Paul's letters that are often misunderstood by some who suggest Paul thought of resurrection differently than just discussed. Because I am limited by space, I can only give attention to the most controversial of those texts: 1 Corinthians 15:42–50.[38] There are two major points of contention in this passage.[39] The first is Paul's statement that the body is sown "natural" (*psychikon*) and raised "spiritual" (*pneumatikon*) (15:44). Some English translations render the first term "physical" instead of "natural."[40] The idea in those translations is the bodies of the dead are physical in nature when buried but are spiritual or immaterial in nature when raised. But is this idea correct?

The term *psychikon* appears 846 times in Greek literature, including the New Testament, written from the eighth century BC through the

---

37. See also 1 Cor 15:42–44.

38. Additional texts are Gal 1:11–19 and 2 Cor 4:16–5:8. I have treated these in-depth in Licona, *The Resurrection of Jesus*, 375–79, 425–37.

39. There are additional contended points in 1 Cor 15: What does Paul mean when referring to Jesus as a "life-giving Spirit"? What does Paul mean by saying "we will be changed"? However, these points are not contested as strenuously as the two I mention in this essay. For an in-depth analysis of these other points, see Licona, *The Resurrection of Jesus*, 415–17, 420–23.

40. For examples, see the *NRSV*, the *Amplified Bible*, and the *Common English Bible*.

third century AD.[41] Only five of the 846 occurrences appear prior to the fourth century BC. Usage of the term experiences an explosive growth in the first century BC and even more in the first century AD. Then we observe its usage grow by 1,000 percent in the second century! There are 1,131 occurrences of *pneumatikon* during the same period.[42] It first appears in the sixth century BC, with an explosive growth in occurrences in the first century AD. There is then an almost 400 percent growth that occurs in the second century.

Space limitations allow me only to summarize findings I have presented in detail elsewhere.[43] From the eighth century BC through the third century AD, *psychikon* and *pneumatikon* each possess a number of meanings. However, *psychikon* is never employed in a sense meaning "physical" or "material." Therefore, in 1 Corinthians 15:44, Paul was not contrasting a "physical/material" body with one that is "ethereal/immaterial." It is also worth observing that Paul had a better term at his disposal had he wished to communicate this sort of contrast. Only a few chapters earlier he writes, "If we sowed spiritual things [*ta pneumatika*] in you, is it too much if we reap material things [*ta sarkika*] from you" (9:11)?[44] If the apostles were providing spiritual teachings to the Corinthian Christians, were they not entitled to receive material benefits like food, clothing, and lodging? Had Paul desired to draw a contrast between physical and immaterial, he could have written "It is sown a *sarkikos* [material] body. It is raised a *pneumatikos* [spiritual] body." And it is certainly worth noting that in both 1 Corinthians 9:7–11 and 15:36–44, the analogy of a seed is being used.

In 1 Corinthians 15:44, Paul was likely communicating that while our present body is animated by natural organs, such as a heart, lungs, a stomach, and kidneys, our transformed body will be animated by the Holy Spirit. This explanation of what Paul had in mind is far more likely

---

41. These and the findings for *pneumatikon* below are the results of a search using *Thesaurus Linguae Graecae* (disk E). This database is now accessible online at http://stephanus.tlg.uci.edu/index.php (accessed June 21, 2019). There were no occurrences of either word in the Oxyrhynchus papyri.

42. Of these, 610 appear in Origen (third century AD), the majority of which describe the "spirituality" of the Law.

43. See Licona, *The Resurrection of Jesus*, 407–15.

44. See also Rom 15:27, where Paul employs a contrast using the same Greek terms: "For if the Gentiles shared in their [i.e., the Jews'] *spiritual things* [*tois pneumatikois*], they ought also in their *material things* [*tois sarkikois*] to serve them." Elsewhere in the New Testament, *sarkikos* appears in 1 Cor 3:3; 2 Cor 1:12; 10:4; and 1 Pet 2:11. Thus, all occurances but one appear in Paul's letters.

than that he used *psychikos* in a sense not employed by Paul in any of his letters or by the remaining New Testament literature or by any known author from the eighth century BC through the third century AD.

Another point of contention in 1 Corinthians 15 is verse 50. Paul states that "flesh and blood cannot inherit the kingdom of God, nor does the perishable inherit the imperishable." Some scholars see a similarity with Paul's statement with what the risen Jesus says of himself in Luke 24:39: "a spirit does not have flesh and bones as you see I have." These scholars interpret "flesh and blood" as a synonym for "physical."[45] However, most scholars agree that the term is a figure of speech—and probably a Semitism—referring to man as a mortal being.[46] The expression "flesh and blood" appears five times in the New Testament (two of which are in the Pauline corpus),[47] occurs twice in the LXX,[48] and is common in the Rabbinic literature, all carrying the primary sense of mortality rather than physicality.[49] That "flesh and blood" is employed in this sense in 1 Corinthians 15:50 is reinforced by the fact that, when the present body is described elsewhere in 1 Corinthians 15, the focus is on its mortality rather than its physicality. Therefore, Paul is stating in 15:50 that *the living cannot inherit the kingdom of God in their present condition.* Accordingly, there is no tension between Paul's statement in 1 Corinthians 15:50 involving "flesh and blood" and Jesus' statement in Luke 24:39 involving "flesh and bone."

---

45. Marcus Borg, *Jesus: Uncovering the Life, Teachings, and Relevance of a Religious Revolutionary* (San Francisco: HarperSanFrancisco, 2006), 289; Raymond E. Brown, *The Virginal Conception and Bodily Resurrection of Jesus* (New York: Paulist Press, 1973), 87; John Dominic Crossan, quoted in James Halstead, "The Orthodox Unorthodoxy of John Dominic Crossan: An Interview," *Cross Currents* 45 (1995–96): 521; James D. G. Dunn, "How Are the Dead Raised? With What Body Do They Come? Reflections on 1 Corinthians 15," *Southwestern Journal of Theology* 45 (2002): 11; Barnabas Lindars, "Jesus Risen: Bodily Resurrection but No Empty Tomb," *Theology* 89 (1986): 95; Donald Wayne Viney, "Grave Doubts About the Resurrection," *Encounter* 50 (1989): 130; and Nigel Watson, *The First Epistle to the Corinthians*, Epworth Commentaries (London: Epworth, 1992), 179.

46. We may think of English idioms that are not to be interpreted literally, such as "cold-blooded" and "green with envy."

47. Matt 16:17; 1 Cor 15:50; Gal 1:16; Eph 6:12; and Heb 2:14.

48. Sir 14:18 (Gk. and Heb.); 17:31.

49. Rudolf Meyer, *Theological Dictionary of the New Testament*, ed. Gerhard Kittel and Gerhard Friedrich, trans. G. W. Bromiley, 10 vols. (Grand Rapids: Eerdmans, 1964–76), 7:116. A nice example is found in b. Berakot 28b in a logion attributed to Yohanan ben Zakkai (late first century AD). Three examples in the Mishna appear in m. Nazir 9:5 (twice) and m. Soṭah 8:1. There are no occurrences of the term in the Qumran texts, the Targums, or Hebrew inscriptions. Thus, we have "flesh and blood" employed in the sense of *mortality* from the second century BC through the end of the first century AD. I am indebted to Craig Evans for his insights pertaining to the Mishna, Qumran texts, Targums, and Hebrew inscriptions.

We have looked carefully at two points of contention in this text and discovered that Paul's thoughts in them do not contradict his clear teaching elsewhere that resurrection involves a transformation of the corpse. Since Paul held that our resurrection will be similar in nature to what Jesus experienced, and we will experience bodily resurrection, it follows that Paul believed Jesus experienced bodily resurrection. Accordingly, Paul's view of the nature of Jesus' resurrection is consistent with what we observe in the Gospels.

Also similar to the Gospels is Paul's teaching in 1 Corinthians 15 that the resurrection of Jesus was a historical event. In 1 Corinthians 15:17–18, Paul states, "And if Christ was not raised, your faith is worthless, you are still in your sins, and then those who have fallen asleep in Christ are lost." In 1 Corinthians 15:29–32, he writes,

> [29] Otherwise, what will those do who are baptized for the dead? If the dead are not raised at all, why then are they baptized for them? [30] Why also are we in danger every hour? [31] By my pride in you, which I have in Christ Jesus our Lord, [I affirm that] I die every day. [32] If I fought wild beasts in Ephesus according to man [i.e., without God's involvement or for his purpose], what does it profit me? If the dead are not raised, let us eat and drink. For tomorrow we die.

We may restate Paul's argument as follows:

If Christ was not raised, we will not be raised.

If we will not be raised, the Christian life is not worth living.

But Christ was raised.

Therefore, we will be raised.

Therefore, the Christian life is worth living.

Paul's argument is incomprehensible if we understand him in any other way than as believing Jesus' resurrection had actually occurred.

Before moving on, I want to assess Paul's view of Jesus' resurrection as portrayed in Acts. It can be granted that the appearance of the risen Jesus to Paul described in Acts differs in nature from the appearances of the risen Jesus to his disciples in the Gospels. In the Gospels, as mentioned above, Jesus appears to others in his physically resurrected body. They can touch him. He can eat and fix meals. He is seen by groups and converses with the percipients. On one occasion, two disciples speak with him as a fellow traveler, because they were prevented from recognizing him (Luke 24:13–32). Earlier that day, Mary Magdalene mistook Jesus for a gardener (John 20:11–17), which could have been for a number of reasons, such as Mary having tears in her eyes; her position in the tomb and proximity to Jesus at that moment, which prevented her from having a clear view of the one speaking to her; or because Jesus may have been standing in a shadow and had his head covered at the moment. Later, Jesus appears to his disciples, who do not recognize him at first, probably because they were in a boat approximately one hundred yards from the beach where Jesus was standing (John 21:4, 8). The point to be made is that, in the resurrection narratives, Jesus looked like any other healthy person when he appeared to his followers after his resurrection.

This is quite different than how Acts portrays Jesus' appearance to Paul. There he appears to Paul with an exceedingly bright light. The term Luke uses in 9:3 and 22:6 is *periastraptō*, meaning "to flash around," which is found only in these two references in the New Testament and in 4 Maccabees 4:10, where it is similar to lightning. In 26:13, we observe the far more common *perilampō*, meaning "to shine around." Although it is difficult to determine whether *periastraptō* is here describing a single flash, similar to lightning yet much brighter, or whether there was a strobe effect or if the light was static for a period, *perilampō* most likely refers to a more static effect. Luke then mentions that Paul heard a voice. We are not told if the voice came from heaven or from the light. Luke says Paul's traveling companions heard the sound of the voice but did not understand it (9:7; 22:9). Accordingly, Jesus' appearance to Paul is narrated in Acts in a manner that's quite different than what we observe in the canonical Gospels. This is most likely because the Gospels and Acts narrate Jesus appearing to others prior to his ascension, whereas the appearance to Paul occurred afterward, perhaps a few years later.

Although Paul's conversion experience of the risen Jesus in Acts differs from what we read in the Gospels, we should keep in mind that, in Acts, Paul is still portrayed as proclaiming Jesus' bodily resurrection.

In Acts 13, he is speaking in a synagogue at Pisidian Antioch. When he comes to mention Jesus' resurrection, he says,

> [32] And we proclaim the good news to you the promise made to the fathers [33] that God fulfilled this [promise] to their children—us, having raised Jesus as it is also written in the second Psalm, "You are my Son. Today, I have begotten you." [34] And that he raised him from the dead, no longer to return to decay, he has spoken in this way, "I will give to you the holy and reliable blessings of David. [35] Therefore, he also says in another [psalm], "You will not allow your Holy One to experience decay." [36] For David, after he served God's purpose in his own generation, fell asleep and was laid with his fathers, and experienced decay. [37] But the one whom God raised did not experience decay. (vv. 32–37)

In short, Paul says that, according to the psalmist, God will not allow his Holy One to decay and that this psalm (Ps 16) could not be referring to David, since David died, was buried, and decayed. It is, therefore, referring to Jesus, who had died, was buried, but did not decay, since God had raised him, which implies that he believed Jesus' physical body had been raised. Of course, this is Luke's rendition of Paul's sermon. But it should also be noted that Paul's conversion experience in Acts is also Luke's rendition of the event. Therefore, it is futile to appeal to the appearance of Jesus to Paul in Acts in order to support the view that Paul did not believe Jesus had been raised bodily without also considering Paul's sermon in Acts 13, which informs us that he thought of Jesus' resurrection as an event that involved his corpse.

In summary, Paul believed Jesus' resurrection was a historical event that included his corpse returning to life and then being transformed. Accordingly, his view of Jesus' resurrection is entirely consistent with the resurrection narratives in the canonical Gospels.

Conclusion

The apostle Paul is our best ancient source for assisting us in answering the most important questions related to the resurrection of Jesus. We have an early source who had an extreme bias against Jesus but became one of his most ardent followers after he had an experience that convinced him Jesus had truly risen from the dead and had appeared to him. Paul's willingness to suffer continually for his gospel proclamation, even to the point of martyrdom, strongly suggests he actually believed what he taught.

We can be confident that Paul had personal connections with the Jerusalem leadership, which included Peter and John—who had belonged to Jesus' innermost circle—and Jesus' own brother James. These certified that Paul's gospel message was aligned with their own. Consequently, Paul's letters serve as a tool by which we may detect some of the content of the preaching of the Jerusalem apostles. Their preaching included the assertion that Jesus' physical, bodily resurrection was a historical event. Therefore, the exclamation "God raised Jesus" was not merely a metaphor to represent Jesus' exaltation in heaven, his perceived continual presence among believers, or the survival of his teachings. We can dispel of the notion that Jesus' resurrection was a later development as stories about him were passed along person-to-person, in some cases carelessly, during the first few decades of the Christian church. We can also reject the long-outdated proposal that Paul had preached a message about Jesus that differed significantly from what the Jerusalem apostles who had known Jesus were preaching. Finally, we can reject the hypothesis that Paul's thinking about the nature of Jesus' resurrection stands in tension with how the canonical Gospels view it.

I can only imagine a very few sources that would be superior to Paul. I can fancy an authentic document from the high priest Caiaphas in which he describes how Jesus had appeared to him after rising from the dead, urging him to teach the Jews to follow him and avoid the forthcoming destruction of Jerusalem, and with Caiaphas replying that Satan had raised him. I can fantasize documents written by Pontius Pilate and Tiberius Caesar describing how Jesus had appeared to them after being crucified, urging them to repent of their evil ways, embrace his teachings, and with their subsequent proposals that the Roman senate recognize Jesus as a god to be worshipped. While such sources belong only to imagination, authentic letters by Paul, from which a wealth of knowledge may be mined, belong to reality.

17

WHAT ASPIRING (AND VETERAN) APOLOGISTS MAY LEARN FROM GARY HABERMAS

"... in whom there is no guile." (John 1:47)

Alex McFarland

I f you've ever been in an older house heated by a furnace, you are familiar with a coal bin. Our house (built in the 1920s) had one. In a corner of the basement, behind a concrete foundation wall, was an area about three times bigger than a coat closet dedicated to storing coal. Just above this dusty space was a sort of steel trap door that opened to the outside. A couple of times per year, a truck would back up to this opening and dump coal down the chute.

Though faithfully offering bursts of hot air in the winter months, the coal furnace also christened everything in the house with a residue of grey film. Everything. And my Mom hated this. Wiping dust was a never-finished chore.

Perhaps it was that coal furnaces had become obsolete, or that my parents decided that black lung was a family trait no longer needing to be passed along, but by my early teens the old coal furnace went the way of the dinosaur. Electric baseboard heaters were installed and, after decades of use, the coal bin lay empty.

My dad decided that the former coal bin could be basement space used for something else. So he decided that a good father/son project would be for us to create an opening in the concrete wall the size of a standard closet door. How would a rectangular opening three feet wide and seven feet tall be cut through concrete wall about eight inches thick?

With a hammer and chisel, of course! One evening after supper, Dad and I went to the basement with our tools. He made a chalk outline of the proposed door, and we began pecking away at what would become a lengthy project.

If time travel were possible, I would like to go back and tell my dad about rental shops and how things like air hammers and power tools were actually available in the 1970s. But if my memory serves me, we spent nearly two months of random evenings chipping away at that concrete. We must have hit thousands of blows scribing that door opening, and I often thought the job would never get done. The hammer and chisel did wonders for my fledgling teenage arms, so that was a benefit. But the job sometimes felt like futility, and the concrete often appeared to be intractable. Some weeks into the job, my mom advised us to "just forget about it."

However, I will never forget the night that my dad said, "Son, watch this." He took the chalk and marked a yellow X in the middle of the rectangle. Handing me the hammer, he said, "Hit right there, on the mark."

"How hard?" I asked.

"Just hit one time," he said. "You won't have to hit too hard."

What happened next inflated my teenage ego immensely. One not-especially-powerful smack on the X in the middle of the wall crumbled the concrete to pieces. All those consistent, intentionally placed taps cut through the hardness, and a barrier wall was felled.

A Tool in the Father's Hands

Why would I begin a chapter honoring Gary Habermas with that anecdote? Because in many ways, an effective apologist is like a tool carefully wielded by the Father's hands. Like cutting through concrete, sometimes it is only through countless gestures, numerous conversations, and long seasons of intercession that unbelieving hearts are opened. The apologist should go about his work with the tenacity of workers chiseling through a stone wall.

Let me tell you about one who has done that.

It has been my privilege to know Gary Habermas since 1990—first as a student, then as a friend, ultimately as a colleague, and always as a brother in Christ. All who know Habermas will agree that he is a first-rate scholar, a meticulous thinker, and a patient listener. I have watched Habermas mentor students amidst their novice ramblings and rescue skeptics blinded by their own wayward logic.

Gary Habermas would be the first to tell you that any good thing emanating from his life and ministry is all due to Jesus Christ. While in graduate school at Liberty University (around 1991–1995), I remember him beginning a class period by commenting on the end of John 15:5: Christ said, "apart from me, you can do nothing." In the content of his teaching, and unmistakably through his demeanor, Habermas lives his Christianity, and this is impossible to miss. I think that is why, even thirty years ago, students were gravitating to him, seeking out his advice, and filling up his courses. We hung on each word and listened to whatever conversation Habermas might be having in the classroom or in the hallways. Time around him was always beneficial.

Please know that the observations and reminiscences of this chapter are not the sycophancies of some former-student-now-fan, though I am both of those. To paraphrase Babe Ruth (who said of his baseball skill, "No brag, just fact"), I would say of three decades of knowing Gary Habermas, "No embellishment, just personal experiences." Many have earned some type of degree in apologetics; Habermas is actually worthy of the title *Christian apologist*. I believe this is because he consistently models all that constitutes what it means to be a disciple of Jesus. Meet Gary Habermas and you will know that I am speaking the truth. The man's life is as authentic as his message. This is what a searching world longs to see and the Scripture itself demands of us.

From the days when Liberty University was just about to hit five thousand students (I think they have that many per dorm floor, now) until now, it has been my privilege to work with Gary in a number of contexts. Many have noted his accomplishments as a scholar, but I speak enthusiastically about the man's walk with Christ because I have been impacted by it firsthand. From classrooms to churches, on stages and in studios, from Focus on the Family to coverage by CSPAN-, Habermas has been a faithful participant with me in many endeavors. Habermas has been a key contributor to the current apologetics movement we see all around us (today, apologetics and worldview titles comprise the fastest growing segments of Christian publishing). But personally, I would also point out that he has been an integral part of the growth of Truth for a New Generation (TNG), the apologetics conferences I began organizing after my graduation from Liberty.

My attempts to organize apologetics conferences for teens began even while I was a student at Liberty. Our vision grew, and by the late 1990s we were renting auditoriums at colleges throughout the mid-Atlantic region and as far south as Florida. Habermas patiently listened to my ideas, made recommendations about content, gave instructive feedback, and helped our ministry visions materialize. If I was making a pest of myself by incessantly calling Gary in Lynchburg, he did not let on. He would dutifully come and speak nearly everywhere I asked him, declining only when some scheduling conflict made his involvement in TNG impossible. I know that in the early days of our ministry, Habermas's involvement lent our fledgling organization enough credibility to draw other major apologists to our events.

Doing Apologetics and Being an Apologetic

To be sure, Gary Habermas has shaped the lives of countless people, my own included. Habermas's accomplishments as an academic, an apologist, and as a Christian public figure are notable. His scholarship about ancient evidence for the life of Christ, near-death experiences, dealing with doubt, or his "minimal facts" defense of the gospel are all significant. Equally compelling has been the Christ-honoring way in which he processed the loss of his wife, Debbie.

As pop-level atheism became a cottage industry in the early 2000s, the skeptic's world was rocked when news broke that one of their champions, Antony Flew, affirmed theism. Habermas's lengthy friendship and dialogues with Flew decisively contributed to this. And how many apologists get written into the scripts of theatrically released feature films?[1] Factor in the significant role he has played in Lee Strobel's journey, and it becomes clear that Habermas is one of the persons most used by God to raise awareness for apologetics over the last two decades.

But what I've learned about apologetics from Gary Habermas goes well beyond refutations of naturalistic theories about the resurrection.

---

1. Habermas is prominently featured in the Lee Strobel biopic, *The Case For Christ* (Scottsdale, AZ: Pureflix Entertainment, 2017). He has also appeared (as himself) in the film *God's Not Dead 2* (2016) and *Send Proof* (2020).

So often, apologetics is assumed to be a pastime of intellectual jousting that takes place among bookish believers. Even many pastors and Christian educators (who would, presumably, be favorable toward apologetics) can be dismissive of this realm of study. "You will never need that C. S. Lewis stuff," a senior denominational leader once said to me, "unless you are on the campus of Yale University. Islam, atheism, trying to prove the Bible—those issues the average believer will never deal with."

That person's low view of apologetics was especially ironic in light of the fact that issues he referenced (Islam, atheism, the authority of Scripture) are, in fact, exactly the topics Christians in the Western world must know how to address. Some complain, "You can't argue someone into the kingdom of God," or, "Apologetics may help reassure believers, but it doesn't win the lost to Christ." I am mindful of the fact that some in the church have not had unfavorable experiences with apologetics, but rather negative encounters with apologists.

Once, while encouraging a group of ministers to bring more apologetics and biblical worldview content before their people, one pastor shared a story that broke my heart. The pastor explained that a two-person apologetics team had come to the church to speak to their youth. During the Q&A time, a teen girl innocently asked a question about Jehovah's Witness literature that had been coming to her house. She said she had been reading their *Awake* magazine, and to her it seemed to make sense. "What do you guys think?" she asked.

The two young men (perhaps well-meaning but misguided) launched into a rapid-fire rebuttal of everything related to the Jehovah's Witnesses. As her youth group friends watched, the speakers did a five-minute "data dump" on the girl, critiquing both the publications and her for having read them. The pastor grew fairly emotional as he ended the story: "Alex, that teen girl was so embarrassed that she left the room crying. The worst part is that the two apologists seemed to show no concern, and they high-fived each other at the end of their talk."

That encounter illustrates how the apologetics and life of Gary Habermas remains so exemplary. The pastor's experience still makes me cringe whenever I think back on it. I agreed with him that the behavior described typifies a sort of apologetics that should never be encouraged. But Christian friend and ideological foe alike will agree that Gary Habermas, the man, is undeniably a credit to the worldview he represents. Habermas proclaims truth; better still, he lives it.

I am reminded of a time that Habermas presented his "minimal facts" argument before hundreds of students at the University of North Carolina, Charlotte.

The standing-room-only crowd listened intently as a long line formed for the Q&A period. In characteristic fashion, Habermas fielded comments, objections, and helped more than a few students who did not quite know how to frame their question. One young man came to the mic and made it clear that he did not like the conclusions Habermas drew from the implications of Christ's physical resurrection.

"If I'm understanding you," the student reasoned, "the resurrection would mean that Jesus is God, and the way of salvation." The young man's tone grew belligerent: "Is that what you're saying?"

"You got it," said Habermas. "You are tracking with me, yes."

The college student appeared more and more agitated as it sunk in that the resurrection would, indeed, validate Christ's messiahship. His volume rising, the student said, "I don't like this! I don't like this!" Half the audience seemed to want the aggrieved student to step aside, and half seemed bemused to watch meltdown in process. Habermas offered, "I get it, you're not comfortable with where this is going. But just to say that you don't like it, well, that's not an argument."

Amazingly, the student waved his hands, as if to say, "Be gone!" to both Habermas and his content. Storming away, the young man growled into the mic, "AARRRGGHHH!" Some snickered at the exchange, and the program concluded. But I watched Gary Habermas seek out the young man, who clearly had no idea he was trying to argue the resurrection with the topic's most astute scholar. It was a powerful sight to watch Habermas, like a gentle big brother, listen to the student, diffuse the young man's anger, and minister the gospel. Apologetics comprises both scholarship and shepherding.

Habermas's repeated visits to Probe Ministry retreats (an apologetics ministry) is what led me to begin this chapter with the story of a hammer, chisel, and repeated blows to a concrete wall. There have been attendees at numerous conferences and retreats who have come for years as skeptics. But Habermas is not a one-and-done witness for Christ. Men have come to faith after years of doubt because of Habermas's faithful witness being used by God to chip, chip, chip away at layers of disbelief and excuses.

Many don't know that Gary Habermas—for all his prolificity—only types with two fingers. Thus, emailing (and especially spending time crafting lengthy emails) represents true investment in the spiritual progress of others. Habermas is a Christian who goes the distance in his interaction with searching people. His sacrificial investment of time on behalf of others has been amazing to watch.

The maturing of one's soul should keep pace with the expansion of his intellect. Studying apologetics can enable a person to accumulate important facts and interesting content. One's vocabulary will expand, and soon, everyday conversation will include words like epistemology, evidential, and empirical. The challenges for a good apologist are to remain humble and also to rely on the Holy Spirit's empowerment, not on any assumed intellectual prowess.

Can even the most sophisticated objections against Christianity be soundly refuted? I believe so. Aquinas was right in noting that every line of argument against the faith has a rational mistake in it somewhere (or as he phrased it, "are the result of conclusions incorrectly derived"). But apologetics should not breed cockiness or arrogance. The preponderance of proof on the side of Christianity in no way deputizes us to treat enemies of the cross abrasively.

Hours of intellectual preparation cannot replace prayer in the life of the apologist (in the crucible of life, do not one day find yourself well-read but spiritually powerless). Apologetics is not a substitute for God's providential work in the lives of unsaved people. It has been said, "You can't argue someone into heaven." Of course not. But the truths presented to people may be used by the Lord in drawing a person to himself.

Intellectual prowess should not be confused with (nor substituted for) spiritual maturity. Galatians 5:23, speaking of the fruit of the Spirit operative in a Christian's life, concludes, "against such things there is no law." This is essentially saying, "You can't argue with that." A skeptic may quibble over some point of content, but when the message is coupled with an authentic and consistently godly life (as with Habermas), the witness is hard to refute.

Much of apologetics study will stretch one's mind, but it should also enlarge his heart. The Bible states that the gospel is not based on "cleverly devised stories" (2 Pet 1:16), but it also says that changed lives and godly actions speak loudly to an often skeptical world (1 Pet 2:15). Apologetics is more than dialoguing with people. It is about loving God and loving people. What could be more practical than that?

Habermas's life shows us that the ultimate goal of the apologist is to glorify God. On this battlefield of ideas, believers are soldiers, fighting to secure hotly contested territories. The souls of people are in the crossfire, and the apologist works to see as many lives as possible brought to salvation in Christ. From Gary Habermas I have learned what God-honoring apologetics is, and conversely, what it is not. Apologetics is:

- A call for one's life to be as unassailable as one's message

- A ministry in which the practitioner himself can be an empirical evidence for the gospel

- A discipline that represents not only defense of the gospel but also worship of the Savior

- Content and methodologies that may be used by the Holy Spirit to equip the saved and persuade the lost

Apologetics is not:

- Intellectual rigor that excuses neglect of personal sanctification

- A means by which Christian opportunists can put themselves on a pedestal

- A license to be a jerk

- A substitute for the prayer to the sovereign work of the Holy Spirit

How wonderful it is that Habermas has invested his time and abilities in spreading the truth for which the human heart longs most. It is no wonder that a video clip we posted online of Habermas proclaiming,

"Death! You got nothin'!"[2] received more than one million hits under a month (and this was when YouTube was in its infancy). Like Job, people everywhere want to know, "If someone dies, will they live again?" (Job 14:14).

The Greek leader of Athens, Solon (638–558 BC), wept over the death of his son. A compassionless person asked, "Why do you weep, since weeping avails nothing?"[3] Solon answered, "Precisely because it avails nothing." Solon's angst would resonate with countless bereaved hearts in this world of loss. The apostle Paul recognized that the only hope for eternal life, reconciliation with God, reunion with loved ones, and hope beyond this world is Christ's resurrection. And if Jesus didn't rise- and there is no hope beyond this world- then, "we are of all people most to be pitied" (1 Corinthians 15:17–19).

Habermas has given people convincing evidences for Christ's resurrection, has compellingly shown reality of an afterlife, and has simply explained how one may be prepared. And he lives his calling in tireless and Christ-like fashion. What lessons are in this for us all!

Gary Habermas inspired his students to not merely acquire knowledge but to pursue wisdom. Heaven forbid that we talk about God without deeply knowing Jesus. God deliver the apologist who knows C. S. Lewis chapter and verse, but who has starved himself of the food that is Scripture. I have watched too many apologists (veteran and novice) who inflict themselves on others, aspiring to save the lost but who needed to be saved from themselves.

Many set out for the summits of scholarship and apologetics; Habermas's life points us to that highest peak of all: *discipleship*. Solomon famously says that the starting point for wisdom is the fear (or reverence) of God. Proverbs 1:7 also warns, "Fools despise wisdom and instruction." Habermas's legacy is rich in knowledge, wisdom, and instruction, as the opening chapter of Proverbs promises, because he has given priority to the most primary thing: the fear of the Lord.

---

2. "Did Jesus Rise From the Dead?" Filmed at Dare2Dig Deeper: The Big Dig apologetics conference, Focus On the Family, Colorado Springs, CO; August 27, 2005.

3. Plutarch's Lives, trans. John and William Langhorne (Cincinnati: Applegate and Co., 1863), 73.

18

WHAT EVERYONE SHOULD LEARN FROM GARY HABERMAS

Frank Turek

Gary Habermas once said something to a skeptic that makes Christianity far more plausible than even most Christians recognize. It happened in Calgary, Canada. Gary and I were both speaking at an apologetics and theology conference there in March 2016. During one of our sessions, an intelligent young man of twenty-five expressed skepticism about the resurrection of Jesus. So Gary and I invited him to dinner.

Not too far into our dinner conversation, I asked the young man the same question I ask any non-Christian with whom I am dialoguing: "If Christianity were true, would you become a Christian?"

This question, if answered honestly, reveals the real reason someone is not currently a Christian. Are there really intellectual obstacles that are keeping the person from becoming a Christian, or is the person not a Christian because he or she has some moral or emotional resistance to Christianity? I have found that, more often than not, reason is not the reason for unbelief. It is more about someone's resistance than a question about God's existence. More on that later.

Anyway, I asked the question, and the young man said yes (a bit reluctantly).

Then Gary said something that, if true, enhances our confidence that Jesus rose from the dead. He said:

> If the New Testament documents are inspired, then obviously Jesus is risen from the dead. If the New Testament documents are merely historically reliable, then Jesus is risen from the dead. But even if the agnostic view is correct, if the New Testament

documents are mostly *unreliable*, then we still have enough good data from those texts to know that Jesus rose from the dead.

I had never heard it put that way before. It was really another way of articulating the implications of Gary's minimal facts approach, which shows that just the facts accepted by even skeptical New Testament scholars are enough to establish that Jesus rose from the dead.

"But isn't that using the Bible to prove the Bible?" the skeptic asked.

No. Gary pointed out that the scholars are not treating the New Testament documents as inspired sources, but like any other historical documents from the ancient world. The question is, do those documents have any truth in them? As we will see, it would seem to take far more faith to think they are complete forgeries. In fact, Gary went on to say, "If I don't quote the New Testament for reliable historical information, Bart Ehrman [the famous skeptical New Testament scholar] will."

Why? Because, as Gary went on to explain, historians have tools that help them mine nuggets of truth out of what they may consider largely unreliable texts. He said it's like a family using tools to uncover treasured possessions in the rubble of their home following a tornado.

Five Tools

What are these tools, and how can they help us get reliable facts even from a text that could be largely unreliable? Habermas and Mike Licona cite five tools in their book *The Case for the Resurrection of Jesus*: multiple independent sources, enemy attestation, embarrassing admissions, eyewitness testimony, and early testimony. Let's take a brief look at how the New Testament documents fare when these tools are applied to them.

Multiple Independent Sources

A saying or event that is recorded by more than one source is more likely to be true. Many events recorded in the New Testament documents, most importantly the resurrection, are found in multiple independent sources. In addition to Matthew, Mark, Luke and John, other first-century sources that cite or allude to the resurrection include Paul, Peter, James, and the writer of Hebrews. And even if the Synoptic

Gospels are drawing some of their facts about the resurrection from the same source, they each contain enough unique information to show a plurality of sources (in fact, if there were not differences in the minor details of the resurrection story, there would be no skeptics claiming the accounts are contradictory).

Habermas also identified that there are oral sources beneath those written sources. In his classic work *The Historical Jesus,* Gary identified more than forty ancient creeds in the New Testament documents that were initially formulated, memorized, and passed orally by the first Christians from about AD 30 to 50—the most prominent of which (1 Cor 15:3–8) names fourteen eyewitnesses of the resurrection and claims that there were five hundred others, many of whom were still alive and could be interviewed.[1]

Enemy Attestation

Whenever someone who has a vested interest against a message admits something that actually advances that message, then that admission is probably true. For example, when Jewish authorities claimed that the disciples stole the body of Jesus (Matt 28:11–15), they were implicitly admitting a fact that advances the message of Christianity—that the tomb was empty.

Did Matthew make this up? No, because if he did, he would have completely discredited himself with the very Jewish audience he was trying to reach by lying about their own explanation for the empty tomb. Moreover, the claim that the disciples stole the body persisted in the centuries after Jesus' death even in a prominent Jewish source (Toledoth Jesu).[2]

Embarrassing Testimony

If a saying or event embarrasses the author or the author's cause, then it is probably true. After all, you are not going to invent details that hurt you or your cause. Have you ever lied to make yourself look good? Of course. But how often have you lied to make yourself look *bad*?

---

1. Gary Habermas, *The Historical Jesus* (Joplin, MO: College Press, 1996), 143–70.
2. Habermas, *The Historical Jesus*, 205–6.

The Jewish writers of the New Testament documents have filled them with embarrassing details that make the writers—and even Jesus—look bad. For example,

- The disciples depict themselves as dimwitted; they fail to understand what Jesus is saying several times and don't understand his mission completely until after the he is already ascended to heaven.

- The leader of the disciples, Peter, is sternly rebuked by Jesus: "Get behind me, Satan!" And later, after pledging to be faithful to the end, Peter denies Christ three times.

- At the crucifixion all but one of the disciples run away in fear.

- The disciples then make no effort to give Jesus a proper burial. Instead, they say a member of the Jewish ruling body that sentenced Jesus to die is the noble one; Joseph of Arimathea buries Jesus in a Jewish tomb (which would have been easy for the Jews to refute if it was untrue).

- Two days later, while the men are still hiding in fear, the women go down and discover the empty tomb and the risen Jesus. What man would invent that he was cowardly while the women were the brave ones who discovered the empty tomb? Moreover, a woman's testimony was not as credible that of a man, yet they are depicted as the first witnesses by all four Gospels. Why say your first witnesses were people considered unreliable, unless it was really true?

- At the climax of the entire story (the Great Commission), some of the disciples of Jesus are doubting Jesus is there, even though the risen Jesus is standing physically right in front of them (Matt. 28:17)! Why would Matthew invent an embarrassing instance of the disciples doubting the risen Jesus?

Other embarrassing claims about Jesus are also unlikely to be invented. For example,

- Jesus has two prostitutes in his bloodline (Tamar and Rahab), an adulterer (Bathsheba), and a king (David) who lies, cheats, and murders to cover up his sins. That's certainly not an invented royal bloodline!

- Jesus is considered "out of his mind" by his own family, who come to seize him to take him home (Mark 3:21,31). Why would they admit this if, as some skeptics claim, the New Testament writers were trying to invent a divine Jesus?

- Jesus is called a "madman" (John 10:20), a "drunkard" (Matt 11:19), and "demon-possessed" (Mark 3:22; John 7:20; 8:48).

- Jesus is thought to be a deceiver (John 7:12).

- Jesus is deserted by many of his followers after he says that followers must eat his flesh and drink his blood (John 6:66).

- Jesus' own brothers do not believe him (John 7:5). (For James, disbelief turned to belief *after* the resurrection. He was martyred as the pastor of the church in Jerusalem in AD 62).

- Jesus turns off Jewish believers so much that they want to stone him (John 8:30–59).

- Jesus has his feet wiped with the hair of a prostitute, which easily could have been seen as a sexual advance (Luke 7:36–39).

- Jesus is crucified despite the fact that anyone who is hung on a tree is "accursed of God" (Deut 21:23).

If you were inventing a Messiah to the Jews, you would not say such unflattering things about him. And that is not all. I have written much more about these embarrassing details elsewhere.[3]

---

3. See Frank Turek, *Stealing From God* (Colorado Springs: NavPress, 2015), 199–203. See also Norman Geisler and Frank Turek, *I Don't Have Enough Faith to Be an Atheist* (Wheaton, IL:

When a text contains verifiable characteristics of eyewitness testimony, historians are more likely to deem it reliable. Many of the New Testament documents contain testimony that only an eyewitness, or someone who interviewed eyewitnesses, could know. For example,

- Roman historian Colin Hemer verified through archaeology and other historical sources that Luke records eighty-four historical and eyewitness details from Acts 13 to the end of the book (Acts 28).[4] Many are obscure details that only an eyewitness could know, such as the names of small-town politicians, local slang, topographical features, specific weather patterns and water depths, etc.

- Luke puts historical crosshairs in his Gospel. In Luke 3:1, he writes, "In the fifteenth year of the reign of Tiberius Caesar—when Pontius Pilate was governor of Judea, Herod tetrarch of Galilee, his brother Philip tetrarch of Iturea and Traconitis, and Lysanias tetrarch of Abilene —during the high-priesthood of Annas and Caiaphas, the word of God came to John son of Zechariah in the wilderness" (NIV). This is obviously not written as a fairy tale. And all eight leaders named in this passage are known from history to be in those positions at that time (AD 29).

- Famed archaeologist Sir William Ramsay began his research skeptical of Luke. But after twenty years of study, Ramsay concluded that Luke "should be placed along with the very greatest of historians."[5] He wrote, "You may press the words of Luke in a degree beyond any other historian's, and they stand the keenest scrutiny and the hardest treatment."[6] Among many other findings, Ramsay noted that Luke references thirty-two countries, fifty-four cities, and nine islands without making a single mistake. That is an

---

Crossway, 2004), 275–83.

4. For the list of the eighty-four details, see Geisler and Turek, *I Don't Have Enough Faith to Be an Atheist*, ch. 10.

5. William Ramsay, *The Bearing of Recent Discovery on the Trustworthiness of the New Testament* (South Africa: Primedia eLaunch, 2011 [1915]), Kindle loc. 2707.

6. Ramsay, *Bearing*, Kindle loc. 1085–86.

outstanding record for historians of any era—and he did all that without the benefit of modern-day maps, charts, and Google Earth.[7]

- John includes fifty-nine historically verified or historically probable eyewitness details in his Gospel.[8]

- The names of several prominent people (such as government and religious officials) appear at various places in the New Testament documents. More than thirty of these people have been verified by ancient non-Christian writers or through archaeological discoveries. They include John the Baptist, James (half-brother of Jesus), Pilate, Caiaphas (whose ossuary was discovered), Agrippa I, Agrippa II, Felix, Bernice, several Herods, those cited in Luke 3 above, Jesus Christ, and many others.

Early Testimony

The closer the testimony to the events described, the more likely the testimony will be accurate, and the less likely exaggeration and legend will have crept in. This is the case with the New Testament documents. Most, if not all, of them were written prior to AD 70. While this is not a majority position, it is gaining steam among scholars for several reasons:

- No New Testament document mentions the Jewish war with the Romans that began in AD 66 and culminated in the destruction of Jerusalem and the temple in AD 70. It is highly unlikely that such cataclysmic events in the history of Israel would be ignored by every biblical writer. Jesus actually predicted the destruction in about AD 30, but no New Testament document reports that his prediction

---

7. Norman Geisler, *Baker Encyclopedia of Christian Apologetics* (Grand Rapids: Baker, 1999), 431.

8. See Craig Blomberg, *The Historical Reliability of John's Gospel* (Downers Grove, IL: InterVarsity Press, 2001). For a listing of the fifty-nine, see Geisler and Turek, *I Don't Have Enough Faith to Be an Atheist,* 263–68.

turned out to be correct.[9] Moreover, this is not an argument from silence, because several New Testament documents presuppose the temple and the city are intact when they were written.[10]

- The book of Acts, which ends abruptly with Paul under house arrest in Rome, appears to have been written no later than AD 62.[11] Luke traces the ministries of Peter and then Paul in the book of Acts. Along the way, he records the martyrdoms of peripheral characters Stephen and James (the brother of John) but makes no mention of the martyrdoms of Peter and Paul, his main subjects. He also makes no mention of the martyrdom of James, the half-brother of Jesus, who, we learn from Josephus and Hegesippus, was killed by the Sanhedrin (the Jewish ruling council) in AD 62.[12]

- We have good evidence that Nero martyred both Paul and Peter sometime in the 60s. I know this is a bit of a stretch, but Paul had to have written all of his books before he died! Due to an archaeological discovery in Delphi, we can pinpoint Paul's travels and his writings.[13] Paul wrote some of his books prior to AD 50 and his first letter to the Corinthians in AD 55 or 56. The problem for skeptics is that Paul appears to quote Luke's Gospel in that letter (compare Luke 22:19–20 with 1 Corinthians 11:23–25), which means Luke must be earlier than AD 55. Since Luke appears to use

---

9. Matthew 24:2. This prediction of Jesus is one of the primary reasons scholars date the Gospels late. Who could predict an event like this with such accuracy? But that's just the result of an anti-supernatural bias, which is unwarranted, as we'll see below.

10. See John 5:2; 2 Thes 2:4; Heb 5:1–3; 7:23,27; 8:3–5; 9:25; 10:1,3–4,11; 13:10–11; Rev 11:1–2.

11. Colin Hemer, *The Book of Acts in the Setting of Hellenistic History* (Winona Lake, IN: Eisenbrauns, 1989), 376–82. Hemer lists fifteen reasons to believe Acts is earlier than many scholars suggest.

12. Josephus (AD 37–100), *Antiquities*, 20:9, and Hegesippus (AD 110–180), *Fragments from His Five Books of Commentaries on the Acts of the Church*, book V, posted here: http://www .earlychristianwritings.com/text/hegesippus.html, accessed February 27, 2014.

13. Archaeologists found a stone inscription at Delphi, in Greece, that mentions that the Roman governor (proconsul) Gallio served in the province of Achaia in AD 52. Paul was brought before Gallio in Acts 18:12. The date allows us to establish where Paul was at certain times.

Mark and Matthew as two of his sources, those Gospels are probably even earlier.

- The names of people in the Gospels mirror those found in Palestine in other first-century sources. This suggests that the writers lived in Palestine in the first century and is difficult to explain if the Gospels were written later and/or in another place.

- Most importantly, the creed mentioned above (1 Cor 15:3–8) predates AD 40, perhaps within a year or two of Christ's death, as even liberal scholars admit. This creed, the many other creeds, and the New Testament documents are far too early to be the results of legend.

There are even more tools that scholars can apply to test New Testament claims. While we don't have space to cover them here, they include: undesigned coincidences, scores of archaeological findings, the explosion of believers out of Jerusalem where Jesus's tomb was known, and the writings of non-Christian sources. These all help confirm that many events of the New Testament actually occurred.[14]

Of course, everything in the New Testament cannot be verified by these tools. But as Habermas has shown, more than 90 percent of New Testament scholars, from atheist to Christian, admit that tools such as these yield the following minimal facts:

1. Jesus died by Roman crucifixion.

2. The disciples had experiences that they thought were actual appearances of the risen Jesus.

3. The disciples were thoroughly transformed, even being willing to die for this belief.

4. The apostolic proclamation of the resurrection began very early, when the church was in its infancy.

---

14. In addition to Turek, *Stealing from God*; Geisler and Turek, *I Don't Have Enough Faith to Be an Atheist*; and Habermas, *The Historical Jesus*; see Lydia McGrew, *Hidden in Plain View: Undesigned Coincidences in the Gospels and Acts* (Tampa: DeWard, 2017).

5. James, brother of Jesus and a former skeptic, became a Christian due to an experience that he believed was an appearance of the risen Jesus.

6. Saul (Paul), the church persecutor, became a Christian due to an experience that he believed was an appearance of the risen Jesus.[15]

Just to reiterate, these facts are accepted even by those who believe the New Testament documents are largely *unreliable*. Habermas believes (as do I) that the evidence shows the New Testament documents are historically reliable. But the main point is this: even if you grant the skepticism of the critics, you wind up with at least with these six facts. The only question is, what is the best *interpretation* of these facts?

If Scholars Admit the Minimal Facts, Then Why Don't They Become Christians?

Aren't the minimal facts best explained by the resurrection? Not for skeptics and New Testament critics; anything but a resurrection is more plausible. Like what? They do not know. Habermas mentioned in a recent radio interview with me that critical scholars are recognizing that naturalistic explanations are increasingly untenable. That is why Bart Ehrman, for example, is now agnostic about how to best explain those facts—he no longer cites a favorite naturalistic explanation because he knows that Christian apologists will point out its massive holes.

So why don't more New Testament scholars become Christians? Habermas believes that some skepticism is the result of an anti-supernatural bias. Peter Williams agrees. He writes, "Were it not for the many miraculous reports in the Gospels, most historians would be very happy to treat their accounts as generally historically reliable."[16] He can say that confidently because the evidence for the events of the New Testament far exceeds evidence of other events from the ancient world that critics have no problem accepting.

---

15. Gary Habermas, *The Risen Jesus and Future Hope* (Lanham, MD: Rowan & Littlefield, 2003), 26–27.

16. Peter J. Williams, *Can We Trust the Gospels?* (Wheaton, IL: Crossway, 2018), 133.

The problem for critics is that their anti-supernatural bias goes against what we know about the universe. Nearly all scientists, including atheists, are admitting that the universe—space-time and matter—exploded into being out of nothing. While atheists will come up with every speculation to avoid God as the cause, it is actually difficult to avoid the conclusion that whatever created space-time and matter must be spaceless, timeless, immaterial, powerful to create the universe out of nothing, as well as personal and intelligent to choose to create a universe fine-tuned from the very beginning.[17] Add to that the moral argument, and you have attributes of an eternal Being like the God of the Bible, who spoke the universe into existence. If a God like that exists, then miracles are possible. And since the greatest miracle has already occurred—the creation of the universe out of nothing—then one must be open more modest miracles, such as the resurrection.

But what about scholars who are open to the possibility of miracles—why are they not Christians? While he obviously cannot speak for everyone, Gary likens their rejection of Christ to people who do not want to get married. A man may find the facts about a potential spouse appealing, but he will not say "I do" because he does not want to be committed to anyone right now. Likewise, many people simply do not want to be committed to Christ. It not really a matter of the head but the heart.

I have found the same in my interactions with atheists and agnostics on college campuses. Many people are not on a truth quest but a happiness quest. They reject Christ because they think he might get in the way of their happiness.

While some have admitted this to me privately, very few will do so publicly. No one wants to admit resisting a truth for moral or emotional reasons. Skeptics and critics, like all of us, would much rather appear to be beacons of reason who are relentlessly following the evidence where it leads. The truth is, none of us are completely rational and often make decisions because of emotional, moral, or other commitments. However, if one wants to be rational, Gary Habermas has shown that there is very good evidence to believe that the resurrection

---

17. For more on this, and for a refutation of atheistic speculations, see Turek, *Stealing from God*, ch. 1.

is true. And if the resurrection is true, then the essentials of Christianity are quite easy to establish.

What Does This Mean for Christians and Christian Apologists?

It is a common belief prevalent among many Christians today that Christianity is true because an inspired Bible says it is true. In reality, Christianity would still be true even if the Bible was never written.

How so? Because Christianity did not originate with a book. Christianity originated with an event—the resurrection of Jesus of Nazareth. In other words, Christianity is not true just because the Bible says it is true. Christianity is true because the resurrection occurred.

While we would not *know* much about Christianity if the reports of the resurrection had never been written, the resurrection preceded the reports of it. There were thousands of Christians before a line of the New Testament was ever written. Indeed, Paul became a Christian before he wrote a word of the New Testament. So did Matthew, John, James, Peter, etc. Why? Not because they had read a book, but because they had witnessed the resurrected Jesus.

Could they have made it all up? Even if you ignore the tools and evidence we have been through, the suggestion is dead on its face. All of the New Testament reporters (except Luke) were observant Jews who would pay dearly for proclaiming the resurrection.[18] Why would people who thought they were God's chosen people for two thousand years invent a resurrection story that would get them excommunicated from the chosen people club, and then beaten, tortured, and murdered?

They wouldn't. They were believers in Yahweh who never expected a resurrected Messiah. Yet they proclaimed it, altered their lives and religion because of it, and later wrote about it, despite the fact that doing any of that would likely get them killed. They had every earthly motive to say the resurrection was *not* true, and no motive to invent it.

---

18. Even if one accepts the unfounded assertion that the Gospels were originally anonymous, there is little doubt that the Gospels were written by Jewish authors who either were eyewitnesses or had access to eyewitness testimony. And no one doubts that undisputed authors of New Testament documents, Paul and James, were Jewish. For the Jewish nature of the Gospels, see Williams, *Can We Trust*, ch. 3. For a refutation of the Gospels being anonymous, see Brant Pitre, *The Case for Jesus: The Biblical and Historical Evidence for Christ* (New York: Image, 2016), ch. 2.

Given this, ask yourself, "Why do the New Testament documents exist at all?" It would be a bigger miracle to have a New Testament written by observant Jews in the first century if Jesus had *not* risen from the dead. Contrary to what some internet infidels might assert, the New Testament writers did not create the resurrection—the resurrection created the New Testament writers.

So what does this mean for Christians and Christian apologists? It means that when you are talking to an unbeliever, you should not lead with or assume an inspired text. The apostles never attempted to convince non-Jews that the Hebrew Scriptures were inspired. Rather, they attempted to show them that Jesus had risen from the dead to prove his claim to be the Savior of the world. That was their apologetic and should be ours. Gary's minimal facts approach can help you do that.

This is not to deny the inspiration of the Bible. It is just that inspiration is a conclusion, not a premise. We first try to discover if the resurrection really happened. If it did, then Jesus is God. Since whatever God teaches is true, it is on Jesus' authority that we can conclude that the documents are inspired.

The key to everything, including salvation, is the resurrection. If Christ rose from the dead, then Jesus is Lord and the essential teachings of Christianity are true on his authority. On the other hand, if he did not rise from the dead, then, as the first-century eyewitness Paul admitted, Christianity is false.

That is why Gary Habermas has made the resurrection the focus of his life's work. We should learn from him about how to establish the world's most important truth with facts even most skeptics will grant.

What We Learn from Habermas
Beyond the Evidence

It is not just Habermas's practical academic work that makes him worthy of the honor that this book bestows. Gary Habermas is also worthy because he wears Christ well. In fact, it is hard not to love Gary, regardless of your theological outlook.

His Christian demeanor is so attractive that even once-hardened atheists, such as Antony Flew, whom he debated several times, are softened by his friendship and concern. It also helps that he stays focused on the essentials (such as the resurrection) and does not get bogged down or divide over secondary issues (something every Christian and apologist should learn).

Then there is the fact that he routinely spends hours on the telephone with people struggling with doubt. These are people he has never met, but he invests his time, expertise, and compassion in them.

Habermas can do so effectively because he has experienced intense suffering and doubts himself. When his wife, Debbie, was nearing death from stomach cancer in 1995, Gary asked God why He didn't heal her. The response he sensed from God impressed Christ's sacrifice and resurrection upon him in a way he hadn't experienced before. His imagined conversation with God went something like this:[19]

> "Lord, Debbie is only forty-three years old, and I have ministry and kids. Why is Deb dying?"
>
> "Gary, we've got something in common. I watched my son die. You know I didn't rescue him from the cross, did I?"
>
> "No Lord, you didn't."
>
> "You know, Gary. He died. I watched my son die. Do you expect better treatment than my Son?"
>
> "Lord, I'm not worthy. You understand. I'm just hurting."
>
> "Gary, what kind of world is this?"
>
> "I guess it's a world where you raised your son from the dead."
>
> "Yes, Gary."
>
> "But Lord, that was AD 30. It's now 1995."
>
> "Gary, it's the same world today in 1995 as it was in AD 30. What does that mean?"
>
> "It means that this is a world where you watched your son die, but then you raised him from the dead."
>
> "Yes, Gary. I'm not going to save you *from* this right now, but I am going to save you *through* it. You will see your wife again."

Gary Habermas's life's work on the resurrection makes belief in that comforting hope a lot more certain. What work could be more important than that? Thank you, Gary!

---

19. This exchange is adapted from a five-minute video Habermas recorded in 2008, "The Death and Resurrection of Debbie," posted here: https://www.youtube.com/watch?v=489i38n1gjU.

LIST OF CONTRIBUTORS

Dale C. Allison, Jr. is the Richard J. Dearborne professor of New Testament at Princeton Theological Seminary. He is the author of, among other books, *Jesus of Nazareth: Millenarian Prophet* (Fortress Press, 1988) and *Night Comes: Death, Imagination, and the Last Things* (Eerdmans, 2016).

David Baggett is a two-time *Christianity Today* book award winner, professor of philosophy at Houston Baptist University, and the author or editor of about fifteen books. His books on moral apologetics with Jerry Walls include *Good God: The Theistic Foundations of Morality* (2011), *God and Cosmos: Moral Truth and Human Meaning* (2016), and *The Moral Argument: A History* (2019), all with Oxford University Press. A more popular version of material on the moral argument is *The Morals of the Story: Good News about a Good God*, co-written with his wife, Marybeth, published with IVP Academic (2018).

W. David Beck is a professor of philosophy at Liberty University, where he served for many years as dean of Graduate Studies. He holds an MA from Trinity Evangelical Divinity School and a PhD from Boston University. He teaches courses in ancient and medieval philosophy and in philosophy of religion, and has published numerous articles, primarily on the cosmological argument. His current interests include the relationship between science, philosophy, and theology, Aristotelian metaphysics, the arguments for God's existence, and God and the multiverse. His book *The Reality of God* (IVP Academic) is forthcoming in 2021.

Francis J. Beckwith is a professor of philosophy and church studies as well as associate director of the Graduate Program in Philosophy at Baylor University. He has written over a dozen books, including *Never Doubt Thomas: The Catholic Aquinas as Evangelical and Protestant* (Baylor

University Press, 2019) and *Taking Rites Seriously: Law, Politics, and the Reasonableness of Faith* (Cambridge University Press, 2015).

Darrell Bock is a senior research professor of New Testament studies at Dallas Theological Seminary and executive director for cultural engagement at the Hendricks Center at the seminary. He is the author of several books related to Luke, Acts, and the Historical Jesus. He is a former president of the Evangelical Theological Society.

William Lane Craig is a research professor at Talbot School of Theology and at Houston Baptist University. He has authored or edited over forty books, including *Assessing the New Testament Evidence for the Historicity of the Resurrection of Jesus* (Edwin Mellen Press, 1989), *Will the Real Jesus Please Stand Up?* (with John Dominic Crossan) (Baker Books, 1995), and *Jesus' Resurrection: Fact or Figment?* (with Gerd Lüdemann) (IVP Academic, 2000), as well as over two hundred articles in professional journals such as *New Testament Studies*, *Journal for the Study of the New Testament*, *Expository Times*, and *Kerygma und Dogma*. Visit his website at www .reasonablefaith.org.

Craig A. Evans is the John Bisagno distinguished professor of Christian origins at Houston Baptist University. He has published several books on Jesus and the Gospels and has appeared in many documentaries and news programs.

Mark W. Foreman is a professor of philosophy and religion at Liberty University. Mark has been a student and then colleague of Gary Habermas for thirty years. He holds a PhD in biomedical ethics from the University of Virginia. His specialties are Christian apologetics, biomedical ethics, and logic. He is the author of *Prelude to Philosophy: An Introduction for Christians* (IVP Academic, 2013), *Christianity and Bioethics: Confronting Clinical Issues* (Wipf & Stock, 1999), and *How Do We Know: An Introduction to Epistemology* (with James K. Dew Jr.) (IVP Academic, 2014).

Craig Hazen is the founder and director of the Christian apologetics graduate program at Biola University. He holds a PhD in religious studies from the University of California, Santa Barbara, and a degree in biological sciences. He is the author of several books, including *The Village Enlightenment in America* (University of Illinois Press, 2000), *Five Sacred Crossings* (Contend, 2008), and *Fearless Prayer* (Harvest House, 2018), and was the editor of the philosophy journal *Philosophia Christi* for the last twenty years.

Michael R. Licona is an associate professor of theology at Houston Baptist University. He is the author of several books, including *The Resurrection of Jesus: A New Historiographical Approach* (IVP Academic) and *Why Are There Differences in the Gospels? What We Can Learn From Ancient Biography* (Oxford University Press). His web site is risenjesus .com.

Sean McDowell is an associate professor of apologetics at Talbot School of Theology, Biola University. He has written or edited over eighteen books, including the recent update to *Evidence that Demands a Verdict* with his father, Josh. Sean is a popular speaker at schools, universities, camps, and churches, and is the co-host for the podcast *Think Biblically*. Sean blogs regularly at seanmcdowell.org.

Alex McFarland is an apologetics-focused evangelist, broadcaster, and conference organizer. He is a graduate of Liberty University and author of eighteen books on apologetics and worldview. His website is alexmcfarland.com.

J. P. Moreland is distinguished professor of philosophy at Talbot School of Theology, Biola University. He received a BS in physical chemistry from the University of Missouri, a ThM in theology from Dallas Theological Seminary, an MA in philosophy from the University of California at Riverside, and a PhD in philosophy at the University of Southern California. He has authored, edited, or contributed papers to ninety-five books, including *Does God Exist?* (Prometheus), *Universals* (McGill-Queen's), *Consciousness and the Existence of God* (Routledge), *The Blackwell Companion to Natural Theology*, *The Blackwell Companion to Substance Dualism*, and *Debating Christian Theism* (Oxford). He has also published over eighty-five articles in journals such as *Philosophy* *and Phenomenological Research, American Philosophical Quarterly, Australasian Journal of Philosophy, MetaPhilosophy, Philosophia Christi, Religious Studies,* and *Faith and Philosophy.* Moreland was selected in August 2016 by *The Best Schools* as one of the fifty most influential living philosophers in the world.

Barrie Schwortz was the official documenting photographer for the Shroud of Turin Research Project (STURP), the team that conducted the first in-depth scientific examination of the Shroud in 1978. Today, he plays an influential role in Shroud research and education as the editor and founder of the internationally recognized Shroud of Turin website (shroud.com), the oldest, largest, and most extensive Shroud resource on the internet, with more than fifteen million visitors from over 160 countries. In 2009 he founded the Shroud of Turin Education and Research Association, Inc. (STERA, Inc.), a non-profit 501(c)(3) corporation, to which he donated the website and his extensive Shroud photographic collection, as well as many other important Shroud resources, in order to preserve and maintain these materials and make them available for future research and study. He currently serves as the President of STERA, Inc.

Benjamin C. F. Shaw (Ph.D. in Theology, Liberty University) is the author or co-author of over a dozen chapters and journal articles, including "What's Good for the Goose is Good for the Gander: Historiography and the Historical Jesus" in the *Journal for the Study of the Historical Jesus* and (with Gary R. Habermas) "Miracle, Evidence, and Agent Causation: A Review Article" in *Philosophia Christi.* He recently coedited (with Habermas) a reprint of Oscar Cullmann's *The Earliest Christian Confessions* (Wipf and Stock, 2018).

Beth M. Sheppard is a professor at the University of West Georgia. She is the author of *The Craft of History and the Study of the New Testament* (SBL, 2012) and earned her doctorate from the University of Sheffield.

Robert B. Stewart (MDiv, PhD, Southwestern Baptist Theological Seminary) is a professor of philosophy and theology at New Orleans Baptist Theological Seminary, where he occupies the Greer-Heard Chair of Faith and Culture and directs the program in Christian apologetics. He has authored or edited twelve books, including *The Quest of the Hermeneutical Jesus: The Impact of Hermeneutics on the Jesus Research of John Dominic Crossan and N. T. Wright* and *The Resurrection of Jesus: John Dominic Crossan and N. T. Wright in Dialogue,* plus numerous of articles in journals and books.

Frank Turek is the president of crossexamined.org and author or coauthor of several books, including *I Don't Have Enough Faith to Be an Atheist* (Crossway, 2004).

Printed in the United States
By Bookmasters